Toward New Human Rights

[**toward**

new human rights:

the social policies of the Kennedy and Johnson administrations

Edited by David C. Warner

Lyndon B. Johnson School of Public Affairs
The University of Texas at Austin

Copyright © 1977 by
Board of Regents
The University of Texas

Price: $5.95

L.C. Card Number: 76-623065

ACKNOWLEDGMENTS

This book is the result of more than a year of planning and discussion and generous support from a number of sources. The idea that a major conference ought to be held to discuss the social programs of the Kennedy and Johnson Administrations originated from a visit by Wilbur Cohen to the LBJ School of Public Affairs in the summer of 1975. Following his visit, the support of the Lyndon Baines Johnson and John F. Kennedy Presidential Libraries and of The University of Texas was enlisted by William Cannon, then Dean of the LBJ School, and planning began for the conference to be held in the fall of 1976.

Two committees were involved in planning the conference. William Cannon chaired the committee that determined which substantive areas ought to be covered and commissioned the papers that appear in this volume. This committee consisted of Victor Bach, Henry David, and myself from the LBJ School, David Austin of the School of Social Work, Robert Hardesty, who was then Governor Briscoe's Press Secretary, Ray Marshall of the Department of Economics, and Harry Middleton, Director of the Lyndon Baines Johnson Presidential Library. Wilbur Cohen was nominally a member of the committee; but coordination difficulties were such that he should not be held responsible for any of the sins of ommission or commission of the committee.

Once the topics were selected and the papers commissioned, the work of planning and coordinating the conference was passed on to a campus-wide committee chaired by Dean Elspeth Rostow. This committee included William Cannon, Robert Hardesty, and Harry Middleton from the first group as well as William Drummond from Physics, Dean Peter Garvie from Fine Arts, Dean Lorrin Kennamer and Melvin Sikes from the School of Education, Stanley Ross then Provost, and Jere Williams from the Law School, Dean Jack Otis of Social Work, and Mike Naeve and Dorthy Territo of the LBJ Library. In particular, this committee selected the panelists for each session, passed on the arrangements for and organization of the Conference, and was available to approve changes in the program. This committee is a standing committee at The University of Texas at Austin which coordinates one University of Texas-LBJ School-LBJ Library conference annually supported by grant funds from the Lyndon Baines Johnson Foundation.

Other funding for the conference came from the Moody Foundation and a Ford Foundation general support grant to the LBJ School of Public Affairs. In addition three of the panels and part of the cost of publishing this volume were supported by grants from government agencies: the panel on "The Right to a Decent Standard of Living" by the Texas Department of Public Welfare; the panel on "The Right to Health and Medical Care" by the Dallas Regional Office of the Public Health Service, Department of Health, Education, and Welfare; and the panel on "The Right to Equal Educational Opportunity" by the National Institute of Education, Department of Health, Education, and Welfare.

At the conference, which took place September 12-16, 1976, the technical papers, which are the chapters of this book served as starting points to frame and organize the discussion by panelists and the audience. Well over a thousand people attended one or more of the sessions and the rapporteurs' reports at the close of each section briefly summarize the discussion which took place during the conference.

Although space does not permit acknowledgment of all who worked on the conference or the book, some must be mentioned. Mike Naeve, Associate Director of the Lyndon Baines Johnson Foundation, arranged for much of the funding and helped organize the conference. Dorothy Territo, Charles Cockran, and Jeri Wayson of the Lyndon Baines Johnson Presidential Library managed the logistics of a five-day conference very well. Kenneth Tolo who was Acting Dean of the LBJ School in the spring of 1976 took Dean Cannon's place on the committee and ably carried out the administrative tasks associated with the school's participation in the conference. Amy Jo Long and Helen Tackett of the University News and Information Service handled publicity and press arrangements.

Hoyt Purvis, Director of Publications at the LBJ School, has done much of the editing and handled the publications arrangements. He has been assisted in this by Gwen Wells. Nancy Horrell designed the poster, program, and stage backdrop for the conference and has been responsible for the design of the book. And finally, Toni Nelson has dealt with a number of crises and unreasonable demands associated with the conference and the book with initiative and skill.

As with all programs of the LBJ School and LBJ Library, we have benefited greatly from the warm encouragement and support of Mrs. Lyndon Johnson which, combined with her strict policy of noninterference, is one of the greatest resources an institution could have.

David Warner

INTRODUCTION

The social programs of the Kennedy and Johnson Administrations were designed to extend basic rights to all citizens and to develop new "social" rights for those most in need. In this book, a number of scholars and policy makers examine these programs, describe how they were initiated and why they developed as they did. These observers evaluate the results of the Kennedy-Johnson programs, and delineate what still remains to be done if many of the objectives of these programs are to be fully achieved. It is hoped that their efforts to put these programs in perspective will help policy makers and citizens in the future by providing a basic understanding of the changes that have taken place during the last 16 years.

The Programs

During the sixties, a period which Vernon Jordan describes as the Second Reconstruction, many citizens were guaranteed for the first time the right to vote and to be served in places of public accommodation, and legislation was passed banning discrimination in employment and housing, even though these rights are still inadequately assured. In addition to classic individual rights or guarantees of equality, the programs of the sixties fostered the growth of what Arthur Schlesinger refers to as social rights—a natural extension of President Franklin D. Roosevelt's economic bill of rights of 1944. The Federal Government took responsibility for guaranteeing a minimum standard of living, housing, and medical care for the groups most in need of these services. And compensatory programs in education and training, to equalize opportunity for groups starting out at a disadvantage were also initiated.

The enormous outpouring of programs in the 1960s was the consequence of a number of related events. Those who had been denied civil rights and those who believed in the justness of this cause became more active. They marched on Washington, held sit-ins in restaurants, confronted authority at Selma Bridge, and rode as freedom riders. The natural sympathy and sense of justice of many was first translated in a major way into legislation after the assassination of John Kennedy. After the deaths of Robert Kennedy and Martin Luther King, nearly five years later, the final Civil Rights Act and other Great Society programs were assured passage. Many programs were perceived as feasible because of the constantly growing economy and low inflation rate of the early sixties so well described by James Tobin. Finally, the strong commitment of President Johnson, combined with his legislative skill, broke what Douglass Cater refers to as the "decades-long legislative log-jam" on many of these programs.

Johnson provided a context in which the private-parochial compromises on Title I of ESEA, the passage of Federal health insurance for at least the old and the poor, the tying together in several programs of the interests of the housing developer and the poor in need of housing were all possible. The legislation passed in every area. In nearly every case it was necessary to combine the carrot with the stick. The Elementary and Secondary Education Act (ESEA) provided huge increases in funds for local schools, especially in urban areas and the rural areas of the poorest states. Medicare and Medicaid were only possible because non-interference with providers was promised. Model Cities programs added to the budgets of nearly every city with a population larger than 100,000. Training programs and other subsidies reduced labor costs to private employers. And that great sleeper of all the programs, Title VI of the Civil Rights Act of 1964, only really became effective as the amount of funds available to localities in return for ending discriminatory practices became too attractive to refuse.

It is not useful here to list all the social programs and initiatives which emerged during the 1960s. The chapters of this book discuss many of them within a more appropriate context. In many cases there is no doubt that there are both redundancies in the programs and gaps whereby certain groups or classes of people are unjustly excluded from particular programs. What is often overlooked is in the extension of rights to groups or citizens there appears to be a moral imperative. Once the right to the good, or income level, or service is established, legitimate debate may only be concerned with providing the commodity or service more efficiently or equitably, not with doing away with it entirely. And by laying down a broad range of entitlements the Kennedy and Johnson Administrations assured that these rights would no longer be subject to debate or "up for grabs."

The Results of the Programs

It is possible to evaluate the effects of these programs using fairly narrow criteria such as the reduction of the number of people living in poverty or the increase in the number employed, or, using broader criteria, by looking at the changes which have taken place in society at large during the last 15 years.

The Great Society programs did not eradicate poverty in the United States. However, as Robert Lampman and Robert Levine both point out, if transfer payments and non-cash tranfers in the form of food, housing, and health care are taken into consideration the poverty income gap (the total dollars required to lift everyone above the 1974 adjusted OEO poverty line) may have been $5 billion or even less by 1974 just before the onset of the 1974-75 recession.

Although differentials between the poor and non-poor have not been eradicated, the poor do now seem to be better off in terms of housing, life expectancy, and the levels of education achieved by their children. Many would argue that these measurable improvements in economic and social conditions alone are not dramatic enough to justify the shotgun programmatic approach of the Great Society in comparison to the benefits which would accrue from a negative income tax or guaranteed income approach which spent the same amount of money. They argue that the guaranteed income approach could wipe out income poverty, narrowly defined, and that the poor would be able to exercise consumer sovereighty in their consumption of goods and services.

But there was another dimension to the Great Society programs and that was equality of opportunity and political participation. Pluralism is generally thought to be the best description of our political system. Every individual or every interest should be represented somehow through access to government agencies, community groups, or elected officials. In the sixties there were large numbers of persons for whom this system did not work, they were permanently excluded—an underclass.

The programs and legislation of the sixties changed much of this. The right to vote was guaranteed and the one-man-one-vote ruling increased the potential returns from participation to those living in districts with low turnouts in elections. In addition, the Great Society programs established jobs for many in such a way that the poor had a stake in the system and some control over the programs. Edelman points out that "about 176,000 of the 362,000 non-professionals mostly aides [employed in public school classrooms] were employed in Title I ESEA programs in 1972 and many of the non-Title I aides were employed because of the popularity of aides employed by Title I." Frieden and Kaplan show that 40 percent of the jobs in Model Cities programs went to the poor. And, with the expansion of the health sector, in part as a result of Medicare and Medicaid, jobs for the poor and relatively untrained have increased rapidly in hospitals and clinics. In addition to jobs in occupations in an expanding service sector, some control over many of these programs has been vested in local residents and consumers of services. With this increased control or voice has come the possibility for many to feel represented, for many to have an organization or person to go to when they need help, and for many to believe they have rights to certain services and to jobs. In a sense just as the programs and accommodations of the New Deal are said to have saved American capitalism, so perhaps can it be said that the Great Society saved American pluralism.

What Remains to be Done?

This is not to say that the work of the Great Society is done or that there are not changes and additions required in order for us to move closer to a just and compassionate society. Many of the changes can be accomplished if Presidential commitment matches the objectives of the programs when they were enacted; others are required to reduce the piecemeal nature of the coverage of the population requiring these services while controlling the escalation in costs, and finally it will be necessary to design a Federal system whereby Federal initiatives and guarantees do not entirely destroy local autonomy and a local presence in the program.

In regard to civil rights, a strong commitment by the President, combined with some fairly straightforward changes in the powers of the Equal Employment Opportunity Commission (EEOC), could lead to great improvement in the guarantee of equal employment opportunity. Clifford Alexander shows how the Civil Service Commission could design tests more applicable to the requirements of the job and less correlated with formal education and parent's socio-economic status. Both Alexander and Burke Marshall point to the huge backlog of complaints regarding employment discrimination at the EEOC. Alexander suggests that this backlog could be more expeditiously handled if the commission were enpowered to issue cease and desist orders. Finally there is a good deal of initiative which could be taken by the President in the implementation of Executive Order 11246. Federal grants and contracts can be cancelled if an employer is not in compliance with the equal employment guidelines, and this is a weapon which should be used when necessary. These are remedies which have been allowed to fall into disuse during the last eight years.

In employment, health, education, and housing there may be approaches which can provide every American with a right to decent entitlement without either destroying incentives or adding too much to current cost levels. With regard to employment and manpower training the cost of guaranteeing everyone a job may be less than the current enormous cost of unemployment insurance, destruction of confidence of the wage earner, and the lack of productive on-the-job training for most inner-city youth. Ray Marshall points out that direct employment programs and training programs tied to specific jobs appear to be approaches which work best.

In health care it has become apparent that, as costs escalate rapidly, large segments of the population are cut out of the market. Recent research shows that it is those who are in late middle age who are not quite eligible for Medicare and those who are poor, but not categorically entitled to Medicaid, who use health services least in relation to their need for them. Entitling every citizen to health care will require some concomitant controls on the health delivery system. Some of these would have to include, if costs are to be controlled, moderating the fee-for-service system, changing the carte blanche nature of hospital reimbursement, eliminating cream-skimming behavior of both health insurers and health-care providers, and providing incentives to alternative organizational forms for care. Alternatives which emerge from the book as first steps toward comprehensive national health insurance are "kiddie care," for all mothers and young children, which is advocated by Cohen and Marmor, and universal care for the medically indigent, which Davis would provide to all those below a certain income level.

With the recent environment of Federal permissiveness in both education and community development, the compensatory programs of the Great Society have been eroded by local school administrators or local governments which have redirected the additional resources to groups other than those stipulated in the original legislation, and often to the least deprived in the target population. In both cases, more active Federal monitoring of ongoing programs would have reduced this mobilizing of resources away from the poor. As Edelman and Frieden and Kaplan show, a Federal presence and Federal regulation are necessary in order to stiffen the backbones of local officials who want to do right but cannot in the context of local political realities.

Even with stringent controls and fulfillment of the letter of the law many would be excluded from housing and education programs. Two-thirds of the substandard housing in the nation is in rural areas and there are inadequate means available to solve that problem. Similarly, as John Gallery points out, solutions for the community development program cannot come just from resuscitating the Model Cities programs of the sixties—the approach must also take into account the design of new employment and economic development programs at the local level. Similarly, in education many students who require some compensatory education do not live in the right school district or attend the right school to receive it. As Albert Shanker comments, it may be necessary to design totally new kinds of programs for children who reach third grade and who still cannot read and write.

Finally, as the Federal role and entitlements become more and more important, we as a nation will have to guard against the possibility of too much control and the possibility of basic freedoms being eroded. This can be done, in part, by designing some autonomy and local democratic participation into these programs—at the local level. This will serve to provide for local input and choice and, hopefully, will also be a means of reducing the hegemony of professionals over such programs. The Federal regulations can remain as guidelines to which state plans and local performance must conform, but they should not be laid down in a way that stifles innovation and improvement. An improved delineation of roles of all actors in the Federal system is a prerequisite before more comprehensive programs can be appropriately put in place.

John Gardner said in a letter to Harry Middleton, director of the LBJ Library,

> I see a society learning new ways as a baby learns to walk. He stands up, falls, stands again, falls and bumps his nose, cries, tries again—and eventually walks. Some of the critics now sounding off about the Great Society would stop the baby after his first fall and say "That'll teach you. Stick to crawling."

In the last 16 years we have learned many new ways of providing for those least able to provide for themselves and of ensuring basic rights. We have rid ourselves of much that was unacceptable to our vision of ourselves. In the years ahead we must consolidate the gains made in ensuring all citizens basic rights and access to government while developing a system in which local initiative and individual rights are nurtured.

David Warner

CONTENTS

The Right to Health and Medical Care

The Right to a Decent Home in a Decent Community

The Right to Equal Educational Opportunity

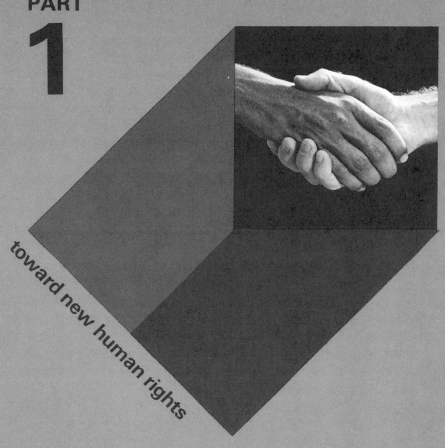

toward new human rights

Vernon Jordan

1 The Evolution of Social Rights

Two-hundred years ago Americans rose in armed revolt against the British Crown, basing their actions upon the philosophical premise that "all men are created equal, that they are endowed by their Creator with certain inalienable rights, that among these are life, liberty, and the pursuit of happiness."

The leaders of that revolt were largely drawn from the elite of colonial society. For many of them, the "inalienable rights" inherent in all men were rights they themselves denied to black people whom they owned as chattel, whose lives and labor they commanded.

But if the men who gathered to declare their independence from English rule were blind to the hypocrisy of their position, those whom they held in bondage were not. Two years before the Virginia slaveowner, Thomas Jefferson, enshrined the concept of "inalienable rights," a group of black people petitioned the Massachusetts General Assembly for their freedom, declaring:

We have in common with all other men a natural right to our freedoms without being deprived of them as we are a freeborn people and have never forfeited this blessing by any compact or agreement whatever.

Thus, masters and slaves agreed on the common concept of man's natural right to freedom, and the history of our nation has largely been the record of the fight to reconcile the ideals of freedom with the reality of its denial to significant segments of the population. Our first century was characterized by the struggle to extend the most elementary rights to all Americans, and it took a long and bloody civil war to do it. Our second century was marked by the struggle to break the bonds of a narrow interpretation of the meaning of those God-given "inalienable rights" in order to extend to larger and larger portions of the population the rights and privileges enjoyed by the few.

This effort may be seen as an illustration of Lincoln's dictum that the "legitimate object of government is to do for a community of people whatever they need to have done but cannot do at all or cannot do so well for themselves in their separate and individual capacities."

Governmental power is thus seen as an intervening force to help right the balance between the powerful and the powerless. But government has never been neutral; indeed, it has often been the instrument to deny rights to people without the wealth, status, and education that characterize the powerful. It was state power that made formal freedom for blacks relatively meaningless, and it was Federal power that enshrined "separate but equal" as the law of the land, that encouraged rapacious "robber barons" and discouraged social and economic equality for blacks and for working people of all races.

With the coming of the New Deal and World War II we saw more active Federal action on behalf of the dispossessed and a new awareness of the need to widen basic human rights. The shared agonies of the Depression, the hardships, sacrifices and democratic rhetoric of the war experience, and the large-scale economic rearrangements caused by both events, helped to open our society to the winds of change.

For black people, the mass migration from southern agriculture to northern urban industry, the growth of the union movement, the New Deal reforms, and the experience of fighting for democracy in a segregated army resulted in a new insistence that rights are not a function of whiteness, and that the Constitutional guarantees enjoyed by white people must be extended to blacks and other minorities.

The civil rights movement of the 1950s and 1960s fought for those rights, but even while demonstrating against segregated buses, segregated drinking fountains, and segregated schools, there was a basic awareness that beyond the basic rights of equality before the law, was the need for equality of opportunity in every sphere of human life. It is often forgotten that the slogan of the 1963 March on Washington was for "Jobs and Freedom," and not for an otherwise empty "freedom" alone.

Second Reconstruction

Without access to jobs, economic security, quality education, and other means of exercising political rights, our traditional rights would wither and die. And because traditional "rights" are empty without the ability to use them, the struggle to secure what may be called "social rights" has become the focus of our attention. Indeed, from the Declaration of Independence's insistence that "all men are created equal" comes the natural conclusion that those elements basic to securing equality of opportunity are rights as fundamental as those enshrined in the Bill of Rights.

It is a measure of the vision of the architects of the New Frontier-Great Society era that much of their energies were devoted to extending economic and social rights to those denied them. This Second Reconstruction combined executive orders, judicial decisions, and Congressional actions to dismantle some of the barriers to equality, and to confer upon the poor and the powerless some small measure of economic security.

The Second Reconstruction swept away laws and practices that denied civil rights to blacks and other minorities, extended the right to vote, enabled access to schools and housing to those denied them, and provided for Federal programs of health, housing, education, and economic security designed to assist groups disadvantaged in those areas. Through the War on Poverty, it stimulated organization of the poor and increased their access to the judicial system and to public policy-making, in addition to concrete programs to improve their neighborhoods.

This was a significant era in our national history, one that will be seen as effecting a revolution in the status of minority groups. It enabled the South to finally rejoin the Union. And by stressing the economic prerequisites for a more equal society it helped win greater acceptance for the concept of social rights, and for their extension to all citizens.

If history will judge those Kennedy-Johnson years favorably, it must be admitted that our own day does not. Today the period of the sixties is widely regarded as a time of unwise social experiments, unfair advantages to minorities, and undue governmental interference in the economy and in private decisions.

Such a view is mean-spirited and wrong. It is the natural response of many forced to share their monopoly on rights and privileges. It elevates the right to oppress and to discriminate above the right to equality.

What concerns me most is not the attack on the reform of the 1960s by last-ditch segregationists and the radical right. Such a last gasp of venom is expected from those unwilling to admit black people's right to vote and to work.

What distresses me is the failure of moderates and liberals to take pride in the accomplishments of reforms they helped institute and supported. There is a fatal flaw of compromise and timidity in conventional liberalism that today takes the form of retreat from the uncompleted battle for equality and in the overly defensive reaction to unfounded criticisms of the reforms of the sixties.

It cannot be said too often—the Second Reconstruction was a success. Whatever the failings of this or that specific program, the overall thrust to extend equality, increase community initiatives, focus attention on the real problems of our society and to mobilize national efforts to solve those problems constitute one of the few periods of our national history of which we can be proud.

The social programs of the Kennedy and Johnson Administrations did not bring about full racial equality, they did not end poverty, they did not build a new Jerusalem. No eight-year-long effort can be expected to overcome centuries of poverty, neglect, and discrimination. No social thrust as underfunded as were the programs of the sixties and so bitterly opposed by so large a segment of the population, could possibly achieve all its goals. And like other periods of social reform—Wilson's New Freedom and Roosevelt's New Deal—the Second Reconstruction ended on the battlefields of a far-off war, untimely killed before it could achieve its ends.

For black people, the era of the sixties was a period of unprecedented advances. The numbers of the black poor were reduced from over half the black population in 1960 to a third in 1969. Median black income, half that for whites in 1960, rose to over 60 percent of white income by the end of the decade. Black college attendance doubled. Black gains in housing, political participation, job distribution, and other indicators all showed startling improvements.

So black people are not inclined to be apologetic about the experiences of the sixties. We are not inclined to be overly critical of the Kennedy-Johnson social programs although they were too few and too underfunded to fully solve the problems they tackled.

But the changes of the sixties did not bring equality to black people. They did remove the restrictions imposed by race on crucial civil rights. They did provide the impetus for developments that made it possible for that portion of the black community that had skills and educaton to win a measure of economic progress. And they provided some measure of assistance to the majority of blacks chained in the prisons of poverty.

The Beneficiaries

It is all too often conveniently forgotten that the real beneficiaries of the social reforms of the sixties were white people. Even in those programs popularly believed to be "black," the majority of participants were white. The so-called "black" War on Poverty became a major instrument for reducing white poverty faster and in greater numbers than black poverty.

It is a truism that some poor whites raised to middle-class status by the New Deal wound up cursing "that man in the White House" for his liberalism. So too, in the sixties, we saw the weird phenomenon of white people trained by manpower programs and placed in well-paying jobs, who bought their homes with Federal loans and guarantees, whose children went to college on federally-financed scholarships and grants, and whose entire well-being was made possible by the programs of the Kennedy-Johnson era, now castigating those same programs as being for black people.

To the extent that blacks benefited in disproportionate numbers from those programs it is because blacks were disproportionately poor. But by sheer weight of numbers, those programs were white programs, just as today the so-called "black" welfare system has more whites than blacks on its rolls.

At the end of the sixties a great gap between whites and blacks remained, a gap that has grown wider with each passing year. The reason for that gap is not hard to find. Without positive intervention on behalf of the poor and the powerless, the wealthy and the powerful will increase their share of both wealth and power.

This has been proved through recent experience. The abdication of Federal responsibilities has been followed by intolerably high levels of unemployment, accelerated urban decay, and by increased black disadvantage. Today, every fourth black worker is unemployed, two out of three black young people cannot find jobs, the numbers of the black poor are increasing, and a people who, just a few short years ago, were glibly characterized as "middle class" are once again struggling simply to survive.

Lyndon Johnson understood that it is not enough just to say "we won't discriminate any more." I was at the Civil Rights Symposium in 1972, shortly before he died, when he said: "To be black in a white society is not to stand on level and equal ground. While the races may stand side by side, whites stand on history's mountain and blacks stand in history's hollow. Until we overcome unequal history, we cannot overcome unequal opportunity."

And Johnson concluded by saying "It's time to get down to the business of trying to stand black and white on level ground. In specific areas we must set new goals, new objectives and new standards."

It is indeed time our society stopped the rear-guard warfare against affirmative action programs that compensate for an unequal past. It is time our society scrapped the outmoded myths of limited government and neutral market forces and replaced them with policies based on the new realities of the complex economy we live in today. And it is time, long overdue, for our society to build upon the pioneering reforms of the past 40 years to finally build a nation of political, social, and economic justice for all.

A prerequisite for such an effort is the formulation of an extended concept of rights, a concept that includes the traditional rights embedded in the Constitution but goes beyond them to assure economic and social rights so long withheld from those excluded from privilege based on wealth, class, and race.

A New Bill of Rights

Thus, I suggest the necessity for a New Bill of Rights that extends traditional American freedoms to include the natural rights that truly enable groups and individuals to enjoy "life, liberty, and the pursuit of happiness."

The New Bill of Rights for America's third century would include:

The right to education, preparing all children for fuller, freer lives;

The right to economic security, which includes the right to a decent job at a decent wage for all and an income maintenance program that replaces the welfare system;

The right to health, and the need for a national health policy that ensures decent health care for all;

The right to family stability, enabling families to survive the relentless pressures of poverty and discrimination;

The right to representation, enabling minorities to achieve full participation in the political process; and

The right to safe communities, so that no neighborhood need live in fear of crime and violence.

And implicit in these rights is the *right of our cities to survive,* to prosper, and to flourish as the centers of our economy and of our civilization, thus fulfilling their historic role in human history.

I suggest these new rights not as vague formulations, unattainable goals toward which to strive, but as essential elements of true democracy to be enjoyed—*as rights*—by all of our citizens. There is no reason why this, the world's richest nation, cannot implement them within a short, realistic time frame. There is no reason why we cannot have zero-level involuntary unemployment, and not the four percent level that is supposed to be "full employment," a level incidentally, that means 8-10 percent black joblessness. There is no reason we cannot have an income maintenance program built into a reformed tax structure, health and educational systems that deliver quality services to all, or a Domestic Marshall Plan that restores urban viability.

Despite the warnings against too much government, the Federal share of the gross national product is about what it has always been since the 1950s. Despite alarmist warnings about higher national debt, it is lower in proportion to GNP than in the past. Despite the warnings against inflation, there is plenty of slack in the economy and we suffer not from classical inflation but from underproduction and from wasted resources.

There is a view of Federal responsibilities I have called "the new minimalism." It is a view that insists on less government, less social programs, and—ultimately—fewer rights and freedoms for those on the bottom half of our social ladder. It is a view that is incompatible with a desire to extend and reinforce social rights, for it sees as exorbitant spending programs what are really basic investments in our nation's future, investments in America's third century.

We of the Urban League movement have experience with the kind of investment in human resources that pays off, and pays off well. For the past nine years, our Labor Education Advancement Program (LEAP) has been recruiting and training young people for jobs in the construction trades. Some of these young people were on welfare. Some of them were on street corners and some of them, yes, some of them were keeping body and soul together in hustling and in crime. Many were high school dropouts. Most were on the outermost margins of our society, part of the growing pool of invisible black people ignored by the statistics-keepers.

Over the nine years of LEAP's life, the government has invested $22 million in the program. Last year alone, LEAP's 16,000 placements paid $31 million in taxes—or $9 million more than Washington's total investment over nine years. Over the whole nine years, LEAP's placements earned a cumulative $380 million and their total taxes have come to $90 million. That means for every dollar the government put into LEAP, it got four back.

So social programs, Federal spending, and a new Bill of Rights are perfectly compatible with sound resource management and practical human investment policies. The social devastation we see around us today, the blasted hopes and embittered dreams of so many millions of our people, the hunger and homelessness and bleakness that characterize so many of our cities, must inspire us to reject the prophets of the new minimalism, to restore the social concern and activism of the Second Reconstruction, and to devote our energies to securing new human rights in our third century.

A hundred years ago, on the occasion of the Centennial, Thomas Huxley said:

As population thickens in your great cities and the pressure of want is felt, the gaunt spectre of pauperism will stalk among you. . . Truly America has a great future before her: great in toil, in care, and in responsibility; great in true glory if she be guided in wisdom and righteousness; great in shame if she fail.

History will record that the Kennedy and Johnson Administrations strove to take our country to the high road of care and responsibility, that their energies, accomplishments, and even their mistakes, were all informed by the desire to capture for America the greatness that is based on decent and righteous behavior.

It is my hope that in these first days of our third century Americans will revive that dedication and take their first steps on the long arduous journey toward the true equality and justice for all.

Arthur Schlesinger, Jr.

2

The Evolution of the National Government as an Instrument for Attaining Social Rights

It is a risky business to discuss new human rights at a time when so many people appear willing to renounce a number of the old and when even some who retain their belief in social rights are skeptical of the national government as an instrument for attaining them. Still, as the prophet used to say, let us reason together. My assignment is to set forth an historian's view of the changing role of the national government in the quest for social rights—a story that might be briefly called from rags to riches to revaluation, if not to repentance and recantation.

No one, even in the present retrogressive mood, challenges the obligation of the national government to protect traditional personal rights to life, liberty, law, property, and the pursuit of happiness. We are concerned here not with such rights in the individual sense but rather with their redefinition in terms of the high-technology society—with what are variously called "new human rights" or "social rights." These can perhaps be held to begin with the enumeration of rights, incomplete as it was, made 30 years ago by Franklin Roosevelt in his "economic bill of rights" of 1944.

FDR's Economic Bill of Rights represented a crystallization, precipitated by the Great Depression, of 40 years of analysis and agitation by reformers, journalists, social workers, professors, and practical politicians. It also represented something of a departure from 19th century ideas of the proper role of the national government in economic and social affairs. So perhaps it would be well to start with some reminder of the way the American democracy has dealt with economic and social crisis, distinguishing as best we can myth from reality; for traditions, in part at least, determine possibilities.

Economic crisis is a shattering experience for any society, and especially shattering, at least psychologically, for the American. After all, the vast majority of people in this planet live in routine and permanent poverty of a sort that would strike most Americans as economic crisis of the most intolerable nature. As David Potter argued in a notable book 20 years ago, we are a "people of plenty." We regard affluence and upward opportunity as the normal condition of life. Even our poor are affluent compared to the poor of the Third World.

So, when anything threatens or upsets that affluence, Americans are more than usually staggered by it. Economic crisis is an affront to the whole theory by which we have been historically conditioned to live. If it has by no means been absent from our history, it was an intruder so irrelevant to the normalities of life that, when the unexpected visitor arrived, we simply waited around for him to go away. Government, which always felt free to act in the support of business enterprise, rarely intervened in the event of economic collapse.

This was more than a consequence of laissez-faire ideology. Here we must distinguish between myth and reality. The myth is that American economic growth was the product of unfettered private enterprise—as if we sprang, by immaculate conception, from the loins of Adam Smith. The fact is that government played a vigorous role in the American experience of what we now call economic development. Indeed, the first great prophet of the United States as an industrial society was also our first great champion of affirmative government. Alexander Hamilton had deep faith in the dynamics of individual acquisition when tempered by a measure of public control. His countrymen, he wrote, had "a certain fermentation of mind, a certain activity of speculation and enterprise which, if properly directed, may be made subservient to useful purposes but, if left entirely to itself, may be attended with pernicious effects." His effort was to establish the necessary framework of proper direction. In so doing, he placed government policy behind those who he thought would make the most socially beneficial use of capital. Hamilton certainly did not believe in leaving the market alone. Through most of the 19th century, the protective tariff, one of his great bequests, sought systematically to transfer capital to those most likely to use it to accelerate national growth. It was a program of government redistribution.

Government, especially state government, played an indispensable role in the creation of the transportation net that developed the internal market. Of the $245 million required to build the 9,000 miles of southern railroads that existed in 1860, public authorities furnished 60 to 70 percent of the capital (and much of the rest came from overseas in an early form of foreign aid). A number of state governments went into direct public enterprise—state-owned and operated—of which New York's Erie Canal was only the most celebrated. The corporation itself, which became in later days the stronghold of the private sector, actually began as an instrument of state activity—as a means by which the commonwealth could guide the allocation of private economic resources. Early corporations were chartered by individual legislative enactment and in the main to provide social overhead for quasi-public purposes. The stipulations in each charter generally provided for detailed legislative oversight of the ensuing activity. Land policy, of course, was another means by which government stimulated growth. A series of laws from the Ordinance of 1785 to the Homestead Act of 1862 and beyond invited the settlers to occupy and cultivate the western lands. Government land subsidies after the Civil War helped build the great transcontinental railroads.

Government was seen as the indispensable partner of entrepreneurial initiative and private greed in American economic development. John Quincy Adams stated the nationalist view of these matters in his first annual message: "The great object of the institution of civil government is the improvement of those who are parties to the social compact, and no government, in whatever form constituted, can accomplish the lawful end of its institution but in proportion as it improves the condition of those over whom it is established." Here one sees the roots of what we moderns call the welfare state.

I go into all this simply to make the point that 19th century Americans were by no means laissez-faire doctrinaires. They had no inhibitions, theoretical or practical, about calling on government to promote business enterprise and open up economic opportunity. But the early welfare state was essentially a welfare state for business (and to a degree for the farmer). What impresses one in retrospect is the general unwillingness to call on government to play a role in times of economic calamity.

Government and Social Rights in the 19th Century

The United States suffered more or less serious depressions in 1819, 1837, 1857, 1873, and 1893. Even John Quincy Adams, the great believer in "the system of internal improvement by means of national energies," could see no remedy for the Depression of 1819. "Government can do nothing," he thought, ". . . but transfer discontents and propitiate one class of people by disgusting another . . . The healers and destroyers, Time and Chance, must bring the catastrophe or the cure." The classic statement of the 19th century American attitude about government and depression was made by President Martin Van Buren in the midst of the Panic of 1837. The crisis was severe enough for him to call a special session of Congress. But his message to the special session was by contemporary standards exceedingly bleak. Van Buren said:

Those who look to the action of this Government for specific aid to the citizen to relieve embarrassments arising from losses by revulsion in commerce and credit lose sight of the ends for which it was created and the powers with which it is clothed . . . All communities are apt to look to government for too much . . . If, therefore, I refrain from suggesting to Congress any specific plan for regulating the exchanges of the country, relieving mercantile embarrassments, or interfering with the ordinary operations of foreign or domestic commerce, it is from a conviction that such measures are not within the constitutional province of the General Government, and that their adoption would not promote the real and permanent welfare of those they might be designed to aid.

Two years later, depression still persisting, he reaffirmed this view:

Relief is not to be found in expedients . . . It is only by retrenchment and reform—by curtailing public and private expenditures, by paying our debts, and by reforming our banking system—that we are to expect effectual relief, security for the future, and an enduring prosperity.

You may well wonder why, if Van Buren thought the national government so impotent in the face of depression, he bothered to call Congress into special session at all. But he did recognize one way in which government was involved in the business cycle—through monetary policy. He explained depression as a result of inflation—of "excessive issues of bank paper and . . . other facilities for the acquisition and enlargement of credit." The banking reform he had in mind was the separation of the government and the banks through the establishment of an independent treasury system and the return, as far as practicable, to hard money. The national government, in short, should try and bring about deflation. That, so far as he could see, exhausted its power to act against depression. He saw no role for the national government in dealing with the human consequences of economic crisis. There was no conception in the modern sense of social rights.

You may also wonder why an old Jacksonian like Van Buren should have taken what we would regard today as so rigid a position. For one thing the United States in 1837 was predominantly an agricultural society. This fact attenuated and diffused the social impact of economic collapse. Unemployment was less devastating when most people could still subsist on the produce of their own farms. For another, Van Buren and his generation were familiar with government intervention chiefly as a means of the promotion of business enterprise. It was something that, from the time of Alexander Hamilton, had been undertaken for the benefit of and generally at the behest of the business community. Men in the Jeffersonian tradition had been taught by their master that, if they could establish the principle that government should not intervene in the private economy, this would protect the plain people, the producing masses, of the republic.

Ironically, in this very period, the business community itself was retreating from the Hamiltonian conception of publicly guided private enterprise. Businessmen had been angered and alarmed not only by Andrew Jackson's novel and aggressive idea of presidential power but by the use to which he put this idea in disciplining and ultimately dispossessing the great contemporary symbol of American capitalism, the Second Bank of the United States. In the states, Jacksonians were displaying an irritating penchant for economic regulation and administrative experiment. The age of Jackson, in short, was demonstrating that the

Hamiltonian state could turn from the servant into at least the rival, if not the master, of business. So businessmen began to discern a belated charm in the Jeffersonian proposition that government was best that governed least. An exception was naturally made when government aided business, as through the protective tariff and other forms of subsidy. The rise of the versatile American idea of "free enterprise," so different from the simplistic laissez-faire theories of contemporaneous England, can be traced in the brilliant and resourceful explanations of the economist Henry C. Carey.

More fundamentally the rise of laissez-faire was the consequence of what Walt Rostow has taught us to call the "takeoff" into self-sustaining economic growth. As private enterprise began to generate its own capital, the need for public capital receded. The problem now was less the provision of social overhead than the maximization of production and innovation. Here the private sector came into its own. So the Hamiltonian tradition of state intervention in the economy faded away, while the Jacksonian practice of state intervention was never codified. As a result, the laissez-faire creed emerged to govern public reactions to economic and social crisis for a century after Van Buren, finally hardening in the hands of such able writers as William Graham Sumner and Edwin L. Godkin into a dogma that rivaled the Manchester school in rigor of application and surpassed it in liveliness of expression.

So, when depression struck again in 1857, President James Buchanan alleged his personal concern for "the suffering and distress prevailing among the people. With this the Government cannot fail to sympathize, though it may be without the power to extend relief." He blamed the depression, as Van Buren had, on the banking system, adding gloomily, "The Federal Government can not do much to provide against a recurrence of existing evils." A year later: "No government, and especially a government of such limited powers as that of the United States, could have prevented the late revulsion." President Ulysses S. Grant was similarly stoical during the bitter, grinding depression that began in 1873. Again he saw currency as the answer. "I believe frankly," he told Congress, "that there can be no prosperous and permanent revival of business and industries until a policy is adopted . . . looking to a return to a specie basis."

Grover Cleveland, re-elected to the Presidency shortly before the Panic of 1893, had the same restricted notion of the power of the national government. This was another long and hard depression. About 13 percent of the labor force was unemployed in an economy grown far more urban and industrial than the one over which Van Buren had presided half a century earlier. In his inaugural address Cleveland sententiously attacked the "popular disposition to expect from the operation of the Government especial and direct individual advantages." The lessons of "paternalism", he said, had to be unlearned, "and the better lesson taught that while the people should patriotically and cheerfully support their Government its functions do not include the support of the people."

In this spirit, as depression got worse, Cleveland, like Grant, Buchanan, and Van Buren before him, blamed the trouble on the monetary system and contended that the only legitimate role of government was to secure the integrity of the currency. Like his depression-bound predecessors, he pleaded for a return to hard money, denouncing those who "insist that the cure for the ills now threatening us may be found in the single and simple remedy of the free coinage of silver."

As Cleveland's condemnation suggests, even his main opponents still saw the currency system as the key to the business cycle and proposed that the national government act against depression only in that limited area. Throughout the 19th century people considered the currency problem crucial and proposed to resolve it, if they were creditors, by restricting, or, if they were debtors, by expanding the money stock. In retrospect most economists today would say that the 19th century inflationists were generally more to the point. To call them inflationists, however, is misleading. They were, to put it more precisely, what used to be called in New Deal years reflationists; that is, they were trying to restore prices to previous levels, not to raise them indefinitely beyond those levels. In the 1890s the free silverites wanted to stabilize the dollar and the burden of debt in an era of falling prices. The silverties saw the money stock as the key to the problem. In a way they were premature Friedmanites.

We must not forget that the wholesale price index (1910–1914 = 100) had declined from 193 in 1864 to 82 in

1890—a drop of 111 points in 36 years. This fantastic deflation showed how far the money stock was lagging behind economic expansion—and why William Jennings Bryan was more correct on these questions than Cleveland or McKinley. Yet, however correct the reflationists were on the narrow issue, their argument with the sound-money men still respected the limits Van Buren had set for governmental responsibility in the face of economic crisis.

From the Populists to FDR

This was a situation in which something had to give. Though the post-Civil War years had been an age of striking industrial expansion, they had also been marked by hard times of a severity previously unknown in American history—not only the protracted industrial depressions in the 1870s and 1890s but recession in the 1880s and deepening agricultural depression in the 1880s and 1890s. Hard times in due course led to a demand for governmental action beyond the accepted limits. This was a critical moment in the development of social rights. The active force was the Populist Party.

I know it has become fashionable in recent years, even among historians, to deplore the Populists as a rabble of clamorous, xenophobic, backward-looking demagogues yearning for some extinct and primitive agrarian utopia. I would submit, on the contrary, that they were considerably more modern-minded than the Republican and Democratic Parties of the period. One has only to compare the platforms adopted by the three parties in 1892. For both Republicans and Democrats the tariff was the supreme issue. The Populists, dismissing the "sham battle over the tariff," favored not only reflation but a graduated income tax, the nationalization of the railroads, telephone, and telegraph, the initiative and referendum, and other measures addressed, well or ill, to the emerging problems of industrial society. These measures followed from the premise carefully stated in the platform: "We believe that the powers of government—in other words, of the people—should be expanded . . . as rapidly and as far as the good sense of an intelligent people and the teachings of experience shall justify, to the end that oppression, injustice, and poverty shall eventually cease in the land."

The Populists thus formulated the fusion of Hamiltonian means with Jeffersonian ends toward which the Jacksonians had been vaguely groping 60 years before. Populism expressed a new mood; and this mood, in its eastern and urban variant, hit the White House early in the 20th century with the accession of Theodore Roosevelt. "Only the National Government," TR said, could exercise the "needed control" over the anarchy of modern industrial society. "This does not represent centralization. It represents merely the acknowledgment of the patent fact that centralization has already come in business. If this irresponsible outside power is to be controlled in the interest of the general public, it can be controlled in only one way—by giving adequate power of control to the one sovereignty capable of exercising such power—the National Government."

Roosevelt, under instruction from muckrakers and social workers, broadened this thesis in time to initiate the 20th century idea of social rights for workers, consumers, country dwellers, women, and other oppressed groups. The first comprehensive political statement of social rights is to be found in the platform of the Progressive Party in 1912 with its ringing dedication to "the conservation of human resources through an enlightened measure of social and industrial justice." Oddly, Roosevelt confined his thesis to the normal operations of society, making, any more than his benighted predecessors, no special dispensation for the business cycle. During the Panic of 1907—considered a fairly sharp setback at the time, though the 8.5 percent unemployed would be, it appears, accepted as routine today—he offered nothing specifically addressed to the economic problem. Depression remained the aberration, the irrelevant intruder who would go away if everyone ignored him, rather than a chronic crisis of the system requiring organized government counteraction.

This remained the situation during much of our own lifetime. The ratification of the Sixteenth Amendment in 1913 and the establishment of the Bureau of the Budget in 1921 created a new weapon for use against depression—fiscal policy. But the contracyclical possibilities of budgets and taxes were not understood in the 1920s, except by a few heretics like Foster and Catchings. In the main, thinking about the role of the national state in economic society had hardly advanced from the days of

Van Buren. In case of trouble government must retrench, batten down, and wait for the storm to blow over. No one in political or economic authority believed government could do much to stop depressions in advance or end them after they had begun. Depression was an uncontrollable natural calamity. Economic fatalism was the ruling creed.

As Van Buren in 1839 had spoken of the therapeutic virtue of retrenchment, of curtailing public and private expenditures, so Calvin Coolidge in 1924: "In my opinion, the Government can do more to remedy the economic ills of the people by a system of economy in public expenditure than can be accomplished through any other action." This remained the prevailing orthodoxy after the worst of all depressions assaulted the country in 1929. The next year Herbert Hoover issued a ringing declaration of governmental impotence: "Economic depression cannot be cured by legislative action or by executive pronouncement. Economic wounds must be healed by the action of the cells of the economic body—the producers and consumers themselves." Hoover did his best to cut government spending, rejected any notion of Federal responsibility for the unemployed, raised the tariff, and relied in general on exhortation and voluntarism. Balancing the budget became his obsession. Vetoing a bill intended to provide relief for those who could not find work, he said, "Never before has so dangerous a suggestion been seriously made to our country." For the national government to assume what ought to be local responsibilities, he said, would be to undermine "the very basis of self-government."

It is against this long historical background, this conviction of governmental impotence, this surrender to economic fatalism, that the contribution of Franklin Roosevelt must be measured. For, while ideologues in Washington were disclaiming up to the end both power and responsibility to act against the economic and human devastation of depression, Roosevelt, as governor of New York, was insisting that government had the duty to act. As he told the New York legislature in the depths of the downturn,

I assert that modern society, acting through its government, owes the definite obligation to prevent the starvation or the dire want of any of its fellow men and women who try to maintain themselves but cannot . . . To these unfortunate citizens, aid must be extended by government, not as a matter of charity, but as a matter of social duty.

It was this spirit that he carried to Washington in March, 1933. He now charged the national government with a double task: to revive the economy; and to relieve the human and social impact of depression. No previous President had ever acknowledged such obligations. No previous President had ever proclaimed such duties. The revolution FDR wrought in our attitudes has been so complete that it is hard to imagine today any President turning his back on economic collapse and social misery.

The experience of the depression decade led to the promulgation of the Economic Bill of Rights in 1944. This, I have suggested, was an early formulation of "social rights." Obviously the right to employment was fundamental. As Winston Churchill had written, "The problem of unemployment is the most torturing that can be presented to a civilized society." But other rights were coming to seem of equal significance: the right of every family to a decent home; the right of adequate medical care; the right to a good education; the right to protection from the economic fears of sickness and old age. The startling omission in FDR's list inadequately covered by the expressed hope that these rights would be established for all "regardless of station, race, or creed," was any clear and definite assertion of the right to full equality of opportunity for women and for non-white minorities.

There developed in the postwar years broad agreement on FDR's listing of social rights. Even conservatives accepted them in general as proper ends of society, if not of government. And there developed too, at least among liberals, broad agreement on the central role of the national government as the instrument for attaining these rights. It was in this faith that Harry Truman launched his Fair Deal, John Kennedy his New Frontier, and Lyndon Johnson his Great Society. The extraordinary rush of legislative achievement under Johnson's leadership in the mid-sixties marked the high point of belief in the national government.

The Role of the National Government

That was only a decade ago. In the years since we have seen a singular revulsion, even among liberals, if not against the social rights affirmed by the second Roosevelt, Truman, Kennedy, and Johnson, then certainly against the idea that government—above all, the national government—is the appropriate instrument through which to seek them. By 1976 the candidate of the party of the New Deal had made a leading theme in his quest for the nomination the proposition that, as he put it to the California legislature in the spring, "Washington has become a huge, wasteful, unmanageable, insensitive, bloated, bureaucratic mess." In the states liberal Democratic governors vied with each other in lowering expectations, cutting budgets, cutting services, proclaiming the end of days of wine and roses. The far left joined the far right in fulminating against the national government and celebrating the virtues of decentralization. Public opinion polls reported widespread distrust of Washington and big government. Small became beautiful, in E. F. Schumacher's rewrite of Louis D. Brandeis. Everyone vigorously denied being such an idiot as to suppose problems could be solved by throwing money at them—a phrase we owe, I think, to the late Richard M. Nixon. We are entrapped today in the mood that Vernon Jordan has called "the new minimalism" in which national goals become less government, less spending, less regulation, less public protection, fewer public services.

The logical end of this mood would be the end of the effort initiated by Theodore Roosevelt to humanize industrial society and a return to the laissez-faire policies of the late 19th century. Of course it will not be carried so far. Few people, least of all the voters, want to dismantle the national structure of service and control that has grown up in the last 40 years. Polls regularly show that Americans favor less government spending only when it is not seen to deny them personally public help they seek. By large margins they want more government money spent on health care, on Social Security, on education, on assistance to the poor, on consumer protection, on housing assistance, on mass transit. Nor, much as they think they are opposed to government regulation in the abstract, would they wish to abolish the specific Federal standards that keep our competitive system from reverting to the jungle world of King Kong trusts stamping out the smaller animals, of fetid sweatshops, verminous products and stinking slums, that brought about the Progressive counter-revolution at the turn of the century.

Still no one can doubt the deep, urgent, and widespread dissatisfaction that has fixed on big government and, to some degree, on the social programs of the sixties as symbols. The very existence of this dissatisfaction signals the need for reevaluation. The buoyant and innocent faith of our youth in big government is nearly as dead as the buoyant and innocent faith in no-government that it superceded. What we must do is to understand the reasons for the latter-day revulsion against the national government as an instrument for attaining social rights—which means, among other things, sorting out the real from the fictitious reasons and tackling the real reasons with the same fervor with which the Progressives and the New Dealers tackled substantive conditions of inequality, unemployment, and social misery.

Let us begin by clearing the fictitious reasons off the board. Big government, we are told, led inexorably to Vietnam, Watergate, and the Imperial Presidency; therefore let us abandon the social welfare state. One senses here a disjunction between premise and conclusion. Standing by itself, the premise has a certain plausibility. But the big government and massive public spending that led to Vietnam and Watergate evolved not at all on behalf of social programs, but on behalf of the Pentagon, the Central Intelligence Agency, the Federal Bureau of Investigation, and other branches of the national security establishment. This form of big government was demanded and cherished by the very people who most passionately opposed affirmative policies on behalf of the defenseless and the dispossessed. It is not the welfare state but the warfare state that has produced the overweening bureaucracy and supine citizenry so bewailed by the enemies of social programs.

Still the myth persists that the combination of government spending for the poor and government regulation of the rich is hurrying us down the road to serfdom. Last year President Ford promulgated a crusade against the awful state of "regulatory bondage" in which, as he saw it, the American government was holding the oppressed and helpless American businessman. "I hear your cries of anguish and desperation," he told one audience of capitalists as if they were inmates of a Soviet forced labor camp. Alas, he showed far less sympathy for Solzhenitsyn.

As an historian, I can only observe that this is not the way nations go totalitarian. Thurman Arnold long ago scoffed at "the absurd idea that dictatorships are the result of a long series of small seizures of power on the part of a central government." The exact opposite, he observed, was true: "every dictatorship which we now know flowed into power like air into a vacuum because the central government, in the face of a real difficulty, declined to exercise authority." One must add that, far from decreasing individual freedom and opportunity, affirmative national government has vastly increased these things for the great majority of Americans in the 20th century.

Of course the resort to the national government appears to contradict the Jeffersonian faith that the governments closest to the people would be most responsive to popular needs. But, in practice, local government has characteristically been the government of the locally powerful, not of the locally powerless. The best way the locally powerless have discovered to sustain their rights against the locally powerful—against the local planters, bankers, and industrialists and their legal and political agents—is through appeal to the national government. That is why history has proven Jeffersonian means inadequate to attain Jeffersonian ends—why Wilson declared his confidence that "if Jefferson were living in our day he would see what we see . . . Without the watchful interference, the resolute interference of the government, there can be no fair play."

Without the national government, for example, black Americans would still be fifth-class citizens; actually, without the national government, most blacks would still be slaves. It is the national government that has protected the Bill of Rights against local vigilantism. It is the national government that has protected natural resources against local greed. It is the national government that has civilized our industry, that has secured the rights of labor organization, that has defended the livelihood of the farmer. Only the national government can relieve such problems as racial justice, unemployment, inflation, urban decay, environmental protection, and the nation's needs for health care, education, housing, and welfare. The individual freedoms destroyed by the increase in national authority have been in the main the freedom to deny a tenth of the population their elementary rights as citizens, the freedom to loot and waste our resources, the freedom to work small children in mills and immigrants in sweatshops, the freedom to offer squalid working conditions and pay starvation wages, the freedom to lie in the sale of goods and securities—all freedoms, one would suppose, a decent country can easily do without.

Another common charge against big government is that government spending leads to inflation. Let me say at once that I am decidedly among those who consider inflation a most serious issue. I do not feel that 5-6 percent annual inflation is a reasonable price to pay for full employment (or that it would be even if inflation at that level produced full employment, which it does not). Inflation seems to me indeed a more troubling problem than unemployment. This is only partly because it affects more people and falls with particular force on the pensioners and the poor. It is fundamentally because we know more or less how to cure unemployment—through deficit spending—whereas we have no clear idea how to cure inflation, except through inducing unemployment or through imposing controls. Both these solutions exact their social costs—unemployment, it seems to me, far heavier costs than controls. On the other hand, we have not yet managed to work controls very well except in a war economy. We will, I believe, have to try in the future.

I think it is a most superficial analysis that makes government spending the prime cause of our recent inflation. Actually government spending, as a proportion of the gross national product, has not risen all that dramatically; the increase has only been from 18.2 percent in 1955 to 20.1 percent in 1975. It seems to me that modern inflation, far from being temporary and fortuitous, is rooted in the arrangements and structure of the post-war economy. The inherent propensity toward inflation may have one set of triggers one year; another, the next year. But, whatever form inflation takes, whether it is commodity-based or price-based or wage-based or demand-based or Arab-based, it is beyond all question the disease to which the post-war economic organism most readily and habitually succumbs. As depression was endemic in the classical economic system, inflation is endemic in the modern economic system. In my judgment, it presents almost as strong a threat to the survival of the system as depression presented 40 years ago. And, precisely because it is structural in its nature, the notion that the reduction of social spending will dispose of the threat of inflation seems to me frivolous.

There is also the cant about over-selling, over-promising, raising people's expectations and so on. This point is perennially raised against every movement of social advance from the New Deal to the Great Society. It assumes that, had it not been for political leaders stirring them up, the poor would have been happy in their misery and the blacks in their subjugation. What an absurd conception of the social process! I would guess that television had far more than Lyndon Johnson to do with raising people's expectations in the 1960s. It also assumes that voters are such fools that they take political rhetoric as an exact and literal prediction of what will happen next week. Of course they don't: they take political rhetoric as a signal of the direction in which the political leader wants to move. They perfectly understand that, in the words of Emerson, "Nothing great was ever achieved without enthusiasm." All large undertakings in America begin with expansive benedictions. The idea that, if we lower expectations, problems will go away seems of most dubious validity.

Yet the existence of fictitious reasons for the revulsion against the affirmative state does not mean that there are not real grounds for concern and complaint. A good deal of popular unease springs, I think, from the vision of endlessly enlarging social commitments going remorselessly through public budget ceilings. While I do not share the apocalyptic expectations of Caspar Weinberger about the future of social spending, I have no doubt that there is a very real problem here. In New York City, for example, pension arrangements negotiated in moods of careless optimism—there were once days of wine and roses—will, unless revised, inexorably consume a large and larger share of a budget already under intense strain to provide ongoing services and protection in the troubled metropolis. We must deal with the fact that the proportion of the retired and aged in our population is steadily increasing, especially as the birth rate declines, and that the potential costs of pensions and particularly of medical care are almost unlimited. Moreover, more and more of the Federal budget is already untouchable in the sense that the spending is mandated by law and beyond executive control. Though democracy produced the laws, the consequence may be profoundly anti-democratic by limiting the power of future generations to make their own choices among social priorities.

Making Social Programs More Effective

We are far from having become a nation collapsing under the burden of social benefits. Yet something here demands attention and rectification. One contributing factor is that, in practice, a good deal of the money involved in social programs never gets to those for whom it is intended but is siphoned off along the way by the middle-class professionals who administer the services. Daniel Patrick Moynihan and others have argued that, in general, the social programs of the sixties served the needs of the poor less efficiently than they served the interests of the professionals who gained jobs and prestige from the programs and research grants to assess the results. Administrative costs rise faster than the number of beneficiaries. This general point has been exaggerated, but it is a real point all the same.

For the social program of the sixties unquestionably fostered a professional constituency inside the technostructure—and this constituency, articulate, organized, purposeful, has often been more effective in asserting itself than has been the weak, diffuse, and inarticulate constituency of the poor. Related to this is the tendency of professionals to spin out in their barbaric argot instructions and regulations that do more to gratify their self-esteem than to enlighten the public. Related too is the tendency of government agencies to stay in business after their ineffectuality has been demonstrated or their function has disappeared. The 'sunset laws' of which we hear so much these days seem to me altogether too simple an answer to this problem. But we deceive ourselves if we do not suppose that the problem is a significant source of revulsion against the national government as an instrument for attaining social rights.

Considerations such as these no doubt played a role in the famous shift from the 'services' to the 'income' strategy a few years ago. But this shift created problems of its own. Food stamps and other direct transfers to poor families do little to alleviate such structural sanctions of poverty as racism, poor education, poor job training, poor housing, poor transportation. Moreover, the flow of large sums of money, whether in connection with income or with services, always attracts crooks—a proposition that seems not to have sufficiently impressed the high-minded people who designed the social programs of the sixties. One of the triumphs of the New Deal in retrospect was the astonishing lack of graft in the disbursement of Federal funds. I do not recommend that we return to the days of Harold Ickes, who used to wiretap his employees to make sure that no one was cooking PWA contracts. Still nothing has discredited the affirmative state more than the rip-off issue—the impression people have that the public money is being stolen and no one cares.

The *New York Daily News* had a headline recently about the medical community of New York City: "Report Shows 108 Docs Got $167M in Medicaid." The headline in the *Times* was "New York Officials Place Medicaid Frauds at 20%." The thoughtful reader would understand that this unscrupulous rip-off is an argument *against* devolution to the states and communities and *for* centralization in Washington, because Medicaid is essentially a state-managed program, while the federally-managed Medicare has been, so far as we know, less marked by such gross abuse. But many readers will take the random revelations of the Moss Committee as one more argument against social spending and the affirmative state. And there has been, heaven knows, sufficient evidence of corruption in housing and urban development programs and other Federal activities.

Liberals have always had a blind spot about crime. We have been traditionally involved in sentimental theories of the social origins of criminality. Crime itself has seemed somehow unseemly and irrelevant, an issue for conservatives to demagogue about. Yet the fact that conservatives invoke crime for their own purposes does not mean that the issue is not terribly real and does not, and for good reason, deeply bother a great part of the population. As yet the social programs have been invaded mainly by white-collar crime. As the money flow swells, we can be reasonably sure that organized crime will figure out ways to get into the act. I assure you that the protection of social programs against rip-off is a matter of the highest urgency not only on its own merits but as a means of restoring faith in the integrity and equity of government.

Yet *The New York Times* tells us that the Department of

Health, Education, and Welfare had not before this year assigned a single person full-time to the problem of Medicaid fraud. Perhaps the White House or the Office of Management and Budget should establish an Inspector General with authority to inquire into everything from the conduct of an agency to the capacity of its officials to write an intelligible English sentence. Perhaps the FBI should move on from the Socialist Workers to social work and investigate the rip-off scandals. Certainly one would wish for objective and thorough congressional oversight.

I conclude in an expression of perplexity. I have no doubt that the national government must remain central in our quest for social rights. The dream of decentralization of authority seems to me a dead end. Centralization is less vulnerable to selfish local pressure; it assures the most economical use of specialized public personnel; it offers greater flexibility in the transfer of resources; it provides the only means of establishing national standards. Yet the public discontent tells us that something has gone badly wrong, and we must listen.

The time has come for a comprehensive reassessment of the condition to which social policy from the New Deal to the Great Society has brought us. We have been marching too long into the quagmire without a battle plan. Clearly our traditional social programs need much more in the way of careful administration, responsible oversight, effective policing and unremitting attention to racial justice and to what used to be called in foreign aid programs "end-use." Perhaps David Lilienthal's old phrase about the "decentralized administration of centralized authority" provides a clue worth more systematic exploration. Or perhaps the present type of program is simply too superficial in its effect. Perhaps social policy must cut a great deal deeper and at last confront the distributive problem. The distribution of income in the United States has remained static for 30 years. Perhaps this will be the issue that characterizes the next great period of social advance.

What the nation requires is a new framework within which to consider the problems of social equity and justice. The old framework has served us well. We would not throw it on the scrap heap. But it has not completed the job. Not that the job will ever be finished: but let us pray that the next generation will learn from our experiments and press forward with their own.

James Tobin

3

The Political Economy of the 1960s

I shall concentrate on the general macro-economic design and strategy of the Kennedy and Johnson Administrations, especially during the period 1961-1965 before the Vietnam War and its financing dominated the scene. The macro-economic strategy of those years was, I think, the indispensable foundation for the important advances in domestic social policy of the two Presidents. As those innovations are the main subject of this book, I shall allude to them only in the briefest and broadest terms. At the outset I should also confess the obvious. I come to this subject with the bias of an economist who served on President Kennedy's Council of Economic Advisers in 1961-62 and was associated with the Council for some years thereafter.

Kennedy-Johnson Macro-Economic Strategy

Over the five years from 1961 through 1965 the Kennedy and Johnson Administrations developed, preached, and practiced a remarkable coherent macro-economic strategy. The theme was steady economic growth at full employment, avoiding cycles of recession and inflation. The Administrations regarded growth in national production and income not only as an end in itself but as the fount of economic and fiscal resources for meeting national needs. With new resources unendingly provided by growth, public services could be expanded and upgraded, social insurance and income assistance extended, a war on poverty launched—all without divisive conflicts over taxes, the size of the public sector, defense spending, and the distribution of income and wealth. Stable, rapid, noncyclical, non-inflationary growth was to be the underpinning of the Great Society.

I must now make an academic but important distinction, one which the Council taught from the outset in 1961, not always successfully. The distinction is between the growth in the economy's capacity to produce goods and services and the quarter-to-quarter or year-to-year growth in actual production and real income. The growth of capacity is limited by the growth in the labor force and its productivity, determined by trends in the size of the population, its availability for work, its skills and education, and in the rate of technological advance, capital accumulation, and the supply of land and other natural resources. The trend growth rate of potential output changes very slowly; in the United States since World War II it has been between 3½ and 4¼ percent per year, of which 1¼ to 1½ points are attributable to the growth of labor input and the remainder to the various factors raising the productivity of labor. On the other hand, the short-term—quarter-to-quarter or year-to-year—growth of actual output has varied drastically, from rates as high as 10 percent per year to negative figures. Accompanying these variations are extreme changes in the rate of utilization of the labor force, reflected in fluctuations of unemployment rates, and of industrial plant. These oscillations are due to instability in the growth of aggregate demand for goods and services; while potential supply grows quite smoothly, actual demand advances unevenly and sometimes indeed falls.

In the short run, if there is a lot of slack in the economy in the form of unemployed labor and underutilized plant and equipment, production can respond to rapidly expanding demand and grow more rapidly than its long-run trend. This is what happens in a recovery from recession; indeed there cannot be a true recovery unless output does grow faster than capacity, for otherwise unemployment and excess capacity will not be reduced. But rates of growth greater than the growth of capacity cannot be sustained; once the recovery is complete and the economy is again operating at potential, output will be limited to the capacity growth rate, 4 percent more or less in this country.

The distinction is essential to understanding the macroeconomic design of the Kennedy-Johnson Administrations. There were basically three objectives. (1) Taking office at the trough of the fourth post-war recession, with unemployment at 7 percent the Kennedy Council naturally saw rapid and full recovery, with high short-run growth of actual output, as its prime goal. (2) Once that was achieved, moreover, the Council aimed to keep the economy operating at its potential, with demand expanding fairly steadily at the sustainable rate of growth of supply. (3) But the Council and the Administration also hoped to accelerate the growth of capacity, not of population and labor force, of course,—that would be determined by demographic and social trends and individual tastes—but of productivity, output per hour of work.

The government's handle for the first objective, recovery, is much more obvious than its ability to achieve the other two. And the second goal is probably easier for government to realize than the third. That is because the first two tasks involve the manipulation of demand, for which the Federal Government has some powerful direct and indirect tools. Influencing supply—technology, efficiency, human and physical capital—was and is a much more uncertain enterprise.

The recovery strategy of 1961-1965 was quite successful, and it was popularly perceived as even more successful than it really was. Five years of uninterrupted advance brought the unemployment rate down to 3.9 percent in January, 1966, achieving the Kennedy Administration's explicit "interim goal" of 4 percent. Real GNP, i.e., production measured in constant prices, grew more than 5 percent per year over the same period, employment by 2.5 percent per year. The percentage of the population living in poverty, as it came to be officially measured, declined from 22.4 percent in 1960 to 14.7 percent in 1966. Corporate profits after taxes rose by 80 percent. Other economic indicators performed just as spectacularly. Meanwhile the inflation rate remained below 2 percent per year.

For the reasons already explained, growth at the 1961-1965 pace could not continue, as the Kennedy-Johnson economists knew and said. Of the total GNP advance, about 27 percent was cyclical recovery, associated with the three point reduction of the unemployment rate. The remainder was growth in the economy's capacity to produce which could be expected to continue. The aim of macro-economic policy was to slow demand in 1966 to the sustainable rate of capacity growth, to keep unemployment close to 4 percent, to avoid both recession and inflationary overheating of the economy. Meanwhile manpower and labor market policies were to pave the way for gradual reduction of unemployment below the interim 4 percent target, and policies fostering the formation of physical and human capital and the advance of technology were slowly to raise the sustainable growth rate.

We will never know whether this was a feasible scenario. The sudden escalation of Vietnam war spending in 1965-66, without compensating tax increases or spending cuts, destroyed the prospects of stable growth not only for the remaining years of the Johnson Administration but for the 1970s as well. Although economists inside and outside recognized in January, 1966, that deficit financing of Vietnam spending was a serious error, no one foresaw how dreadful and durable the consequences would be. The new fiscal stimulus pushed unemployment down as far as 3 percent, with predictably desirable effects on the employment and income of the disadvantaged and poor. But it also generated waves of wage and price inflation of unexpected virulence and persistence. In any case macro policies in 1966-1969, in contrast to 1961-1965, were a scramble to restore stability—a well-managed scramble, but a scramble.

Recovery Policy and Its Obstacles 1961-1965.

I have attributed to the Kennedy and Johnson Administrations a coherent macro-economic strategy, but this was not in place on inauguration day in 1961. The Heller Council of Economic Advisers and its allies in the Bureau of the Budget had a clear conception of the task ahead, but this was far from fully accepted in the White House, Treasury, or Labor Department, much less in the Federal Reserve, the Congress, or influential public opinion. It took 18 to 24 months for the Council's diagnosis and prescriptions, modified in internal and external debate, to become dominant Administration policy. Not until 1964 did the centerpiece of New Economics fiscal policy, the $12 billion tax cut, take effect.

As a result, the 1961-1965 recovery was, for worse or better, slower—and at times more fragile and uncertain—than its economist architects desired. I point this out today because the 1961-1965 episode is widely cited as a model for the current recovery, in particular to support the view that slower is better and longer. The fact is that there were some anxious days in 1962-1963, when luck, together with whatever fiscal stimulus could be smuggled into conservative budgets and whatever monetary support a gold-conscious central bank could be induced to provide, kept recovery from petering out.

The Council's prime objective was to restore full employment defined for the time being as 4 percent unemployment. According to Council estimates which proved correct in the event and are known to all economics students as Okun's Law, the requisite three point reduction of unemployment would yield a 10 percent increase in GNP, on top of the normal annual increment from growth of labor force and productivity. In the Council's view the country had the labor power, skills, technology, and plant to produce the extra 10 percent, and failure to utilize these resources was an inexcusable massive waste.

The Council was, of course, concerned by the human predicaments of people who could not find jobs. But unemployment was also seen as a general barometer of the country's economic health. Business profits, state and local finances, farm incomes, real wages, stock market value—all would look much rosier if prosperity were restored and maintained. Because of the 1957-58 recession, the aborted recovery of 1959-60, and the recession of 1960-61, the economy had not achieved 4 percent unemployment since 1957 and was in danger of prolonged stagnation.

To the Kennedy economists the means were as obvious as the end. Federal fiscal policy and Federal Reserve monetary policy should stimulate aggregate spending, public and private, by some combination of new government expenditure, tax reduction, and easing of credit and interest rates.

Fiscal expansion meant, in the short run at least, larger budget deficits. But these were innocuous and appropriate in an under-employed economy, even one commencing a cyclical upswing. Indeed one of the reasons for the post-1957 stagnation, in particular the 1960 recession, was "fiscal drag"—the natural growth of the economy was raising the potential Federal tax take at full employment faster than Federal expenditures were increasing. Yet the potential revenues were not realized because the taxes detracted from private spending and depressed the economy. The Council pointed out, with emphasis if not originality, that the budget should be judged not by the actual deficits yielded in recessions but by the deficit or surplus it would produce at full employment.

Although the New Economics remains identified in the public mind with the active use of fiscal policy for stabilization, the

Council also strongly advocated the use of monetary measures. The Federal Reserve was urged to lower interest rates, especially long-term bond yields, and to abandon its self-imposed rule of intervening only in the market for Treasury bills. The Treasury was urged, unsuccessfully, to adopt debt management tactics that would lower long-term rates. The Council was not monetarist, but it was not "fiscalist" either, if that term has the symmetrical meaning that the other tool is viewed as useless. The Council recognized the efficacy and importance of both kinds of macro-economic policy, not only for promoting recovery but for restraining aggregate demand if the economic situation were reversed.

Regarding the mixture of public spending, tax reduction, and easy monetary policy as recovery instruments, there was some disagreement in the Administration. J. K. Galbraith's prime concern was to nourish the public sector; the only expansionary measures he favored were those that increased government spending. He opposed the tax cut of 1964, and he had little faith in monetary policy. Some of us took quite seriously the expressed objective of raising the long-run growth rate of the economy's capacity to produce. We stressed the importance of public and private investments in human skills, technology, and physical capital. Encouragement of capital formation, as a contribution both to recovery and to long-term growth, was a major motivation for the investment tax credit enacted in 1962. For the same reasons, we stressed the importance of monetary policies which would stimulate investment with low interest rates. We hoped to have a Federal budget surplus, augmenting the saving available for capital information, once full employment was restored. Walter Heller was, I think, somewhat skeptical of the economic, as well as the political, feasibility of a policy mixture strongly oriented to investment. He thought the surest road to recovery was direct stimulus by public spending or private consumption induced by tax cuts.

These differences of emphasis were largely resolved by practical constraints on the policy mix. No Galbraithian burst of Federal civilian spending was in the political cards. To be sure, the Kennedy Administration made use of opportunities to increase some Federal spending. Social Security benefits were increased ahead of schedule and ahead of the matching payroll taxes; at the time this could be done without cosmetic damage to the administrative budget. No one wanted to use defense spending as a demand stimulus. But when the Berlin crisis of 1961 evoked a modest increase of military outlay, the Council successfully blocked the instinctive urge of many high Administration officials to raise taxes to match. Monetary policy was also constrained. Because of anxieties about the U.S. balance of international payments, the Federal Reserve could not or would not pursue an aggressively easy monetary policy. For major expansionary stimulus, tax reduction for private consumers and business investors was the only avenue open.

Inflation and the Wage/Price Guideposts

The major serious justification of the restrictive monetary and fiscal policies that led to the two recessions of 1957-58 and 1960-61 was the need to cool off the 4 percent inflation rate reached in the mid-1950s. Inflation had subsided to a negligible 1.5 percent per year. The Kennedy Council did not regard a revival of inflation as likely early in the recovery. But it did not want to take any risks, and the mid-50s were a warning of what might happen as unemployment was reduced again to 4 percent. To be quite candid, the Council feared rises in price index less for their own sake than for the damage they would do to the credibility and acceptability of a full recovery and full employment policy within the Administration, the Federal Reserve, the Congress, and in general public opinion. To the customary objections to inflation would be added the deterioration of the U.S. competitive position in world markets and of the U.S. balances of trade and payments.

Like most economists, the Council members were well aware that full employment in an advanced democratic captialist economy was likely to give wages and prices an inflationary tilt. By themselves monetary and fiscal policies to regulate aggregate demand cannot be sure to achieve both full employment and price stability. This is definitely not a recent revelation.

The Council's answer was the "guideposts for non-inflationary price and wage behavior" set forth in the 1962 Economic Report. The guideposts were standards for management and labor. Perhaps more important, they were standards for government officials in their inevitable interventions in labor disputes, We did not want industrial peace at any price level. The guideposts had no legal force. But the President, the Council, the Secretary of Labor, and cabinet officers deployed their persuasive powers to keep announced prices and wage bargains of national importance in approximate compliance.

This policy began as early as 1961, when the President—largely on the initiative of the late Kermit Gordon, a member of the Council at the time—began urging restraint on the steel industry and its union. These contacts culminated in the moderate steel wage contract of 1962 negotiated with the active participation of Secretary Goldberg. President Kennedy's confrontation with the industry, when major steel companies announced price increases before the ink was dry on the union contract, is an oft told tale.

Through 1965 the recovery was virtually free of inflation. Whether the policy of guideposts supported by moral suasion deserves any credit remains debatable. Perhaps the slack in the economy sufficed to restrain wages and prices. In comparison with subsequent periods, however, the stability of the early 1960s now appears exceptional. History has vindicated the Council's view that some kind of incomes policy is an essential complement to fiscal and monetary management of demand. Without it—pessimists will say with it too—full employment and inflation control are all too likely to be incompatible. The experience also suggests that incomes policies should be in place when there is still slack in the economy, not imposed when the pot is already boiling.

A weakness of the guideposts is that they were not developed with the participation of business and labor leaders; they were indeed opposed by most of them. This was not because the Administration did not try. It was intended that the President's Labor-Management Advisory Committee, with business, labor, and general public members, would seriously confront the problem. But the climate was not favorable; the Committee preferred to debate general issues of economic policy among themselves and with Federal officials. After the disheartening experiences of the last decade, I suspect the climate today is much more favorable for joint formulation and support of guideposts.

The outbreak of excess demand inflation in 1966 put impossible strains on the open mouth operations of the Johnson

Administration. Under such pressures even full-fledged controls would have given way.

Fiscal Conservatism and the New Economics

The principal obstacles to the macro-economic design of the Kennedy economists were conservative fiscal and financial tenets prevalent in the Administration itself, the Congress, and influential public opinion. At the beginning of a new Democratic Administration, after an uncomfortably close election, with a reliable majority in Congress, highly suspect in the business and financial community, JFK was not ready to do battle for New Economics. Planned deficit spending was taboo, especially after the recession had "bottomed out." Budget deficits initially were okay only if they could be blamed on Eisenhower. Even when minds were later liberated, Ike's $12 billion deficit in fiscal 1958 became an upper limit.

The 4 percent unemployment target was widely challenged, from the right and from the left. Federal Reserve Chairman Martin attributed the growth of unemployment in the 1950s not to demand inadequacy but to structural maladjustments in labor markets. For different reasons this view also appealed to the top leadership of Kennedy's Labor Department. Prophets like Robert Theobald laid the increase of unemployment to automation and detected a trend toward technological obsolescence of human labor. These issues are discussed further below.

Conservatives contended that the count of the unemployed was swollen by undeserving cases, and even deliberately exaggerated by the government. JFK was moved to appoint a blue ribbon committee to defend the purity and intertemporal comparability of the statistics.

Reenforcing the grip of conservative fiscal opinion was the suspicion and hostility of the business and financial community toward a new Democratic Administration after eight years of Eisenhower. It was easy to read the confrontation with Big Steel as confirming their worst fears. The extent of mistrust was exemplified by the organized opposition of industry to the investment tax credit proposed by the Administration, a bonanza now highly prized and resolutely defended. These political attitudes accentuated a general failure of confidence in the American business future, initially bred by the stagnation of the late 1950s and the nation's international economic difficulties. The mood of 1962 was very similar to that of 1975. But there was less reason for discouragement then, and pessimism was quickly transformed into euphoria in 1963-1965.

The Dollar, Gold, and the Balance of Payments

Potentially the external position of the dollar and defense of the country's dwindling gold stock were serious constraints on domestic economic policy. As it was they constrained the mixture of demand management policies more than the overall thrust, and they compromised the traditional liberal position of the United States in international economic relations.

Convertibility of dollars held by foreign governments into gold at the established price was considered, in the Federal Reserve and the Treasury and in private financial circles, a sacred commitment and absolute priority. Its precedence over other policy objectives was never to be questioned, even behind closed doors, lest doubts arise at home and abroad regarding the Administration's determination to defend the parity, doubts which could trigger further speculation against the dollar. Like non-conservative governments in other countries—the first Administration of Harold Wilson is a notable and notorious example—the Kennedy-Johnson Administration felt particularly vulnerable to charges of softness and amateurism in international finance. To demonstrate soundness and firmness, such governments over-react. Just as, for similar political reasons, it eventually took a Republican President and Secretary of State to crack open the door to China, so it took Nixon and Connally to cut the tie between dollar and gold. When they did it in 1971, it was heralded as a famous victory.

In the early 1960s gold and the balance of payments constituted a powerful argument against all expansionary policy, but particularly against expansionary monetary policy. Our friends in Europe, notably in the influential Working Party Three of the Organization for Economic Cooperation and Development, came to understand and to accept the value to the world as well as to the United States itself of a strong sustained American recovery. They thought it should be fueled by fiscal policy, and their acceptance of deficits along the way defused some of the domestic opposition and official hesitation. However, they supported the Federal Reserve's view that U.S. interest rates should rise, certainly not fall, in order to avoid outflows of funds in search of higher yields in Europe. This position stood in the way of the policy mixture preferred by some Kennedy economists, which featured easy monetary policy for a high-investment recovery oriented to long-run growth. The investment tax credit, and the largely futile effort to twist the interest rate structure toward higher short-term rates, to keep funds at home, and lower long-term rates, to encourage domestic investment, were attempts at reconciliation.

Once fears of deficits and inflation were neutralized, the balance of payments was not a serious inhibition on economic expansion *per se*. The reason was a variety of ad hoc measures: direct controls to limit foreign exchange demands by government and private citizens, and international arrangements to defend the dollar against speculation and to limit actual conversions into gold (except by DeGaulle) while maintaining formal convertibility.

Throughout the period the Council argued, mostly unsuccessfully, that the gold-dollar parity should not be allowed either to interfere with domestic recovery and growth or to erode the historic American commitment to unrestricted international trade and capital movement. With one hand, the Kennedy and Johnson Administrations were ostentatiously carrying forward the 30-year-old policy of negotiating mutual reductions of tariffs and other trade barriers. These efforts encountered increasing domestic resistance, as more and more American industries and workers found themselves no longer competitive at the established exchange rates. Organized labor, especially resentful of the "export of jobs" by overseas investments of American corporations, became increasingly protectionist. With the other hand, the Administrations were busy defending the exchange rate and American producers by informal quotas on textile imports and other products, by insisting that foreign aid be tied to purchases in the U.S., by discriminatory rules on military procurement, and other devices. Likewise the Treasury was compromising the position of the United States as an international center of finance and capital by restrictions on foreign lending by American banks, tariffs on flotations of foreign securities, and on direct investment by U.S. companies.

The Council's argument was that the risk of dollar devaluation and exchange depreciation should be accepted, because the consequences would be anything but disastrous if these events ever came to pass. When they finally did, in 1971, the truth of the argument was demonstrated. Meanwhile, the Council thought, the U.S. should use more of its diplomatic weight to negotiate improved international monetary arrangements, augmenting international liquidity and assigning a proper share of adjustment responsibilities to the surplus countries of Europe and Japan. In restrospect it really is a shame that our government did not have the courage and foresight to float the dollar in 1961, instead of 10 years later.

Policies to Reduce Unemployment and Poverty

The Kennedy-Johnson Council economists were from the beginning confident that the American economy, adequately stimulated by policies to expand aggregate demand, could create enough jobs to restore 4 percent unemployment. Jobs were required not only for the two million workers representing the excess of unemployment over the target but also for the growth of the labor force from demographic trends and from the increased availability of jobs. In fact the economy generated nine million new jobs in the five years 1961-1965.

Critics inside and outside the Administration thought that the Council overstressed its macro-economic remedies for unemployment and underplayed micro-economic cures. The Council's main concern was to refute the influential views in vogue at the time, that the economy had undergone a change of life rendering macro-economic stimuli ineffective against unemployment. I recall an Undersecretary of Labor, later Secretary, who argued that there was no *general* unemployment problem, but as many specific problems as there were unemployed individuals. Of course no specific programs, oriented to particular jobs and individual workers, could ever have generated nine million new jobs in five years.

Actually the Council always recognized that there were limits to macro policies, that 4 percent unemployment overall implied excessive rates for some demographic groups and geographical regions, and that general prosperity left all too many people either out of the labor force—not even counted as unemployed but discouraged or unemployable because of discrimination, disability, location, lack of skill or of education—or for similar reasons employed sporadically at substandard jobs and wages. The Council always supported the Administration's micro-economic employment policies: development assistance to depressed areas like Appalachia, equal employment opportunity, improvement of labor exchange to match jobs and workers more quickly and efficiently, federal assistance to urban schools, youth employment, training on and off the jobs.

The hope was that these programs would eventually make it possible for macro policies to aim at lower rates of unemployment than 4 percent. Unfortunately the hope has not been realized. Whatever their individual successes, labor market policies collectively have been a disappointment. Certainly they have not lowered the feasible non-inflationary unemployment rate. Meanwhile demographic trends have worked the other way, raising the fractions of the labor force of workers—young, female, nonwhite, single—who whether through discrimination, disqualification, or personal preference are highly susceptible to spells of unemployment. The structuralists who in 1961 claimed this had already happened were premature, but it has happened since 1966. Likewise urban pockets of unemployables, chronically outside the mainstream of American economy and society, have grown. It is even more evident today than in the 1960s that general prosperity and growth will not by themselves solve these problems. The economy cannot be stimulated to such a pitch that jobs are created for those at the end of the queue or beyond it, without igniting inflationary fires that the society at large will not tolerate.

This truth does not justify today, any more than in the 1960s, the discard of macro policies of expansion. Anemic recovery and stagnation will surely worsen the plight of disadvantaged workers and add new cohorts of adults who cannot get a job because they never had one. In spite of the disappointments of the past, specific job programs are even more essential today than fifteen years ago. But they will have two, maybe three, strikes against them if macro policies hold the economy at 8 percent unemployment, or 7, or 6 percent.

That in 1959 nearly a quarter of the population lived in abysmal poverty was a disgrace to the affluent society. Kennedy-Johnson economists knew that general economic expansion and progress were the most powerful forces for reduction of poverty. The two Presidents knew that it was much less divisive to aid the poor from the fruits of economic expansion than from explicit redistribution of the existing pie. The unpopularity of redistributive programs today, in an economy stalled for several years, confirms the soundness of their instincts. Yet Presidents Kennedy and Johnson agreed with Walter Heller and his colleagues that overall recovery and growth, essential as they were, would not diminish poverty fast enough. The War on Poverty embodies their determination to enable all Americans to share the general prosperity of the country.

I shall confine myself to two comments about the War on Poverty. First, in the grand design, the maintenance of prosperity, full employment, and growth was always regarded as necessary though not sufficient. The necessity is confirmed by the increases in incidence of poverty accompanying recent macro-economic reverses. Second, I regret that the Johnson Administration never supported systematic universal income guarantees and income-conditioned cash transfers—yes, a "negative income tax." This reform was not inconsistent with War on Poverty programs, and it would have brought victory in the war appreciably closer. In eschewing this approach—belatedly endorsed by the Heineman Commission appointed by President Johnson—the Administration carried to extreme its reluctance to face squarely the issue of income redistribution. Moreover, Democratic fears of conservative backlash almost defaulted this innovation, like the overture to China and the floating of the dollar, to the next Republican administration, in the form of Nixon's Family Assistance Plan.

Stable Growth at Full Employment

The Kennedy-Johnson Administrations hoped to break permanently the post-war cyclical rhythm of the American economy. The Council was confident that fiscal and monetary management of aggregate demand, supported by incomes policies, could hold the economy within a fairly narrow band around its full employment growth track. "Fine tuning" was, I believe, not Walter Heller's own phrase but a journalistic caricature, but it did succinctly capture the faith of the New Economics in the efficacy of discretionary macro-economic policies and in the wisdom of policy-makers.

However, the policy-making apparatus was inadequate. As for fiscal policy, Congressional procedures for appropriations and taxes were too slow, too decentralized, too preoccupied with issues extraneous to economic stabilization. They seldom added up to rational overall fiscal policy, or provided prompt and measured counterweights to fluctuations of private spending. The long delays in enacting the tax reduction of 1964 are a case in point.

A remedy proposed by Presidents Kennedy and Johnson was limited Presidential discretion to make temporary changes of income tax rates in a pre-arranged format, or, failing such a delegation of power, agreed streamlined procedures for speedy consideration of Presidential requests for temporary tax changes for purposes of economic stabilization. These proposals got nowhere—unfortunately in my view. However, other ideas for making fiscal policy more responsive to economic conditions—notably extension and enlargement of unemployment benefits in recession—have been adopted. Moreover, the new Congressional budget procedures and staffs promise greatly to increase the rationality of Federal fiscal policy.

As for monetary policy, the tools are generally adequate, flexible, and capable of quick response. The problem is the independence of the Federal Reserve, which can follow a macro-economic policy quite different from that of the Executive and the Congress. The Fed does read the election returns, and informal relations with the President, Council, and Treasury were generally good during the Kennedy-Johnson years. (The big exception was in December, 1965, when a restrictive move by the Fed surprised the Administration. In retrospect, I think the Fed was right in substance, although I did not think so at the time.) Yet its independence, and the exclusion of other economic officials from its deliberations, gives the Fed's position a greater weight in overall policy than other government agencies, and for that matter foreign central banks, enjoy. Independence is a sensitive political issue. The Kennedy Administration could not even get Congress to make the Federal Reserve Chairman's term coincident with that of the President, although that reform was endorsed by Chairman Martin and his colleagues. Recent efforts for reform have also lost to the lobbies of banks and financial interests. But Congress and Committees have been making the

Fed more accountable; and now that Congress makes fiscal policy with explicit economic objectives and forecasts, it probably will not tolerate Federal Reserve policies which pull the economy off course.

The Keynesian views of the Kennedy-Johnson economists regarding the need and efficacy of discretionary policy stand in contrast to what may now be once again the prevailing orthodoxy of economists, a doctrine that certainly exerts heavy influence in Washington today. This is the faith that the private economy is intrinsically stable, that cycles and fluctuations are mainly the reflection of instability in government fiscal and monetary policies themselves, that discretionary variation of these instruments, fine tuning or coarse, is unnecessary and counterproductive. The prescription of the new-old orthodoxy is to follow a steady fiscal and monetary course, unvarying with economic conditions and outlooks, in the belief that the economy will settle down in adjustment to the fixed policy and that wherever it settles, whatever the rate of unemployment, is the optimal outcome.

I point out the contrast, but I do not debate the issue here. I remain of the view that the economic vessel has been, will continue to be, buffeted by many strong winds and currents other than those of the pilots' own making. Poor helmsmen steer wavy courses, but that is not a convincing reason to lock the rudder. Nothing in the history of capitalist economies suggests that they are inherently stable or that they can unguided achieve and maintain a tolerable volume of employment.

Long-Run Economic Growth

The third objective I mentioned at the beginning was to raise the sustainable rate of growth of productivity. Like the reduction of unemployment and poverty, this was to be attempted by a combination of general and specific measures. As I have already explained, a growth- and investment-oriented mixture of macro policies was for the most part ruled out by the international constraints on monetary policy. While the investment tax credit undoubtedly accelerated capital formation during the recovery, nothing was done to augment the saving available for capital formation at full employment. The tax cut of 1964 worked in the opposite direction, and so, of course, did the deficit financing of Vietnam War expenditure, only partially mitigated by the belated temporary tax increase of 1968. Consequently tight monetary policy, discouraging to investment, bore the brunt of anti-inflationary restraint. As for specific pro-growth policies, there were modest efforts to speed up technological and scientific advances and their diffusion, and I am afraid that no perceptible success can be claimed for them. Agriculture is the model here, but no one knows how to copy the successes of agricultural experiment stations and extension services in other industries.

Of course, under the best of circumstances it would be difficult to detect policy-induced changes in long-run growth trends for the economy as a whole. We are talking about fractions of percentage points; measurement is imperfect, and other influences, probably more powerful than policies, are at work. The trend of productivity is probably much the same now as in the 1960s.

In the early 1960s, the vision of economic growth as the source of ever improving material well-being for ever larger majorities of the population was unclouded by the concerns prevalent today over environment, energy, and resource limitations. Growth is no longer a popular word. To many persons, especially among the young, the Kennedy-Johnson enthusiasm for growth seems misguided and insensitive. The failure of those Administrations to develop environmental, energy, and resource policies was certainly a grievous omission.

Yet the 1960s commitment to growth was motivated by the same considerations as the conservation movement, namely giving future generations a fair deal or better. Overall economic slowdown is a terribly wasteful way to diminish pollution, conserve energy, husband natural resources. The problems are micro-economic, not macro-economic. The solution is not to cut back in production and employment indiscriminately, as the advocates of zero economic growth suggest. The solutions are incentives, regulations, and programs that prohibit or limit the use of processes and products which damage the environment and waste scarce resources. With specific remedies in place, the case for full employment and for overall progress in technology and productivity is as strong as ever. The composition of national output will be different from the past, and the nation's capacity to produce may grow more slowly, at least temporarily.

Economic Aspects of the Vietnam Tragedy

The 1960s began with high promise for American life, but much of it was lost in Vietnam. The economic dimension is perhaps the least important, but serious enough. The War on Poverty petered out, the dream of the Great Society was not fulfilled, the grand macro-economic design was discredited. The economy resumed an unstable course, with stubborn inflation and, in the 1970s, excessive unemployment too.

Lyndon Johnson bravely fought to combine guns and butter, to prevent his Great Society programs from being sacrificed for military spending. In a sense he was quite right: the society could well afford both. Vietnam War spending was never a large fraction of GNP, and at its height the total defense budget was smaller relative to the economy than in the 1950s. But in 1966 the economy could not finance both without an increase in taxes. Deficit financing overheated the economy and began the era of inflation and instability still afflicting us.

The President's motive was to save his domestic programs from the cuts which a request for higher taxes would, as experience later showed, surely have invited. But in the longer run politics of the country, his aim was not achieved. The standard mythology today, erroneous in my opinion, forgets the war and its financing and blames inflation and instability on the economic design itself, on Great Society programs, on government spending and deficits *per se*.

The war tragically rent the fabric of American society, the bonds of trust and compassion among citizens and between citizens and governments. The political economy of the 1960s did not expect citizens to be altruistic. But it did assume a widespread popular faith that government and the economy would give all individuals and groups a fair deal, and a fair share of the fruits of a growing economy. The willingness of the taxpaying majority to help less fortunate citizens depended on such attitudes. But the faith has been eroded by the war and its economic consequences, as well as by Watergate and other betrayals of trust and justice. The 1970s display more selfish, group-interested, militant behavior of every kind—economic, social, political. Today the people yearn for leadership to restore the spirit of community to American life.

PART

2

the right to a decent standard of living

Robert A. Levine

4

An Overview of the Policies and Programs to Guarantee a Decent Standard of Living

Since many of the sins of the Kennedy and Johnson Administrations were rhetorical (and therefore perhaps less than mortal) it should be noted at the outset that this chapter covers primarily the anti-poverty programs of the two Administrations, which may or may not be a less rhetorical rendition of the topic, "Programs to Guarantee a Decent Standard of Living." The point is not trivial because: (a) terminology is important, and a major theme of the chapter will be the tension between the "anti-poverty" terminology and the "provision of opportunity" description of many of the programs. These labels are not the same but they were applied to the same programs; (b) The initial objective of the anti-poverty programs, except in the most rhetorical way, was not to *end* all poverty (i.e., to *guarantee* a decent standard of living). That came later.

The best description of how the poverty programs came together has been provided by James Sundquist:

> The measures enacted, and those proposed, were dealing separately with such problems as slum housing, juvenile delinquency, dependency, unemployment, illiteracy, but they were separately inadequate because they were striking only at surface aspects of what seemed to be some kind of bedrock problem, and it was the bedrock problem that had to be identified so that it could be attacked in a concerted, unified, and innovative way. Perhaps it was Harrington's book that defined the target for Kennedy and supplied the coordinating concept—the bedrock problem, in a word was "poverty." Words and concepts determine programs; once the target was reduced to a single word, the timing became right for a unified program.[1]

The trouble is that it did not stay even that simple. The section of the basic anti-poverty law (The Economic Opportunity Act of 1965), that sets forth the declaration of purpose says:

Although the economic well-being and prosperity of the United States have progressed to a level surpassing any achieved in world history, and although these benefits are widely shared throughout the Nation, *poverty* continues to be the lot of a substantial number of our people. The United States can achieve its full economic and social potential as a nation only if every individual has the *opportunity* for education and training, the opportunity to work, and the opportunity to live in decency and dignity. It is the purpose of this Act to strengthen, supplement, and coordinate efforts in furtherance of that policy. (emphasis added)

Thus the objectives of combating poverty (doing something for people at the lower end of the income scale, including those needing not opportunity but just money), and providing opportunity (doing something for people whose opportunities were substantially less than those open to their fellow Americans, including people like blacks with income above the poverty line, who were still far worse off than whites with equal capabilities) were well mixed from the beginning. Nonetheless, because of the shorthand Sundquist refers to, most of the rhetoric was in terms of fighting poverty, and low-income poverty programs tended to dominate opportunity programs.

The idea of *ending* poverty did not enter in a major way until 1966, two years after the beginning of the anti-poverty program and the Office of Economic Opportunity (OEO). In that year, the second anti-poverty plan presented to OEO Director Sargent Shriver by his economic planners led by Joseph Kershaw, stated as the clear goal, putting an end to poverty within 10 years. Shriver embraced the goal, recommended it to the White House, and discussed it in Congressional testimony.

"Ending poverty in 10 years" has frequently been taken as the prototype of the Great Society's "overpromising." In fact, given the sort of definition used for poverty, income below a stated dollar level (about $3,100 for a family of four at that time, now $5,500) the promise was entirely feasible economically. The magic that would make it happen was an income maintenance plan of the negative income tax type which in 10 years would bring its minimum income guarantee level up to the poverty line. The costs, although not small, were not considered economically impossible—about $30 billion a year added to anti-poverty programs by 1971 and $15 billion more by 1976. Although the income maintenance program was the final mop-up, making the guarantee good, a wide variety of other programs for training, education, other means of individual assistance, and community help was expected to take the pressure off the negative income tax as the sole program. All of this was intended to set up goals which were technically feasible, even though it was well recognized that it was politically very doubtful that they would be adopted. The overpromising came in two ways. First, goals were adopted rhetorically, but not pragmatically. Second, the fuzziness of the distinction between "anti-poverty" and "opportunity" meant that many took the goal to be equalizing opportunity—particularly for minorities and poor communities— in 10 years and that would have been much more difficult to do. No simple mop-up programs like the negative income tax have been thought of to end discrimination and the other reasons for inequality of opportunity.

Given all of these distinctions between programs and rhetoric, and between the two program goals, how did the United States measure up against these goals, looking back with a dozen years of hindsight? The measure, of course, must be as of now, not as of 1969, since most of the programs of the Great Society have been continued for the last eight years, and many of them require substantial periods of time to work out their full effects. Indeed, some programs attributable in large measure to the Great Society did not even begin until after President Johnson had left office. Public Service Employment, for example, was begun on a pilot basis in the 1960s but first put into being on a large scale by Congressional initiative in 1971.

Examining first the definable anti-poverty goal—the effort to raise family incomes above the poverty line (which has increased over the last 10 years almost entirely because of inflation rather than redefinition), the answer, if ambiguous, is at least consistent with some degree of success in moving toward these objectives.

Figure I shows why. It is, of course, tricky to generalize from 11 years of data. At the end of the Great Society in 1969, it was even trickier to generalize from the five years since the passage of the Economic Opportunity Act. In those five years, poverty had gone down drastically, but so had unemployment, and it was obvious that these two movements had something to do with one

FIGURE 1 Poverty and unemployment rates

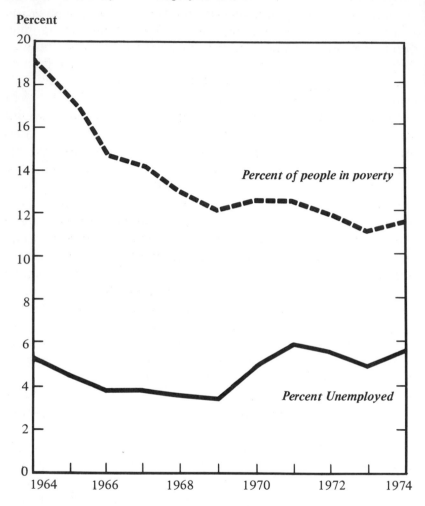

another. Under the circumstances, it was impossible to separate out as causes of the decrease in poverty, the unemployment rate and the programs of the War on Poverty. In summing it up in 1970, the author stated:

It has thus proved impossible so far to measure directly in any rigorous way that part of the anti-poverty improvement of the last few years directly attributable to explicit anti-poverty programs [as compared to lower unemployment] ... It still seems likely that some of the credit ... should go to the anti-poverty programs themselves. This is a weak statement, however. The only strong statements that can be made are that poverty has dropped sharply since 1964, that the War on Poverty was associated with this drop, and that the extent of causation cannot at present be known.[2]

The chart for 1964 through 1974 still seems to bear out. the same weak statement. After 1969, unemployment shot up. That poverty was still strongly related to the level of unemployment is shown by the fact that in subsequent years, the level of poverty went up and down year-by-year with the level of unemployment. That the programs of the Great Society may have had some lasting effect, however, is indicated by the fact that poverty in the 1970s never showed any tendency to rise back to the levels of the early 1960s, but rather, stopped falling and tended to level off. It thus seems possible that the War on Poverty did engender a structural change by making poverty less sensitive to even very high unemployment than it had been before. Although 1975 poverty data became available too late to put on the chart, the relatively modest rise in percentage of poverty (10.8-12.3) caused in part by the very sharp rise in unemployment (5.8-8.5) tends to bear out this decreased sensitivity.

Turning then to the specific programs that might broadly be included within the goal of decreasing poverty defined as low income, it is useful to distinguish between those programs designed to increase earning capabilities of those poor people who might be in the work force or capable of entering it, and those designed to help the poor for whom work is unlikely. The paper will then turn to the broader equal opportunity objective of the War on Poverty.

Earnings-Oriented Programs

Increasing the opportunity for the poor to earn their own way was the dominant theme of the manpower programs and the educational programs of the Great Society. In both cases, the background was, as suggested by Sundquist, a set of old ideas developed into new models.

Manpower. For manpower, these ideas consisted of providing training for better jobs for those in need of better jobs. At least with regard to the problems of poverty, little direct evidence exists for the success of these programs. The initial objective of the programs, starting with the Manpower Development and Training Act (MDTA) of 1962, had little to do with poverty, except perhaps of the quite temporary variety. Rather, the primary objective was to *retrain* relatively skilled workers in obsolete industries or with obsolete skills who had been working and earning above poverty levels but had been left behind by the economy. By the end of the 1960s, the MDTA program (administered by the Department of Labor) had been changed in some measure to an anti-poverty program assisting those with few skills to begin with, but the program produced little anti-poverty impact that could be demonstrated. Although rigorous evaluation of such programs almost always falters because of technical difficulties having to do with control groups and other matters, some evidence does exist that MDTA programs did increase earnings of participants.[3] However, the evidence is thin and what it does show is relatively small earning increases, which when multiplied by the small size of the anti-poverty portions of MDTA (as compared to the poverty problem), led to overall results that must be counted as being insignificant.

The two major manpower programs of that portion of the War on Poverty directly under the aegis of the Office of Economic Opportunity were the Job Corps and the Neighborhood Youth Corps. The Job Corps, a program of residential training camps for youth, patterned on the Civilian Conservation Corps of the New Deal, was plagued initially by scandals and by overpromising. After it settled down the question became whether it was worth the very high cost, estimated variously between five and ten thousand dollars per enrollee-year. (Most individual enrollees did not stay for a whole year, which was part of the problem.) How much the Job Corps aided those who went through it depends on analysis of nonexistent data; certainly if George Foreman, who took up boxing in the Job Corps, is included in the before-and-after incomes sample, it was a success, but otherwise the issue remains in doubt. The Neighborhood Youth Corps (NYC), in some ways a local neighborhood analog of the Job Corps, run for OEO by the Labor Department, was a much larger program with far less intensive training. NYC, which had components for out of school youth, those who were in school, and those looking for summer jobs, became known as a holding operation to keep kids off the street and give them a little money. Its training component was thin, where it existed at all, and evidence of lasting effect on its enrollees does not exist.

Most of the other manpower programs of the Office of Economic Opportunity were small and conjectural. New Careers for the Poor followed a theory that new jobs could be provided for poor people as "paraprofessionals"—aides to teachers, doctors, policemen, and other professionals. On a very small scale, the program worked, but it was clearly not appropriate for most of the job-needing poor. Other programs funded in large measure by OEO like the Opportunities Industrialization Corporation (OIC), begun in Philadelphia, worked for some things some places, but not as breakthroughs into overall manpower programs. Local poverty agencies (Community Action Agencies) set up a wide variety of manpower programs. A 1967 attempt to "coordinate" all the local programs funded by OEO and the Department of Labor under the heading of "Comprehensive Employment Programs" failed almost completely.

One program begun in 1968, the last year of the Great Society, was called Job Opportunities in the Business Sector (JOBS). JOBS, which provided a subsidy to private employers to train the poor, seemed very promising for a while, but neither in its first year or thereafter provided very much data to demonstrate anything,[4] and after 1969 became the victim of the rapidly rising rate of unemployment. Like many of the other programs mentioned here, it still exists as a small and probably useful institution, but with only a faint resemblance to the original dream.

Indeed, that can serve to sum up the manpower programs of the Great Society: Some of them worked somewhat; few of them were large enough to have had a significant impact on poverty had they worked well, none of them was strong enough to resist rising aggregate unemployment. It should be noted that the major anti-unemployment program in use today—Public Service Employment—was recommended by the planners of the Great Society, but was not brought into being until later, as a Congressional initiative. In any case, although it is difficult to demonstrate success of impact for any one of the manpower programs, it still remains possible, as noted, that they should get some credit for the failure of poverty numbers to rise in the 1970s as unemployment went up sharply.

Education. In a longer-run sense, the education programs of the Great Society were also intended to increase earning capacity. Because of the timing, however, it it impossible to even guess whether they have done so. Most of the beneficiaries of the Great Society's education programs are only coming into the work force now. The first cohort of enrollees in the preschool Head Start program is just turning 16. In general, internal evaluations of the effects of the programs in increasing learning capabilities have been mixed. Head Start evaluations showed that children enrolled in it year-round at least seemed to enter school better off than their contemporaries, but that the contemporaries then caught up.[5] The major Great Society investment in compensatory education for the poor—Title I of the Elementary and Secondary Education Act—was (and is) a diffused program of Federal funding through states and local school districts for a myriad of different school programs in schools with a lot of poor kids. Although such a program is even more difficult than a relatively homogeneous one to evaluate as a whole, some recent evaluations do tend to show that the program as a whole can be credited with significant learning gains for some of those in Title I programs.[6]

Regional Development. Before leaving the job-creating efforts of the War on Poverty, mention should be made of one program category sometimes included here which probably ought not be. The programs are the regional development attempts both of the Area Redevelopment Administration, begun in the early 1960s and transformed to the Economic Development Administration in the mid-sixties, and the Appalachian and other regional commissions. Because of one overriding phenomenon, no attempt is made here to evaluate the job-creating success of these efforts. They may have done it in large numbers—but the evidence that exists shows that a job created in a poor area like Appalachia is not necessarily a job created for a poor person. Indeed, the indications have been all along that successful regional economic development of this sort has assisted with the legitimate objective of stemming the unemployment-induced outflow of the children and young adults of the middle and working classes, but this is different from an anti-poverty objective.

Health Care. Another kind of program affecting the work-force poor as well as those unable to work was in the health area. Because of the concentration of this chapter on poverty and the standard of living, it will not go into any detail here. Rather, the relevant effect of the Great Society can be summarized by saying that the Medicare and Medicaid programs have made for major transformation in American health care systems and costs. Medicaid in particular has made medical care far more accessible to the poor than it would otherwise have been.[7] However, the price paid for the increase in total demand for medical services associated with these programs has been very rapidly accelerating medical costs all along the line. Beyond this, the specific health efforts associated with the more narrowly defined programs of the War on Poverty (those run by OEO and allied agencies) were not markedly successful. The Comprehensive Health Centers sponsored on a pilot basis by OEO provided one prototype for Health Maintenance Organizations (HMOs) that some look to as the solution for the efficient organization of health care. Few HMOs however, have provided substantial evidence of success thus far.

Non-Earnings Programs

The definition of "non-working-poor" in itself implies that the central program must be transfer payments, which are payments other than for work or other services rendered. The non-working poor obviously include those too old, too young, or too sick to work, but beyond that the boundaries of the category dissolve in controversy. Such questions as: "What mothers of children of what ages 'should work'?" "What constitutes disablement beyond obvious crippling?" "What about alcoholics and addicts?" were not resolved by the analysts of the Great Society, nor have they been resolved yet. Until they are resolved definitionally for general categories, mechanisms have been set up for resolving them satisfactorily on an individual case basis, or it has been decided to ignore the distinctions between "working" and "non-working" poor and provide transfer payments to people simply because they are poor, major welfare reform will escape us.

Nonetheless, the Great Society did make two major beginnings on improving the transfer payment system and several minor ones, as well as beginning the sort of planning that could eventuate in major reform. One major change was Medicaid; the other was the introduction of the food stamp system of providing quasi-money to the poor to help them purchase this chief necessity. Food stamps were introduced as a pilot program in 1961 and as a full-scale alternative (at the discretion of local welfare authorities) to distribution of surplus foods to the poor, in 1964. After major publicity and debate over hunger in the last year of the Great Society, the food stamp program was shifted to a more solid basis in 1971 by making the program mandatory nationwide. Food stamps, although subject to some abuse, have been an important factor in making the system of transfer payments to the poor flexible and national, while awaiting major reform.

The lesser changes took place mainly in Social Security— increases in minimum benefits and the like. These helped the aged poor, and also helped many non-poor aged who were receiving Social Security minimums because their primary pension coverage had been under other systems such as Civil Service. This concentration on Social Security, as well as many other political factors, drove out serious attempts to institute other transfer payment reforms in areas such as public assistance.

What the Great Society also did, however, was to restart for the first time since the 1930s serious thinking about the role and structure of transfer payments. Much of this revolved around the negative income tax concept invented in the late 1950s by Milton Friedman and Robert Lampman. In the Johnson Administration, OEO and HEW, together with the Council of Economic Advisors, developed the negative income tax idea to a point at which the Nixon Administration was able to pick it up and turn it into the proposal for a Family Assistance Plan. It was brought into the Nixon Administration in large measure by the same people who had developed it in the Johnson Administration, the major addition to the team being Daniel Moynihan. The Family Assistance Plan failed to pass, but the concepts were applied at least to transfer payments for the aged above and beyond Social Security, under Nixon's Supplemental Security Income program. The net result at the end of the Nixon Administration was that the major improvements for the non-working poor were based on the earlier beginnings or Medicaid and food stamps. Yet overall system reform remained elusive.

Summary on Poverty

Indeed, to sum up: the record of the programs begun by the Great Society to end poverty defined as low income is by no means one of failure, but the record is mixed and its evaluation is obscured by the depression of the 1970s. For the working poor, the fact that poverty failed to rise to its early levels when unemployment shot up may indicate some success, but it is very difficult to find evidence for major successful impact of any one of the Great Society's programs to which this improvement might be attributed. For the non-working poor, the Great Society made beginnings which were expanded in the Nixon years, but major overall change is not yet here.

Opportunity

On the other major objective of the War on Poverty, the improvement of opportunity—or, not to be euphemistic, the attempt to equalize opportunity among the races—there also seems some progress attributable to the programs initiated by the Great Society, but again, the record is mixed and ambiguous. Again, also, long-run trends are very much obscured by the business cycle, particularly by the depression of the 1970s. Black unemployment remains a multiple something like two times white unemployment, and the absolute difference between the two percentages (black unemployment rate minus white unemployment rate) rises in recession as it always has, although the ratio of the two (black unemployment rate divided by white unemployment rate) may fall slightly. It seems possible that the differentials are narrowing over time, but the differences between the late 1960s and the first half of the 1970s are so obscured by the differences between prosperity and depression that any statement about long-run trends must be very weak.

Nonetheless, various long-run indicators, particularly those associated with education, show apparent improvement. Roughly the same proportions of the races now complete high school, but black completion of four years of college and black graduate education still lags. (The statistics for the other major ethnic minority—Spanish-Americans—do not look as good in the educational area.)

For minority groups in general, the differentials between incomes may be decreasing (and much is sometimes made of the fact that in certain restricted categories, like young married adults in the North, black income levels are quite close to white), but there too the depression raises an obscuring cloud.

What does seem to be less ambiguously the case and what can be directly attributed in part to the Great Society is the change in the power relationships of minority and majority groups. Indeed, instituting and helping engender such change may be the greatest social achievement of the 1960s. Before the 1960s, blacks in the South were not only powerless but almost entirely voteless. Blacks in the central cities of the North had the vote but with a very few exceptions, very little power going with that vote. In the South, the drastic changes in this situation engendered by the civil rights revolution were aided by the Kennedys and pushed much further by President Johnson. The changes from 1960 to 1968, and the subsequent changes attributable in large measure to the momentum from the earlier period (particularly the momentum begun by making black voting possible and effective in the South for the first time) are quite obvious.

What happened in the inner-city ghettos of Northern cities is less obvious but perhaps equally important. Before the mid-1960s, minority groups and minority areas in cities were not much heard from economically or in terms of political power. In *Beyond the Melting Pot*[8], Nathan Glazer and Daniel Moynihan pointed out that the black poverty groups in ghettos in New York were quite unlike the earlier Irish, Italian, and Jewish poverty groups and areas, in that the white poverty groups built a vigorous internal institutional life (around the Irish bar and political club, the Italian church and hometown society, the Jewish settlement house and workman's group, for example.) For blacks, however, at the time Glazer and Moynihan wrote the book in the early 1960s, such institutions existed only thinly in Harlem and Bedford-Stuyvesant. One result of this thinness of inner institutional life was a shortage of nodes around which to build outwardly-directed institutions of political power, and a consequent shortage of such black political power. And New

York was comparatively well off; other inner cities had much less.

It is clear that this urban situation has undergone drastic change, change that has been necessary for equal opportunity. Now minority institutions and minority political power exist on relative independent bases throughout the nation's cities. There are many reasons for this. One stems from the simple demographics of increasing blackness of Northern cities; black urban power necessarily exists where black votes become a majority in any political unit. A second cause is the overlap and overflow of the civil rights revolution of the 1960s from the South, where the first targets existed, to the Northern cities. Not part of the civil rights revolution but related were the urban riots of the 1960s, which sensitized the cities and the nation to the needs of the ghettos.

But the Great Society programs as such also formed a major part of the impetus toward minority urban institutions and political power. The earliest and most important program was the Community Action Program (CAP) of the Office of Economic Opportunity. CAP was the part of the War on Poverty designed and controlled in local areas, in some cases by local governments but more often by non-profit Community Action Agencies. Because of sheer geography, most Community Action Programs were in rural areas, but the vast bulk of the money went to urban concentrations of poverty, and with a few exceptions, cities were where the programs were most effective. CAP was three different things:

- It was a seedbed for new ideas, starting with Head Start, and including innovative health programs, manpower programs, etc. As had been noted, it is difficult to find evidence of substantial success for most of these programs, but one crucial exception should be noted. The Legal Services Program innovated by CAP had a major effect in procuring for the poor their legal rights in such areas as housing, welfare, and even marital relations. As such, Legal Services had an important effect in changing the conditions and causes of poverty.
- CAP was also supposed to have been a center for careful local planning well-thought-through and well-meshed anti-poverty programs. This was the particular hope of those in the Bureau of the Budget who held strong beliefs in favor of

planning and felt that since centralized Federal planning could not get into the detail necessary for successful administration of thousands of local programs, local planning was needed. In practice, however, local planning and the planning requirement for applications for Federal money rapidly became a charade.

- The third aspect of Community Action, the building of institutions and political power in the ghettos, was in some measure unintended. Although it had conceptual roots in the juvenile delinquency programs of Robert Kennedy's Department of Justice and in the Ford Foundation's "Gray Areas" program, many of those who pushed and voted for the OEO bill, including Community Action, were not aware of this institutional thrust. Had they been aware of it, many of them would have voted against it because of their fear of engendering intergroup conflict. Moynihan points out in *Maximum Feasible Misunderstanding*[9] that such conflict did occur, although he fails to make clear that most of it occurred under the predecessor programs to Community Action or in the very early days of Community Action itself, and that in its three or four years under the Johnson Administration, the Community Action program worked out most of these conflicts.

In any case, Community Action did work in substantial measure to create new minority institutions in every city with a concentration of minority poverty, and it did work to create new political power bases. Some of this effectiveness stemmed simply from drawing political attention to problems that had existed for a long time; some of it came from political confrontation. The different programs of local Community Action, ranging from Head Start through Legal Services to a bewildering variety of community centers and self-help institutions formed the nuclei around which power concentrated. Perhaps the famous phraseology about "maximum feasible participation" of the poor, criticized by Moynihan as a small statement of democratic intent deliberately exaggerated in action (but certainly intended from the beginning by many), had something to do with it. However, it seems likely that at this time in history, given the activities themselves and the thrust of minority groups, the phrase was not all that important. What was much more important was the independent funding of a lot of local organizations that naturally tended to try to create power for themselves.

Indeed, when it was felt that CAP confrontation had gone too far, the resultant efforts to change the actuality by changing the law had little effect. By 1966, a feeling in the Administration that independent Community Action was vastly overdoing its thing led to the creation of the Model Cities program, much more firmly under the control of local mayors. In 1967, the passage of Representative Edith Green's amendment to the Economic Opportunity Act gave city governments the option of taking over existing non-profit Community Action programs. Not many programs were taken over, and although Model Cities agencies were controlled differently from Community Action agencies, they ended up doing much the same sort of things.

To my mind, Community Action and the surrounding institutions and activities provided the greatest achievement in the War on Poverty portion of the programs in the Great Society. They helped create and accelerate an irreversible once-for-all change in the face of urban America. It seems entirely unlikely that cities or Federal programs having to do with cities can ever revert to the indifference to poverty and minority problems that characterized these areas through the early 1960s.

Looked at now, however, this history may suggest some reasons for concern about the future. The late 1960s were a time of great racial ferment, accompanying and in part affecting the changes discussed here. But, to be quite speculative about subsequent events, if these changes were as important as has been suggested here, then they may have been the major cause of the relative racial peace that has existed since the late sixties. It is really quite remarkable that after the confusion and confrontation and urban violence of the sixties, the subsequent combination of the slowdown in progress in racial equality plus a major economic depression hitting blacks worse than others has coincided with a period of racial peace. Unfortunately, following this line of speculation may lead to the hypothesis that the slowdown, the depression, and the general decline of central cities will lead to new racial turmoil following its causes with the same four-year time lag as between the racial progress of the late sixties and the racial peace of the late seventies.

In any case, to summarize this section on Community Action and community change, it may well be that what in a way were the least logical, least thought through, least planned programs of the Great Society, may have been much the most significant. The programs least amenable to careful planning by professional planners, economists, etc.—programs like voting rights and Community Action that affected political process and bargaining power rather than programs designed to assist in individual opportunity—were the ones that seemed to work best. This thought might just possibly make planners a bit humble. It also seems an appropriate transition to a brief discussion of some of the planning aspects of the Great Society's programs.

Planning

As has been clear, the programs discussed here were an ecletic collection of old ideas like manpower training and educational improvement, planning theorists' concepts like the importance of local planning, and the beliefs of a variety of social theorists. The late 1960s were also marked by attempts to put all of these strands and others together under one variety or another of central grand planning. The collective name for most of these attempts was the Planning-Program-Budgeting System (PPBS). This is not the place for a comprehensive statement on PPBS, but a brief examination of planning in the context of the programs discussed here will serve to round out the picture. The PPB System was brought into being in 1965 by directive of President Johnson. It was supposed to have been an extension to all Federal agencies of principles that had been applied in the Department of Defense by Secretary McNamara in the previous four years.

The general record of PPBS is dismal; in most places it worked very poorly if at all. Two of the agencies in which it is reputed to have had the greatest success, however, were ones with cognizance over the programs discussed here—the Office of Economic Opportunity and the Department of Health, Education, and Welfare. (That this relative success took place in regard to these programs, however, must be marked something of a coincidence. In two other key agencies responsible for programs in this area—the Department of Labor and Department of Housing and Urban Development—PPB worked not at all.) In examining how the planning systems worked in these two agencies, where they did work, it becomes clear, however, that what worked was not the whole elaborate five-year mechanism of the new budget system, but rather PPB as a cover for some good economic and social policy analysis. It was not that the comprehensive plan was effective in itself; it was that the razzle-dazzle of comprehensive planning provided a cover for some bright people to think systematically about some real problems. (The five-year anti-poverty plan discussed earlier in this paper might be considered an example of coherent comprehensive programming, but it is better characterized as systematic structuring of a dream.)

The separate analyses under the cover of PPB were at first based in large measure upon relatively conventional ideas about earnings-increasing programs in the areas like manpower and education where as has been indicated the programs themselves did not work very well. On the other hand, the very important work on transfer payments discussed above stemmed in large measure from these analyses carried out in OEO and HEW. And to reverse the field back again, the Community Action ideas which I have characterized as being in my opinion the most successful of the Great Society programs, far from originating in these planning analyses, were out ahead of these analyses, with the planning analysts only catching up with them much later.

Thus the social analysis carried out under PPB has a rather mixed record: Not very useful in manpower and education; after the event in Community Action; but very important in the transfer payment area. This probably sums up to at least one important gain from this type of planning at the cost of only a relatively small waste of resources.

These analyses and analysts had one more significant effect, however—one which was almost casual in its origin and quite mixed in its results. This was the origin of a new kind of social experimentation—new in that it was rigorously controlled and designed to produce policy information that could be carefully analyzed. The experimental thrust began with the belief of the advocates of the negative income tax sort of comprehensive income maintenance program that the chief political obstacle to such a program was the popular belief that it would cause able-bodied men to quit work and live on the dole. To test the real importance of this work-reducing effect, an income maintenance experiment, sited in New Jersey, was carefully designed and set up. Substantively the primary result of the experiment was to cast substantial doubt on the importance of such anti-work-incentive effects. However, the other result was to make experimentation look very interesting. The Nixon Administration picked up the idea and began carrying out such experiments in a number of areas—health, housing, education, and welfare. In the minds of the advocates, such experimentation was considered a substitution of analysis at costs of tens of millions of dollars for frequently unsuccessful major programming like that of the Great Society, costing billions of dollars. In the minds of its opponents, social experimentation of this kind was a substitution of long years of inaction for action to combat social ills. Now, as the experimental thrust of the Nixon Administration winds down, it is becoming clear that both sides are right. On the one hand, important information for program design and program choice has been gained from the experiments. On the other hand, were such experiments continued indefinitely instead of social action, the results for the social fabric of this nation could be tragic.

For the bottom line on the analysis on the programs of the Great Society designed to provide better standards of living for those most in need is that many of them did work. The programs that look in retrospect as if they worked best were those most difficult to define precisely or to quantify, but that is frequently the way with social progress.

References

The author wishes to thank John Ellwood, Robinson Hollister, Walter Williams, and Robert Reischauer for their comments.

[1] James L. Sundquist, *Politics and Policy* (Washington, D.C.: The Brookings Institution, 1968), pp. 113-114.

[2] Robert A. Levine, *The Poor Ye Need Not Have With You: Lessons From the War on Poverty* (Cambridge: MIT Press, 1970), pp. 96.

[3] See, for example, John H. Goldstein, *The Effectiveness of Manpower Training Programs: A Review of Research on the Impact on the Poor*, Paper No. 3 in United States Congress, Joint Economic Committee on Fiscal Policy, Studies in Public Welfare, 1974, and Orley Ashenfelter, "The Effect of Manpower Training on Earnings: Preliminary Results" in *Proceedings*, 27th Annual Meeting of the Industrial Relations Research

Association, 1975. In an unpublished paper "The Economic Benefits of Four Manpower Training Programs (May, 1976) Nicholas Kiefer finds that MDTA benefited primarily female trainees.

[4] Kiefer, *op. cit.*, does suggest that some data show that JOBS, like MDTA, had measurable benefits primarily for female trainees.

[5] The best single evaluation of Head Start remains the 1969 study reported in Westinghouse Learning Corporation/Ohio University, *The Impact of Head Start: An Evaluation of Head Start on Children's Cognitive and Affective Development*, Bladensburg, Maryland, July, 1969. The controversy this stirred up is discussed in Walter Williams and John Evans, "The Politics of Evaluation: The Case of Head Start" in *The Annals* of the American Academy of Political and Social Science, September, 1969.

[6] This is hinted, somewhat tantalizingly, by the Office of Education in their fiscal year 1975 *Annual Evaluation Report on Programs Administered by the U.S. Office of Education*, in a discussion of a study by the Educational Testing Service supposed to be released in September, 1976.

[7] See, in particular, Karen Davis, "Medicaid Payments and Utilization of Medical Services by the Poor" in *Inquiry*, XIII, 2, June, 1976.

[8] Nathan Glazer and Daniel Patrick Moynihan, *Beyond the Melting Pot*, (Cambridge, MIT Press, 1963).

[9] Daniel Patrick Moynihan, *Maximum Feasible Misunderstanding* (New York, The Free Press, 1969).

Ray Marshall

5

Microemployment Programs
of the 1960s

Let me dispose of some definitional problems before addressing myself to an evaluation of the manpower and other selective employment programs of the 1960s. I will conclude with some observations on what seems to me to be the future directions of selective employment policies. The problem of defining "manpower" programs is complicated. The term "manpower program" has been applied only to training. In addition, the concept changed considerably during the 1960s as the dynamic and complicated nature of the job matching process became clearer as a result of the experimental and demonstration projects of those years. Finally, the use of the term "manpower" is objected to by many because of its sexist connotations.

What previously was called manpower policy is more appropriately called employment policy. The Manpower Administration of the U.S. Department of Labor has therefore changed its name to the Employment and Training Administration, and the National Manpower Policy Task Force has become the National Council on Employment Policy. Employment policies may be divided into general, or macro, and selective, or micro, policies. The new policies of the 1960s stressed selective or microemployment policies because of the conviction that aggregate (monetary-fiscal) policies could not produce full employment.

In order to avoid confusion created by these diverse concepts, we should be fairly explicit in our definition. As I use the term "selective employment programs," it applies to programs which seek to match workers and jobs. The match might be accomplished either by getting workers ready to fill vacant jobs or by creating jobs for workers who do not have adequate employment opportunities. More specifically, selective employment policy includes the following components:

(1) *Labor Market information systems* are essential to economic policy, both for employers seeking workers and for workers seeking information about jobs. Labor market information also

is necessary for effective employment planning.

(2) *Skills training* seeks to improve economic activity and job opportunities by increasing workers' skills. Training may be "institutional" (classroom), on-the-job, or some combination of the two. Traditional vocational or technical training has been institutional, while apprenticeship training stresses some combination of these approaches. Certain skills, such as those useful for clerical and office jobs, mathematics, and theoretical aspects of the job, usually can be more effectively taught in classrooms, while on-the-job instruction can be more useful for teaching manual skills. Apprenticeship, generally considered to be the best form of skilled training, combines institutional and on-the-job training.

(3) *Public employment programs* can create jobs for people who cannot find employment in the private sector. The traditional way to combat unemployment has been through general labor market programs based on monetary-fiscal policies. Experience demonstrates that these general policies can do much to motivate private employers to hire workers, but these measures usually reduce unemployment by creating inflation. Efforts to eliminate chronic pockets of unemployment or underdevelopment might therefore generate intolerable levels of inflation while doing little about unemployment. A better, and much less inflationary policy is the placement of the unemployed in jobs on useful projects. At all times, public employment projects are useful for reducing pockets of chronic unemployment. In times of general, cyclical unemployment, they are just as valuable.

Public employment programs can take several forms: (a) public service employment, whereby workers are employed directly by governments to provide public services; (b) public works, whereby governments sponsor the construction of public facilities by private contractors; (c) supported work, whereby governments sponsor jobs for particular groups to provide work experience and/or training. Thus, public employment programs can have a variety of forms, all of which have different effects.

Expenditures on public employment programs can be more cost effective than tax cuts of equal magnitude in reducing unemployment. The Congressional Budget Office (CBO) has estimated the impact of these approaches (in a report entitled *Temporary Measures to Stimulate Employment: An Evaluation of Some Alternatives* which was published in 1975.). The CBO's study implies that the net cost to society of a job generated by tax cuts after 24 months is in the range of $17,000 to $21,000. The net cost of a public service job after 24 months was between $2,600 and $3,500. The lower cost of public service jobs implies that more jobs can be created with less inflationary pressure through public employment than through tax cutting.

Moreover, the effects of tax cuts are diffused throughout the economy, while public employment programs can be targeted on particular groups of unemployed workers.

(4) *Pre-employment and pre-training programs* are necessary when qualified workers are excluded from the procedures through which workers are recruited and trained, or when workers have personal problems which impede their participation in training programs or in holding jobs. Service for personal needs can include: medical care, literacy training, transportation, orientation to work, etc.

(5) Selective employment programs also seek to *improve* the *operation of labor markets*. This might be done by eliminating such artificial barriers to entry as discrimination by improving labor market information, by eliminating legal and other barriers to labor market operations, by rationalizing labor markets to provide better or more regular jobs, or by conducting programs to move workers from labor surplus to labor shortage areas.

(6) Finally, selective employment policy must concern itself with manpower *delivery mechanisms.* The logical division of labor between levels of government and between public and private organizations is one of the unsettled issues in employment policy. A lesson of the 1960s was that there is a need to decentralize manpower programs away from Washington. At the same time, the Federal Government, which probably is better suited than state and local governments to provide funds to pay for selective employment programs, must formulate national employment policy and see that it is carried out.

Coordination of all employment and development programs is required for accomplishing economic and community development. Frequently many of the necessary ingredients for development are present in an area, but there is no catalyst to bring them together with the necessary outside development resources. Concerted Services in Training and Education (CSTE) provides an example of a catalytic employment mechanism designed to promote development.

Delivery mechanisms have important implications for the outcome of a particular program. If private employers undertake employment programs, their decisions are likely to be related to the profit motive, which means they will seek to recruit and train the most productive workers. If units of government operate programs, the outcomes are likely to conform with the operating procedures and motives of those units of government, which might be to reduce taxes, build physical facilities, or to reward political friends. Thus, ordinary private and governmental procedures often bypass disadvantaged people. It might therefore be necessary to have programs operated by organizations specifically concerned with putting the disadvantaged to work. For example, the Farmer's Union, through the Operation Mainstream program, gave a larger share of public employment jobs to the disadvantaged than did state and local governments through the Emergency Employment Act program. Similarly, specialized local outreach groups might do more for the disadvantaged than the Employment Service, and a community development corporation might be more effective than state governments in extending "start-up" training programs to the disadvantaged.

Early Programs

Although selective employment programs increased dramatically in number and in scope during the 1960s, there had previously been a number of such programs. These traditional activities included vocational-technical programs, apprenticeship training operated mainly by unions and employers, and the labor market information system operated by the Federal-State Employment Service. However, most of these traditional efforts were considered to be unresponsive to the problems of the poor, the disadvantaged, and blacks and minorities, and were inadequate supplements to the general or macroemployment policies which were developed in the 1930s. There was particular concern that these traditional labor market institutions and procedures perpetuated racial discrimination. The new programs therefore attempted to establish new delivery mechanisms as well as to deal with pressing labor market problems.

The Context of the 1960s

Among the general economic problems addressed by the new labor market programs was the problem of full employment and price stability. The labor market programs of the 1930s had done much to reduce the problem of unemployment. At the macroeconomic level, the depression taught policy makers the value of monetary and fiscal policies as means of stabilizing the economy and reducing unemployment. The New Deal programs also attempted to protect workers from the adverse effects of labor markets by providing income in the form of unemployment insurance, income assistance for those who could not work, or retirement benefits for those covered by the Social Security Act. The Employment Act of 1946 created the Council of Economic Advisors to advise the President on means to achieve full employment.

For a brief time, the New Deal programs created the impression, at least among economists, that the nation's main economic and social problems had been solved. The safety nets placed under people by the protective labor legislation seemed to offer some security for those who could not (or should not) work. The macroeconomists, who predominated on the Council of Economic Advisors, often gave the impression that despite some minor problems of forecasting and timing, they had the problem of economic stability pretty much in hand. If things did not go right, economists could always blame it on the politicians who refused to accept their advice, or blame it on "market imperfections." The solution was therefore either to educate the politicians or to remove the imperfections by vigorously enforcing the anti-trust laws or other measures to increase competition. The main macroeconomic problem was considered to be how to generate sufficient aggregate demand to absorb the bountiful supply of goods and services the economy could produce at full employment.

Fortunately for the economists, but unfortunately for the economy, the pressures of World War II and the Korean War obscured the weaknesses in the oversimplified view of the world held by orthodox neoclassical and Keynesian economists. The defects in traditional economic analysis and in the economy were revealed by events during the 1960s. One of the most important of these defects was the economy's apparent inability simultaneously to maintain full employment, stable prices, and a society in which wages and prices went unregulated. It was discovered that the actions that reduced unemployment tended to increase purchasing power faster than the supply of goods, thereby generating inflationary pressures on the economy.

Most of the measures developed during the New Deal period to combat unemployment and recession were designed to *increase* prices—economists did not know how to handle the problem of rising unemployment and inflation. Indeed, a British economist, A.E. Phillips, discovered that there was a long-run inverse relationship between unemployment and inflation. This does not, however, necessarily imply causation.[1] Many economists considered this relationship to be such a basic principle of economics, that the only solution to inflation was unemployment and the only solution to unemployment was inflation.

Some economists and policy makers in the United States and Europe thought that the inflation-unemployment dilemma could be resolved through wage and price controls, or "incomes" policies, as they were called in Europe. The only problem with this approach was the requirement that "natural" market forces be controlled by regulating wages and prices in order to prevent incomes from increasing faster than productivity at full employment levels of income.

Some people even thought we could have all of our cake and eat it too by relying on "voluntary" wage and price constraints. However, those who held this strange concept of power and human conduct were quickly disillusioned wherever voluntary constraints were tried. Union leaders cannot be expected voluntarily to restrain demands for higher wages where full employment conditions give them the power to improve their members' earnings and benefits. Those union statesmen who adopt this position are likely to have very short tenures in office. Their members are likely to vote such officials out in favor of leaders who promise to be more vigorous in the use of the unions' power to improve wages, hours, and working conditions, especially where, as is probable, prices are increasing faster than wages.

Wage and price controls, voluntary or involuntary, operate

against the basic pressures on the demand as well as the supply side of the market. Profit maximizing employers are asked to hold the line on prices when they have the power to raise those prices and maximize profits. Employers also are asked to resist wage increases and risk strikes at a time when sales are brisk, profits are rising, and higher wages could be passed on to consumers in the form of higher prices.

Because they must oppose such strong basic motivations and market forces, voluntary wage and price controls have no chance of succeeding for very long, and governmental controls—short of an all-out planned economy—have little more chance. Freedom of action by unions, employers, and workers tends to undermine wage and price controls. Without going into the technical details, experience in the United States and Europe demonstrates that a general wage-price freeze can temporarily restrain wages and prices but that controls are very difficult to implement except under war-time conditions. It is difficult to design a workable formula for wage and price controls that will not create problems in product or labor markets. Labor market pressures also are likely to cause upward adjustments in wage payments even though wage rates are unchanged.

Experience also demonstrates that wage and price controls can succeed where they are made an adjunct of collective bargaining, as was true under the Construction Industry Stabilization Committee led by John Dunlop. In this case, unions and employers had motives to accept controls, because inflation creates serious political problems for union leaders. Since selective employment programs enhance labor market efficiency, they tend to work *with* basic labor market trends rather than *against* them. Except for public employment, selective employment programs can do little directly to reduce unemployment, but they can reduce the inflationary pressures created by monetary-fiscal policies. Moreover, selective employment programs can be designed to deal with specific problems in specific labor markets while monetary-fiscal policies are general and have less ability to differentiate between labor markets. In other words, because of labor market segmentation, general policies might generate inflationary pressures in some labor markets in the attempt to reduce unemployment in others. Selective employment policies can be adapted to specific problems in specific labor markets. Although selective employment programs serve as a valuable component of general employment policy, their main objective is to help improve job opportunities for individual workers and to lower the cost, and to improve the availability and quality of labor for individual employers. Not only can selective employment programs improve the skills of workers, but they also can rationalize labor markets in order to provide better jobs for workers and more dependable supplies of labor for employers.

Expansion of Selective Employment Programs

There was a dramatic increase in Federal expenditures for selective employment programs during the 1960s—from $450 million in 1964 to $2.6 billion by fiscal 1970[2] and over $9 billion by 1976.[3] The Manpower Development and Training Act (MDTA) of 1962 was initiated to provide retraining for workers displaced by technological change, but during the 1960s it was altered to provide more aid to the disadvantaged.

This expansion of selective employment programs was provided for in several major laws. The Economic Opportunity Act (EOA) of 1964 created a number of programs for the poor: the Neighborhood Youth Corps (NYC), to provide work and training for in-school and out-of-school youths; the Job Corps, to provide comprehensive services for disadvantaged teenagers in a residential setting; the Work Experience and Training Program, to provide work experience and basic education for the poor. One of the most successful public employment programs, Operation Mainstream, was created in 1965 mainly to provide jobs for older workers constructing a wide array of useful facilities for nonprofit organizations and government. The New Careers program, established in 1966, provided for the restructuring of private nonprofit and public jobs in order to provide better jobs for paraprofessionals.

One of the most important selective employment programs was Title VII of the Civil Rights Act of 1964, which outlawed discrimination in employment. Indeed, this law was the only serious Federal effort to intervene actively in labor markets. Because civil rights laws operate only on the demand side of the discrimination problem, however, it soon became clear that initiatives also were required on the supply side if excluded workers were to be able to take advantage of employment opportunities opened up by the lowering of racial barriers. Many of the training and supportive programs of the 1960s were designed mainly to help racial minorities. Perhaps the most effective of these labor supply efforts was the development of outreach programs to recruit, train, and place minorities in skilled, professional, and technical jobs. The outreach efforts started with apprenticeship programs in the construction industry and spread to other areas.[4]

The rapid growth of employment programs during the 1960s led to administrative problems and confusion. There were fears that programs were leading to waste, duplication, and inefficiency and not doing as much as possible for the target groups. There also was growing concern that programs designed in Washington would not fit local realities. Manpower authorities and political leaders of both major political parties therefore began to advocate decentralization and more comprehensive approaches. The Concentrated Employment Program of 1967(CEP), attempted unsuccessfully to solve the coordination problem by providing block grants to local groups to plan, operate, and coordinate local programs in selected low-income areas.

Another major concern of policy makers during the 1960s was the growth of welfare rolls and costs. The Aid to Families with Dependent Children (AFDC) program was of particular concern to cost-conscious lawmakers and the public. AFDC expenditures increased from about $1 billion in 1961 to $4.9 billion in 1970; enrollment increased from 3.1 million to 9.7 million during this period. The news media gave considerable, though usually superficial, attention to this problem, creating the erroneous impression that large proportions of those on welfare either could or should work. The result was the Work Incentive (WIN) program, created by a 1967 amendment to the Social Security Act, designed to make welfare recipients self supporting.

The WIN experience provides some insight into the prospects for using selective employment programs to get people off the welfare roles and into the labor market.

The 1971 Amendments to the WIN program authorized a 20 percent tax credit to private employers on wages paid AFDC recipients (these tax credits could be combined with training subsidies). However, these tax credits did not cause employers to hire many welfare recipients. Jobs proved very difficult to find for welfare mothers, especially when many experienced workers were unemployed.

Work incentives have not been any more effective. Reducing the high marginal tax rate on welfare recipients has produced limited results. The WIN provision allowing welfare recipients to retain $30 and a third of monthly earnings before losing welfare payments lowered the marginal tax rate from 100 to 67 percent.

Despite what appears to be a substantial incentive, the impact was small: The proportion of welfare recipients who worked was 15 percent in 1967, 15 percent in 1971, and 16 percent in 1973.

It is doubtful that any further reduction would produce different results, especially in a slack labor market.

In addition, lowering the marginal tax rate would increase those eligible for welfare. If there were a minimum guarantee of $2,000, a 67 percent marginal tax rate raises eligibility to $3,000; a 50 percent rate raises it to $4,000. A 50 percent tax rate rather than 67 percent under the Family Assistance Plan (FAP) would have increased beneficiaries over 50 percent.

If tax and earnings incentives do not work, it is doubtful that reducing the benefits would induce more people to work. A great reduction in benefits to induce a few welfare recipients into the labor market would cause a deprivation for those who cannot work.

Combining welfare and employment programs faces serious administrative problems. Labor market specialists know little about and are not always sympathetic to those in need of public assistance and welfare specialists know very little about labor markets. Attempts to merge these systems have not been very successful.

Implications

— The best way to reduce welfare rolls is to move toward full employment.

— Incentives should be left in the system to encourage employers to hire welfare recipients and the recipients to work, but I would not devote much administrative and political energy to this problem.

—It makes more sense to concentrate on full employment and making work significantly more attractive to welfare recipients by improving the quality and quantify of jobs available to them.

— Experimental and demonstration programs should be continued. The supported work concept seems particularly promising.

— All welfare recipients should be eligible for supported work or training programs. I would not make a distinction between "employables" and "unemployables". These distinctions are arbitrary.

There also was growing concern during the 1960s that the private sector could be much more effective than public agencies in providing jobs for the poor and disadvantaged. It was reasoned that the permanent solution to the employment problem would have to come through jobs in the private sector. In order to involve private employers in this effort, President Johnson established the Job Opportunities in the Business Sector (JOBS) program, providing subsidies to private employers to induce them to hire and train the disadvantaged. The National Alliance of Businessmen (NAB) was created to administer the JOBS program. Despite an appearance of success, however, these private efforts were plagued by a number of problems, including (1) their inability to create jobs and to give employers incentives to create good jobs, and (2) nothing was done to change employers' basic operating procedures so there was no assurance that employers were not simply subsidized to do what they would have done in tight labor markets without the program—i.e., they hired essentially the same kinds of people and bypassed the truly disadvantaged.

There also were some important education initiatives during the 1960s. Many training programs included an adult basic education component to overcome the educational deficiencies of disadvantaged adults. The Great Society programs revealed serious deficiencies in the nation's education establishment, especially that it tended to be a closed system with values and procedures which perpetuated social and economic segmentation and which bore very little relationship to the employment needs of workers and employers. Indeed, the system concentrated mainly on perpetuating its own values, so that conformity with those values was the main criterion of success; this usually conveyed a strong bias against manual work and placed an emphasis on preparing people for the next academic level rather than training their intelligence to deal with life and work.

The bias against manual work was translated into a very low status for vocational education within the system. Vocational education concentrated far too much attention and resources on non-labor market programs, such as homemaking, or declining occupations such as agriculture, and practically ignored emerging occupations, good work habits, and healthy attitudes toward work. Congress attempted to reform vocational education by Amendments in 1963 and 1968. In 1968 the vocational rehabilitation program was extended to the economically as well as mentally and physically handicapped.

Critique

The widespread bipartisan support for selective employment programs began to dissolve during the late 1960s. The efforts to coordinate programs and make them more responsive to labor market needs of workers and employers did not silence the critics on the left or right. The left-wing critics argued that the programs were not very effective in reforming the society's basic institutions. Conservatives favored efforts to reduce welfare rolls and shift more responsibility to the private sector and state and local governments. President Nixon was particularly critical of the Job Corps, which he charged was too expensive and accomplished very little. The Job Corps and other Office of Economic Opportunity employment programs were transferred out of the OEO, estensibly to make them more effective, but really to reduce the control of groups representing the poor. The Comprehensive Employment and Training Act of 1963 (CETA) formally transferred major responsibility for employment programs to state and local governments.

Despite those shifts, total outlays for selective employment programs continued to rise, reaching $5 billion in fiscal 1973, $6 billion in 1975, and over $9 billion in 1976 (see Table 1). Most of these increases were for public employment programs designed to deal with rising unemployment, the NYC summer program, and the vocational rehabilitation program.

Program Evaluation

The growing criticism of training programs during the 1960s and 1970s led to numerous efforts to evaluate these programs in order either to settle controversies, or, as was more often the

TABLE 1 Outlays for microemployment programs

	1964	1967	1970	1973	1974	1975	1976 (est.)
Total (millions)	$450	$1,775	$2,596	$4,952	$4,666	$6,177	$9,053
Department of Labor							
U.S. Employment Service	181	276	331	431	390	423	482
MDTA-Institutional	93	221	260	358			
Job Corps	---	321	144	188			
JOBS	--	----	86	104			
Jobs Optional	5	53	50	73	1,419[1]	2,118	2,690
NYC In-School	---	57	58	73			
NYC Summer	---	69	136	220			
NYC Out-of-School	---	127	98	118			
Operation Mainstream	---	9	42	82			
Public Service Careers	---	----	18	42			
Concentrated Employment Program	---	1	164	129			
Work Incentive Program	----	----	67	177	218	304	365
Public Employment Program	--	----	----	1,005	598	1,083	3,035
Program Administration, Research and Support	23	118	143	209	162	168	196
Department of Health, Education and Welfare							
Vocational Rehabilitation	84	215	441	636	755	885	807
Work Experience and training	---	120	1	---	----	8	9
Other Programs							
Veterans' Programs	12	19	141	292	351	352	355
Other training and placement programs	15	116	277	382	377	341	545
Employment-related child care	37	53	141	433	398	495	569

[1] Programs now authorized by Comprehensive Employment & Training Act.
Source: U.S. Office of Management and Budget.
From: Levitan, Mangum, and Marshall, *Human Resources and Labor Markets: Labor and Manpower in the American Economy,* Harper & Row Publishers, revised edition, 1975, Table 12-1, updated January, 1976.

case, to demonstrate that the programs had either succeeded or failed. The basic evaluation technique used was the so-called human capital approach which assumed that the returns to investments in training or other employment programs could be measured. Most of the early studies using this approach to evaluate training programs found the returns to be substantial and positive for both the enrollees and society. Nine major studies of institutional training under the MDTA found benefit-cost ratios ranging between 2 and 12.[5] On-the-job-training was found to be even more profitable. Benefit-cost ratios for five major studies of the JOBS program ranged from 1.5 to 4.3 and two studies of the MDTA-OJT program found ratios between 5.9 and 9.2.[6]

These positive findings were not very welcome or convincing to the coalition of policy makers and academics who wanted to cut these programs. The policy makers were concerned about costs and direct intervention in the economy, while the academics and related professionals were concerned because specific labor market interventions required technical skills and training they did not possess, and were based on assumptions contrary to their theoretical economic beliefs. Since the state-of-the-art in program evaluation does not permit as much rigor or precision as many of its advocates and practitioners would like to have people believe, it was very easy to challenge the conclusions reached by the studies which showed positive results. It is equally easy (if not easier) to challenge the conclusions reached by the critics of training programs. There are always serious data limitations. Influences other than the training programs can never be controlled for with precision. There is no convincing way to specify or measure either the programs' costs or their benefits. Indeed, it was generally agreed that some of the most important program results (reducing institutional discrimination, improving the operation of labor markets, changing the attitudes and behavior patterns of disadvantaged teenagers, facilitating the employment effects of macroemployment [monetary-fiscal] policies at lower levels of inflation than otherwise would have been possible) could not be measured in monetary terms. Even quantifiable program outcomes and inputs depended heavily on debatable assumptions about elements on the cost and benefit side, and about the time allowed for program impacts to be measured. Indeed, human capital theory, the conceptual under-pinning of benefit-cost analyses of both the critics and supporters of training programs, is highly questionable on theoretical and logical grounds. [For a critique of the human capital approach see reference 7.]

One of the major studies used by the critics of training programs to justify arguments for retrenchment was a massive study based on 10-year earnings histories, taken from Social Security data of 57,000 persons enrolled in training programs in 1964. These were compared with the earnings histories of a control group of persons not enrolled in training programs. The results of this study were not as favorable to the training programs. MDTA institutional enrollees had average annual earnings of $68 less than the controls in the five years before training, but $152 less in the five years after training. White females and blacks benefited relatively more than the controls, while male completers and all noncompleters lost relative to the controls. Moreover, participants in other programs, like the Job Corps, fell further behind the controls through time. Although this study was never officially released by the Manpower Administration, it was leaked to critics and widely quoted.[8]

As is true of all such studies, however, the one based on Social Security data had serious methodological problems. For one thing, the Social Security data have serious defects for program evaluation. All earnings are not reported, since not all earnings are covered by Social Security. The earnings gaps are therefore filled through projections, which create technical problems. More importantly, however, information on some very important variables is not available in the data. This is particularly important for variables like educational attainment and family wealth and income. Without this kind of information for controls, young college students were compared with the high school dropouts from poor families who were more likely to be in the manpower programs. Both groups might have low and unstable earnings before training, but the college group clearly would be expected to have high earnings following training.

Moreover, statistical biases were introduced in the Social Security study because the controls were from higher income groups, who would be expected to achieve higher absolute earnings over the long-run, and because of the fact that the trainees' generally low earnings of the year before training were dropped on the questionnable assumption that the trainees were experiencing special difficulty that year. Dropping the year prior to training had the effect of matching enrollees with higher income people in the control group. This is a questionable procedure, because without the training the enrollees might have continued to have employment difficulties and therefore the prior year would have been an entirely legitimate inclusion.

The influence of these data and methodological biases is suggested by reexamination of the data using different assumptions and approaches. The impact of dropping the prior year is suggested by the fact that a reexamination using a 1959-1963 base (rather than 1958-1962) found that participants gained absolutely and relatively.[9] Similarly, a longitudinal study using Social Security data and controlling for the control group bias in the original Social Security study by comparing enrollees with people who were eligible for the manpower programs (and signed up for them but did not show up) found that the average earnings of male participants rose by two-thirds more than the earnings of the no-shows. Female enrollees gained even more relative to no-shows.[10]

Thus, while the overwhelming weight of evidence and logic supports the conclusion that the manpower programs were cost effective, controversy continues because the state of the evaluation art makes it impossible to lay this matter to rest with perfect certainty.

Conclusions

My critique of the evaluation procedures is not meant to argue against program evaluation. Evaluation efforts must continue because we need to know what works and why in order to make the programs more efficient. Since we cannot achieve absolute precision, we should follow the example of the legal profession and require the *best possible evidence* for the conclusions reached. We should, moreover, carefully examine, and discount appropriately, the biases of the advocates for and against programs. The most effective test to apply to these programs after the best evidence is presented is judgment and common sense. Since logic is clearly on the side of the selective employment programs, the burden of proof should be on those who argue that these activities have not worked.

Selective employment programs were experimental and small relative to need, the size of the work force, and the Federal budget—they never reached over 10 percent of the target population, or 1 percent of the work force, and never accounted for more than 2 percent of the Federal budget.

The logic supporting selective labor market programs has not been seriously challenged by the experience of the 1960s and 1970s. If anything, the case for specific interventions has been strengthened. It cannot seriously be argued that monetary-fiscal policy alone can achieve full employment without inflation. Nor can it be convincingly argued that wage and price controls effectively prevent inflation under conditions of full employment. Specific employment efforts are needed to improve the effectiveness of labor markets.

The human problems which prompted the Great Society programs still persist. Despite the arguments about "new" unemployment (which presumably is less of a burden (a) because it hits teenagers, women, minorities most heavily and (b) because of the safety nets placed under workers by the New Deal programs) unemployment is still correlated with rising levels of poverty, suicide rates among middle-aged men, incarcerations in prison, family breakups, confinements to mental institutions, and infant mortality. Moreover, too many workers are still restricted to bad jobs from which they and their children have considerable difficulty escaping. In addition, although there has been some improvement, minorities, women, and older people continue to be discriminated against for reasons unrelated to productivity. Similarly, although there has been some improvement in traditional labor market institutions like vocational-technical training and the Federal-state employment service, much room for improvement remains.

Finally, the New Frontier and Great Society programs did not solve all employment problems; there were many false starts, much waste and inefficiency, and much more was promised than could be delivered. Solutions to employment and other national problems seemed much simpler in the early 1960s than they do in the late 1970s. The compassion for those who suffered employment disadvantages often obscured the technical problems involved in solving specific labor market problems. Nevertheless, without the compassion and energy of the Great Society there would be more human misery than we now have and less understanding of what remains to be done. It is now very clear that providing full employment and decent jobs for all willing and able to work is a very difficult objective to achieve, but do we dare not to try it?

Lessons

The main lessons of the selective employment programs of the Kennedy-Johnson years were:

1. Inflation and unemployment are twin evils and must be attacked simultaneously. While inflation does not necessarily originate in labor markets, there is no doubt that the operation of labor markets could be inflationary. Improvements in the operation of labor markets through selective employment programs, could therefore make it possible to have lower levels of unemployment and inflation.

2. The concept of selective employment programs was broadened considerably during the Kennedy-Johnson years. In particular, after some controversy and disagreement over priorities, it became generally accepted that selective employment policies were needed as supplements to general macroeconomic policies. During the 1960s, "manpower" programs became synonymous with training, but were broadened during those years to include labor market information systems; supportive programs to get people ready for training, education, or work; public employment (including special government jobs for particular groups of unemployed workers, supported work, and public works programs); antidiscrimination programs; and programs to improve the operation of labor markets (relocation projects, decasualization, deseasonalization).

3. Although the experiences of the 1960s improved our knowledge of selective employment programs, and formed the basis for future programs and policies, much more needs to be done to transform these programs from logical concepts to operational mechanisms. There is a special need to make programs as efficient as possible in order to minimize their inflationary impact and to maximize their effect on target populations.

4. In order to improve labor markets and employment

mechanisms it will be necessary to collect much better labor market information and develop better measurement and evaluation techniques. It will not be possible to measure selective employment impacts with perfection, but much stronger evidence must be developed for program impact. If programs are logical, the burden of proof should rest with their critics, but better policy decisions will be made if their critics and supporters present the best possible evidence.

5. A major unsettled issue which is not likely to be easily resolved, is the appropriate agents to operate selective employment programs. Clearly, however, a variety of public and private agents will be required, including new private organizational forms and public and private consortia. The appropriate division of labor between public and private agents and the appropriate level of government (Federal, state, or local) also will continue to be an issue. The appropriate agents and the appropriate program mix will vary with time, place, and circumstances.

Although many issues remain to be solved, a number of conclusions may be drawn from the experiences of the 1960s:

- Full employment and reasonably stable prices are not likely to be achieved by general (monetary-fiscal) policies alone.

- Training programs can (and have) improved (d) the employment and income positions of program participants.

- At low levels of unemployment, some kind of incomes (wage-price) policy can moderate inflationary pressures. However, general wage-price controls are not likely to be effective. A more effective approach is likely to include standby controls and continuous negotiations and study of programs geared to particular industries or sectors.

- It is very costly in material and human values to ignore unemployment.

- It is not clear that full employment and stable prices can be achieved through the use of a combination of general and selective programs, but there is enough evidence to justify the attempt.

References

[1] Ray Marshall and Richard Perlman. *An Anthology of Labor Economics.* New York: John Wiley & Sons, 1972.

[2] Sar Levitan, Garth Mangum, and Ray Marshall. *Human Resources and Labor Markets.* New York: Harper & Row, revised, 1975.

[3] Sar Levitan and Robert Taggert. *The Promise of Greatness.* Cambridge: Harvard University Press, 1976.

[4] Ray Marshall and Vernon Briggs. *The Negro and Apprenticeship.* Baltimore: John Hopkins University Press, 1967.

[5] Jon H. Goldstein. *The Effectiveness of Manpower Training Programs.* Washington, D.C.: U.S. Congress Joint Economic Committee, 1972, p. 29.

[6] Joe N. Nay, John W. Scanlon, and Joseph Whaley. *Benefits and Costs of Manpower Training Programs.* Washington, D.C.: Urban Institute, 1972.

[7] Ray Marshall, Allan Cartter, and Allan King. *Labor Economics.* Homewood, Illinois: Richard D. Irwin, Inc., 1976, chapters 10 and 11.

[8] David J. Farber. "Changes in the Duration of the Post Training in Relative Earnings Credits of Trainees." Washington, D.C.: Manpower Administration, U.S. Department of Labor, August 1971, mimeo.

[9] Orley Ashenfelter. "Progress in the Development of Continuous Performance Information on the Impact of the Manpower Development and Training Act." Washington, D.C.: Manpower Administration, U.S. Department of Labor, 1973, mimeo.

[10] Edward Prescott and T.F. Cooley. "Evaluating the Impact of MDTA Programs on Earnings under Varying Labor Market Conditions." Washington, D.C.: Manpower Administration, U.S. Department of Labor, 1971, mimeo.

Kenneth Clark

6

Community Action and the
Social Programs of the 1960s

The task of doing full justice to the social concerns of the Johnson and Kennedy Administrations is one which must be left to future historians, political scientists, and social scientists who will assume the responsibility of examining the documents and the consequences of these programs in the detail required for objective scholarship.

All that is possible for me to do is to approach this topic from the perspective of my personal involvement in these programs. I will try to make some contribution to the present and future understanding by sharing some of my personal observations of those aspects of these programs in which I had the privilege of being involved. I am presumptuous in assuming this approach to the problem. I justify this approach only on the assumption that history basically is a mosaic, a pattern of individual activities, reflecting the contributions, the strengths, the weaknesses, the cumulative impact of individuals working together or in conflict on social problems and social issues.

The Kennedy-Johnson period in American history was a period of hope, of promises, of concern with making the American democratic system more effective, more real. It was a period when one sought to extend the benefits of democracy to groups of human beings who previously had been either excluded or involved only to a minimal degree. It is appropriate that the Kennedy-Johnson period of 1961 through 1968 was designated as the period of "The New Frontier" and "The Great Society." The verbal aura of "The New Frontier/Great Society" period was established by the words of Kennedy's Inaugural Address with the quotable phrase, "Ask not what your country can do for you—but what you can do for your country."

In retrospect, this seems to be a somewhat paradoxical theme, because, while it stimulated many American citizens to become involved in the social programs of that time, it stimulated concerned Americans to see government as a partner in defining and working toward positive social goals, particularly for the benefit of the underprivileged. It stimulated the mobilization of the resources of the power of the government toward the attainment of social stability and social justice. The unstated rallying cry of the period was "for the fulfillment of the promises of American democracy."

President's Committee on Juvenile Delinquency

The social mobilization of that time was not just verbal. President Kennedy established the President's Committee on Juvenile Delinquency. This committee, which was chaired by Robert Kennedy, the Attorney General, sought to deal with the problems of juvenile delinquency by encouraging local groups to plan programs and develop techniques for helping young people to live more constructive lives. The basic assumption of this committee was that if young people were somehow constructively involved in their society, they would not become victims of frustration and disillusionment and therefore would not have to resort to delinquent and criminal behavior. In looking back on the assumptions of the President's Committee on Juvenile Delinquency, one sees that the whole approach encouraged by this committee was totally antithetical to the subsequently popular racist code words such as "crime in the streets" and "law and order." Rather, the committee took the affirmative posture of trying to help local groups and young people develop techniques for helping themselves, for overcoming negative dependence and making positive contributions to their neighborhoods and to society as a whole.

A pioneer project which came out of the President's Committee on Juvenile Delinquency was the Mobilization for Youth Project on the lower east side of Manhattan in New York City.[1] This project was directed by such outstanding social scientists as Lloyd E. Ohlin and Richard A. Cloward. As its basic theme for the control of juvenile delinquency, it developed a program for providing constructive opportunities for young people. It was believed that if the society assumed the responsibility of providing these opportunities for young people, they would become constructive members of the society and would not be required to resort to delinquency. At the end of the planning stage of Mobilization for Youth, the White House under the Kennedy Administration had a well-publicized promotional ceremony. The directors of the Mobilization Program were invited to Washington and the President greeted them and announced the allocation of the—at that time, unprecedented—funds to support the successful operation of the Mobilization for Youth program on the lower east side of Manhattan.

Harlem Youth Opportunities Unlimited, Inc.

Soon after the launching of the Mobilization for Youth program, another important program in New York City was funded by the President's Committee on Juvenile Delinquency. The HARYOU—Harlem Youth Opportunities Unlimited, Inc.—program, which I had the privilege of directing during its planning phase, centered on problems of delinquency in Harlem. The founders of HARYOU obtained a planning grant from the President's Committee of Juvenile Delinquency.

In order to understand the aura of the early stages of the Kennedy Administration, it might be of value to give a brief, historical background of the HARYOU program. It did not emerge directly out of the Mobilization for Youth program, but rather out of a specific confrontation and incident which I, at that time, called "social work colonialism." The officials of the City of New York who were responsible for the allocation of funds for youth services in 1962 made the decision to give to a well-established social agency in New York City a substantial amount of funds to work with adolescents in three or four areas of New York City, including the Harlem area. This social service agency, which received these funds and mandate, was not based in Harlem.

My wife, Dr. Mamie Phipps Clark, and I were heading a Harlem social agency, the Northside Center for Child Development, at that time. We were working with emotionally troubled children who were having difficulties adjusting in school or at home or in the community. We struggled to obtain support for the work of the Northside Center through funds and contributions from individuals and private foundations. In our work at the Northside Center we cooperated with a number of the social agencies in the Harlem district, such as the YMCA, the YWCA, the New York Urban League, and the Harlem Neighborhoods' Association.

When we learned through the newspapers of the city's decision to import an out-of-neighborhood agency to work with Harlem youth, we protested publicly. We called meetings with the heads of all of the Harlem agencies to mobilize their power to protest the importing of an out-of-neighborhood agency to work with Harlem youth. The controversy was long and sustained, but we insisted that it would be better not to have a program at all rather than to have it under these conditions of "social work colonialism." Our protests were heard. Out of this first community-based protest against social service colonialism came the decision to fund the planning of a HARYOU program to control juvenile delinquency in Harlem.

The HARYOU Approach to Community Planning

The basic structure and assumptions of HARYOU were similar to, but, I think, somewhat different from, the Mobilization for Youth program. From the very beginning, the HARYOU approach involved the cooperative efforts of all of the Harlem social agencies. The Harlem Neighborhoods' Association was a basic foundation for the HARYOU program from its planning stage up until its actual operational stages. HARYOU involved church leaders; civil rights groups, such as the local Urban League, the National Association for the Advancement of Colored People (NAACP); municipal officials, such as James Dumpson, the Commissioner of Welfare, and political leaders, such as J. Raymond Jones and Percy Sutton. HARYOU even had the quiet backing of such militant leaders as Malcolm X. It, without question, was an early experiment in the attempt to bring together the wide spectrum of community leadership in the planning and operation of a serious program of delinquency control.

Early in the planning stages of HARYOU, it became clear that delinquency control could not be isolated from the larger problems of community health and stability and justice. An important part of the HARYOU planning stage was the bringing together of a highly competent professional staff. Dr. James Jones, a brilliant young black sociologist, is presently a professor of the Columbia University School of Social Work. I pirated him from Mobilization for Youth and appointed him the HARYOU research director. The late Dr. Kenneth Marshall of the Columbia

University School of Social Work assumed the responsibility of program director and Cyril Tyson, who had many years of experience on the Mayor's Commission on Human Rights in New York City, was brought over as administrative director. These three young men, working under my direction and with an interracial staff, assumed primary responsibility for planning HARYOU and developing the program which was published under the title, *Youth in the Ghetto*[2].

The HARYOU operation had its basic financial and psychological support from the Federal Government—the President's Committee on Juvenile Delinquency. David Hackett, an assistant to Robert Kennedy, was in constant communication with our planning staff. In fact, his involvement was such that it could be accurately described as that of an adjunct member of the HARYOU staff. The municipal government, Mayor Wagner and the Deputy Mayor for Administration, presently Federal Judge Tenny, and his deputy, Henry Cohen, were active participants and cooperators in the planning stages. There was an aura of excitement and optimism and hope in this planning which was encouraged and supported by the President's Committee on Juvenile Delinquency and by the municipal officials of the City of New York.

Another characteristic of the HARYOU planning stage was that for the first time the youth of Harlem were actually involved in the activity. These young people were brought in, not only to be interviewed, but also to participate in a series of discussions concerning the problems of the community, the relationship between these problems and the perspectives, the attitudes and the behavior of youth. These young people, in fact, became volunteer members of the staff and, in some cases, were paid for their activities. Their preliminary projects were supported and they became identified with HARYOU in a way in which they felt that this was their club or a community betterment activity of which they were an integral part.

Some of the basic assumptions of HARYOU were:

— Delinquency was not an isolated phenomenon but had to be understood as a symptom of the larger problem of a community. In Harlem, delinquency appeared to be a symptom of the powerlessness of the community to control its own destiny and to control the behavior of its youth.

— A serious program to control delinquency had to take into account the total pattern of community strengths, weaknesses, and pathologies.

— Delinquency control had to be seen as part of a total civil rights struggle—the struggle for social justice, racial equality and the equality of educational and economic opportunity.

The central assumption of the whole HARYOU planning approach was that the community and the society as a whole had to be involved in a constructive struggle for social justice; that the welfare and social services programs which encouraged dependency and powerlessness of human beings were counterproductive to a serious approach to the stability of the community and the stability of the individuals who were essential to the control of delinquency.

The HARYOU approach raised critical questions concerning the traditional "lady bountiful," social services' approach to helping economically and educationally deprived communities. It asserted that traditional public welfare and voluntary social services tended to increase dependency, contributed to the stigmatization of individuals, intensified social class distinctions and thereby intensified the social and community problems which spawned delinquency and crime in the total pattern of community pathology. The HARYOU program sought to break this cycle of dependency, dehumanization, and community pathology in which crime and delinquency were merely symptoms of a total pattern of social instability, frustration, and powerlessness.

The report which came out of this planning stage took two years to prepare and was published in the summer of 1964. It was submitted to the President's Committee on Juvenile Delinquency. It was read carefully, praised and the general and specific programs outlined in that report were accepted and funded for a demonstration HARYOU program in the Harlem community.

If one is to be objective, one cannot end the description of the HARYOU saga with the Hollywood "positive" ending. A number of things occurred soon after the completion of the HARYOU planning stage and the submission of the *Youth in the Ghetto* report. Near the end of that program, President Kennedy was assassinated and Lyndon Johnson became President. It was clear from the beginnings of the Johnson Administration that the positive social programs of the Kennedy Administration would not only continue but would also be intensified as far as possible. The Johnson Administration adopted the Great Society as its slogan for the continuation of the New Frontier emphasis. The President's Committee on Juvenile Delinquency under Kennedy gave way to the War on Poverty under Johnson. The focus of the War on Poverty was directly compatible with the socially holistic perspective and emphasis of the HARYOU "Youth in the Ghetto" program.

The Approach of the War on Poverty

Sargent Shriver was appointed director by President Johnson and given the responsibility of developing the apparatus and the approach for the War on Poverty. He talked with me a number of times during this period of planning the War on Poverty. It was obvious that he and his planning staff had read *Youth in the Ghetto*. From the earliest talks with Mr. Shriver and some of his staff it was evident that the War on Poverty program would emphasize "community action programs" and would seek "maximum feasible participation" of the poor in planning for the improvement of their status in their society. It was apparent also that the War on Poverty programs would put particular emphasis on programs for disadvantaged young people and would seek to broaden their perspectives and their chances of constructive involvement in their larger society.

Specifically, the Head Start program, which was strongly supported by Lady Bird Johnson, is part of the total pattern of the War on Poverty and is quite similar to the community day-care programs for young children described so vividly as the "Pre-School Academy" in the *Youth in the Ghetto* document.

There is no question that Lyndon Johnson's insistence on the development of a War on Poverty was the critical, if not the nuclear, component of his Great Society program. In its initial stages the War on Poverty raised the aspirations and stimulated positive activity among the poor and the deprived. Individuals who previously seemed to have had no hope for being a part of the decisions affecting their destiny were now not only given hope, but seemed also to be encouraged, stimulated, and organized in seeking to effect positive changes in the lives of their children and themselves.

Again, it would be desirable if one could accurately conclude this description of the War on Poverty approach of the Johnson Administration with an unalloyed positive ending. Unfortunately, one cannot. A number of problems interfered with or blocked total positive results of the War on Poverty. Among the major problems which seemed to me to have reduced the effectiveness of the War on Poverty are:

1. Rising involvement and expenditures of the war in Vietnam. In spite of the desire, it was not possible to resolve the fiscal dilemmas of that time in the direction of the ability to have both guns and butter. In that conflict it appears as if guns won out over the needs of the poor.

2. The second, and probably equally important social and psychological problem, was that the conflict between the newly stimulated, indigenous poor and the entrenched political power brokers and controllers of political systems in local communities soon emerged as a major problem which had not been adequately anticipated or prepared for. The untrained poor sought to assert their power and found that, in fact, they really did not have the controlling power which the community action programs, including the HARYOU program, promised them. Anti-poverty programs became political pork-barrel type programs and were taken over by sophisticated middle-class bureaucrats. In some cases, upwardly mobile working class individuals became either the products of or the puppets of the more sophisticated middle-class political controllers of these programs. Sometimes the upwardly mobile indigenous became sophisticated anti-poverty hustlers.

The War on Poverty programs did not benefit the masses of the urban poor to the extent hoped for by those who planned these programs. This particular set of problems which emerged as dominant ones in the War on Poverty should have been anticipated by the very effective way in which Adam Powell moved in and took control of the HARYOU program in Harlem. This first dramatic intrusion of a local anti-poverty program was a prototype for the general pattern which affected the anti-poverty programs as a whole. The poor were not trained and did not have the power to cope with the entrenched decision making and controlling power of the established political bureaucracy. The poor tended to vent their hostilities, resulting from the frustrations of the promises of the anti-poverty program, by developing random and at times self-destructive forms of hostilities toward the controllers of the anti-poverty programs.

It is probably not just coincidental that the urban riots of the late 1960s (1964-1968) came in the wake of the anti-poverty programs. Furthermore, black nationalism, the rise of the racial militants, and black separatism, was part of this pattern wherein American deep-seated racism resulted in the combination of the anti-poverty programs becoming for the most part, if not exclusively, perceived as programs reserved for blacks and Hispanics. It was a fact, nonetheless, that the blacks who were in need of the fulfillment of the promises of these programs were not in control of them and therefore tended to react with sporadic, widespread, or restrictive violence.

Some of the Successes

In spite of these very real problems which certainly limited the effectiveness and the attainment of the desired goals of the anti-poverty programs, one cannot conclude that the War on Poverty, the nuclear ingredient of the social programs of the Johnson Administration, was a total failure. There were some positive residues of the Great Society and the War on Poverty programs. There were aspects of social sensitivity and concern of Lyndon Johnson and his Administration which took root and are still affecting positively contemporary American society.

For example, the whole community action approach of the War on Poverty program did, in fact, give a new dimension to the civil rights movement. Attempts to involve the poor and to encourage the indigenous members of the community to partici-pate in seeking positive solutions to their problems awakened in many of these individuals a sense that they did have certain rights and could make certain demands and could develop groups and organizations to seek amelioration of their problems.

It is now fashionable among many social scientists, functioning in the role of Monday-morning quarterbacks, to assert that the fact that the War on Poverty did not succeed and that the poor were unable to mobilize their resources and develop a constructive community consensus of positive action was because these programs were inherently unrealistic. Some of these critics maintain that we now know that there is no possibility that a systematic government-sponsored attack on the problems of poverty and ghetto pathology can work. Some of these analysts dare to suggest rather explicitly that these programs reflect the inherent inferiority of those who are presently caught in the mesh of economic deprivation. They contend that the negative experiences of the social programs of the "Great Society" period provide empirical support for the contention that poverty is a manifestation of personal deficiency.

These conservative political arguments do not take into account the fact that the experiments to involve the poor in participation in the solution of their personal and community problems did not really get off the ground. These social programs were blocked by a number of unresolved problems including the fact that nowhere in the planning of these programs was allowance made for the training of the indigenous groups to deal with the inevitability of conflicts, disagreements, and power competitions among the individuals in these groups. They were unprepared for the clashes which emerged as part of the process in developing community programs eventually seeking solutions for community problems. Those of us who were involved in the planning of these community action programs must confess a certain amount of naive and sentimental projection of spontaneous capacities among the poor. We tended to assume greater clarity in their understanding of complex social, political, and economic problems than could possibly exist among individuals who had been excluded from even the minimal level of middle-class involvement in their society. Probably most important, we did not take into account the debilitating, inhibiting effect of the most persistent and stark factor in American poverty; namely, the factor of criminally inferior education in the public schools in low-income areas of our cities. In our desire to avoid any suggestions of condescension in working with the poor, we went to the uncritical extreme of a sentimental view of the poor as being prepared to function effectively in dealing with their problems—by virtue of their poverty.

In spite of this critical error in planning and perspective, the anti-poverty movement did leave a positive residue of, admittedly imperfect, community control, concerns, rhetoric, and organizations among the poor. Groups of individuals in economically depressed areas did become more concerned with what was happening to their children in their neighborhood public schools. It would not seem to be an exaggeration to say that the movement toward the decentralization and community control of the public schools in New York City is a direct spillover from the community action component of the anti-poverty programs. Unfortunately, the evidence today reveals that this decentralization and community control has not yet resulted in any observable increase in the academic achievement of poor children in these public schools.

While one cannot with absolute confidence conclude on the basis of available evidence that the rise of systematic political activity among minorities is a direct consequence of the anti-poverty programs of the sixties, the passage of the Voting Rights Act of 1965 caused a marked increase in the number of black elected officials throughout the United States. Within the past 10 years, the number of these officials has moved from less than 300 to nearly 4,000. There have been black mayors in such major American cities as Cleveland, Los Angeles, Detroit, Atlanta, Newark, and Gary, Indiana. There are presently two black lieutenant governors. The number of blacks in Congress has increased from 3 to 18—17 members of the House and one senator. These figures do not tell the whole story, not only because they reflect still a very small percentage of black involvement in the political decision power of our nation, but also because they mask the extent to which blacks and other minorities are becoming increasingly involved and organized to participate in the overall democratic political process.

It might be of interest to also point out that during the Kennedy-Johnson period, the number of blacks appointed to the Federal courts increased dramatically. Prior to 1960, only five blacks were members of the Federal Judiciary and three of them were appointed to the Federal court in the Virgin Islands and to the U.S. Custom Court. William Hastie was the only black serving in the Federal court in the continental United States at that time. In the Kennedy-Johnson period, there were 15 blacks serving in the U.S. Federal Judiciary. One of these, Thurgood Marshall, was appointed to the U.S. Supreme Court by Lyndon Baines Johnson, and two, Spottswood Robinson and William Hastie, to the U.S. Circuit Court of Appeals.

Another historic appointment for a black during the Great Society period of Lyndon B. Johnson was the appointment of Robert Weaver as the first black to serve in the cabinet of a President of the United States.

Some Longer-Run Effects

While one must agree with the fasionable revisionist social philosophers who now conclude that positive social change through systematic government planning and programs is difficult, this observer continues to insist that it is possible. What most of the pessimistic critics seem to ignore and consistently deemphasize is the inescapable fact that the New Frontier/Great Society/War on Poverty period, initiated during the Kennedy Administration and sustained and intensified during the Johnson Administration, had a tremendously positive social and psychological effect upon the masses of economically and socially deprived Americans.

These programs brought with them hope and expectations for the possibility of positive changes. The aspirations of a critical percentage of American citizens were increased. Human beings who previously were consigned to pervasive deprivation, a sense of hopelessness, powerlessness, frustration, and despair, were given a governmentally supported basis for the belief that their status could be improved. In spite of the fact that these rising expectations were not fully realized, they generated a social climate of optimism and confidence which often manifested itself in the turbulence of demands and confrontations. It is important that the "benign neglect" strategy of the Nixon Administration did not reverse the uphill gains stimulated by the Johnson social programs. Backlash, neoconservatism, urban eruptions, and racial polarization did not destroy the motivation for positive change within the framework of the American democratic system.

Summing up the positives and the negatives of the Kennedy-Johnson social programs, one can objectively conclude that their overall effect remains positive. The problems that arose demonstrate that social progress and the struggle for social equality do not proceed on a straight, upward line. Social progress must be charted with ups and downs, but with the general trend toward up. The contribution made by the social programs of the Kennedy-Johnson Administrations is in providing a basic foundation upon which future social progress can be built. These programs will remain an important historical monument to Lyndon Baines Johnson.

Future historians, I believe, will interpret these governmentally supported social programs as a reflection of two Presidents who were, in fact, deeply concerned with raising the status and the quality of life of their fellow human beings. These programs and their consequences will demonstrate, in spite of the tragedy of the war in Vietnam, that these two Presidents sought to use the power of their office and their personalities to mobilize the Federal Government to assist otherwise powerless human beings in developing a capacity to help themselves and thereby to make constructive contributions to society. By displaying their profound concern for all of their fellow citizens, these two Presidents demonstrated that this pervasive concern, when acted upon, will benefit all Americans. They built upon the past ideals of the moral uniqueness of American democracy and strengthened them as the basis for future action.

References

[1] The staff prepared a planning report under the title: "A Proposal for the Prevention and Control of Delinquency by Expanding Opportunity." Mobilization for Youth, Inc., 1961-1962.

[2] *Youth in the Ghetto: A Study of the Consequences of Powerlessness and a Blueprint for Change*. Harlem Youth Opportunities Unlimited, Inc., 1964.

Robert J. Lampman

7

Changing Patterns of Income, 1960–1974

What changes in the level of income—and of publicly provided goods and services—have occurred since John F. Kennedy took office? What differences are apparent in the incomes of rich and poor, old and young, black and white, North and South? To what extent were these differences caused by the social programs of the Johnson and Kennedy Administrations? Do the benefits of the changing pattern outweigh the costs of achieving it?

Levels of Production and Income

Between 1960 and 1974 the population of the United States increased by 31 million, from 181 to 212 million. While the population increased by 17 percent, the labor force swelled by 30 percent, from 72 to 93 million. The larger labor force produced 64 percent more goods and services; that is, the gross national product (GNP) rose from $737 billion to $1,211 billion, in 1972 dollars, between 1960 and 1974.[1] Almost half this increase occurred in the five years 1962 through 1966, when the year-to-year growth averaged 5.4 percent. In contrast, average yearly growth for the whole 14-year period was 3.6 percent. Per capita GNP went up from $4,082 to $5,711, or by 40 percent. A substantial share—18 percent—of the increased production was allocated to investment and net exports, and 17 percent to government—mostly state and local—goods and services. However, the great bulk of it, two-thirds, went to output for the use of households, and per capita consumption increased by 43 percent.

This extraordinary addition to yearly output was matched by income increases, with labor income showing a slight rise in share, from 77 to 79 percent of the total, and property income, in the form of profits, rent, and interest, an offsetting decline. (For purposes of this calculation, "proprietors' income" is arbitrarily assigned half to labor income and half to property income.) These incomes as earned in the market are reduced by taxes, which grew as a ratio of GNP from 28 to 32 percent, and increased by cash transfers, which changed from 6 to 10 percent of GNP. Disposable personal income (DPI)—income after payment of taxes and after receipt of cash transfers—was 44 percent higher on a per capita basis in 1974 than in 1960.

Non-cash benefits flowing to persons from government programs, e.g., education services and health care services, rose from 5 to 8 percent of GNP. These benefits are not counted in DPI, but they are properly part of a broader income concept. They reflect a re-allocation of productive resources from private markets or from other public uses. These non-cash benefits, along with cash transfers, e.g., social insurance and public assistance benefits, all of which are referred to below as "social welfare expenditures," add up to the grand total of redistribution, i.e., taking income from some persons and giving benefits to others, which the public sector carries out. The two types of benefits together were $178 billion greater in 1974 than in 1960; that amount equalled 37 percent of the increase in GNP which was achieved in the period.

The larger population in 1974 produced substantially more and had a higher average income level than was true in 1960. However, that larger population is very differently composed, located, and occupied than earlier. The average age in the country advanced. The number of children under five years of age declined absolutely. A larger part of the population is 65 years of age or older, yet the proportion of persons in the "prime working ages" of 20 through 64 years is greater. Persons in these ages were 51 percent of the total population in 1965 (the post-war low for this ratio), and 54.5 percent in 1974. This historic turnabout, along with a 50 percent increase in women at work outside the home,[2] explains the disproportionate rise in the labor force, and the increase from 36.3 to 40.5 percent of the total population employed. This greater work effort came about despite younger people staying in school longer and older people retiring earlier. (The labor force participation rate of aged men fell from 32 percent in 1960 to 23 percent in 1974.)

The number of consumer units, or households, grew faster than population. Those living alone, or as unrelated individuals, increased by 70 percent, while the number of families, whose average size declined slightly from 3.7 to 3.5 persons, increased by 22 percent. These changes are related to the startling increase, most of which occurred after 1965, in the proportion of all persons who were in households headed by women, from 12 to 15 percent.

While DPI per capita increased by 44 percent, the median income of families (pre-tax income including cash transfers), increased by only a third (from $9,538 to $12,836 in 1974 dollars), with virtually no change after 1969. Unrelated individuals, on the other hand, saw their median income climb from $2,864 to $4,439, or by 55 percent.

Average hourly earnings in constant dollars went up 21 percent for production workers in private, non-agricultural industries. These workers put in fewer hours at work as the period advanced and had only a 15 percent increase in average gross weekly earnings, and a 9 percent rise in average spendable weekly earnings, i.e., gross earnings less Social Security and income taxes. DPI was enabled to rise more than that 9 percent by the more rapid rise of other incomes, including cash transfers, and by the rapid growth of the numbers at work.

Certain historic trends continued throughout the period. Thus, the population became more urbanized. Two million people moved out of agricultural employment and the share of the population living in metropolitan areas continued to increase. On the other hand, the flow of population appeared to shift away from the East toward the South and West, rather than toward the North and West. With education levels rising, more people moved into skilled, technical, and professional occupations. The production of services, as opposed to goods, continued to occupy a larger and larger share of all workers. The most rapidly growing employment was in state and local government. Many of these shifts have undoubtedly worked to the disadvantage of the less educated and less skilled members of the labor force. The racial composition of the population also continued to change, with races other than white increasing from 10 to 12 percent of the total.

Inter-group Income Differences

These trends are consistent with an observed narrowing of some traditional income differences. Thus, farm residents' incomes now average over 80 percent of non-farm income, and the North-South income difference is less than it was. For example, Mississippi's per capita income rose at 1.6 times the national average. In 1960, the per capita income of the poorest region (the East South Central region) was only 57 percent that of the richest (Middle Atlantic) region. By 1972 it was 69 percent. During the 1960-1974 period, black family incomes rose from 52 to 62 percent of white family incomes, and blacks' share of total income increased from 7 to 8 percent. The median income of families of Spanish origin probably also rose in relation to the national median and now stands at 74 percent. The median educational difference between whites and blacks narrowed from 2.7 years to 2.0 years, and the narrowing was even more marked for younger adults. At the same time, at least up to 1970, it seems that the income advantage associated with additional schooling remained unchanged, with men having four years of college earning 1.91 times at much as those with only eight years of schooling.

One important inter-group income difference that has not been reduced is that between males and females. Incomes of women working full-time, year-round were 60 percent those of men in 1960 and 57 percent in 1974.

There is some evidence that wage differentials have widened for prime age males within and among occupational groups in recent years and that the distribution of wages among all earners has become somewhat more unequal. This may be explained in part by the changing age distribution of the labor force and by the increasing number of women workers, which may offset the equalizing effects of lessened disparity of educational attainment and of retreat from some low-paying occupations and regions. In any event, there seems to be a growing consensus among close observers that the current trend is toward greater inequality in earnings of persons, the distribution of which underlies and largely determines the distribution of family income.

The growth of cash transfers at a rate in excess of the growth of average earnings meant that, in some cases, the difference in income between those at work and those not at work was narrowed. This was particularly true for retired persons. In 1960, less than three-fourths of the aged received Social Security benefits, but in 1974, nine-tenths of them did. For the average wage earner who retired in 1963, the average benefit was $121 per month, or 29 percent of his last year's monthly earnings; the similar worker retiring in 1972 had a benefit of $210, or 32 percent of his earnings (Levitan and Taggart, 1976). Benefits for the lowest-income aged and disabled persons were improved by President Nixon's Supplemental Security Income program, which went into effect in 1974.

The Aid to Families with Dependent Children (AFDC) program had an even greater rise in participation than did Social Security; in 1960, only one-third of low-income families headed by women with children were participating, but by 1974 three-fourths of them were. At the same time, AFDC average benefits rose relative to median family income. In 1974, they were $720 per person per year. Veterans benefits were also improved relative to average wages. Unemployment insurance coverage and benefit levels were not changed notably after 1960 until 1974, when eligibility was broadened and the duration of benefits was temporarily extended.

In 1974, cash transfers amounting to $112 billion were paid to about 50 million people. Over two-thirds of these benefits went to aged and disabled persons; one-fourth went to families broken by death or separation; and only about 5 percent went to persons whose only "qualification" was unemployment. These transfers tend to offset between a fourth and a third of the aggregate income lost due to the great hazards to income continuity of old age, disability, loss of family breadwinner, and unemployment.

The median family money income, as noted earlier, was $12,836 in 1974. Sixty percent of all American families were clustered in a narrow range between $6,500 and $20,445. The lowest fifth, with incomes below $6,500, received only 5.4 percent of total family income, while the top fifth, with incomes above $20,445, received 41 percent of the total. The top five percent, whose incomes start at $31,948, had 15.3 percent of all family income.

The existing pattern of inequality is better understood by a look at the differing compositions of the several income groups. The top 10 percent is disproportionately comprised of families headed by white, prime-age, working males; multiple-earner families; families residing in northern metropolitan areas; and families headed by those of high educational attainment who are in managerial, professional, and technical occupations. The bottom 10 percent of families—which is not quite the same as the

12 percent of the population currently below the official poverty lines—is disproportionately made up of aged, nonwhite, and female-headed families; southern and nonmetropolitan residents; and those with low educational attainment and relatively unskilled occupations. Contrary to the popular impression, income increases with increased family size up to five persons. The top fifth of families ranked by income has 20 percent of all the children and 27 percent of the earners; the lowest fifth has 16 percent of the children and 11 percent of the earners. In 1974, 44 percent of all the income going to the bottom fifth of families ranked by income was in the form of transfer payments.

This pattern of inequality has remained virtually constant throughout the post-war period in spite of the changes in the size, composition, and geographic location of the population and in the industrial and occupational distribution of the labor force. As we mentioned earlier, there is some evidence of a trend toward more inequality in earnings. That trend is entangled with some demographic changes which tend to increase inequality of family income. Among these are changes in the age-income profile and in the age-composition of the population (Paglin, 1975). Other demographic changes that are relevant include the trend toward separate living arrangements for aged parents and young adults, earlier retirement, and the increasing number of broken families (Danziger and Plotnick). However, these disequalizing trends seem to have been offset by the increases in transfer payments, and by the growth in the number of working wives, who have tended to strengthen the middle of the income distribution. (In the future, if more wives of high-income men work, this may be disequalizing.)

A changing relationship between income and family size, which is masked by the conventional way of measuring income inequality, may have lessened inequality of per capita income. Family size declined more for the lowest fifth of families than for other families, and unrelated individuals (left out of the family count) increased as a proportion of the population. Moreover, income inequality among unrelated individuals shows a decided decline since 1964. Adjusting for family size and including unrelated individuals does reveal an upward trend in the per capita income share of the lowest fifth of households, from 4.1 to 5.2 percent between 1948 and 1973 (Thurow, 1975).

Another argument in support of the idea that there was a hidden trend toward less inequality is that the recent increase in cash transfers, which was concentrated in the lowest fifth of households, is consistently under-reported to the Bureau of the Census. Moreover, a case can be made for counting as income certain non-money benefits, such as food stamp bonus values, the insurance value of Medicare and Medicaid, and public housing subsidies, all of which tend to go to lower-income people. The increasing importance of such benefits means that they would, if included, tend to reduce reported inequality through time. On the other hand, the increasing tax burden is not accounted for either in the distribution of money income. As of 1966, the combined Federal, state, and local tax system was roughly proportional in the income range containing 90 percent of families and progressive through the top 10 percent of incomes (Pechman and Okner, 1974). The new emphasis upon payroll and sales taxes means that the tax system has become less progressive. This means that accounting for taxes paid directly and indirectly does little to support the notion that there is a hidden trend toward less inequality.

One scholar who has examined these matters concludes that the share of the lowest fifth of families in "adjusted relative income," after adjusting for family size, taxes, under-reporting of cash transfers, and after including non-money benefits, did rise (from 8.8 to 11.7 percent) between 1962 and 1972 (Browning, 1976). However, another study concludes that there is little reason to believe that post-fisc inequality has decreased in recent years. "Factor markets remain the primary determinant of trends in income inequality . . . we find no major changes in final income distributions despite rapid growth of government, (and) sizable changes in the composition of taxes and expenditures . . ." (Reynolds and Smolensky, 1975). As of the time of this writing, the question must be reported as unsettled (Taussig, 1976, and Sawyer, 1976).

Income Poverty

While measured income inequality has been remarkably constant, there has been a decline in poverty as measured against the fixed purchasing power poverty-income lines drawn by the Social Security Administration. These lines vary by family size and turn around a base of $3,000 of money income in 1962 dollars for a four-person family.[3] In 1974, this amounted to $5,038 in current dollars. In that year, 24.3 million people, or 11.6 percent of the population, were below these lines. In 1959, 39 million persons, or 22 percent of the population, were in income poverty, but by 1969 this number had fallen to 24 million, or 12 percent of the population. The next four years were years of slow reduction of poverty and 1974 and 1975 saw a reversal of the trend.

The composition of those counted as poor in 1974 differed from the rest of the nation in a number of ways. The poverty population was disproportionately located in the South (44 percent) and in what have been designated as "poverty areas" (44 percent). It was relatively poorly educated, with 32 percent of family heads having 8 years or less of schooling. It was also disproportionately non-white (31 percent). About half of all the poor were single women or in family units headed by women. One-fifth of the group were unrelated individuals. Half the poor families were headed by a person out of the labor force.

The frequency of poverty was two or more times as high as the overall average of 11.6 percent for the following groups: unrelated individuals, female heads, Negroes, families with 5 or more children, farmers and farm laborers, and families where the head did not work during the year. Interestingly, the frequency of poverty was near the national average for families headed by a person 65 years of age or older. And for families where the head was unemployed, the frequency of poverty was only slightly above the average at 16.1 percent.

The composition of the poverty population has changed significantly since 1965. Particularly, the aged have declined in numbers, while unrelated individuals and female heads have increased. The latter two groups have increased relative to the total population, but the aged have been taken out of poverty in large numbers by cash transfers. With regard to location, the poor are now more heavily concentrated in metropolitan areas; the share in such areas rose from 47 to 59 percent.

It is important to envision "the poor" as not static either in terms of aggregate numbers or of composition. Some people leave poverty every year and some enter it. We say that poverty declines when more leave than enter. Hence, it is as misleading to speak of "the poor," as it is to speak of "the unemployed," as if they were a permanent class. The University of Michigan Survey Research Center followed 5,000 households over a five-year period. Of those households that were poor in 1967, only 32 percent were poor for the following four years, 42 percent were not poor for at least one year but with no consistent pattern, and the remaining 26 percent were not poor after 1967, although many did not rise far above the poverty-line. Many non-aged families moved in and out of poverty in the five-year period, in most cases because of a change in family composition, the incurring of a disability, or the passing of age 65.

It was noted earlier that poverty was not strikingly higher among the unemployed than among the population at large. Conversely, families with an unemployed head made up only 9 percent of the poor (compared to 5 percent in the total population). Unemployment is not the most prominent characteristic of the poverty population. Looking at the figures another way, one is impressed by how many of the poor are employed. 3.2 out of 5.1 million poor families had at least one earner in 1974; 1.0 million had two or more earners. 1.2 million poor family heads worked the full year, while another 1.5 million worked part of the year. Of the latter group, only 643,000 gave unemployment as the reason for not working; the remainder cited such reasons as disability and family responsibilities. The reasons for not working given by low-income persons 14 years old and over show that the poor differ from the non-poor chiefly with respect to disability and school attendance. Low-income persons who did not work for reasons other than school, illness, or family responsibilities represent only about 5 percent of all poor persons of working age.

The fundamental ingredient of poverty-reduction is growth in per capita capacity to produce (Lampman, 1971). Such change in productivity is believed to arise out of improved education and training, more capital and natural resources per worker, technological advance, and better management. Of lesser importance in the long run is a declining unemployment rate, which cannot fall steadily year after year. Interacting with the rate of economic growth and the level of unemployment, are the following determinants of the year by year process of poverty reduction. (1) The moves people make in search of higher incomes, i.e., from one location, occupation, or industry to another; (2) demographic changes such as shifts in age and family size; and (3) changes in cash transfers, which offset income loss and supplement low earnings.

During the 1960s, poverty-reduction proceeded at a good rate because of a relatively high gain in productivity per worker, particularly in the years 1962-1966, a short-term fall in the unemployment rate, a rise in the share of the population at work, and strenuous moving about by millions of people in search of higher incomes. Some demographic changes were favorable (more young, well-educated workers), but they were partially offset by others that were unfavorable (more female-headed families). Poverty-reduction was also facilitated by a rapid growth of cash transfers.

Cash transfers are part of a broader set of social welfare

TABLE 1 Social welfare expenditures under public programs, all levels of of government, by purpose, selected fiscal years (1960-1974)

Expenditure	1960	1965	1970	1974
Total, net[a]	52.3	77.2	145.8	239.3
Income maintenance (cash)	26.3	36.6	60.8	107.7
Health	6.4	9.5	25.2	40.9
Education	18.0	28.1	52.0	73.4
Welfare and other services	1.6	2.9	7.8	17.4
Total in constant (1975) prices	**86.7**	**121.0**	**195.2**	**264.6**
Total as percent of GNP	**10.6**	**11.8**	**15.3**	**17.7**

Source: Alfred M. Skolnik and Sophie R. Dales, "Social Welfare Expenditures, 1950-75," *Social Security Bulletin*, vol. 39, no. 1, January 1976, Table 10, p. 19.

[a]Total expenditures adjusted to eliminate duplication resulting from use of cash payments to purchase medical care and educational services.

expenditures, which include outlays by all levels of government for Social Security, public aid, health and medical programs, veterans' programs, education, housing, emergency employment, manpower training, and other social services.[4] An alternative classification of these same social welfare expenditures is displayed in Table 1, which sets forth the outlays by broad purpose. It shows that cash transfers, or income maintenance benefits, were over half the total in 1974, and that they had quadrupled in current dollars since 1960.

One careful estimate is that both in 1965 and 1972 over half of cash transfers went to the fifth of the population who would have been poor in the absence of such transfers. (See Table 2.) However, individual programs vary considerably in their emphasis on the poor. Public assistance paid out virtually all of its benefits to the poor, but unemployment insurance devoted only a fifth of its benefits to that group. In 1972, 53 percent of all cash transfers, or $42 billion, went to the pre-transfer poor.

This $42 billion, given the fact that some pre-transfer poor got more than enough cash transfers to take them over the income-poverty line for their family size, resulted in 12 percent of the population being poor after transfers, in contrast to the 19 percent counted as poor pre-transfer. It is a shocking fact that in spite of the enormous increase in cash transfers between 1965 and 1972 (from $37 billion to $80 billion in current dollars), the share of the population in post-transfer poverty only fell from 15.6 to 11.9 percent. This is due in part to the failure of pre-transfer poverty to decline much at all, in fact by only about a million persons, and to the rise in the pre-transfer income deficit, that is, the difference between actual earnings and poverty line earnings, from $29 billion to $34 billion in 1972 dollars (Plotnick and Skidmore, 1975). Most demographic subgroups showed little change in the frequency of pre-transfer poverty. However, the frequency decreased for families headed by non-white males under 65, while it increased for families headed by white females under 65.

In spite of the slow reduction of pre-transfer poverty during the 1965-1972 period, there was, as previously mentioned, some progress against poverty in post-transfer terms. Cash transfers moved 33 percent of pre-transfer poor households out of poverty in 1965, and 44 percent in 1972. While 69 percent of the group

TABLE 2 Public social welfare expenditures of all levels of government, by type, with percentage spent on pre-transfer poor, 1965 and 1972 (in billions of dollars)

	1965 Total Expenditures	Percentage Spent on Pre-Transfer Poor	**1972** Total Expenditures	Percentage Spent on Pre-Transfer Poor
Total	**$72.2**	**43**	**$181.7**	**42**
Cash Transfers	36.6	57	80.1	53
Social Security and railroad benefits	17.6	62	40.4	58
Public employee retirement	5.1	52	11.7	38
Unemployment insurance	2.5	24	6.8	21
Workmen's compensation	1.8	27	3.8	33
Public assistance	4.8	89	10.8	87
Veteran's benefits	4.1	52	6.2	43
Temporary disability	0.3	25	0.4	21
Non-cash benefits	36.1	28	101.6	35
Nutrition	0.9	37	3.7	70
Housing	0.3	51	1.8	55
Health	5.7	55	24.6	56
Welfare and OEO services	1.4	64	5.3	72
Employment and manpower	.7	63	3.9	72
Education	27.1	18	62.2	19

Source: Robert Plotnick and Felicity Skidmore, *Progress Against Poverty: A Review of the 1964-1974 Decade,* New York, Academic Press for the Institute for Research on Poverty, 1975, pp. 52-53 and 56-57.

received a transfer in 1965, in 1972, 78 percent did so. This percentage varied considerably by demographic group, however. Less than half of poor able-bodied fathers, couples without children, and unrelated individuals received a transfer. These facts are often cited as evidence of unfair treatment by the cash transfer system (Barth, *et al.,* 1974).

The effectiveness of the cash transfer system in relieving poverty for some groups in 1965 and 1972 is indicated by Table 3. Closer analysis reveals that blacks are less likely than whites to receive enough cash transfers to take them out of poverty. Those living in the South, those with limited education, and unrelated individuals are also less likely than the average to move out of poverty via cash transfers.

The poverty-income gap remaining after cash transfers was cut by only a billion dollars between 1965 and 1972 and stood at $12.5 billion in 1972. This amount equalled about one percent of GNP, a relationship which indicates how close we were to the elimination of income poverty.

TABLE 3   Anti-poverty effectiveness of cash transfers, by demographic groups, 1965 and 1972 (numbers in thousands)

| | Pre-Transfer Poor Households | | Pre-Transfer Poor Households Made Non-poor by Cash Transfers | | | |
| | | | Number | | Percent | |
	1965	1972	1965	1972	1965	1972
All Households	15,609	17,640	5,161	7,682	33	44
With aged heads	7,512	8,643	3,801	5,461	51	63
With non-aged male heads, with children	2,761	2,011	302	464	11	23
With non-aged female heads, with children	1,395	2,210	302	503	22	23
With non-aged heads, with no children	3,943	4,776	756	1,254	19	26

Source: Robert D. Plotnick and Felicity Skidmore, *Progress Against Poverty*, Table 6.4, pp. 146-147.

It can be argued that we were, in fact, closer to that goal than the money income figures indicate. One scholar estimates that after adjusting for under-reporting of incomes (which is particularly large for cash transfers), intra-family transfers, and taxes paid, the poverty-income gap was really only $9 billion in 1972. Further, he finds that if one takes account of non-cash transfers in the form of food, housing, and health care (which increased from $9 billion in 1968 to $16 billion in 1972), then the poverty-income gap was only $5 billion (Smeeding, 1975; c.f., Browning, 1975). Following this line of reasoning, and noting the advent of Suplementary Security Income (SSI) and the expansion of food stamps in 1974, one can conclude that the goal of eliminating income poverty as stated by President Johnson in 1964 had been virtually achieved before the onset of the 1974-75 recession.

By referring back to Table 2, one can see that the poor were recipients of substantially increasing non-cash benefits. The total of such benefits almost tripled between 1965 and 1972, and the share received by the pre-transfer poor increased from 28 to 35 percent. It is reasonable to conclude that the poor were getting a somewhat larger share of the nation's output of such vital services as housing, health care, legal services, job-training, and education in the early 1970s than they were in the 1960s.

What Caused the Changes in Income Patterns?

GNP in 1974 was $474 billion greater in constant dollars than it was in 1960. This enabled an increase for an expanding population of 43 percent in per capita GNP. This extra production was widely shared. Income differences narrowed among regions, races, some occupational groups, and between earners and non-earners. There appeared to be no substantial change in the sharing of money income among families ranked from high to low income. The tax system seems to have become less progressive. However, a changing relationship between income and family size, and a more egalitarian distribution of a rising total of non-cash government benefits suggest that the combined total of money and non-money "income" may have become less unequal on a per capita basis. Income poverty was significantly reduced and, again, if non-cash benefits were to be counted as income, it could be said that poverty was nearly eliminated by 1974.

It can at least be argued that the production increases from beginning to end of the 14-year period would not have been as great as they were without the aggressive fiscal policy practiced by the Kennedy and Johnson Administrations. It can also be argued that the wide sharing of income would not have occurred without the social policy initiatives of the New Frontier and the Great Society, some of which were extended in the Nixon period. These initiatives included the affirming of new rights and the helping of people to exercise them. They encouraged submerged minorities to aspire to greater economic as well as social and political participation. These initiatives may well have facilitated a part of the nation's most sustained period of high economic growth (Levitan and Taggart, 1976).

The Great Society dedicated the powers of the Federal Government to the attainment of national minimums of money income, and of health care, educational, and other key services. This idea was new, but in its pursuit use was made of institutions developed in Franklin D. Roosevelt's New Deal. Again, it can be argued that reaching out to help the disadvantaged regions and groups via cash and non-cash benefits may interact favorably with aggregative fiscal measures to yield a more sustained and harmonious growth.

It is, of course, impossible to know what the patterns of income would have been like in 1974 had the domestic policy initiatives of Lyndon B. Johnson never been tried. We cannot re-run that chapter of history with all else the same, excluding only those policies and all their interactions. But it does seem fair to conclude that these policies as carried out did contribute, along with earlier social policies with which they were not inconsistent, to a wider sharing of the fruits of economic progress. That wider sharing, in itself, was a primary benefit of the Great Society.

Some critics fault these policies with assertions that secondary, or indirect, benefits were too low, and that the direct and indirect costs associated with them were too high (Lampman, 1974). Thus, they claim that while additional health care and educational services were received by the poor and presumably valued by them, the indirect benefits to society in the form of improved health standards and academic performance were not significant. Further, these critics argue that the true cost of cash and non-cash benefits includes not only the taxes to pay for them but also increases in price, e.g., for health care, occasioned by the extra demand associated with government policy. A further element in indirect cost is any loss in production due to idleness or any reduction in saving induced by social benefits. Finally, some claim that a still different form of cost must be assessed in evaluating these policies. They allege that crime and disorder, the weakening of family solidarity, and a breakdown of inter-racial community feeling all result from these policies.

It is, of course, quite wrong to regard redistribution as costless; and indirect consequences and costs, correctly assigned and appraised, are relevant to the comparison of costs and benefits. But the final judgment will tend to rest on the subjective value that the observer, and the voter, place upon the fact of redistribution itself. The question posed by President Johnson is: How much is it worth to us to have the national government affirm new rights and pursue redistributional goals?

Today's Questions

Further questions for political judgment are thrown out to this generation by the experience since 1960. How much must the Federal Government try to do itself and how much is better delegated to state and local and private agencies? What balance should be sought between cash and non-money benefits? Should future expansions of social welfare expenditures emphasize a negative income tax, further development of the social insurances, including health insurance, or innovation of a massive child day-care program or a set of housing allowances? Should new forms of benefits be designed to meet the income needs of male-headed families and of disadvantaged youth entering the world of work? Should such benefits take the form of tax credits, as in the 1975 income tax law provision for low-income wage earners, or of public job creation? How much emphasis should social welfare expenditures place on offsetting income loss as opposed to sup-plementing chronically low income as opposed to helping people buy key services such as housing and college educations? How closely can how many different benefits be scaled simultaneously to a beneficiary's income before all monetary incentive to work is destroyed? How seriously should we take the idea that bene-fits, like taxes, should fall evenly on all persons similarly placed?

(There are numerous horizontal equity problems associated with social welfare programs.)

These and related questions of today involve identification of goals, choice of processes and strategies, and technical considerations (Rivlin, 1975). They owe their vitality to the openings of earlier years and to latter-day reactions. In these questions—and in other ways—the Great Society lives.

References

[1] Throughout this section, incomes are cited in dollars of constant purchasing power. It should also be noted that 1960 and 1974 are both recession years, with unemployment at about six percent of the labor force.

[2] GNP does not, of course, include a valuation of housewives' services at home. To the extent that their services at home declined, the increase in total production is overstated by GNP.

[3] President Johnson set it as a national goal in 1964 to eliminate income poverty as thus defined.

[4] It is worth pointing out that some Federal Government outlays for these purposes merely replaced state and local government and private outlays.

Bibliography

Michael C. Barth, George L. Carcagno, and John L. Palmer, *Toward an Effective Income Support System: Problems, Prospects, and Choices,* Madison, Institute for Research on Poverty, 1974.

Andrew F. Brimmer, *The Economic Position of Black Americans: 1976,* Special Report No. 9, National Commission for Manpower Policy, Washington, 1976.

Edgar K. Browning, *Redistribution and the Welfare System* Washington, American Enterprise Institute for Public Policy Research, 1975.

Edgar K. Browning, "How Much More Equality Can We Afford," *The Public Interest,* No. 43, spring, 1976.

Council of Economic Advisors, *Annual Report, Together with Economic Report of the President* Washington, 1976.

Sheldon Danziger and Robert Plotnick, "Demographic Change, Government Transfers, and the Distribution of Income," Discussion Paper 274-75, Institute for Research on Poverty, 1975.

Robert J. Lampman, *Ends and Means of Reducing Income Poverty,* New York, Academic Press for the Institute for Research on Poverty, 1971.

Robert J. Lampman, "What Does It Do for the Poor: A New Test for National Policy," *The Public Interest*, No. 34, winter, 1974.

Robert J. Lampman, "Employment versus Income Maintenance," *The American Assembly on Manpower Goals for American Democracy*, Eli Ginzberg, ed., New York, Prentice-Hall, 1976.

Sar A. Levitan and Robert Taggart, *The Promise of Greatness: The Social Programs of the Last Decade and Their Major Achievements*, Cambridge, Harvard University Press, 1976.

M. Paglin, "The Measurement and Trend of Inequality, A Basic Revision," *American Economic Review*, September, 1975.

John L. Palmer and Joseph J. Minarik, "Income Security Policy," in *Setting National Priorities: The Decade Ahead*, Charles Schultze, ed., Washington, Brookings Institution, 1976.

Joseph A. Pechman and Ben Okner, *Who Bears the Tax Burden?*, Washington, Brookings Institution, 1974.

Robert D. Plotnick and Felicity Skidmore, *Progress Against Poverty: A Review of the 1964-1974 Decade*, New York, Academic Press for the Institute for Research on Poverty, 1975.

Morgan Reynolds and Eugene Smolensky, "Post-Fisc Distribution of Income: 1950, 1961, and 1970," Discussion Paper 270-75, Institute for Research on Poverty, 1975.

Alice M. Rivlin, "Income Distribution—Can Economists Help?" *American Economic Review*, May, 1975.

Malcolm Sawyer, "Income Distribution in OECD Countries," *OECD Economic Outlook*, July, 1976.

Timothy R. Smeeding, "The Economic Well-Being of Low-Income Households: Implications for Income Inequality and Poverty," *Augmenting Measures of Economic Welfare*, Marilyn Moon and Eugene Smolensky, eds., New York, Academic Press, forthcoming.

Michael K. Taussig, "Trends in the Inequality of Well-Offness in the United States Since World War II," Discussion Paper, Institute for Research on Poverty, 1976.

Lester C. Thurow, "Lessening Inequality in the Distributions of Income and Wealth," unpublished mimeo, May, 1975.

U.S. Bureau of the Census, *Current Population Reports, Consumer Income,* Series P-60, No. 99, July, 1975; Series P-60, No. 101 and 102, January, 1976.

SUMMARY David Austin

The Kennedy-Johnson years were an era of innovation and experimentation. It was an era comparable to the Progressive Era from 1893 to 1916, described by Arthur Schlesinger, Jr., as one of those times when national crisis led to significant and continuing changes in the American society. During the 1960s there was a complex mixture of political leadership that pointed the way toward goals of national greatness, program initiatives by the Federal Government, and local mobilization.

As part of the assessment of the New Frontier-Great Society there was an effort to define the consequences of the anti-poverty/manpower programs of the 1960s, and in part a comparison between those years and the years since.

The Strategy

The first issue addressed was that of the underlying strategy of the anti-poverty/manpower programs and its appropriateness. Robert Levine defined the social initiatives of the New Frontier-Great Society as spanning two broad concerns. The first was the problem of poverty; that is, the lack of an adequate income on the part of millions of Americans. The second was the problem of barriers to opportunity; that is, the existence of blockages to economic opportunity resulting from racial discrimination, inadequate education, language differences, and geographic location.

At the heart of the anti-poverty/manpower program strategy were those persons who existed at the intersection of these two concerns. This meant in particular black Americans, and those who were part of other ethnic groups that faced the handicaps of both poverty and discrimination. The initiative for action to deal with these two interrelated issues of poverty and discrimination came in part from political and professional leaders in the Federal Government as Dean Jack Otis pointed out in describing the early development of the President's Committee on Juvenile Delinquency. However, Frances Piven emphasized the importance of the "peoples' movement," generating pressures from the local level for action on the problems of unemployment, poverty, and discrimination, in forcing national political leaders to take action.

It was a recurrent theme that the strategy for attacking the interrelated problems of poverty and discrimination did not emerge as a fully developed plan carefully worked out in detail before Federal action began. The various anti-poverty/manpower programs, in fact, emerged only as many persons, including presidential advisors and the two presidents themselves, became aware that macro-economic interventions were not sufficient. The problems of unemployment and poverty, had become severe by the end of the 1950s. Lisle Carter pointed out that Federal domestic policies in the 1950s, in particular the subsidized mechanization of agriculture and suburbanization of urban areas, had aggravated the national pattern of economic inequality, with particular consequences for black families. The first proposals pointed to the use of Federal fiscal policies to stimulate the economy. The decision to use fiscal policies in a deliberate effort to strengthen the economy was itself a major shift from the policies of the 1950s, claiming for the Federal Government a central role in the management of the economy.

However, it was evident to a number of persons at the Federal level that a general rise in the level of economic activity could not resolve problems of unemployment as long as wide-spread discrimination in employment persisted. Nor could an increase in general employment demands overcome structural unemployment problems resulting from inadequate education or from the long-term economic decline in some rural areas and in central city districts in older metropolitan areas. In the panel discussion both Frances Piven and Earl Johnson emphasized the fact that macro-economic interventions can not reach particular groups shut off by barriers of discrimination and that such interventions do not deal with injustices in the distribution of economic benefits.

Not only were there problems in unequal access to the economic opportunities in the private sector created by an affluent society. It was evident to many that lack of effective access by blacks, and those of other ethnic minority backgrounds, to the local political system directly affected access to economic opportunity. In part, this was because access to the political system was necessary to obtain access to local public employment. Lack of effective access to local politics also affected the distribution of public resources in such areas as public education. Moreover, there began to be an awareness that high rates of unemployment among adults, lack of access to the political system, and the general condition of "powerlessness" that Kenneth Clark has spoken to, all played significant roles in shaping the attitudes and behaviors of black youth. There was a direct link between these problems and such issues as juvenile delinquency, school failure, and unemployment among black youth. As Jack Otis pointed out, this analysis led to a focus on the need for changing social conditions, rather than on changing individuals in the approach taken by the President's Committee.

The strategy of the New Frontier-Great Society initiative that emerged under Presidents Kennedy and Johnson was to combine stimulation of the general economy with the establishment of a series of selective, targeted programs directed at structural aspects of the poverty/racial discrimination/unemployment problem. A critical aspect in this strategy was presidential leadership in identifying the issues, educating the public on the nature of the issues, and supporting individuals and groups who were working on these problems at all levels of government.

The establishment of this dual strategy was itself a major innovation in Federal policy. For the first time the principle was established, through both presidential and congressional action, that problems of chronic poverty, racial discrimination, and persistent unemployment were a responsibility of the Federal Government. Both Steven Minter and Mayor Maynard Jackson noted in their discussions the importance of the fact that during the 1960s poverty and "the rights of the poor" became an official subject of Federal concern. Even during the Progressive Era and during the 1930s, ongoing Federal responsibility for leadership and initiative in regard to these problems had never been established as a basic principle.

It was noted, particularly by Steven Minter, that the 1960s strategies of both macro intervention and selective programs directed at the problems of poverty, unemployment, and discrimination did not deal directly with the problems of those

American families that were outside of the labor force. The Kennedy-Johnson strategies did not give serious attention to the development of a basic universal program of income maintenance for those persons who could not gain access to an adequate income through employment. Except for the programs of Medicaid and Medicare, designed to deal only with the rising costs of medical care, the financial provisions of the state-administered, federally financed and regulated public assistance programs for single parent families, the blind, the disabled, and the elderly remained relatively unchanged throughout the 1960s.

It is evident that, as in the 1960s, there are still significant differences among persons with similar social concerns about poverty and discrimination as to the balance that should be struck between macro-economic initiatives and specialized programs targeted at particular problems. It is also clear that the events of the 1960s, as well as the events of the years since, have not resolved differences of opinion about the division of responsibilities between the Federal Government and state and local governments, and voluntary local efforts, in addressing the pervasive issues of poverty and discrimination. Governor Anderson, in particular, spoke to the regressive tax effects that follow when Federal funding is reduced and responsibility for programming is thrown back upon the states. Mayor Tom Bradley, however, proposed that city officials have the major role in determining program priorities.

The Effectiveness

The second major issue addressed was the question of the effectiveness of the anti-poverty/manpower programs. It was evident that it is very difficult, if not impossible, to separate individual program elements of the New Frontier-Great Society strategy and arrive at a definitive judgment about the exact level of accomplishment of a single type of program, isolated from all others. There are a number of reasons why the assessment of individual programs is so difficult, and why sweeping conclusions about either absolute success or absolute failure are impossible to substantiate. First, in many programs it is not clear what statement of objectives should be used as the criteria for assessment. There was usually a substantial difference between the formal legislative objectives and the operational or administrative objectives of the programs once the programs were established. In other instances, the objectives were stated in very ambigious language or redefined a number of times over the life of the program. The provisions in the Office of Economic Opportunity (OEO) legislation regarding "maximum feasible participation" were among the more extreme examples of ambiguity in program goals. In these instances, the assessment of results is normally lost among the continuing arguments about what were the true objectives of the program.

Second, in most of the anti-poverty/manpower programs, the basic program concept included a simultaneous emphasis on Federal initiative and guidance and on local planning and decision making. This was characteristic of the juvenile delinquency prevention demonstration programs under the President's Committee, the community action agencies, the Model Cities program, and even of the Head Start program. This ensured that there would be wide variations in the characteristics of local programs, making a true nationwide assessment relatively meaningless. It also meant that where individual local programs could be identified as "successful," it was unclear whether this was the consequence of a particular combination of local conditions and the technical competence and administrative ability of local program leaders, or of the effectiveness of the Federal guidelines, technical assistance, and supervision.

Third, it is also evident, that outcomes of each of the program elements was affected by other events during the 1960s. Important among these events was the civil-rights/black-power movement, including actions at the Federal level involving the President, Congress, and the courts. There was also the impact of the Vietnam War on the economy, on specific population groups most directly affected by military service, and on the stimulation of political and protest movements during the late 1960s. Not only were individual programs affected by concurrent events of the 1960s but the long-term cumulative effects of these programs have been significantly affected by events during the 1970s, including the Nixon-Ford policies intended to cutback the programs and the economic recession of the early 1970s.

Given these complexities in any effort to assess success or failure for an individual type of program, it is not surprising that various authors and political figures have arrived at widely different conclusions. The discussion, however, did point to some individual programs that appear to have had a substantial degree of success. Several persons, including Earl Johnson and Mayor Maynard Jackson, placed strong emphasis upon the results achieved through the Legal Services program. Earl Johnson pointed out that the Legal Services program established a basis for legal enforcement of general principles of human rights, particularly as these applied to black citizens and low-income persons. He pointed out that the program also had significant effects on raising the standard of living for many families by striking down administrative barriers to obtaining benefits under such programs as public assistance and food stamps. He also noted that this program, which used constitutionally established mechanisms for dealing with injustice, had been maintained with governmental subsidies long after many other programs which were also directed at social change, such as neighborhood organizing, had been eliminated. Some of the manpower-training programs, as noted by Ray Marshall, also had demonstrably effective results. Mayor Tom Bradley commented on the importance of the manpower programs, as he had observed them in Los Angeles, as well as the significance of "citizen participation" in developing a new generation of civic leadership.

The major conclusion about the issue of effectiveness that emerged is that it must be viewed as applying to the total patterns of outcomes from the events that took place during the 1960s rather than as an additive process based on assessing each program separately. Robert Lampman, looked at the cumulative consequences of the programs of the 1960s for income levels and patterns of income distribution. It is his judgment that there is evidence of the positive impact of the anti-poverty programs of the 1960s on some aspects of the pattern of income distribution. However, these gains which can be identified are modest and as he points out the economic events of the 1970s have, in part, offset those gains. In other areas for example, the pattern of the total distribution of income among all households and the relative earning rates for male-headed households and female-headed households have changed not at all since the early 1960s.

However, it was the political changes, not the economic changes, that were most frequently referred to in the panel discussion, in assessing the impact of the anti-poverty/manpower

programs. Frances Piven, early in the panel discussion, emphasized that the important outcomes of the anti-poverty/manpower
programs were the secondary, or unintended, outcomes directly
linked to the entrance of large numbers of black citizens and other
ethnic minority groups into the processes of local politics.
Whether the process of political education and political mobilization took place within anti-poverty programs under the label of
"maximum feasible participation" or took place within protest
movements challenging efforts of existing political organizations
to control and manipulate anti-poverty programs, the end result
was a large scale movement of black voters and other ethnic
minority groups, into the political mainstream by the end of the
1960s.

A number of the panel members also pointed to the
development of a substantial group of political leaders, both men
and women, who began their public life through community
action programs, Head Start programs, and manpower programs.
Many of them became new black political leaders of the 1970s.
Mayor Bradley of Los Angeles pointed to the importance of the
anti-poverty programs in his own emergence as a political leader
in Los Angeles. Mayor Jackson pointed out that when the
expectations raised by the anti-poverty programs, and the
political rhetoric that accompanied them, could not be met, the
effect was to generate pressure for political coalition-building that
led directly to the election of black and other ethnic minority
candidates, particularly at the local level.

Although none of the anti-poverty/manpower programs had,
as its primary objective, the political education and political
mobilization of low-income citizens, a number of aspects of the
New Frontier/Great Society programs contributed to this important outcome. Frances Piven pointed out that community action
programs and other programs provided funding in low-income
neighborhoods which supported indirectly the process of political development. Steven Minter referred to the power of political
rhetoric in stimulating change. A number of the panel members
referred to the role of presidential leadership in identifying social
problems and supporting local efforts to deal with those
problems.

Specific programs had specific effects. Community action
programs provided a base for organization at the neighborhood

level, particularly in low-income urban areas in those cities with some degree of political consciousness in the black community. Legal Services provided, in many instances, legal support when efforts were made to quash an incipient pattern of political development. The Model Cities program brought the residents of inner-city areas into intense political competition with the established political system in many cities, as well as providing education in grantsmanship and in the tactics of bureaucratic conflict. Moreover, as both Mayor Jackson and Frances Piven pointed out, the anger and the violence in the cities, that arose in part from the broken promises of the anti-poverty programs, created a readiness at the national political level to take into account the political aspirations and demands of black citizens. One of the most direct and dramatic results was the process of internal change that took place within the Democratic Party in its process of selecting delegates in the years following 1968. This in turn, has had long-term effects on both state and national politics in the mid-1970s.

The panel discussion reflected an agreement that the anti-poverty/manpower programs did have a profound and permanent impact on the position of poor and minority citizens. The most clear-cut and dramatic impact, however, was not in the economic arena, but in the political arena. Many members of the panel saw this as an essential forerunner to any long-term change in the patterns of access to economic opportunity, and as Lisle Carter stated, the central issue is the pattern of economic inequality.

The Problems

The discussion did not ignore the problems and failure of the anti-poverty/manpower programs. Many of the failures constituted important lessons for the future. There were "ripoffs." Some of these were purely examples of greed and fraud. Others, as Kenneth Clark has pointed out, were instances of political exploitation. Steven Minter pointed out, that from his experience as administrator in public welfare during the 1960s and 1970s, the most greedy and difficult groups with which he had to deal were not the poor but organized providers and contractors, including medical care providers. Other references were made to the frauds involving business interests under the Section 235 housing program. Mayor Bradley noted that the choice was often between taking some risk of financial losses through fraud or over staffing the administration of the programs to the extent that the total number of bureaucrats at Federal, state, and local levels outnumbered the beneficiaries three to one.

There were middle-class college graduates and professional specialists, both black and white, who used the programs primarily to promote their own careers. For some programs the costs were clearly out of proportion to the benefits realized. This was probably to be expected in a period of innovation and experimentation. Moreover, as Mayor Jackson pointed out, the total amount of funds involved nationally was very small in relation to the scale of the problems being addressed, and in relation to other aspects of the national economy.

The experiences of the 1960s did raise critical questions about the feasibility and effectiveness of systematic comprehensive, planning procedures as a prerequisite for action programs. The demonstration projects of the President's Committee, the locally based community action programs, the requirements for regional coordination of manpower programs, and the Model Cities program, all required the use of formal, systematic planning procedures and the preparation of planning documents. In some instances, such as in most community action programs, there never was a systematic planning process. In other programs, such as Model Cities and the President's Committee projects, where there was extensive planning activity, the plans did not determine the pattern of actual events. One of the clearest lessons of the 1960s was that rational planning activities dealing with human service programs that were not directly linked to the political and administrative offices that controlled financial allocations and that set actual program guidelines had little impact on the programs that emerged.

Among all of the weaknesses of the New Frontier-Great Society programs, the most frequently referred to in this discussion was the failure to take seriously the problem of program administration. Legislation was often passed that assumed that the legal description of the program would, in effect, be self-implementing. It was often assumed that both Federal legislation and regulations could bring about instant restructuring of local programs, ignoring the realities of day-to-day administration. The priorities within the many programs emphasized participation in policy making over effective program administration. Earl Johnson pointed out that a very large proportion of the cases dealt with under the Legal Services program are those that are a direct consequence of the divided and confused pattern of administration in the public assistance and food stamps programs. Too often, he pointed out, it has been necessary to go to court to get actions which should have been accomplished through administrative decisions.

There was general agreement that the failures and problems, as critical as they were in some programs, do not constitute an argument for Federal withdrawal from dealing with the problems of poverty and discrimination. They do point to the importance of learning from the past in design of new efforts in these areas.

The Reaction

The end of the 1960s was marked by wide-spread attacks on the anti-poverty/manpower programs of the Kennedy-Johnson era. There were charges that the programs themselves were failures, that they involved large-scale waste of public funds, and that they had led to massive violence in some cities. Members of the panel pointed out, however, that it was the successes, rather than the failures of the anti-poverty/manpower programs that led to the bitter reactions that emerged at the end of the decade, the "backlash" as many writers called it. As Mayor Bradley said, the fact that the programs did concentrate primarily on those who were victims of both poverty and discrimination brought charges that such persons were receiving more than their share of public attention. Earl Johnson suggested that in part the reaction was a consequence of the failure to reform Federal tax policies during the 1960s so that it was primarily middle-income persons, rather than higher-income persons, who were being asked to finance the War on Poverty.

Mayor Jackson pointed out that it was, in fact, the indirect success of the anti-poverty programs in stimulating political participation on the part of blacks, and other ethnic minority citizens, that brought the most violent reaction. It was not the program failures but their most important accomplishment that threatened to disrupt existing balance of power relationships among political factions within the Democratic Party, and within local, state, and Federal governments. It was the potential challenge of these political changes to the existing political system for distributing the costs and benefits of public programs that brought forth the critical, and sometimes vitriolic, reactions from many of the liberal political leaders and academicians and professionals who earlier had been in the forefront of demands for social justice and social change. The glorification of "black power" and demands for affirmative action in public employment and in higher education brought heated protests from many of the early supporters of the New Frontier-Great Society programs. Yet the comments of the panel pointed to the conclusion that it was the "empowerment" of blacks and other ethnic minority citizens which was the most significant and far-reaching consequence of the anti-poverty/manpower programs.

Panel members commented on the extent to which, during the eight years that followed the Kennedy-Johnson era, there was a continuous effort to reestablish "normalcy." Efforts were made to limit Federal involvement in the issue of poverty and unemployment to macro-economic policies. Responsibility for specialized, targeted programs directed at aspects of structural unemployment were defined as the primary responsibility of states and local communities. Control of inflation was assigned a higher priority than dealing with the problem of unemployment. A conscious policy of deemphasizing Federal involvement in the issue of racial discrimination, otherwise identified as a policy of "benign neglect" was urged. A minimal level universal income maintenance program was proposed instead of specialized programs directed at barriers to the access to opportunity.

The conclusions of those involved in this assessment of Kennedy-Johnson programs are that eight years under policies of normalcy resulted in higher unemployment, a reversal of the trend toward lessening the number of persons below the poverty line, massive deterioration of the central cities in the older metropolitan areas of the Midwest and East, and a slowdown in the process of full assimilation of blacks and other ethnic minority groups into the mainstream of American political life. At the end of these eight years, the problems appearing in newspaper headlines, including the growth of juvenile delinquency and gang violence, resembled those at the beginning of the 1960s.

The Total Impact

The Kennedy-Johnson years brought decisive changes in American society. The New Frontier-Great Society programs began with a concern for the persistent problems of poverty and discrimination and their consequences for the social and economic health of the nation. A major part of this concern reflected the increasingly aggressive demands of blacks and poverty groups across the country for action on these problems.

The programs were diverse; the results from individual programs varied widely. There were successful community programs and failures. Some specialized programs stood out, and have been continued, such as Legal Services. Others have been abandoned.

The real importance of the anti-poverty/manpower programs, however, is not determined by the success or failure of individual programs, but by the total impact. There is evidence that there were some economic consequences, particularly in the relative income levels of black and white households, but it is clear that these are gains which are difficult to sustain when recession strikes. More conclusive is the evidence of the impact of these programs on the political mobilization of black citizens and on the structure of the political system at the local level. The importance of these changes is evident in the violence of the criticism directed towards the New Frontier-Great Society programs by persons who are threatened by these changes. Yet it is clear that it is these political changes which are the most permanent contribution of the Kennedy-Johnson era to the continuing effort to deal with the problems of poverty and discrimination in the United States.

the right to health and medical care

Wilbur Cohen

8

From Medicare to National Health Insurance

Medicare and Medicaid were not programs which originated in the inner circle of the architects of the Great Society. Neither the New Frontier nor the Great Society could avoid an idea whose time had come and some have said whose time had come and gone.

The basic idea of a Federal law providing for some kind of national health insurance coverage arose in the New Deal of Franklin Delano Roosevelt after the U.S. Supreme Court upheld the constitutionality of the Social Security program in 1937. Once it was clear that it was constitutional to enact a tax and a benefit program, either together or separately, which could be called an insurance program, it was inevitable that the idea should be applied to the controversial health and medical area as well as to old age.

So it was that in 1943 the Wagner-Murray-Dingell bill was introduced in Congress. It was a comprehensive social insurance proposal covering old age, disability, death, and health care which was referred to by its critics as a "cradle to the grave" plan.

The immediate stimulus to the bill was the plan developed by Sir William Beveridge in Great Britain in 1942, in the midst of the war, for the development of a comprehensive, universal, and rational plan of social insurance. This plan, backed by Winston Churchill, was implemented in the post-war period with the support in England of both the Tories and the Labor Government. A partial national health program had been in existence in Britain since 1905, and World War II, with the killing and maiming of people from Hitler's bombing, resulted in a general acceptance in England of a universal, comprehensive national program, an idea which captivated the interest of the United States people at the time. The absence of these factors in the United States resulted in the opposition to the idea and the acceptance of a laissez-faire policy by the returning veterans, their families, and the presidential administration of 1953-1960.

The Legislative Struggle

My principal entry into this storm center came about as one of those who, with I.S. Falk, helped draft the Wagner-Murray-Dingell bill of 1943. I shall never forget when, as a young man, I delivered the omnibus measure to Senator Robert F. Wagner, with the draft of what I thought was a brilliant speech for his introduction of the bill in the Senate. I had enthusiastically and wholeheartedly devoted hours to participating in the social policy incorporated into this monumental and historic leviathan of public policy—a bold and innovative combination of creative ideas which came second only to Thomas Jefferson's imaginative proposals incorporated in the Declaration of Independence.

Then Senator Wagner and I sat around in his office discussing trivialities for about an hour. When, in my youthful impatience I asked the Senator if he was going to look at the bill or the draft statement or he wished to discuss any policy options with me, he said no; he said it would take a number of years before the bill would ever be enacted—it would be re-drafted innumerable times and his role was to introduce it so that future members of Congress could carry it forward to realization long after he was gone.

And so it was. How insightful Senator Wagner was of the complexity of the legislative process.

Senator Wagner, was one of those great figures in social reform in the United States who had known the ups and downs of the health insurance movement in the U.S. which began, in about 1910, the great period of social reform in this nation. It was then already 33 years—a third of a century—that people such as himself and Frances Perkins, John B. Andrews, and John R. Commons, and many others had been fighting for the social reforms which had originated in the Roosevelt-Taft-Wilson era in the reaction to the industrialization and urbanization of the emerging economy.

The Wagner-Murray-Dingell bill succumbed to the massive opposition fired by the American Medical Association (AMA) in 1950, despite the heroic efforts of President Truman to mobilize public support for the plan. President Truman had become the first President to issue a separate special health message to Congress in 1945. While several of his important recommendations have been implemented, his major controversial proposal for national health insurance is still available for future enactment.

With the demise of the Wagner-Murray-Dingell bill, Oscar Ewing, then the Federal Security Administrator, asked the staff for some other options. It was my responsibility to prepare this memo in 1950 in which one of the options I mentioned was a plan for national health insurance solely limited to the aged. Ten minutes after Mr. Ewing received the memo he telephoned to see how soon he could have a bill carrying out the idea. The logic of limiting it to the aged, which he saw immediately, was one which Congress itself recognized.

When Dr. Falk had completed the draft, Mr. Ewing asked me to find sponsors in Congress. I first went to see the Chairman of the House Committee on Ways and Means, Robert L. Doughton, who was not receptive. Then I went to see Representative Jere Cooper. He said no. Then I went to see Representative Wilbur Mills. He said no. Then I went to see other members of the Ways and Means Committee. Finally, Mr. Dingell said he would introduce it. It was not until 1957 that another member of the Committee, Aime Forand, of Rhode Island, sponsored the bill, at the request of the AFL-CIO. It was not until 1960 that a Democratic candidate for President, John F. Kennedy, supported the proposal. I should say that a bill is not significant until it is introduced by a member of the Congressional committee which will handle that bill. It is of some significance that Adlai Stevenson did not advocate the idea in either 1952 or 1956. Despite the increasing cost of hospital services in the post-war period, neither the Republican nor Democratic presidential candidates in 1952 or 1956 took leadership in health policy. This probably reflected the apathy of the electorate on this issue and the intense fear of the political importance of the AMA and its supporters. This group had attacked any health plan since 1917 as socialistic, communistic, and a form of regulation, intervention, and interference into the sacred doctor-patient relationship.

Those who today validly criticize the omissions, failures, and difficulties of Medicaid and Medicare simply do not either know or understand or recall the virulence of the opposition in the 22-year period before the enactment of Medicare and Medicaid. Most progressive physicians with even a partial degree of interest or support of any aspect of the concept of national health insurance had to stay away from the movement for fear of losing referrals from other physicians or losing staff privileges in hospitals. Only a very few highly independent physicians such as Doctors DeBakey, Spock, Esselstyn, Mott, and Furstenberg could publicly endorse the idea without losing their professional practitioner status. As late as the early 1960s there were fewer than 50 practicing physicians out of some 300,000 physicians in the United States who publicly supported the King-Anderson Medicare bill advocated by President Kennedy and later by President Johnson.

When I was appointed a professor at the University of Michigan in 1955, several physicians opposed my appointment on the grounds I was a socialist and a communist and indicated that they would discontinue their voluntary contributions to the medical school. In Michigan two of the most knowledgeable and respected members of the faculty of the School of Public Health were denied appointments at the state and local levels because of their support for national health insurance. My own long participation in these activities was due in large part to the fact that I was *not* a physician. I did not lose my livelihood. In fact, my status grew in certain quarters as I was unjustly accused of being a communist.

Most of those persons who currently complain of the initial faulty structure of Medicare and Medicaid were nowhere to be seen in 1960, 1962, 1964, or even in 1965 when Congress was voting on these measures. The ideological intensity of the opposition to controls and cost restraints would have been recorded at a level of 8.5 on a legislative Richter scale. You can study the several great social reform issues of this century— abolition of child labor, Social Security, woman suffrage, civil rights, Federal aid to education—and none of them exceeded the hostility, intensity, and character assassination which national health insurance evoked prior to 1965. Only the current abortion and busing issues compare with the emotion shown by those who opposed national health insurance and neither of these issues have resulted in collecting the amount of money which the AMA had to oppose national health insurance.

The sponsors of Medicare, including myself, had to concede in 1965 that there would be no real controls over hospitals or physicians. I was required to promise before the final vote in the

Executive Session of the House Ways and Means Committee that the Federal agency would exercise no control. There was virtually no voice in or out of Congress when the Ways and Means Committee adopted an amendment over the opposition of President Johnson and the the Department of HEW in 1965 allowing the radiologists, pathologists, and anesthesiologists to be independent entrepreneurs instead of being considered as hospital employees, thus permitting them to greatly increase their incomes. There was no voice in Congress for effecting constraints on physicians' incomes, hospitals costs, nursing home charges or profits, or for any basic change in the health delivery system. (As a matter of fact, I promised very conscientiously that I would see to it there was no change in the basic health delivery system because so far as the AMA and Congress were concerned, this was sacred.) These demands for change came only after the program was enacted and implemented.

The Medicaid program was based upon state implementation because welfare had been a state and local prerogative in the United States for more than 300 years, deriving its basic form from the Elizabethan Poor Law of 1601 and its subsequent variations. There not only was no Federal welfare system but since 1935 Senator Harry F. Byrd, Sr., of Virginia had opposed the proposed Federal benefit standards in welfare. In 1965 he was the influential chairman of the Senate Committee on Finance. No one—but no one—pressured Senator Byrd to impose Federal benefit standards on the welfare program. Even today, the state unemployment insurance laws—another component of the Social Security Act—after 40 years do not contain Federal benefit standards. Employers vigorously oppose them in unemployment insurance, have never supported them in the welfare or the health insurance system and, along with the AMA, were vigorously opposed to that kind of Federal intervention and control.

The enactment of Medicare and Medicaid must be considered a great legislative achievement by President Lyndon Baines Johnson when it is realized that the proposal was defeated in 1960, 1962, and again in 1964. It was opposed in 1960 by President Eisenhower, when the Secretary of HEW, then Arthur Flemming, recommended to President Eisenhower that he endorse it. It was opposed by Wilbur Mills and a majority of the

House Committee on Ways and Means in 1961, 1962, 1963, and 1964. It was opposed by Senator Byrd, the Chairman of the Senate Committee, in 1960, 1961, 1962, 1963, 1964, and even in 1965 when it passed. In 1965 Gerald R. Ford voted against it in the House on passage and voted against it on adoption of the conference report.

President Johnson required all his skill to get passed what we now consider a limited proposal which at that time was viewed as radical. Only the great tactical genius of President Johnson, when he invited Senator Byrd to the White House, made it possible. He said to Senator Byrd, "I know you are opposed but you are surely going to allow the bill to be reported out." In front of the television audience the Senator could only say "Yes." I must say that Senator Byrd was always a gentleman in allowing a bill to be considered even though he personally opposed it. President Johnson knew that and thus was able to obtain prompt consideration in the Senate.

Implementing the System

Yet despite the vigorous oppostion to the legislation, within a short period of time after passage, the ideological hostility largely evaporated. I cannot think of another issue in which opposition evaporated that fast. The propaganda against the legislation just did not turn out to be true. No physician nor hospital was socialized. There was no communist takeover of the health system of our country. No Federal official became involved in the destruction of the doctor-patient relationship. The physicians who honestly believed the propaganda that was circulated against the legislation were utterly amazed when what they believed would happen did not occur. And besides they had more patients than before and, marvel of marvels, they even made more money than ever before.

The one-page form we devised for reimbursement of physicians, for which I would like to take a little credit, was a model of simplicity. I became convinced you could offset a great deal of opposition if you had simple forms. More physicians today and more people are opposed to government forms than to the ideological issues involved in controversial public policy. We invited the AMA and the insurance industry into the process of criticizing the forms and regulations. We used Blue Cross-Blue

Shield and commercial insurance carriers as fiscal intermediaries in making payments.

The opposition to Medicare collapsed shortly after 1965. By 1970 the AMA was sponsoring a national health insurance plan of its own, although it had supported an "Eldercare" plan late in 1965 as a counter to Medicare. Imagine the AMA using "big brother" to cover everyone in the nation for health insurance protection. It was a plan—not a very good one from my point of view, but it was a Federal plan—which used the Federal Government to attain its objective and the Federal Treasury to finance it. Today the AMA, the U.S. Chamber of Commerce, the private health insurance industry, the Committee on Economic Development, and the American Hospital Association each has a national health insurance proposal. So did President Nixon, so do Senator Long and Senator Ribicoff, and Senators Javits, Cranston, Brooke, Kennedy and numerous others in the Senate and House. I believe this was one of Lyndon Johnson's main achievements. He broke the power of the opposition. It took 55 years—from 1910 to 1965—to enact the limited Medicare program of 1965. Then it took only 5 years for the AMA to change its fundamental policy on national health insurance. So what social reformers, senators, and presidents tried to accomplish for 55 years, Medicare and Medicaid accomplished in 5 years. I consider that a phenomenal achievement which will become even more significant as time goes on.

But what about the frauds, the gaps, and the overruns in Medicare and Medicaid that we see today? They are there and there are a lot more that have not been disclosed. I have every confidence that there will be amendments which will attempt to close those loopholes. But I am also certain that the ingenuity of the American businessman, the lawyer, and the taxpayer will discover new loopholes that we have not yet seen. Those who long for perfect legislation in the American environment do not recognize the imagination, creativity, genius, and conspiracy which exists in the mind and heart of one or two percent of our adult population.

The overruns and frauds in Medicaid and Medicare probably are no greater than those in which Boeing, Lockheed, Gulf, or the milk producers have been involved. As a matter of fact, the physicians see around them the advantages or loopholes which other entrepreneurs in oil, construction, milk, aircraft, and other areas have utilized, and they want to show that they are equally expert in finding and using loopholes.

But there is one other very important contribution of Medicare and Medicaid which has not received public notice—the virtual dismantling of segregation in hospitals, physicians' offices, nursing homes, and clinics as of July 1, 1966. The signs over waterfountains, restrooms, and lunchrooms in hospitals which said "For White Only" came tumbling down overnight. There was very little resistance. There was no legal opposition. A major and monumental change in the way health care was administered to black men, women, and children was implemented without a serious challenge. If Medicare and Medicaid had not made another single contribution, this result would be sufficient to enshrine it as one of the most significant social reforms of the decade.

When I was in the People's Republic of China recently, I was impressed with Chairman Mao's analysis of contradictions in society. His programs were based upon the policy that there were contradictions in both capitalist as well as communist societies.

Today we see political leaders, the media, scholars, young people, and older people attacking government. Yet, at the same time they favor a comprehensive national health insurance system, gun control, more discipline in the schools, more money for education, more police protection, a crackdown on crime, drugs, and delinquency, and welfare reform.

All these involve more governmental intervention and more public sector financing. We observe a contradiction in our electorate.

There is an ebb and flow in social reform—a cyclical process at work in the American environment. Our hopes and enthusiasm rise high. Expectations exceed performance. We try for the millennium and we do not succeed in achieving it. Then a reaction sets in. We are crushed by human inefficiency and human failures. The reactionary and conservative forces are unleashed. The Federal Government is made a political football. Inadequacies are built up into major policy complaints. A new generation comes along and wants to throw out everyone over age 35 who had some part to play in the failures of the past.

Prospects for National Health Insurance

Then a new generation takes hold of the reins of political power. They reinvent the wheel because they are deficient in their historical knowledge and understanding. The rallying cry is that it is time for a change—a slogan used by conservatives against liberals and equally by liberals against conservatives.

The cyclical change in power ushers in a new era. But irrespective of rhetoric and philosophy, irrespective of the political leadership, the only option open is to build upon the past. Change it here and there; add something; change its name; cut off some fuzzy edges; and then proclaim the new day is here in which a new approach has been unveiled to overcome the mistakes of the past.

Now there is substantial public support for basic changes in the health delivery system—something which no one could have advocated before a committee of Congress in 1965. Yet, despite the widespread support for changes in the health delivery system, I really doubt whether Congress will enact such basic changes in the near future which would involve, for instance, repealing the fee-for-service basis for reimbursement of physicians to provide for some kind of per capita payment through health maintenance organizations. And even though President Nixon and President Ford and some of the leadership in HEW since supported the health maintenance organization idea, it really has not gotten off the ground, even though most of us who have been supporting it for 40 years are still supporting it. There is little support among the practicing physicians, and I might add, very little support among the patients.

The record of Congress in dealing with social reform and particularly in the medical care field, tends to be more in the direction of being incremental, categorical, evolutionary, and not comprehensive, universal, or millennial.

The Congress of 535 people must look to the President to lead and to propose while the Congress criticizes, responds, modifies, and amends. My experience in going before various committees of Congress is to have received a lecture from time to time on the American political system which goes somewhat like this: A President of the United States is really only a short-time occupant on the national scene. At the most, he's around for 4 years, and on a few occasions 8 years, and some for only 2 years, but influential members of Congress, particularly in the past, chairmen of the committees, remain for 18 or 24 or even 30 years, long after the President has gone.

I have heard them tell me that they will remain in Congress long after a President is gone; that they do not need to respond to every whim of a President; and that they will, as Members of Congress, still be there to correct any of the evils which will evolve from the President's proposals. That attitude, in many cases, is what makes it difficult when people say, "Well if you knew there were going to be all these abuses and all these problems, why didn't you correct them all in the initial legislation?"

The attitude I find among the members of Congress is that they want to have something to do for the future. They believe that they would like to run again in two, four, or six or other years on the basis of correcting the evils that they found previously. And I say I find that argument convincing. I am very anxious to see Congress continue to have a job to do. And one of the jobs they have to do is the oversight and the correction of the fundamental concepts that were developed at an earlier time.

If you try to sell a key conceptual objective at the same time that you try to handle all the nitty-gritty of details to implement it, you will get neither. You must, in a sense, make the sacrifice or the compromise, if you want to call it that, when you are selling a fundamentally new idea. If you will wrap it up in another hundred pages of detail that will correct every abuse, the Congress will not be able to swallow all of that at one time. And therefore, of course, those of us who had problems in trying to persuade Congress, particularly in the fields of health, education, and welfare, many times have to make a very difficult decision. Do we want the fundamental ideas or do we want the millennium? And usually the choice comes down—we would rather get started on the new program and hope for the millennium to come along in due time.

I would guess, if I had to make a prediction on the basis of what has now happened, after 55, 65 years of struggle over this issue, that when the Great Society is re-examined again in 15, or 20 years, there will be in place a comprehensive national health security program for all the people of the United States.

It will have been built upon the experience of Medicare and Medicaid. It will be a tribute to Lyndon B. Johnson. It may well be quite different from any of the national health insurance plans being proposed in Congress today. If I could make a prediction, the national health insurance plan that will be adopted by Congress, hopefully in the next Administration, has not yet even been introduced. It does not yet exist even in the mind of any influential person who will pursue it, because it is most likely to be some kind of amalgam of ideas that are floating in the ethos today. And whatever anyone will say, it will be evolved probably pragmatically out of trial and error. And although every industrial nation in the world has some kind of national health insurance or national security plan, I will also make a prediction that the American plan will not be identical with the plan of Great Britain, Germany, the Soviet Union, or Canada or any other country. It will be an American plan worked out by the American Congress on some kind of an evolutionary basis.

There are in my opinion three rather big issues that will have to be decided before we take the next step. First, will we adopt a comprehensive plan to go into effect all at one time, whatever the nature of it may be, or will we phase it in over a period of time?

My own personal view is that it would be a catastrophe if we tried to put it all into effect on what the British call the "appointed day." To extend a national health insurance program on one day to 225 million people is a gigantic undertaking. I will only make one comment: I do not have that much faith in the computers. The experience we have had with the Supplemental Security Income (SSI) program which only involves 4 million people is ample testimony that the American faith in computers should be re-examined.

I also believe there is not the managerial genius in the American system to cover medical care and dental care and out-patient care and ambulatory care and mental health care and long-term care all at once, despite what we think of both private enterprise and governmental ability.

My own view is that it would be much wiser for us to start with mothers and children, at the other end of the Medicare scale, a proposal which Mr. Johnson did make in 1968 when he referred to it as "kiddy care." I believe we should reach the objective in a series of steps, although one piece of legislation, being based upon the firm realization that we can get to a great objective by taking small steps rather than by taking one gigantic step which will run us into very great problems.

The second public issue which has to be decided is whether the extension of national health insurance is going to be exclusively a public responsibility or basically be a private responsibility? This issue can be best seen in analysis of the Nixon plan which provided for mandating employers a single type of national health insurance plan which the employers had to impose, in effect, upon their employees by the purchase of private insurance.

I happen to be opposed to that idea. I think once the Federal Government decides that everybody is going to be insured there is no need for a private insurance company to go out and sell coverage to people who are mandated to obtain it. And, therefore, the concept of an actuarial or financial base of using private insurance agencies to achieve the public responsibility seems to me to be wasteful and unnecessary, imposing an additional cost of at least a billion dollars a year on the program without any essential advantage.

I think the issue can be handled as it has been in Medicare if the private sector is to assume a responsibility on the managerial side rather than on the actuarial insurability side. You can use Blue Cross, Blue Shield, Aetna, or any other plans as the fiscal intermediaries to make the payments to doctors so that they do not get a Federal check—they get the Federal money, but they are not humiliated by receiving a Federal check. I am perfectly willing to make that compromise, which has been made in Medicare, but I would open the door a little more by allowing stage agencies to be fiscal intermediaries along with the insurance companies and Blue Cross and Blue Shield. I would change the law to make it competitive, based on contractual and observeable information. And I would see that the contracts were renewable each three years on the basis of demonstrated competitive costs and quality of service and thus attempt to achieve centralized responsibility and equality of treatment throughout the United States but with decentralized administration at the local level.

Now, as difficult as these two issues are, the third one is even much more difficult. And that is the substitution for our present fee-for-service system, an arrangement that assumes some kind of responsibility on the part of a group to deliver medical care on a unit basis or on a per-capita basis or on a salary basis or some combination rather than the fee-for-service basis. Out of 330,000 physicians, I do not think there would be 30,000 physicians in the United States who would support that idea at the present time and to get 300,000 to favor it would take a monumental effort. If we could get 100,000 in the near future to favor it, I would feel pretty good about it.

So I believe that it is going to be very difficult, at least in the immediate period ahead, for us to have a very radical change in the delivery system. It is for that reason that I favor, if we do have a choice, starting with mothers and children first. I believe pediatricians are among the most socially responsible group of physicians out of the more than 300,000 physicians.

I would begin with maternal and child health care because I believe some pediatricians in the country would accept a per-capita or salary or per-unit basis of some kind rather than fee-for-service.

As I said, I believe that in the next few years we will make a very major change in the way health care is financed, organized, and developed in this country.

The major issue has been decided. Do individuals have a right to medical care by virtue of their being a citizen of the United States, a human being? I think that answer has been given. Today what we have to do is to implement that great principle which Lyndon Baines Johnson wrote into law, that every individual in the United States shall have the right to access to the highest quality of medical care that it is within our capacity to provide the men, women, and children of the nation. And we cannot as we think about the future, fail to realize that it was Lyndon Baines Johnson who saw that this right would be enshrined in the basic legislation of our country.

Theodore Marmor
with James Morone

9

The Health Programs of the
Kennedy-Johnson Years:
An Overview

This chapter addresses its topic from both philosophical and political perspectives. The first section analyzes the concept of a right to health in the context of other, competing, principles for the distribution of medical care. The second section places the major health financing initiatives of the Kennedy-Johnson years—Medicare and Medicaid—in an historical perspective. It outlines the political forces which dominated the vitriolic debate over government's involvement in financing personal medical care services and notes their effect on several generations of health insurance proposals. The concluding section appraises the medical policy initiatives of the Kennedy-Johnson Administrations in the light of the dispute over the government's proper role in guaranteeing the "right to health."

THE RIGHT TO HEALTH AND MEDICAL CARE

In its most egalitarian expression, the right to medical care means the equal access of all citizens to equivalent medical services.[1] In this formulation the distribution of services should vary solely with the degree of sickness. Other socioeconomic factors—wealth, race, geographical location, etc.—ought not to prevent the same response to similar medical conditions. Treating similarly ill persons similarly does not mean that all illnesses be treated. Rather, the egalitarian criterion requires that rationing of access be made by category of ailment, not by the social class of the ill.

There are two features of this formulation that require immediate clarification. First, the guarantee addresses medical services, not health. The stipulation that equally ill persons be equally treated does not entail that action be taken such that various socioeconomic groups have equal chances of avoiding

*The author expresses appreciation to Jenny Brorsen and Lynn Carter for their assistance in research and editing.

illness. Insuring equal access requires far more intervention than guaranteeing that once ill, citizens will be treated equally. Almost all of the 20th century debate over the "right to *health*" in fact has addressed issues concerning not health *per se* but the distribution of access to *medical care*.[2] Secondly, note that the right asserted is associated with citizenship, not merit, contribution, or any other indicator of deservingness. At its simplest, the egalitarian medical care argument asserts the injustice of permitting access to so fundamental a service to depend on anything but the "need" for it.

Like many egalitarian arguments, the right to equal care is open to the criticism of failing to distinguish among individuals on the basis of their *merit*. Some persons deserve better treatment than others, according to this view, though the basis of individual desert varies with meritarian philosophers. Even if the basis of merit were agreed to—a daunting task itself—there are strong arguments against distributing medical care on merit grounds. Gene Outka has argued that the equalities of medical need and of merit require different responses: those called for by need and those earned by effort.[3] Ill health—cancer, heart disease, and stroke to name only the most frightening—strikes some in all groups regardless of merit; the substantial differences in the probabilities of some being sicker—the poor for instance—does not invalidate the proposition that persons unequal in merit will find themselves equally in need of care. If merit is largely irrelevant in the origins of illness, it is wrong to apply that criterion in the distribution of the corresponding good. The relevant criterion would be medical condition.

There are two familiar responses to this criticism of the merit principle of distributing medical care. One, recalling the old fable about the industrious ants and the lazy grasshoppers, holds that the prudent who with foresight and discipline prepare for the possibility of illness, deserve superior treatment. Unlike the fable's inevitable winter, however, the worst crises of health tend to be unpredictable. Second, the capacity to cope with the unpredictable costs has as much to do with wealth as foresight and discipline.

A more profound objection to the egalitarian position arises when the premise of illness' unpredictability is questioned. The assumption that health crises are random, that the patient bears no blame for his condition, is in some cases simply false. Many reckless drivers are maimed in auto wrecks, many lungs corroded by nicotine and livers by excess alcohol. If patients are sometimes partially responsible for their medical "needs,"[4] then questions of desert are not so irrelevant. Egalitarians concede such patient responsibility. But they argue that employing this knowledge in the allocation of medical care is excruciatingly difficult. Outka has outlined a series of emergency cases which bring out how perplexing the access to medical treatment issue is. The cases illustrate how people

> suffer in varying ratios the effects of their natural and undeserved vulnerabilities, the irresponsibility and brutality of others, and their own desires and weaknesses:

> (1) A person with a heart attack who is seriously overweight; (2) a football hero who has suffered a concussion; (3) a man with lung cancer who has smoked cigarettes for 40 years; (4) a 60-year-old man who has always taken excellent care of himself and is suddenly stricken by leukemia; (5) a three-year-old girl who has swallowed poison left out carelessly by her parents; (6) a 14-year-old boy who has been beaten without provocation by a gang and suffers brain damage and recurrent attacks of uncontrollable terror; (7) a college student who has slashed his wrists (and not for the first time) from a psychological need for attention; (8) a woman raised in the ghetto who is found unconscious due to an overdose of heroin.[5]

Thus even when the merit criterion is relevant to the distribution of medical services, it may for all practical purposes be impossible to apply.

A more precise meritocratic view of medical care can be extracted from the free market tradition in economic theory. If one accepts the view that workers earn their marginal product and that marginal product measures social contribution, then the distribution of goods purchasable by earned income reflects the social contribution of citizens. Free market theorists regard medical care like any other valued item; individuals purchase either care or insurance out of earnings in whatever amounts they choose, given their income levels. The free market claim is that government programs to redistribute medical care distort individual choices. Different people, it is argued, want varying amounts and types of medical care—beyond some minimum—and will treat medical services differently. One might prefer the most expensive surgery available despite the fact that the more routine procedure is 98 percent as effective; his neighbor might forego the advantage to have more disposable income for other purposes. By failing to distinguish care according to willingness to pay, the argument goes, there is no measure of the marginal benefit of a given treatment to a given person.[6] Ultimately, free market theorists expect to maximize both freedom of choice and efficiency through the interplay of a medical market left to itself; they argue that government should finance no more than some minimum health care to the genuinely (and demonstrably) needy.

There is, of course, some merit in this critique of government intervention in the medical care market. Yet there is an enormous gap between the rhetoric of freedom of choice and the realities of purchasing medical care. The important fact about critical medical care—at birth, near death—is not what one would prefer but what doctors choose and patients can afford. Most analysts do not consider medical care a typical market good. In important cases, consumers (patients) have urgent needs and little information on which to base their choices. Physicians make many of the significant decisions; indeed, their professional discretion is fundamentally based on the knowledge gap between the patient and the provider.

Furthermore, it can be argued that since medical care is so fundamental a need, it is more appropriately viewed a prerequisite rather than a consequence of societal contribution. What someone can afford—even if it truly measures societal contribution—should be considered irrelevant. This suggestion returns us to something like the completely egalitarian "right of all citizens to equivalent medical services".

Clearly, the right to medical care is entangled in a number of vexing theoretical problems. The issue of equal treatment reaches to the most controversial questions about the role of the state in promoting equality. The argument over whether access to medical care should be a need- or merit-based claim proves particularly vexing when questions are raised about the extent to which illness is randomly distributed as opposed to patient-caused. The right to a minimum amount of health care—a physician's obligation under the Hippocratic oath—raises far less controversial issues than the equal right to equal treatment. And finally, the structuring of individual options by a government pursuing an ideal of equal access provokes the whole range of free-market arguments against the expansion of the role of the modern state. Some of these theoretical issues were crucial to the battle over government-financed medical insurance; others remained implicit through most of the debate.

BACKGROUND TO THE HEALTH POLICIES OF THE KENNEDY-JOHNSON YEARS

To appraise the health initiatives of the Kennedy and Johnson years, it is necessary to understand them in historical perspective. First, we will trace the legacy of government health insurance proposals, from the sweeping plans of Harry Truman to the far more modest ones of the late fifties; then we will consider the style and tone of the political forces which combined to produce the policy outcomes of those years.

Throughout the government health insurance debates, reformers espousing the right to medical care sought to overturn the prevailing view that, above some relatively meagre minimum, one deserved the medical care one could afford. They asserted that it was government's duty to reduce financial barriers between illness and care and proposed some form of national health insurance as the means to do so. For 60 years, national health insurance was the most deeply divisive issue in which the right to medical care played a part; at the same time, other government actions which affected the distribution of care—local support of hospitals, public health measures, research support particularly after World War II, and later financial support to the medical training centers—never produced the broad political and philosophical cleavages which the various demands for national health insurance provoked.

From National Health Insurance to Medicare

As noted previously, American demands for government involvement in health insurance date back to the first decade of this century. But it was not until the Great Depression, in an atmosphere of general concern for economic insecurity, that a sustained interest in government health insurance reappeared. The evolution of what became the 1965 Medicare and Medicaid programs reaches back to this New Deal period. To understand the form government health insurance took in the 1960s and to understand the two preceding decades of controversy one must begin here.[7]

The source of renewed interest in government health insurance was President Roosevelt's Advisory Committee on Economic Security, created in 1934 to draft a social security bill providing a minimum income for the aged, the unemployed, the blind, and the widowed and their children. The result was the Social Security Act of 1935 which, in addition to proposing insurance protection against the loss of workers' income, broached the subject of a government health insurance program.

Roosevelt's fear that the controversial issue of government health insurance would jeopardize the Social Security bill kept him from sponsoring the health insurance plan.[8] For many of his advisors, however, the discussions of this issue in the mid-thirties marked the beginning of an active interest in the subject. The divorce of compulsory health insurance from the original Social Security Bill had alerted critics within the medical world to the possibility of attempts to get a "foot in the door for socialized medicine." On the other hand, passage of the Social Security Act freed social insurance activists to address the question of how unequally medical care was distributed in post-Depression America. From 1939 on, their activities were reflected in the annual introduction of bills proposing compulsory health insurance for the entire population. An unaccomplished task of the New Deal, government health insurance became one of the most prominent aspirations of Harry Truman's Fair Deal.

Although compulsory health insurance was originally raised in conjunction with Social Security income protection, New Deal-Fair Deal advocates viewed health insurance primarily as a remedy for the unequal distribution of medical services. The proponents of the Murray-Wagner-Dingell bills took for granted the egalitarian argument noted before, the view that financial means should not determine the quality and quantity of medical care a citizen received. "Access to the means of attainment and preservation of health," Truman's Commission on the Health Needs of the Nation flatly stated, "is a basic human right." The health insurance problem in this view was the degree to which the use of health services varied with income, and not simply with illness. In contrast, for those who considered minimum accessibility to health services a standard of adequacy, the provision of charity medicine in doctors' offices and general hospitals represented a solution, and the problem was to fill in where present charity care was unavailable.

The Truman solution to the problem of unequal access to health services was to remove the financial barriers to care through government action. A radical redistribution of income was, in theory, an alternative solution, but not one which the Truman Administration felt moved to advocate. Rather, as he made clear in his State of the Union message in 1948, Truman's goal was "to enact a comprehensive insurance system which would remove the money barrier between illness and therapy . . . [and thus] protect all our people equally . . . against ill health." But on the issue of comprehensive health insurance for all Americans there were simply too few legislative supporters for enactment of Truman's plan and his demands were repeatedly frustrated. Truman responded to stalemate with vitriolic criticism of the American Medical Association (AMA) as the public's worst enemy in the effort to redistribute medical care more equitably. But the fact was that Truman could not command majorities for any of his major domestic proposals—lambasting the AMA was one way of coping with this executive-legislative impasse.

The persistent failure of Truman's health proposals had made the need for a new strategy evident; a plan was developed which limited health insurance to the beneficiaries of the Old Age and Survivors Insurance program. It was hoped that a broader program could be incrementally built on this foundation— precisely what conservatives feared. The American public's apparent acceptance of Social Security programs made the content of the new strategy appear politically feasible. Thus the stage was set in early 1951 for what came to be called "Medicare" proposals. Millions of dollars spent on propaganda, the activation of a broad cleavage in American politics, the framing of choice in health insurance between socialism and "the voluntary way," the bitter, personally vindictive battle between Truman's supporters and the AMA-led opposition—these comprised the legacy of the fight over general health insurance and provided the setting for the emergence of Medicare as an issue. What had begun in the 1930s as a movement to redistribute medical services for the entire population was now a proposal to help defray some of the hospital costs of some of the elderly. Still, the fight was just as bitter; the specific arguments—on either side—very much the same.

The Appeal of Focusing on the Aged

The selection of the aged as the problem group is comprehensible in the context of American politics, however distinctive it appears in comparative perspective. No other industrial country in the world has begun its government health insurance program with the aged. The typical pattern has been the initial coverage of low-income workers, with subsequent extensions to dependents and then to higher income groups. Insuring low-income workers, however, involves use of means tests, and the cardinal assumption of Social Security advocates in America has been that the stigma of such tests must be avoided. Seeking to avoid both general insurance and humiliating means tests, the Federal Security Agency strategists had to find a socioeconomic group whose average member could be presumed to be in need. The aged passed this test easily; everyone intuitively knew the aged were worst off. Wilbur Cohen was later to say that the subsequent massing of statistical data to prove the aged were sicker, poorer, and less insured than other adult groups was like using a steamroller to crush an ant of opposition.

Everyone also knew that the aged—like children and the disabled—commanded public sympathy. They were one of the few population groupings about whom the moralistic arguments of self-help did not apply. One could not say the old should take care of their financial-medical problems by earning and saving more money. The Social Security system makes unemployment (except for limited part-time work) a condition for the receipt of pensions, and a fixed retirement age is widely accepted as desirable public policy. In addition, the post-war growth in private health insurance was uneven, with lower proportions of the aged covered, and the extent of their insurance protection more limited, than that enjoyed by the working population. Only the most contorted reasoning could blame the aged for this condition by attributing their insurance status to improvidence.

Retirement forces many workers to give up work-related group insurance. The aged could not easily shift to individual policies because they comprised a high-risk group which insurance companies were reluctant to cover except at relatively expensive premium rates. The alternative of private insurance seemed in the 1950s incapable of coping with the stubborn fact that the aged were subject to inadequate private coverage at a time when their medical requirements were greatest and their financial resources were lowest. Under these circumstances many of the aged fell back upon their children for financial assistance, thus giving Medicare's emphasis upon the aged additional political appeal. The strategists expected support from families burdened by the requirement, moral or legal, to assume the medical debts of their aged relatives.

The same strategy of seeking broad public agreement was evident in the benefits and financial arrangements chosen. The 1951 selection of hospitalization benefits reflected the search for a "problem" less disputable than the one to which the Truman plans had been addressed. General health insurance was a means for solving the problem of the unequal distribution of medical care services; its aim was to make health care more equally accessible by removing financial barriers to utilizing those services, an aim broadly similar to that of the British National Health Service. A program of hospital insurance identifies the aged's problem not as the inaccessibility of health services, but the *financial consequences of using those services.* The provision of 60 days of free hospital care only indirectly encourages preventive health measures and cannot allay financial problems of the long-term chronically ill. The hospital benefit was designed, however, not so much to cope with all the health problems of the elderly as to reduce their most onerous financial difficulties. This shift in emphasis left gaping inadequacies. But, in the context of the early 1950s, reformers accepted the political realities which made broader conceptions of the aged's health problems unsusceptible to governmental solution.

The differences between making health services more accessible and coping with the financial consequences of hospital utilization were continually revealed in the next 15 years. The statistical profiles of the aged—first provided by the Truman health commission of 1952—uniformly supported the popular conception of aged Americans as sicker, poorer, and less insured than their countrymen. Health surveys reported that persons 65 and over were twice as likely as those under 65 to be chronically ill, and were hospitalized twice as long. In 1957-58, the average medical expenses per aged person were $177, more than twice the $86 average reported for persons under 65. As age increases, income decreases, producing an inverse relationship between medical expenses and personal income. While slightly more than half the persons over 65 had some type of health insurance in 1962, only 38 percent of the aged no longer working had any insurance at all. Moreover, the less healthy the aged considered themselves, the less likely they were to have insurance; 37 percent of those in "poor health" as opposed to 67 percent who evaluated their health as "good" had health insurance. Of those insured aged, a survey of hospital patients reported, only one-fourteenth of their total costs of illness was met through insurance. There could be no question that the aged faced serious problems coping with health expenses, though it was easy to point out that averages conceal the variation in illness and expenditures *among* the aged.

For those who saw Medicare as prevention against financial catastrophe, the vital question was which bills were the largest for any spell of serious illness. The ready answer was hospital care. Not only was the price of hospital care doubling in the decade 1951-1961, but the aged found themselves in hospital beds far more often than younger Americans. One in six aged persons entered a hospital in a given year, and they stayed in hospitals twice as long as those under 65, facing an average daily charge per patient bed of $35 by 1961. Hospitalization insurance was, according to this information, a necessity which the aged had to have to avoid financial catastrophe. But what the advocates did not point out was that financial catastrophe could easily overtake 60 days of hospital insurance. Such a catastrophe is defined by the gap between medical bills and available resources. Medicare's protection against the high unit costs of hospital care drew attention away from the financial costs of unusually extensive utilization of health services, whether high or low in average prices.

The concentration on the burdens of the aged was a ploy for sympathy. The disavowal of aims to change fundamentally the

American medical system was a sop to AMA fears, and the exclusion of physician services benefits was a response to past AMA hysteria. The focus on the financial burdens of receiving hospital care took as given the existing structure of the private medical care world, and stressed the issue of spreading the costs of using available services within that world. The organization of health care, with its inefficiencies and resistance to cost reduction was a fundamental but politically sensitive problem which consensus-minded reformers wanted to avoid in 1951 when they opted for 60 days of hospitalization insurance for the aged under Social Security as a promising "small" beginning.

The Legitimacy of Social Security: Earned Rights

The use of Society Security funding was an obvious effort to tap the widespread legitimacy which OASI programs enjoyed among all classes of Americans. But it was a tactic with an equally obvious defect. Proof that the aged were the most needy was based on calculation for *all* persons over 65. Yet Social Security financing would in 1952 have restricted Medicare benefits to 7 million pensioners out of the 12.5 million persons over 65. This would have meant not insuring 5.5 million aged whose medical and financial circumstances had been used to establish the "need" for a Medicare program in the first place. Nonetheless, Social Security financing offered so many other advantages that its advocates were prepared to live with this gap between the problem posed and the remedy offered.

The notion that Social Security recipients pay for their benefits is one traditional American response to the charge that government assistance programs are "give-aways" which undermine the willingness of individuals to save and take care of their own problems. Medicare advocates thought they had to squash that charge if they were both to gain mass public support and to shield the aged from the indignity of a means test. The contributory requirement of Social Security—the limitation of benefits to those having paid Social Security taxes—gives the system a resemblance to private insurance. Thus Social Security members would appear to have paid for hospital insurance. In fact, Social Security beneficiaries are entitled to pensions exceeding those which, in a strict actuarial sense, they have "earned" through contributions. But this is a point generally lost in the avalanche of words about how contributions, as a former Commissioner of Social Security, Robert Ball, once remarked, "give American workers the *feeling* they have earned their benefits."[9] The notion that contributions confer rights analogous to those which premiums entail within private insurance was one which deeply permeated the advocacy of Medicare.

The public legitimacy surrounding the Social Security program made it an ideal mechanism for avoiding the stigma attached to most public welfare programs. The distinction between public assistance for the poor and Social Security rights for contributors is, in fact, less clear in law than might be expected. Rights are prescriptions specified in law, and welfare legislation—for any class of persons—confers rights in this sense. But those who insist on the distinction between public assistance and Social Security focus less on the legal basis of rights than on the different ways in which these programs are viewed and administered. Social Security manuals insist on treating beneficiaries as "claimants," and stress that the government "owes" claimants their benefits. The stereotype of welfare is comprised of legacies from charity and the notorious Poor Laws, a combination of unappealing associations connected with intrusive investigation of need, invasion of privacy, and loss of citizenship rights. The unfavorable stereotype of welfare programs thus supports the contention that Social Security funds are the proper financing instrument for providing benefits while safeguarding self-respect.

Pressure Groups and Medicine:
The Lobbying of Millions

Serious congressional interest in special health insurance programs for the aged developed in 1958, six years after the initial Medicare proposal. From 1958 to 1965, congressional committees held annual hearings which became a battleground for hundreds of pressure groups. The same intemperate debate of the Truman years (and often the same debaters) reappeared. The acrimonious discussion of the problems, prospects, and desires of the aged illustrated a lesson of the Truman period: the Federal Government's role in the financing of personal health services is one of the small class of public issues which can be counted on to activate deep, emotional, and bitter cleavages between what political commentators call "liberal" and "conservative" pressure groups.

For all the important differences in scope and content between the Truman general health program and the Medicare proposals. the lineup of proponents and opponents was strikingly similar. Among the supporters, organized labor was the most powerful single source of pressure. Organizations of the aged were the result more than cause of these heightened Medicare demands. The AMA sparked the opposition and framed its objections in such a way that disparate groups only tenuously involved with medical care or the aged could rally around the AMA. A small sample, representing a fraction of all groups involved in the lobbying, illustrates the continuity between the broad economic and ideological divisions of the Truman fight and that over health insurance for the aged:

For:	Against:
AFL-CIO	American Medical Association
American Nurses Association	American Hospital Association
Council of Jewish Federations and Retired Workers	Life Insurance Association of America
American Association of Retired Workers	National Association of Manufacturers
National Association of Social Workers	National Association of Blue Shield Plans
National Farmers Union	American Farm Bureau Federation
The Socialist Party	The Chamber of Commerce
American Geriatrics Society	The American Legion

Three features of this pressure group alignment merit mention. First, the adversaries who are "liberal" and "conservative" on that issue are similarly aligned on other controversial social policies like Federal aid to education and disability insurance. Second, the extreme ideological polarization promoted by these groups has remained markedly stable despite significant changes in the actual objects in dispute, such as the much narrower scope of health insurance proposals since 1952. Proposals for even incremental change in a disputed social policy typically fail to avoid disagreement about "first principles." The polarization of pressure groups on Medicare illustrated the typical structure of conflict over "redistributive"[10] issues in America; the sides, in tone and composition, resembled the contestants in an economic class conflict and framed issues in what some call the terms of "class war." Finally, public dispute continued to be dominated by the AFL-CIO and the AMA. Since the 1940s these two chief adversaries have engaged in what *The New York Times* characterized as a "slugging match," a contest where, as in the fight between public and private power advocates in America,

> The sides have little use for one another. They distrust each other's motives; they question each other's integrity; they doubt each other's devotion to the national good.[11]

Both the AFL-CIO and the AMA have the membership, resources, and experience to engage in multi-million dollar lobbying. Their members are sufficiently spread geographically to make congressional electioneering relatively easy to organize.

During the debates of the 1940s and early 1950s, the AMA and its allies in big business and commercial agriculture found it a relatively successful tactic to focus the debate on the evils of collectivism and socialized medicine. The narrowing of health insurance proposals from universal coverage to the aged, however, set new constraints on the anti-Medicare campaigns. In response to the Medicare bills, the aged themselves began to organize into such pressure groups as the Senior Citizens' Councils and the Golden Ring Clubs. Although these groups lacked the financial and membership resources which characterized the better organized lobbies, it was far more difficult for the AMA to engage in open warfare with them than it had been for the doctors to do battle with the powerful AFL-CIO. When critics of governmental Medicare proposals seized on broad ideological objections, they now had also to take into account the possibility of being labeled the enemy of senior citizens. One effect attributable to this set of circumstances was the appearance of a conservative willingness to offer alternatives. In the late 1940s, Republicans and their allies in big business and organized medicine offered nothing but the *status quo* in opposition to the health insurance schemes of that period. By the 1950s, a change of tactics was in order: it was one thing to write off socialism, but the risks of writing off the aged would give the wise politician some second thoughts.

THE HEALTH AND MEDICAL PROGRAMS OF THE
KENNEDY-JOHNSON ADMINISTRATIONS

The details of the political struggles that culminated in the 1965 passage of Medicare and Medicaid are not relevant to this essay's focus and have been described elsewhere.[12] But the fact that it was the dominant health preoccupation in the Kennedy and early Johnson Administrations is relevant. Indeed, as President Johnson later said, the overriding "importance" of the struggle over Medicare was the "revolutionary change in our thinking about health care" it "foreshadowed." The meaning of health insurance for the aged, in Johnson's view, was the country's beginning recognition that "good medical care is a right not a privilege."[13]

Appraising the contributions of the medical programs of the Kennedy and Johnson Administrations means beginning with what they regarded as their largest achievements. First, we will review the programmatic expression of the health insurance struggle in Medicare and Medicaid and then turn to the numerous other health initiatives which the budgetary outlays for these programs have dwarfed.

The enactment of Medicare and Medicaid was obviously shaped by the electoral landslide of 1964. The Johnson victory guaranteed the passage of Medicare legislation which congressional stalemate had denied the Kennedy Administration. But the assurance of passage did not mean the absence of surprise in the details of the Medicare statute or the Medicaid program that was unexpectedly tacked on.

The older struggle over health insurance for the aged sharply limited the range of alternatives open to the Johnson Administration, even in the flush of election triumph. That long debate—focused on the aged as the problem group, Social Security versus general revenues as financing mechanisms, and partial versus comprehensive benefits for some or all of the aged—structured the content of the statutory innovations. The character of more than a decade of dispute over health insurance for the elderly explains the programmatic features of the final bill that Representative Wilbur Mills helped engineer, President Johnson took pride in, and the conservative critics in Congress and the AMA inadvertently helped to ensure.

The new law (PL 89-974) was broader than its predecessors in benefit structure, but it did not provide payment for all or even most ordinary expenses for the elderly. It reflected the "insurance" as opposed to "comprehensive prepayment" philosophy of medical care financing. The former assumes that paying substantial portions of large medical bills is sufficient; the problem which Medicare in fact addressed was unbudgetable financial strain (though many of the aged expected more). The prepayment philosphy advocated separation of financing from medical considerations, harkening back to the egalitarian view of the Truman period. On this standard, the fact that Medicare came to finance between 40 and 50 percent of the medical expenses of the aged reflected programmatic inadequacy. Only the complete removal of financial barriers to medical services satisfies the strict standard. Medicare's range of deductibles, exclusions, and coinsurance provisions all reflect the private health insurance benefit models.

Medicare's Impact

The impact of Medicare on the elderly is the subject of another chapter in this volume and I will not repeat its findings. But it is worth noting in connection with the "right to health" theme that Medicare's differential impact should have surprised no one familiar with its provisions. The program's emphasis on financing large medical expenses shows in its impact on the aged's increased use of hospitals. As Table 1 indicates, hospital days per aged person rose by nearly 50 percent in Medicare's first three years, while hospital days among the nonaged actually declined. Physician visits do not reflect this marked redistribution across age groups, not surprising in the light of Medicare's deductible and coinsurance provisions for physicians' services (Table 2).

None of this utilization is surprising in the light of Medicare's statutory provisions. But much of Medicare-Medicaid's programmatic implementation was a surprise for the administrators who for years had been anticipating a program insuring the aged against 60 days of hospitalization expenses. The methods of paying physicians were among the most intractable issues facing the Social Security Administration in the first years of Medicare; for years no one had imagined paying physicians under a Medicare program and no office of HEW had thought out how this burden could best be borne. The Medicaid program of

TABLE 1 Hospital utilization by age* and income** before and after the introduction of Medicare/Medicaid

	1965-66	1968
Age	Hospital days per thousand	
65 and over	2,029	2,993
Under 65	828	787
	(20.5% of all days)	(28.3% of all days)
Income	Number of persons hospitalized per thousand	
Under $3,000	107	123
$3,000–4,999	106	107
$5,000–7,999	106	97
$8,000–9,999	96	94
$10,000 or more	89	82

Source: Joseph P. Newhouse, "Health Care Cost Sharing and Cost Containment," Testimony prepared for the Subcommittee on Public Health and Environment, Committee on Interstate and Foreign Commerce, U.S. House of Representatives," April, 1976, p. 26.

*"Persons Hospitalized," *Health Interview Survey, Series 10, Numbers 50 and 64,* Tables 4, 26, and 28.

**Ibid.*, Tables D and B.

TABLE 2 Percentage of persons seeing a physician and physician visits per person per year, by age and income, before and after the introduction of Medicare/Medicaid

	Percentage seeing a physician		Annual visits per person	
Age	1963-64	1969	1963-64	1969-1971*
Less than 65	65.9	69.2	4.3	4.4
65 and over	68.3	71.3	6.7	6.4
Income				
Under $3,000	59.5	66.2	4.3	4.8
$3,000–4,999	64.2	66.8	4.5	4.5
$5,000–6,999	67.1	68.2	4.5	3.9
$7,000–9,999	69.8	69.5	4.7	4.1
$10,000–14,999	71.8	71.8	4.8	4.2
$15,000 or more	75.4	74.5	5.8	4.5

Source: "Physician Visits" and "Current Estimates," *Health Interview Survey,* Series 10, Numbers 72, 75, and 79. 1969 population weights were used to compute the age figures. Income figures are unadjusted for inflation.

*1969-1971 were averaged because the annual figures show some variance. Prepared by Joseph P. Newhouse, *Ibid.*, p. 27.

1965—itself an afterthought addition to the familiar Medicare bill—brought with it serious controversy over exactly who would be designated as medically indigent and how generous the state plans could be.

Perhaps most unexpected was the conflict between assuring the aged access to care and insuring that the facilities they use were not racially discriminatory. In the two decades of debate over government health insurance, almost no one pressed the issue of racially segregated medical services. Yet in the first weeks of Medicare's operations, the question of certifying Southern hospitals took up more time of HEW's top health officials than any other feature of the program. Besides satisfying standards designed to ensure a high quality of care, institutions providing services to Medicare beneficiaries had to offer proof that its services were rendered on a non-discriminatory basis. These requirements frequently posed cruel choices where hospitals unable or unwilling to meet the certification standards were also the only facilities available to the elderly. Civil rights lawyers saw Medicare as a powerful instrument for change, and, though there certainly were and are Southern hospitals not in compliance, a major unanticipated effect of the 1965 legislation was to desegregate the bulk of Southern hospitals.

What Medicare surely did accomplish was practical universalization among the aged of health insurance. That insurance reduced the financial barriers to care for much of the aged population and sharply reduced the fear of pauperization from health expenses among almost all of the aged. But Medicare did not, as President Johnson hoped, mean "good medical care" was a right in the egalitarian sense discussed at the outset of this essay. While the words were the same as Truman's, the health insurance proposals of the Kennedy-Johnson years reflected substantial shrinkage from the ambitions of the Fair Deal. The two sides of the battle used familiar ideological weapons to dispute vastly different programmatic initiatives. That is part of the reason President Johnson wrote of how the country had *begun* to think of medical care as a right with Medicare's passage. While the debate was about broad abstract issues concerning government's responsibility in medical care, the political struggle was conducted at the practical level of securing supporters and defeating opponents. It should come as no surprise that those who measure Medicare's accomplishments by the rhetoric of equal rights to care will be disappointed.

Medicaid

Medicaid, by contrast, was the great program afterthought of 1965. As a scheme for financing the medical care of poor Americans, it was not innovative either programmatically or philosophically. It carried over the tradition of vendor payments for the aged poor, but expanded the minimum eligible population to all of the poor eligible for Federal-state public assistance programs. It employed the traditional public welfare mechanisms of Federal guidelines and state-county administration. But few anticipated the financial, medical, or political consequences when Medicaid began in 1966. From the outset Medicaid was paradoxical. Unexpectedly expensive, Medicaid has been lampooned for actually accomplishing some of the program's stated purposes, including the provision of health financing to a very substantial portion of the welfare population. As the welfare companion to Medicare, Medicaid was expected to grow slowly. That expectation of slow growth presumed that programs for the poor are unpopular and that, as with Kerr-Mills, the states would restrain both program benefits and eligibility. This approach meant that Federal legislators could assume in 1965 that broad language about making medical care available to all the poor by 1975 was safe and HEW regulation writers could presume that Federal rules expressing that intent would not be political dynamite. No one fully anticipated the impact of either general medical inflation or the dramatic increases in the welfare rolls.

Medicaid's two announced purposes were to increase the access of poor people to medical care and provide that care in the mainstream of American medicine. The increased use of physician services by the poor is strikingly impressive. In 1964, the year before Medicaid, those whose family income was below the Federal poverty line averaged 4.3 visits per year. By 1971, visits for the same group had risen to 5.6, compared to 4.7 and 4.9 for middle- and upper-income family members, respectively. Equally, the poor are hospitalized more frequently.[14] Still, even though Medicaid substantially expanded the poor's access to care, it failed to bring them into the mainstream of providers.

These changes do not establish that the poor have attained

meaningful parity of utilization or quality of care. The poor are sicker; equal access to care for the same conditions would mean even higher rates of utilization than now obtained. Moreover, the poor (and rural) are markedly less likely to have a regular source of care than the non-poor (and urban). Children from central cities and rural areas are less likely, according to 1970 data, to see a physician at least once during the year. Perhaps most important, the poor have fewer physician visits in response to days of disability than the rest of the population. Yet the improvement in access associated with the expansion of Medicaid is undeniable.[15]

Whether the care the poor receive equals that of the rest of the population is far more problematic. What is clear is that the poor receive their care in different types of settings and from different sorts of physicians. Medicaid has not markedly improved the access of poor children to private sources of care and has exerted minimal impact on the current pattern of locating and providing care to the poor.[16] The most frequent users of hospital outpatient services are poor children, particularly racial minorities in the central cities. While in 1974, approximately 12 percent of the outpatient visits by the general child population were to hospital-based facilities, the percentage was twice that among poor children in central cities.[17] While the poor use more outpatient departments and general practitioners for their care, the more affluent disproportionately receive specialist care in physician offices. The quality implications of these differences are arguable; the differences in pattern of use are not.

Whatever Medicaid's announced goals, political attention has centered on its costs. Total expenditures have far exceeded official estimates, rising from some $25 million in 1967 to $11 billion in 1974.[18] Similarly, dramatic increases have marked the Medicare program for the elderly, but the political controversy over it has not matched Medicaid's. And part of the reason is that the state-Federal financing of welfare programs decentralizes fiscal conflict, while Medicare's Social Security financing centralizes political oversight at great geographic remove from state and local tax disputes.

Other Health Programs

Despite the political differences between Medicare and Medicaid, they comprise the major programmatic legacy of the

Kennedy-Johnson years. In budget terms their preeminence is stark, overshadowing all of the other programs, as Table 3 shows, by the end of the Johnson Administration. This budgetary predominance by no means reflected the perspective of the Kennedy-Johnson initiators. They were proud, as President Johnson himself reported, of the widespread efforts to reach problems across all the areas of the health industry. More legislation was, to these minds, better government: Johnson stated "during my administration, 40 national health measures were presented to the Congress and passed by the Congress— more than in all the preceding 175 years of the Republic's history."[19]

Though interpretable as features of a comprehensive health strategy, the initiatives of the Kennedy-Johnson years reflected a diversity of both political origins and programmatic fates. Some prospered, others quickly faded. Some grew, others faced budgetary constraints. All experienced review and criticisms by

TABLE 3   Federal health expenditures, 1969 (in millions of dollars)

	1969	1974
Medicare	$6,598*	$9,195*
Medicaid	2,284*	4,405*
Maternal and Child Health Services	209**	580*a
OEO Health and Medical Programs (includes neighborhood health centers)	126*	a
Alcohol, Drug Abuse, and Mental Health Administration	51*	319*
Health Manpower Training	805*	1,240*
Health Related Construction	634*	381*
Health Research	1,475*	1,839*

Sources: *Russell et al., Federal Health Spending, 1969-74, Center for Health Policy Studies, National Planning Association, Washington, D.C., 1974. pp. 3, 55, 56, and 63.

**Department of Health Education and Welfare, Annual Report, 1969.

aFunding through HSA when programs transferred; unavailable breakdown for OEO.

the Republican Administration of the 1970s. And none have the kind of national salience Medicare began with and Medicaid came to have.

This retrospective sobriety differs sharply of course from the enthusiasm with which the Johnson Administration directed itself to a range of health concerns: medical research, providing care in poor areas, special problems of heart disease, cancer, stroke, and mental illness, and the gap between scientific medical knowledge and the care Americans received. For each problem there was a programmatic response, and, unbeknownst to the reformers, an uncertain future.

The neighborhood health centers initiated in 1965 by the Office of Economic Opportunity were to play a major role in making health care delivery a reality in poor urban neighborhoods. The centers were established in high poverty areas and tailored their services to fit local needs. Their aims were ambitious—to overcome a variety of non-financial barriers to medical care: the lack of medical providers in low-income neighborhoods, inadequate transportation to health care centers, discrimination against the poor, and lack of education. The centers provided comprehensive medical and dental care and some initiated programs to ameliorate inadequate housing, sanitation, sewage, or nutrition. But although intended as companions to Medicaid, they were quickly overshadowed by it.[20] Initial estimates were 25 million individuals served by 1973.[21] Yet, by that time a twentieth of that number—1.3 million people—were registered at 100 centers and annual expenditures were declining. Ultimately, the program was a victim of the budget austerity of the Republican years.

The Maternal and Child Health Programs of the mid-1930s were significantly expanded during the Johnson Administration. Comprehensive care for mothers and infants was introduced at neighborhood centers in an effort to reduce the relatively higher infant mortality rate among the poor; special attention was given to young unwed mothers. In 1965, comprehensive health care was extended to children and youth with a special emphasis on preventive medicine and early treatment. The Crippled Children's Program, which had been included in the original Maternal and Child Care Program of 1935, grew from $62.3 million in 1960 to $152.9 million in 1970. By 1970, 491,000 children were being served. Though enormously helpful for certain groups, the comprehensive children and youth projects have never reached a large proportion of poor Americans and have also experienced budget reductions in the 1970s.

Some ambitious programs have never experienced significant growth. The Early and Periodic Screening, Diagnosis, and Treatment Program (EPSDT), for example, enacted in 1967 was advertised as the first Federal policy mandate of comprehensive preventive health services for children. Yet final regulations for the program were not issued until November, 1971, and bureaucratic wrangling, strong professional opposition, and a state disinclination to bear EPSDT's potentially considerable costs have continued to block the successful implementation of this program.

In the area of mental health, there has been both drastic change and subsequent controversies. The Community Mental Health Centers Act of 1963 sought to replace large mental institutions with community mental health services. Subsequent provisions were made for alcohol and drug abuse. By 1974, 626 programs were serving 1.4 million people;[22] the programs were initiated with Federal funds and expected to be self-sufficient within 10 years, although special arrangements were made for centers in low-income neighborhoods. Yet, the Nixon and Ford Administrations announced their intention to phase out this legacy of the Kennedy-Johnson years.

Other programs took up the problems of distribution of providers and medical research. The Health Manpower Training Program was instituted in 1965 to increase the number and improve the specialty and geographic distribution of health care providers. Researchers, physicians, nurses, dentists, and para-medics were trained with government funds; $717 million was allocated in 1969, $1.4 billion by 1973. The Federal Government had actively funded the construction of medical care facilities since World War II; during the 1960s its contribution rose from $195 million (1960) to $4.056 billion (1970).[23] Likewise, the scope of federally funded research (particularly in cancer, heart, and lung diseases; mental health and environmental health) was enormously expanded.

In order to hasten the translation of research breakthroughs into health care practice, the Regional Medical Program Service

(RMP) was established. Focusing on the three largest causes of death in America—heart disease, cancer, and stroke—the program attempted to coordinate researchers, medical schools, hospitals, and other health care institutions by disseminating new information about diagnosis and treatment. Finally, in an effort to integrate the burgeoning number of health programs, the Comprehensive Health Planning and Service Act of 1966 (CHP) established health planning agencies in all of the states. By 1972, more than 200 such agencies were in operation.[24]

While of central importance to professionals directly affected, none of these programs dramatically altered the distribution of access to medical care services. In individual communities, a local health center might be the difference between real and financial access to care. Nurse practitioners reached some rural residents where no doctors were available. But nowhere was the commitment to directly provide health services and personnel comparable to the Medicare and Medicaid commitment to pay for it.

Conclusion

The appeal to medical care rights has, as we have seen, been a familiar feature of 20th Century American health politics. Though commonly invoked, the concept of a right to care remains philosophically vexing and only loosely related to public policy debate and practice. In the disputes over Medicare, the rhetoric of equal access to care—a legacy of earlier health insurance debates—was evoked in defense of plans that by their nature could not satisfy this standard.

In practice, Medicare and Medicaid highlighted the discrepancy between the language of equal rights and the content of public programs. Medicare—by providing equal insurance benefits—insured both that medical care would impoverish fewer of the aged and that, through supplementation of its benefits and regional and racial variation in services provided and financed, the aged would not receive equal consideration. Medicaid, by removing entirely financial barriers to care for some of the poor, moved the nation towards greater equalization of access across income classes. But it did not do so equally by state, region, or type of poverty, thus leaving a legacy of uneven improvement, rapid expenditure escalation, and political controversy.

Whatever Medicare and Medicaid did for their beneficiaries,

they helped to worsen the inflation problem in medicine.[25] Unwittingly, both programs have contributed to the problems other Americans are having with financial access to care and helped to inflate the costs of any national health insurance plan that might now attempt to make medical care equally accessible financially. Medical inflation constitutes a major current problem for both patients and government. Part of its impact shows up in the reduction of real levels of spending in the health delivery, educational, and research programs of the Kennedy-Johnson years. Medicare and Medicaid reflected an incrementalist approach to extending the "right to medical care." Enormously helpful to some Americans, the very expansion of those programs have made the practical obstacles to national health insurance more formidable than the disputes over the right to care which seemed so central in the middle of the 1960s.

References

[1] See Gene Outka, "Social Justice and Equal Access to Health Care," *Journal of Religious Ethics*, 2 (1974), pp. 11-32.

[2] Blue Cross Association. *Conference in Future Directions of Health Care: The Dimensions of Medicine*. Sponsored by the Blue Cross Association, The Rockefeller Foundation, and the Health Public Policy Program, University of California School of Medicine, December, 1975, p. 4.

[3] Outka, *op. cit.*, p. 4.

[4] Blue Cross Association, *op. cit.*, pp. 1-3.

[5] Outka, *op. cit.*, pp. 16-17.

[6] See for example, Robert Sade, "Medical Care as a Right: Refutation," *The New England Journal of Medicine*, 285 (December, 1971).

[7] This section draws extensively on T. R. Marmor, *Politics of Medicare*, (London: Routledge and Kegan Paul, Ltd., 1970).

[8] For an account of this episode, see Daniel Hirschfield, *The Lost Reform: The Campaign for Compulsory Health Insurance in the U.S. from 1932-1943*, (Cambridge: Harvard University Press, 1970).

[9] Robert M. Ball, (1964) "The American Social Security Program," *New England Journal of Medicine*, 170 (January 30, 1964), pp. 232-236.

[10] Theodore J. Lowi, "American Business, Public Policy and Political Theory," *World Politics*, 16 (1964).

[11] Aaron Wildavsky, *Dixon Yates: A Study in Power Politics*, (New Haven: Yale University Press, 1962), pp. 5-6, 304-305.

[12] Theodore Marmor, *The Politics of Medicare*, (Chicago: Aldine Publishing Co., 1973); Eugene Feingold, *Medicare: Policy and Politics*, (San Francisco: Chandler Publishing Co., 1966); Richard Harris, *A Sacred Trust*, (Baltimore: Penguin Books, 1969).

[13] Lyndon Johnson, *The Vantage Point: Perspectives of the Presidency, 1963-1969*, (New York: Holt, Rinehart, and Winston, 1971), p. 220.

[14] Karen Davis, *National Health Insurance, Benefits, Costs, and Consequences*, (Washington, D.C.: The Brookings Institution, 1975), Tables 3-10, p. 43.

[15] Lu Ann Aday and Ronald Andersen, *Access to Medical Care*, (Ann Arbor, Mich.: Health Administration Press, 1975).

[16] See Karen Davis and Roger Reynolds, "The Impact of Medicare and Medicaid on Access to Medical Care" in Richard Rosett (ed.), *The Role of Insurance in the Health Services Sector*. A Universities NBER Conference.

[17] See the data prepared by the National Center for Health Statistics for the Child Health Task Force.

[18] U.S. Social Security Administration, Compendium of National Health Expenditure Data DHEW (SSA) 73-11903, Table 8, pp. 58, 66.

[19] Lyndon Johnson, *op. cit.*, p. 220.

[20] See Karen Davis, "A Decade of Policy Developments in Providing Health Care for Low-Income Families" in Robert Haveman (ed.), *A Decade of Federal Anti-Poverty Policy: Failures and Lessons*. Institute for Research on Poverty, University of Wisconsin, forthcoming.

[21] U.S. Department of Health, Education, and Welfare, Office of the Assistant Secretary for Planning and Evaluation, "Human Investment Program, Delivery and Health Services for the Poor," processed, 1967.

[22] U.S. Social Security Administration, *op. cit.*

[23] See Alfred Skolnk and Sophie R. Dales, "Social Welfare Expenditures, 1972-73," *Social Security Bulletin*, vol. 37, no. 1 (Jan., 1974), Table 6, p. 14.

[24] Both RMP and CHP legislation expired in 1974 and were replaced by the National Health Planning and Resources Development Act (PL-93-641).

[25] This problem is explored much more fully in Michael Zubcoff (ed.), *Health—A Victim or Cause of Inflation*, (New York: Prodist, 1976).

Karen Davis

10 Health and the Great Society: Successes of the Past Decade and the Road Ahead

The Great Society and the War on Poverty held out the promise of great change in American society. Poverty was to be eliminated, and all Americans were to have an equal opportunity in the race for economic well-being. Minorities and the disadvantaged were to gain greater control over the institutions affecting their lives—in employment, in education, and in the quality of daily living.

Disillusionment, as change has not lived up to high expectations, has blinded many of the genuine progress which has been achieved. Poverty was substantially reduced in the 1960s, if not eliminated. Job opportunities for minorities were expanded. Political representation and participation in political processes by the poor and disadvantaged did occur in increasing numbers.

In the 1970s, however, much of the steam went out of the engines for social change. Concern with the Vietnam War, concern with the economy, and budgetary pressures on Federal, state, and local governments redirected attention away from the social problems of the poor and disadvantaged. Poverty ceased to decline, and many governmental programs to assist the poor were eliminated, downgraded, redirected, or cut back in funding.

This experience is perhaps most vividly exemplified by the War on Poverty and Great Society health programs. These programs, aimed at extending the right to lead a healthy, productive life to all Americans, also raised great expectations. Illness and incapacity among the poor were to be eliminated, enabling them to take advantage of educational and employment opportunities. The quality of life for the poor and the aged was to be improved through access to decent, human health care.

Fulfillment of this dream has not occurred. The poor continue to die at a much greater rate than others, and their lives continue to be burdened by chronic illnesses and disability to a far greater extent than that of more advantaged persons.

But failure to achieve all that was hoped should not be a signal for despair. Extension of an equal opportunity for a healthy life to all is not an easily obtainable goal, nor is it one that can realistically be expected to take place in a decade or perhaps even in a generation—as past neglect takes its toll for long periods ahead. Significant improvements in the health of the poor have been made, and the gap has been narrowed, if not eliminated.

We should take heart from the progress which has been achieved, learn from mistakes and places where we have stumbled, and make a renewed commitment to move again toward the goal of enabling all Americans an opportunity to lead productive, healthy lives.

Successes of the Past Decade

It is difficult to assess the full measure of what has been achieved in 10 year's experience with Federal health programs.[1] Despite these programs, in many ways the United States has become an unhealthier place in which to live. Increased urbanization has led to greater crowding, pollution, and stress. Death rates for cancer, alcoholism, suicide, and homicide have risen. More accidents have taken place. Rising food and fuel costs have contributed to poor nutrition, mounting environmental hazards, and heightened vulnerability of the weak. The physical and psychological stress generated by unemployment and inflation has taken its toll. It has been a world where holding one's own has required great exertion.

The U.S. has more extensive statistics on the state of the nation's health than perhaps any other country.[2] Yet, much remains unknown about how the poor have been affected in the last decade relative to other groups. Even with the best statistics, however, much of the change that has occurred is not quantifiable. The limitations of social sciences to detect and document change makes any description of past successes tenuous and incomplete.

The evidence available, however, portrays substantial improvement. Death rates from causes which are amenable to improved health care and which traditionally have been higher among the poor than others have declined substantially. Infant mortality rates have declined 33 percent between 1965 and 1974, with even more rapid reductions in deaths of young babies between

TABLE 1 Infant and maternal mortality, United States, selective years,
1950-1974

	1950	1960	1965	1970	1974	Percentage change 1950-74	1965-74
Maternal mortality (deaths per 100,000 live births)	83.3	37.1	31.6	21.5	20.8	-75.0%	-34.2%
Infant mortality (deaths per 1,000 live births							
Under 1 year	29.2	26.0	24.7	20.0	16.5	-43.5	-33.2
Under 28 days	20.5	18.7	17.7	15.1	12.1	-41.0	-31.6
28 days to 11 months	8.7	7.3	7.0	4.9	4.4	-49.4	-37.1

Source: U.S. Department of Health, Education, and Welfare, National Center for Health Statistics, *Monthly Vital Statistics Report*, "Provisional Statistics, Annual Summary for the United States, 1974, Births, Deaths, Marriages, and Divorces," vol. 23, no. 13, May 30, 1975.

the ages of one month and one year (see Table 1). Deaths from gastrointestinal diseases among babies have declined 50 percent, influenza and pneumonia 58 percent, and immaturity 61 percent over this period. Maternal mortality has been cut by a third. Young children between the ages of one and four have also experienced reduced death rates particularly for cancer (down 26 percent) and influenza and pneumonia (down 48 percent)— although accidents have taken an increasing toll.[3]

Progress has been made for most causes of deaths in the adult population. Age-adjusted death rates for heart conditions have declined 16 percent, cerebrovascular causes 18 percent, accidents 14 percent, influenza and pneumonia 28 percent, diabetes 7 percent, and arteriosclerosis 37 percent (see Table 2).

These percentage declines are based on the entire population. Separate statistics on experience of the poor are not yet available, but those rates experiencing the greatest declines are for conditions historically much higher for the poor than others. It is possible, therefore, that the experience of the poor has been even

TABLE 2 Age-adjusted death rates per 100,000 population, total and for 15 leading causes of death, United States, selected years 1950-1974

	1950	1960	1965	1969	1974	Percentage change 1950-1974	Percentage change 1965-1974
All causes	**841.5**	**760.9**	**741.8**	**730.9**	**666.2**	**-20.8%**	**-10.2%**
Leading causes with a downturn in mortality							
Diseases of the heart (390-398, 402-404, 410-429)	307.6	286.2	275.6	262.3	232.7	-24.4	-15.6
Cerebrovascular disease (430-438)	88.8	79.7	73.1	68.5	59.9	-32.6	-18.1
Accidents (E800-E949)	57.5	49.9	53.4	55.3	46.0	-20.0	-13.9
Influenza and pneumonia (470-474, 480-486)	26.2	28.0	23.4	24.6	16.9	-35.5	-27.8
Certain causes of mortality in early infancy[a] (760-769.2, 769.4-772, 774-778)	40.5	37.4	28.6	21.4	13.6	-66.4	-52.5
Diabetes mellitus (250)	14.3	13.6	13.5	14.5	12.5	-12.6	- 7.4
Arterioscerosis (440)	16.2	13.2	12.0	9.2	7.6	-53.1	-36.7
Congenital anomalies[a] (740-759)	12.2	12.2	10.1	8.4	6.4	-47.5	-36.6
Nephritis and nephrosis (580-584)	16.6	6.5	5.2	3.9	n.a.	n.a.	n.a.
Peptic ulcer (531-533)	5.0	5.2	4.3	3.6	n.a.	n.a.	n.a.
Leading causes with an upturn in mortality							
Malignant neoplasms (140-209)	125.4	125.8	127.9	129.7	131.8	+5.1	+3.1
Bronchitis, emphysema, and asthma (490-493)	3.7	8.2	11.6	12.0	9.2	+148.6	-20.7
Cirrhosis of liver (571)	8.5	10.5	12.1	14.2	14.8	+ 74.1	+22.3
Suicide (E950-E959)	11.0	10.6	11.4	11.3	12.2	+ 10.9	+ 7.0
Homicide (E960-E978)	5.4	5.2	6.2	8.6	10.8	+100.0	+74.2

Source: U.S. Department of Health, Education, and Welfare, National Center for Health Statistics, *Mortality Trends for Leading Causes of Death, United States, 1950-69,* series 20, no. 16, DHEW Pub. No. (HRA) 74-1853, March, 1974; and *Monthly Vital Statistics Report,* "Advance Report, Final Mortality Statistics, 1974," vol. 24, no. 11, Supplement (HRA) 76-1120, February 3, 1976.

more dramatic than suggested by this data. Blacks, for example, have had even more rapid reductions in these death rates than whites.[4] American Indians, for whom separate statistics are available, had even more marked improvements in death rates from a number of cases conducive to better medical care particularly in the areas of infant mortality, tuberculosis, enteritis, and other diarrheal diseases, and pneumonia and influenza. Despite these gains, however, many rates are still four times as high among Indians as for the U.S. population. Infant mortality rates in states with high poverty rates declined more rapidly than others in the last decade, particularly deaths of babies between the ages of one month and one year.[5]

Chronic conditions, on the other hand, have increased in incidence. In part, this reflects the greater concentration of the aged in the general population. In part, a greater incidence of chronic illness is to be expected when death rates are reduced. Reporting may also be more extensive and accurate when a greater proportion of the population comes into regular contact with the medical system.

Despite this deteriorating picture, however, the poor have made some slight improvements relative to others. Poor children have moved closer to nonpoor children in limitation of activity due to chronic illness (see Table 3). For some types of conditions, such as visual impairment and impairments of back or spine, for which comparable data are available over a long period of time, the poor have made gains relative to the nonpoor.[6]

The incidence of reported acute illness has also increased in the last 10 years, and the poor have lost ground relative to others in this respect.[7] Acute conditions ranging from respiratory illness and gastrointestinal disturbances, to injuries have restricted the activity of the poor at an even greater rate over this period.

The poor, however, have made dramatic gains in their access to medical care services to cope with the illnesses and accidents which they have incurred. Visits to physicians have increased dramatically (Table 4). Low-income families who are covered by Medicaid or other governmental health programs now use health services at about the same level as middle-income families (after adjusting for health condition)—reversing a pattern of many decades of greater utilization of the health system by the relatively healthier high-income population.[8]

TABLE 3 Percent of the population with limitation of activity due to chronic illness, by poor and nonpoor status* and age, United States, 1964 and 1973

	1964	1973
All ages		
Poor	25.1	25.6
Nonpoor	8.9	9.7
Ratio, poor to nonpoor	2.82	2.64
Under age 17 years		
Poor	3.1	4.1
Nonpoor	2.0	3.2
Ratio, poor to nonpoor	1.55	1.28
17-44 years		
Poor	13.3	13.5
Nonpoor	7.2	7.4
Ratio, poor to nonpoor	1.85	1.82
45-64 years		
Poor	36.7	43.2
Nonpoor	16.0	18.2
Ratio, poor to nonpoor	2.29	2.37
65 years and over		
Poor	55.2	49.1
Nonpoor	43.1	37.5
Ratio, poor to nonpoor	1.28	1.31

Source: Unpublished data from the Health Interview Survey, National Center for Health Statistics, reported in Ronald W. Wilson and Elijah L. White, "Changes in Morbidity, Disability, and Utilization Differentials Between the Poor and Nonpoor; Data from the Health Interview Survey: 1964 and 1973," October 21, 1974, Table 11.

*Poor is defined as family income below $3,000 in 1964 and below $6,000 in 1973.

TABLE 4 Number of physician visits per person per year, by family
income and age: FY 1964 and CY 1974

	1964	Number of visits		1974	Number of visits
Age	Income		Age	Income	
All ages	All incomes	4.5	**All ages**	All incomes	4.9
	Under $4,000	4.3		Under $5,000	5.6
	4,000- 6,999	4.5		5,000- 9,999	5.0
	7,000- 9,999	4.7		10,000-14,999	4.6
	10,000 and over	5.1		15,000 and over	4.9
Ratio over 10,000 to under 4,000		1.19	Ratio over 15,000 to under 5,000		.87
Under 15 yrs.	All incomes	4.2	**Under 17 yrs.**	All incomes	4.1
	Under $4,000	3.3		Under 5,000	3.7
	4,000- 6,999	4.3		5,000- 9,999	3.7
	7,000- 9,999	4.7		10,000-14,999	4.2
	10,000 and over	5.5		15,000 and over	4.7
Ratio over 10,000 to under 4,000		1.66	Ratio over 15,000 to under 5,000		1.15
15-44 years	All incomes	4.4	**17-44 years**	All incomes	4.5
	Under $4,000	4.1		Under $5,000	5.8
	4,000- 6,999	4.5		5,000- 9,999	5.2
	7,000- 9,999	4.7		10,000-14,999	4.5
	10,000 and over	4.9		15,000 and over	4.6
Ratio over 10,000 to under 4,000		1.19	Ratio over 15,000 to under 5,000		.79
45-64 years	All incomes	5.0	**45-64 years**	All incomes	5.5
	Under $4,000	5.0		Under $5,000	6.5
	4,000- 6,999	5.0		5,000- 9,999	5.8
	7,000- 9,999	5.3		10,000-14,999	5.2
	10,000 and over	5.1		15,000 and over	5.3
Ratio over 10,000 to under 4,000		1.02	Ratio over 15,000 to under 5,000		.81
65 years and over	All incomes	6.7	**65 years and over**	All incomes	6.7
	Under $4,000	6.3		Under $5,000	6.3
	4,000- 6,999	7.0		5,000- 9,999	6.8
	7,000- 9,999	7.8		10,000-14,999	6.9
	10,000 and over	8.3		15,000 and over	8.5
Ratio over 10,000 to under 4,000		1.32	Ratio over 15,000 to under 5,000		1.35

Sources: U.S. Department of Health, Education, and Welfare, National Center for
Health Statistics, *Physician Visits, by Place of Visit and Type of Service, U.S., July
1963-1964.* PHS Publication No. 1000 - series 10- no. 18, pp. 18, 19 and 29.
– Unpublished data for 1974 from the Health Interview Survey, National Center for
Health Statistics.

The proportion of the poor failing to see a physician over a two-year interval has fallen from 28 percent in the mid-1960s to 17 percent in 1973.[9] Low-income women have increasingly been seen by physicians early in the course of pregnancy (up from 58 percent in 1963 to 71 percent in 1970).[10]

Hospital care for the poor has dramatically increased from 14 hospital discharges for every 100 persons in 1964 to 24 per 100 persons in 1974.[11] The aged have also experienced marked increases in use of hospital services. In 1964, there were 19 hospital discharges for every 100 aged persons; by 1973 there were 35. Surgery rates have also increased among the poor, raising the concern that economic incentives may have led to excessive surgery on the poor and aged in some cases.

Dental care among the poor has improved somewhat relative to others, but a substantial gap in access to dental care persists with high-income persons seeing dentists more than twice as frequently as the poor (albeit contrasted with three and one-half times as frequently in 1964.)[12]

Medicare and Medicaid have brought financial protection against the burden of heavy medical bills for many of the elderly and the poor. Protection against the cost of hospital care—the most costly component of health care—has been particularly effective. Many aged persons and their children would be wiped out financially without this important coverage.

Comprehensive health centers, although established on only a limited demonstration basis, have been remarkably successful at achieving a wide range of goals.[13] They have provided employment to the poor and enabled them to upgrade their educational and job skills. They have been a force for economic development and human resources investment in low-income communities. They have served as a lever for social, economic, and political advancement of minorities. They have demonstrated that quality health care can be provided in low-income communities using innovative approaches to health care, including use of non-physician health professionals, outreach efforts, and community participation in the governance and operation of centers. They have overcome many of the multitude of barriers impeding access to health care and improvements of health of extremely poor communities. They have demonstrated that they can improve health in a variety of dimensions—such as reduced infant mor-

tality rates, reduced incidence of serious illness, and have succeeded in reducing hospitalization among the patients they serve
by 30 percent. Despite the fact that centers have taken a broad-
gauge approach to solving health problems of the poor, they have
demonstrated their ability to be cost effective. Costs per patient
served are comparable to the traditional sector. Cost savings from
reduced hospitalization and improved health indicate that they
are, in fact, a lower-cost alternative than traditional methods of
providing care.

The Remaining Gaps

While much progress has been made in the last decade in improving health care for the poor, it would be as wrong to be
complacent about these gains as it would be to ignore the genuine progress which has occurred. Many problems remain. The
health gap has been narrowed, but not eliminated. That which we
know how to do with modern medicine, some of it quite cheap-
ly, has not been disseminated to all.

Those most left behind in the current patchwork of private
insurance and public programs are the working poor, the unemployed, rural residents, minorities, and poor children. The elderly, even with Medicare, face many gaps in financial protection
against the high cost of illness and disability.

Medicaid is the major program financing health care for the
poor. It extends coverage to 23 million low-income people. Yet,
since it is tied to the welfare system, many are excluded from
benefits. Eligibility is largely restricted to the aged, blind, disabled, and one-parent families. Only 40 percent of the rural poor
and 60 percent of the urban poor fit these categories. The majority of the rural poor and a large segment of the urban poor are
families with both parents in the home, typically unemployed or
underemployed in marginal jobs. An estimated 8 to 10 million
people below the poverty level do not receive Medicaid benefits.
These individuals, and many like them just above the poverty
level, face great difficulty in obtaining even basic health care in a
time when average per-capita health expenditure for the family is
$1,360.[14]

Even for those covered by public programs, many inequities
remain. Medicare payments for physicians services are 60 percent
higher in metropolitan areas than in nonmetropolitan areas, and

85 percent higher in Western metropolitan areas than in nonmetropolitan areas of the South or North Central area (Table 5). Medicaid payments range from $210 per AFDC family in Mississippi to $1,570 in New York (Table 6). Even within states, wide variation in Medicaid expenditures occur. New York Medicaid expenditures per person eligible are 54 percent higher in New York City than in smaller urban and rural counties of New York.[15] Similarly, in Kentucky, Medicaid payments per person eligible are 58 percent higher in metropolitan areas than in nonmetropolitan areas.[16]

TABLE 5 Average medicare reimbursement for hospital and medical insurance by metropolitan-nonmetropolitan residence, 1972.

	Metropolitan counties			Non-metro-politan counties	Ratio, central to city counties to non-metro-politan counties
	Total	With central city	Without central city		
Annual hospital insurance reimbursement per person enrolled					
United States	$281	313	293	224	1.40
Northeast	322	377	316	249	1.51
North Central	283	324	286	236	1.37
South	231	256	243	204	1.25
West	305	328	300	234	1.40
Annual supplementary medical insurance reimbursement per person enrolled					
United States	$108	125	114	78	1.60
Northeast	125	136	126	84	1.62
North Central	88	101	94	73	1.38
South	96	115	100	75	1.53
West	137	150	140	96	1.56

Source: Calculated from U.S. Department of Health, Education, and Welfare, Social Security Administration, *Medicare, 1972, Section 1: Reimbursement by State and County*, DHEW Pub. No. (SSA) 75-11704, 1975, Table 1.1.3.

TABLE 6 Average Medicaid payments for persons eligible on the basis of receipt of aid to families with dependent children, Fiscal Year 1974

	Families	Children	Adults
United States*	$ 870	$190	$420
Alabama	550	90	380
Alaska	560	n.a.	n.a.
Arkansas	390	70	230
California	1,010	250	470
Colorado	520	100	310
Connecticut	800	170	430
Delaware	680	120	420
D.C.	1,120	230	600
Florida	390	70	250
Georgia	520	80	370
Hawaii	760	160	390
Idaho	890	140	640
Illinois	1,290	260	570
Indiana	730	150	410
Iowa	780	180	370
Kansas	950	170	710
Kentucky	540	100	330
Louisiana	390	70	230
Maine	880	150	510
Maryland	800	170	440
Massachusetts	1,000	300	300
Michigan	1,120	190	690
Minnesota	1,020	200	680
Mississippi	210	50	100
Missouri	350	70	220
Montana	680	140	460
Nebraska	790	160	470
Nevada	1,090	170	900

TABLE 6 (continued)

	Families	Children	Adults
New Hampshire	780	140	500
New Jersey	1,090	270	420
New Mexico	640	130	380
New York	1,570	460	440
North Carolina	500	70	420
North Dakota	700	130	480
Ohio	1,520	270	910
Oklahoma	540	160	170
Oregon	490	90	310
Pennsylvania	680	120	330
Rhode Island	930	180	510
South Carolina	400	50	290
South Dakota	500	90	330
Tennessee	400	80	250
Texas	820	130	520
Utah	820	180	440
Vermont	940	170	500
Virginia	800	150	460
Washington	610	140	310
West Virginia	670	130	300
Wisconsin	1,060	280	460
Wyoming	430	80	320

Source: U.S. House of Representatives, Committee on Interstate and Foreign Commerce, Subcommittee on Health and the Environment, *Data on the Medicaid Program: Eligibility, Services, Expenditures, Fiscal Years 1966-76,* January, 1976, pp. 60-61.

*Includes Guam, Puerto Rico, and Virgin Islands. Does not include Arizona which did not have a Medicaid program in 1974.

Inequitable distribution of benefits on the basis of race are also prevalent in both Medicare and Medicaid. The latest national figures indicate that Medicare payments per beneficiary are 35 percent higher for whites than for other elderly persons. For some services, particularly physician services and nursing home services, differentials are substantially greater. Extended care benefits, for example, are twice as high per white Medicare enrollee as for others.

Average Medicaid payments are 70 percent higher for white recipients than for others (Table 7). Again, nursing home services

TABLE 7 Medicaid recipients and payments and poor persons, by race and region, 1969.

	White	Other	Ratio, white to other
Medicaid payments per recipient			
United States*	$376	$213	1.76
Northeast	363	205	1.77
North Central	447	249	1.79
South	322	180	1.78
Ratio of Medicaid recipients to poor persons			
United States*	.53	.69	.76
Northeast	1.68	1.94	.86
North Central	.32	.79	.40
South	.26	.31	.83
Medicaid payments per poor person			
United States*	$200	$147	1.36
Northeast	611	399	1.53
North Central	146	197	.74
South	85	56	1.51

*Based on data for 24 states including: Northeast–Connecticut and New York; North Central–Illinois, Iowa, Michigan, Minnesota, Missouri, North Dakota, Ohio, South Dakota, Wisconsin; South–Delaware, D.C., Georgia, Kentucky, Louisiana, Maryland, Oklahoma, Texas; West (now shown)–Montana, Nevada, New Mexico, Wyoming, and Idaho.

are the most inequitably distributed, with average payments almost 5 times higher for white Medicaid recipients as for others.[17] Recent data from the Georgia Medicaid program indicate that whites average Medicaid payments of $587 for all services, while blacks and others average $271.[18]

Most of the major health programs have been geared toward the needs of poor elderly persons and adults. About 70 percent of all Medicare and Medicaid expenditures go for institutional care. Basic services for poor children tend to receive little attention. Medicaid has implemented an early and periodic screening, diagnosis, and treatment program for Medicaid-covered children. However, this program spends less than three-tenths of 1 percent of all Medicaid funds, and reaches only about 13 percent of eligible children each year. As a result of this limited attention to the needs of children, poor children continue to lag well behind others in access to basic medical services. In 1973, poor children were 57 percent more likely not to have seen a physician in two years than non poor children, and 58 percent more likely not to have seen a dentist in two years. Immunizations against diptheria, tetanus, whooping cough, rubella, and polio are dangerously low among poor pre-school children.

The aged, even with Medicare and Medicaid, also face gaps in health care. Despite these programs and the low incomes of the aged, the aged pay more for their own health than do non-aged adults. Private payments by the elderly averaged $536 per person (including their Medicare premiums) compared with expenditures of $330 made privately by nonaged adults. Medicare and Medicaid have been particularly ineffectual in protecting the elderly against the cost of physicians' services where private payments by the elderly have increased from $66 per capita in 1966 to $156 in 1975 (including the Medicare premium—see Table 8). Exclusion of some services such as prescription drugs, eye glasses, hearing aids, and dentures, and limits on nursing home care in Medicare have added to this financial burden. Some elderly have been excluded from Medicare coverage since they are not covered by Social Security. Open-ended requirements that the elderly pay a fixed proportion of all medical bills, and options which permit physicians to charge patients in addition to what Medicare will pay, make the elderly particularly vulnerable to the cost of physicians' services.

These gaps and deficiencies are all problems which need to be solved. The task remaining is not inconsequential, but it is not insurmountable either. Continued progress will require renewed dedication, and stronger Federal leadership.

TABLE 8 Medical care expenditures of persons aged 65 and older, by type of service and source of payment, 1966 and 1975.

	Per capita		Percentage distribution	
	1966	1975	1966	1975
All medical services	$441	$1,360	100.0	100.0
Public	132	825	29.9	60.7
Medicare premium	— —	67	— —	5.0
Out-of-pocket	234	390	53.1	28.7
Private insurance	70	79	15.9	5.8
Hospital services	$182	$603	100.0	100.0
Public	89	541	48.9	89.7
Private	93	62	51.1	10.3
Physician services	$71	$218	100.0	100.0
Public	5	62	7.0	28.4
Medicare premium	—	67	—	30.7
Private	66	89	93.0	40.8
Nursing home services	$65	$342	100.0	100.0
Public	24	183	36.9	53.5
Private	41	160	63.1	46.8
Drugs	$62	$118	100.0	100.0
Public	5	15	8.1	12.7
Private	58	102	93.6	86.4
Other medical services	$61	79	100.0	100.0
Public	10	24	16.4	30.4
Private	51	56	83.6	70.9

Sources: Marjorie Smith Mueller and Robert M. Gibson, "Age Differences in Health Care Spending, Fiscal Year 1975," *Research and Statistics Note*, Note No. 11, May 17, 1976, Table 2; M.S. Mueller, and R.M. Gibson, "National Health Expenditures, Fiscal Year 1975," *Social Security Bulletin*, no. 2, vol. 39, February, 1976.

The Decade Ahead

In the coming years, Federal health policy faces great challenges. It must try to ensure access to health care for all citizens, guarantee that minimum standards of quality are met, combat ever-rising health care costs, and protect citizens from the financial burdens of high health care costs.

In the next decade, the health policy agenda is likely to focus on three objectives: (1) limiting the rise in health care costs: (2) improving access to primary health services in underserved areas; (3) reforming the financing of health care services. All of these objectives are interrelated, and some policies such as national health insurance can be specifically designed to contribute toward the achievement of all three policy areas.

Limiting the Rise in Health Care Costs

While all of the forces leading to higher health care costs are not well understood, the basic underlying cause is the elimination of private market forces which work automatically to curb inflation in other industries. As private insurance and public programs have expanded, patients have had less and less direct financial stake in the cost of care. Physicians, other health care professionals, and health facilities have responded to this increased purchasing power for health care by expanding the range and quality of health care services available. The vacuum created by the displacement of private incentives to curtail costs has not been filled by nonmarket mechanisms of cost control. Instead, most third-party payers of health care services have been placed in a passive position of responding to the demands of health care providers for adequate levels of compensation for a proliferating range of expensive services.

There is little agreement on how to counter this inflation in health care costs. One approach is to "undo" the growth of private and public coverage for health care services, and recreate direct financial incentives on the part of patients to police the health care system. This would be accomplished by eliminating tax provisions which encourage the growth of first-dollar private health insurance and public provision or private mandating of a national health insurance plan with greater direct patient payments for care.

Other strategies recognize that insurance against at least major medical expenses is both inevitable and desirable. In a day in which the average hospital stay costs $1,200 and many stays run into the thousands of dollars, protecting families against financial hardship quickly becomes incompatible with substantial patient incentives to curtail costs through paying a sizable fraction of the bill.

Thus, most analysts agree that other strategies for cost control must be pursued in lieu of or in conjunction with automatic market incentives. One strategy is reimplementation of the type of cost controls prevalent under the Economic Stabilization Program. While this program was reasonably effective over a short period, it is unlikely that the type of rigid cost controls introduced during that period would have sufficient flexibility to deal with dynamic changes in the health care industry. Enforcement of such controls would be increasingly difficult over time, particularly if the health care industry was singled out for special controls.

Another strategy, which was recommended by the Ford Administration, is to curtail levels of reimbursement for health services provided under publicly financed programs. This strategy is largely ineffectual so long as hospitals, physicians, and other providers have the power to shift the distribution of patients or the allocation of costs. Hospitals will either refuse to accept such patients, or charge other patients more to make up the deficit. Physicians can refuse to accept patients (as they have in Medicaid) or charge patients extra on top of government levels of reimbursement (as they have in Medicare). Thus, this strategy merely shifts the locus of cost away from the Federal Government to covered persons or to other patients, but does little to constrain total costs.

Another strategy is to curtail costs through detailed regulation and review of all services and health facilities to ferret out any which might not be "necessary." Professional standards review organizations and utilization review committees have been established to look at the necessity of hospitalization or surgery and appropriateness of length of hospital stay. Certificate-of-need legislation and health planning bodies have been created to try to restrain the building of hospital beds and acquisition of capital equipment. The effectiveness of this strategy and its implications for access to quality health care have not yet been adequately demonstrated.

One attractive strategy for trying to lower costs over the long term is to emphasize non-medical ways of improving health. This strategy would attempt to reduce long-run costs by effecting health improvements at the individual or community level. Pursuit of good personal health habits, such as moderation in eating, drinking, smoking, and adequate exercise, would be encouraged by public exhortation or financial incentives. Improvements in health through greater attention to occupational health and safety, environmental pollution, hazardous chemicals and additives in food and water would be another avenue toward long-term cost reduction. Unfortunately, there is little information available on the effectiveness of alternative ways to induce behavioral change, or on the tradeoffs involved in tighter environmental and occupational health and safety regulations.

One proven method of achieving reductions in total health care costs is reorganization of the delivery of health care services. Health maintenance organizations which have a financial incentive to provide care efficiently and avoid costly methods of treatment have a record of lower hospitalization rates. Comprehensive health centers which pay physicians on a salary basis, promote the use of non-physician health professionals to substitute for physician time, and combine the provision of medical services with non-medical services such as nutrition, patient education, and counseling, and environmental health activities have been successful in improving health, reducing costly hospitalization, and lowering total cost of care. Greater emphasis upon these and other innovative methods of organizing and delivering health care services may be essential in future years as hospital bed capacity continues to grow and the number of physicians entering practice in the U.S. increases at an unprecedented rate.

Finally, one strategy which would integrate many of these initiatives is a fundamental restructuring of the financing of health care through national health insurance. Under the current system, a number of separate organizations and agencies pay the health care bill. Medicaid pays a portion. Blue Cross, Blue Shield, and a host of private insurance companies pay a large share of the remainder. These organizations are fragmented, and have no unifying policy regarding reimbursement. They are basically in a reactive posture, responding to costs or charges imposed by hospitals, physicians, and other health providers. No one payer can attempt to hold down total costs, for to do so would result in less advantageous treatment of the patients they represent. By consolidating all "purchasers" of health care into a single unit, such as through a national health insurance plan, one agency would have the power to bargain collectively with hospitals and physicians regarding a "fair" level of reimbursement. This agency would be in a position to negotiate the best possible deal for all patients, without concern that preferential treatment would be given to patients financed under another plan.

If carefully designed, national health insurance can be a powerful tool for lowering costs and improving the health care system. In addition to the cost control potential which can be realized as the sole purchaser of health care, there are four major mechanisms through which these goals can be pursued: (1) aggressive use of the reimbursement mechanism to encourage more efficient and responsive provision of health care services; (2) funnelling a fixed share of all expenditures into a health resources development fund to create new resources in under-served areas; (3) promoting some automatic cost control incentives through reasonable patient payments; and (4) using sources of financing which create incentives for efficiency and health improvements.

Toward Improved Primary Health Services in Underserved Areas

Because there are significant obstacles facing improved primary health services, a broad-gauged systems approach will be required to effect permanent change. Many of the past failures in attracting or retaining primary health providers in underserved areas can be traced to their narrow focus on only a single aspect of the health care system. An overall strategy for change should be based upon changing the nature, content, and organization of practice in underserved areas, changing the methods of training health professionals, altering the current methods of reimbursing health care under public and private programs, and changing legal restrictions which impede innovations in health service delivery.

Particular solutions should be designed with the needs of given areas in mind. The best approach for a small rural place is likely to be quite different from that of a larger town. Areas with a concentration of poverty or of particular racial/ethnic barriers may require still different approaches.

While much remains to be learned about the most effective approaches for different types of underserved areas, there are three organizational models of health service delivery which strikes us as promising: (1) primary health centers staffed primarily by full-time primary health practitioners rather than physicians; (2) new types of group health practices and team approaches; (3) comprehensive health centers providing a wide range of health and health-related services.

Comprehensive health centers appear to be particularly appropriate for areas where poverty is deeply engrained, where nutritional and environmental factors are major contributors to poor health, where health care can be used to promote community development, or where discriminatory or insensitive practices on the part of existing providers exclude minorities from adequate primary health services.

Primary health centers work well in small rural places which cannot economically support a physician or which are not attractive to physicians as practice locations. Use of local primary health practitioners can provide a stable source of health care if provided in a community-sponsored organizational setting. This model may also be appropriate in some inner-city neighborhoods, where it is important to have primary health providers familiar with the home and community context of health problems.

Community-sponsored group medical practices using a team approach to care can also be valuable in medium-sized towns serving a larger rural population (6,000 to 20,000 people) or inner-city areas. A professional manager can help make a group practice economically viable, even in relatively low-income areas through promotion of more efficient methods of management, familiarity with sources of funding for center activities, and better collection of patient bills. Delegation of some tasks to lesser trained health professionals can also relieve physicians and make more efficient use of existing physicians. An organizational arrangement which permits time off for continuing education, interaction with professional peers, and supporting services from laboratories and other types of professionals can be attractive to physicians and other primary providers.

All of these approaches try to change the current health care system, rather than working within the current mode of private practice or traditional hospital outpatient departments. They share in common a strong emphasis upon nonprofit organizational structures with community boards, use of primary physicians and primary health practitioners on a salaried basis, and the substitution of less specialized for more specialized personnel wherever possible without undermining quality standards.

Reform of Medicare

Medicare and Medicaid have done much to assist those who are poorly served by the private health insurance system. They have protected many elderly and poor persons from the high cost of medical care, and aided their access to medical care services. Despite these programs, many gaps remain in coverage of needy persons and in adequate ceilings on payments required of the aged.

Sensible reform of these programs is urgently needed—both to eliminate the remaining need of the poor for financial protection and to lay the groundwork for integrating health care for the poor in a national health insurance plan for all.

Reform of Medicare is perhaps the easier task. The Comprehensive Medicare Reform Act introduced by Senator Abraham Ribicoff would go a long way toward eliminating the present deficiencies of Medicare. Under this plan, the hospitalization and supplementary medical insurance parts of Medicare would be merged into a single integrated plan which would be available to all elderly persons without a premium charge. All persons 65 or older would be covered, as well as the disabled currently covered by Medicare.

The range of benefits would be extended to include all services currently covered by Medicaid including unlimited hospital care, outpatient hospital care, skilled nursing and intermediate care services, home health services, dental services, physicians' services, laboratory and radiology services, prescription drugs, medical supplies and devices, ambulance and non-emergency transportation services where special problems of access exist, some mental health day services, and a range of supporting services.

Under the Ribicoff proposal patient copayments would be assessed on all services subject to a ceiling. Rather than the flat amounts established in the Ribicoff plan such as $5 per day of hospital care, it is recommended that patient payments be a fixed percentage of total charges—such as 20 percent for all services. These payments, however, would be subject to ceilings set at reasonable levels in relation to patient income so that no elderly person would face undue financial burden. The ceilings set forth in the Ribicoff proposal vary from zero for a single elderly person with income below $2,110 ($2,730 for a couple) rising to a maximum of $750 for a family income of $12,500 or more. Thus, very low-income elderly persons would not be required to make any contributions toward their care while, with a coinsurance rate of 20 percent on all services, even moderately well-to-do elderly persons would not be required to contribute toward their health care bills after they had incurred a total health expenditure of $3,750 or a net cost to them of $750. That is, patient payments would not exceed 6 percent of income, and that would only occur in the event of serious illness.

Other features of the Ribicoff proposal which should be incorporated are new provisions requiring that all institutions, physicians, and other providers desiring to have their services covered by the plan must file a participation agreement with the Secretary of HEW. Physicians would be required to accept the established charge as payment in full, or not participate at all. However, an effort would be made to set annually predetermined fee schedules in a fair way to ensure adequate participation in the plan.

Such a plan should be financed with a combination of general revenues and payroll tax revenues applied to the Social Security trust fund. General revenues could be set at a level sufficient to subsidize lower ceilings for the elderly with incomes below $12,500. Coverage would be automatic, and no premiums would be assessed.

Cost control measures, such as those contained in the Talmadge proposal should be included in the Medicare reform package. Reforms of reimbursement of hospital-based physicians and other reforms of institutional payments contained in the Talmadge proposal are particularly worthy of inclusion. Prospective methods of reimbursement for hospital services, and innovative approaches to controlling long-term institutional costs should be attempted. Alternatives to long-term care such as promotion of home health services, and better utilization review of nursing home patients should be pursued to curb the high level of resources going to this sector.

More equitable treatment of minorities should be promoted through stricter inspection and enforcement of nondiscriminatory provisions. Physicians, as participating providers, should also be required to be in compliance with Title VI of the Civil Rights Act. Greater informational efforts to advise minority persons of their benefits and rights should be promoted.

Rural residents could be assisted through changes in reimbursement policies and in creation of a special health resources development fund which would receive a portion of Medicare revenues to promote the development of resources in underserved areas. Establishment of a nationally uniform physician fee schedule, rather than local schedules as proposed by the Ribicoff plan, would be one important step. Provision for the coverage of nurse practitioner and physician assistant services rendered in primary health centers meeting certain standards should be made and separate reimbursement policies established for such centers. A fixed percentage of Medicare revenues should be set aside in a health resources development fund to promote the development of innovative methods of health services delivery in underserved areas.

Reforming Medicaid as the First Phase in National Health Insurance: A Recommended Plan of Action

The U.S. health care system is in need of major, widespread reform. Some reform can be achieved by making more efficient use of existing resources. Other changes, while likely to reduce the total health care bill over time, will require an increased public share. In a time of generally scarce governmental budgetary resources, choices among alternative programs must be made with care. It is essential that priority be given to cope with the greatest needs first.

Since national health insurance is a key component of fundamental, system-wide change, I recommend a two-phase National Health Security Plan. The first phase should be targeted on the greatest health needs, as well as lay the essential groundwork for a successful comprehensive national health insurance plan to begin in a second phase two or three years following enactment of the plan. It is important that both phases be legislatively approved now so that sensible plans and steps can begin to move toward health care as a right for all our nation's people.

The first phase would contain three elements: (1) reform of the Medicaid program and creation of a safety net against the possibility of ruinous medical expenses for all Americans in a single, coordinated plan; (2) tighter controls on abuse in Federal health programs and creation of positive incentives for cost control through vigorous use of the reimbursement mechanism; and (3) investment in health resource development to improve performance in the health care system and create additional resources in underserved communities.

The second phase would provide universal, comprehensive national health insurance for all. Continued control of health care costs would be achieved through a unified reimbursement system covering all patients, physicians, other health personnel, and facilities. Continued emphasis upon health resources development and improved health system performance would help assure that benefits are extended to all Americans, that health care costs are contained, and within the financial means of all.

In the first phase, priority should be given to reforming the Medicaid program to provide uniform benefits for all the poor, and at the same time meeting the most important needs of the non-poor in a single, coordinated plan. The plan would provide uniform, comprehensive benefits to all the poor—regardless of employment status, family composition, or geographical location. In addition, it would include some assistance to lower-income working families with inadequate private insurance coverage, and a safety net for even middle-income families without adequate major medical coverage. This would be accomplished through a provision which would assist middle- and higher-income families in paying their bills if out-of-pocket expenses were excessive in relation to their income. Under one illustrative schedule shown in Table 9, a family with income of $8,000 would be assisted if out-of-pocket medical expenses exceeded $750 and even families with $10,000 income or above would be assisted if out-of-pocket expenses exceeded $1,250. Such a plan would not eliminate private insurance plans but would act as a safety net for any one currently excluded from private plans or whose plans contained extensive exclusions and limits.

The first phase would also place major emphasis on health care cost control, through better administration of Federal health programs and restructuring of incentives through reimbursement provisions. The reimbursement structure should be redesigned to discourage costly institutional care and to encourage primary health services. Specific steps include: (1) reduction of physician fees for institutional services; (2) making physicians economically neutral with regard to diagnostic tests and choice of treatment through flat payments per patient served; (3) higher payments for primary health services, particularly in rural areas where physicians are now penalized by the reimbursement systems; (4) favorable reimbursement to encourage the growth of nonprofit, community controlled comprehensive health centers and primary health centers; (5) conversion of hospital-based physicians to reasonable salary reimbursement; and (6) continued experimentation with prospective methods of hospital reimbursement which give physicians, hospital administrators, and hospital employees an incentive to control costs.

The final essential action which should be incorporated in the first phase is the establishment of a health resources development

TABLE 9 Illustrative schedule of patient payments under phase 1 (based on a family of four)

Family income	Deductible* (per family)	Coinsurance	Ceiling on family payments
$5,000 or below	0	0	0
6,000	$250	25%	$400
8,000	750	25	1,200
10,000 and above	1,250	25	2,000

*Deductible is a spend-down provision which requires families to pay 25 percent of their income above the base income ($5,000 for a family of four) before benefits of the plan begin. Only directly incurred, out-of-pocket expenses would apply toward the deductible.

fund which would receive a fixed percentage allotment of all expenditures under the National Health Security Plan. The major objectives of this program would be to create new ambulatory health centers in underserved areas and to provide for the training of community health workers and primary health practitioners recruited from and trained in underserved areas. Different approaches would be tailored to the needs of individual communities. In small towns, primary health centers staffed with new health practitioners have been demonstrated to provide quality primary health services in a system of health care that established training standards, protocols for routine patient care, on-going supervision and quality monitoring, and procedures for referral to more specialized health personnel and facilities where appropriate. In larger towns and cities, group medical practices using a team approach to health care warrants further development. A nonprofit organizational form with community control should help assure that surpluses are devoted to preventive care and to the solution of environmental and community health problems, rather than enhancing physician incomes. In areas of severe poverty where health problems are deeply engrained and linked to inadequate nutrition, limited patient education, and environmental health hazards, a more comprehensive health center approach is warranted. Such centers have documented their cost effectiveness through improved health of patients and reduced hospitalization.

These steps should lay the groundwork for universal, comprehensive national health insurance in the second phase, following within two or three years implementation of more limited coverage. This would provide a single plan for all, replacing private health insurance plans and Medicare for the elderly.

Such a move is essential to achieve strong controls over the ever-escalating health care bill. A single plan covering all patients would be capable of negotiating with physicians, hospitals, and other health care personnel and facilities for a level of reimbursement which is fair both to those providing services and those paying for them. It would replace the current system of private insurance plans and public programs which have proven impotent on an individual basis to deal with escalating hospital costs and the costly use of resources.

This plan, however, would not place the entire burden of cost

TABLE 10. Illustrative schedule of patient payments under phase 2 (based on family of four)

Family income	Deductible (per family)	Coinsurance	Ceiling on family payments
$5,000 or below	0	0	0
6,000	$60	25	$200
8,000	180	25	600
10,000 and above	300	25	1,000

control on the reimbursement mechanism. Patients would continue to pay some portion of their own health care bills, but these payments would be designed in such a way that no family would be subject to financial hardship. Table 10 indicates one schedule of patient payments. Since coverage would be expected to replace current private insurance coverage, rather than merely act as a safety net for gaps in private coverage, only modest patient payments are retained.

The health resources development fund and effective health care cost controls developed in the first phase would be carried over and expanded in the second phase to assure continued conversion of the health care system to a more efficient and equitably distributed system of health care delivery.

Financing such a plan should minimize disruptions in current sources of payment. Employer contributions to private insurance plans should be replaced by tax payments to the plan. Other costs of the plan would be financed out of general revenues accruing from a return to full employment and sound economic growth, and improved efficiency in the production of health and health care. Rather than threatening to bankrupt the Federal budget, as some opponents assert, a moderate public National Health Security Plan could be financed without necessitating increases in personal income taxes. Instead, a carefully designed plan could assure quality health care to all Americans and act as a strong force to promote efficiency and economy in the provision of health care services.

References

[1] For more detailed documentation of the trends presented in this section, see Karen Davis, *Health and the War on Poverty: A Ten Year Appraisal*, Brookings Institution, forthcoming.

[2] See, for example, U.S. Department of Health, Education, and Welfare, National Center for Health Statistics, *Health, United States, 1975*.

[3] U.S. Department of Health, Education, and Welfare, National Center for Health Statistics, *Health, United States, 1975*, pp. 359-61.

[4] U.S. Department of Health, Education, and Welfare, National Center for Health Statistics, *Monthly Vital Statistics Reports*, vol. 24, no. 11, February 3, 1976.

[5] U.S. Department of Health, Education, and Welfare, National Center for Health Statistics, *Monthly Vital Statistics Reports*, vol. 23, no. 13, May 30, 1975.

[6] U.S. Department of Health, Education, and Welfare, National Center for Health Statistics, *Health, United States, 1975*, January, 1976 and PHS Pub. No. 1000, Series 10, no. 48, *Prevalence of Selected Impairments, United States, July 1963-June 1965*, November, 1968.

[7] Ronald W. Wilson, and Elijah L. White, "Changes in Morbidity, Disability and Utilization Differentials Between the Poor and the Non-Poor," data from the Health Interview Survey: 1964 and 1973, table 7.

[8] See Karen Davis and Roger Reynolds, "The Impact of Medicare and Medicaid on Access to Medical Care," in Richard Rosett (ed.), *The Role of Insurance in the Health Service Section*, an NBER-Universities Conference, New York, National Bureau of Economic Research, 1976.

[9] U.S. Department of Health, Education, and Welfare, National Center for Health Statistics, *Health, United States, 1975*, DHEW Publication No. (HRA) 76-1232, pp. 289, 409, 507, 509, and 569.

[10] Ronald A. Andersen, *et al.*, *Health Service Use, National Trends and Variations, 1953-1971*, p. 22.

[11] U.S. Department of Health, Education, and Welfare, National Center for Health Statistics, *Health, United States, 1975*, DHEW Pub. No. (HRA) 76-1232, pp. 309, 413, 513, 515, 185; and *Hospital Discharges and Length of Stay: Short-Stay Hospitals, U.S. July 63-June 64*, PHS Pub. No. 1000, Series 10, no. 30, June, 1966, pp. 36, 37, and 50.

[12] U.S. Department of Health, Education, and Welfare, National Center for Health Statistics, *Dental Visits, U.S., July 1963-June 1964*, PHS Pub. No. 1000, Series 10, no. 23, October, 1965, pp. 18 and 42. Unpublished data for 1974 from the Health Interview Survey, National Center for Health Statistics.

[13] See Karen Davis, *Health and the War on Poverty: A Ten Year Appraisal*, Chapter 5, "Neighborhood Health Centers: A New Approach to Health Care Delivery," Brookings Institution, forthcoming.

[14] Based on two nonaged adults at $470 per person and two children at $210. Marjorie Smith Mueller and Robert M. Gibson, "Age Differences in Health Care Spending, Fiscal Year 1975," *Research and Statistics,* Note No. 11 (May 17, 1976), DHEW Pub. No. (SSA) 76-11701.

[15] New York State Department of Social Services, *Statistical Supplement to Annual Report for 1974,* Pub. No. 1053; and U.S. Department of Commerce, Bureau of the Census, *General Social and Economic Characteristics, Census of the Population, 1970,* table 80, New York.

[16] Kentucky Medical Assistance Program, *Report of Services Rendered, Fiscal Year 1972-73.*

[17] Unpublished state Medicaid reports, 1969.

[18] Unpublished Georgia 2082 Report form based on 5 percent sample, 1974.

David Warner

11

Governing the Medical Care System and the Health Programs of the Sixties

The primary goal of the medical care programs of the Kennedy and Johnson Administrations was to extend mainstream medical care services to the unserved poor and elderly. Subsidiary concerns such as reorganizing the medical care system, or controlling the cost of medical services, were paid lip service; but they were not made the major focus of administrative concern until the late sixties and early seventies. Although these priorities were reasonable in the context of the problems of the early sixties, one consequence of these programs has been the development of a rapidly growing medical care system which has begun to appear to follow its own internal logic rather than the needs of the population at large. Here, we will briefly trace the development and administration of the programs, discuss the evolving medical care system, identify some longer-term trends in manpower supply and medical care organization, and finally suggest some approaches to ensuring more community and individual control over the health services delivered.

The Organization of the Programs

The two principal concerns within the Johnson Administration regarding the success of Medicare were that individuals not be kept from enrolling because of the welfare stigma and that providers of health care provide treatment to enrollees in these programs equal to that received by their other patients. In order to reduce any possible stigma which Medicare might have, and as an insurance program restricted to Social Security enrollees it did not have much, a concerted publicity campaign was launched to sign up prominent elderly Americans. Former President Truman and his wife Bess received the first two Medicare cards. President Johnson had signed the bill at the Presidential Library in Independence, Missouri, and Jimmy Durante, Bob Hope, and other celebrities were enrolled publicly and in a way that undercut any possible intimidation of potential enrollees.[1] The experience in the Medicaid program, which was to be administered by state welfare departments that had an interest in controlling expenditures, was quite different. It was explicitly welfare medicine. And although many citizens received mainstream medical services for the first time, many others did not enroll because they wished to avoid the means test and the welfare label attached.[2]

Efforts to insure equal availability of services under Medicare and Medicaid were particularly important in light of the opposition of the American Medical Association (AMA) and some other portions of the medical care system to their passage. In addition to concern that enrolled individuals receive treatment, the Administration made clear that Title VI of the Civil Rights Act would be rigorously enforced and that even such policies as admission to semi-private rooms would be on a first-come, first-served basis. Information collected by the Department of Health, Education, and Welfare shows that between 1966 and 1969 the number of minority patients in hospitals increased 30 percent, that the number of hospitals serving minorities increased 24 percent, and that the number of hospitals with minority-group physicians and dentists on their staffs increased 61 percent.[3]

These successes in implementing a national program of medical care entitlements did not come without compromise. The Medicare act explicitly prohibited Federal interference with medical practice, guaranteed enrollees freedom of choice of medical provider, and the Administration agreed to compensate physicians on the basis of customary and usual fees. For hospitals and to a lesser extent nursing homes the arrangements were equally attractive. The Bureau of Health Insurance of the Social Security Administration, which was charged with administering the Medicare program, agreed to reimburse hospitals on a cost basis for Medicare patients and to accept Joint Commission on Accreditation of Hospitals (JCAH) accreditation and development of a utilization review plan as sufficient conditions for certification for the program.

Cost reimbursement of hospitals was designed primarily to ensure that the Medicare program was not paying for other patients or subsidizing services such as obstetrics, which Medicare enrollees would clearly not use. Although these regulations gained protection from fraud or rip-offs, they also significantly altered the fiscal environment in which medical institutions functioned. In particular the transformation of those patients, the poor and the old, who had been formerly subsidized by private patients and local charity into holders of open ended vouchers who would be able to pay for any services provided, reduced many of the fiscal constraints upon hospital expenditure. In the short run this change especially benefited institutions which already had a large endowment, large expenditures, an indigent population to serve and were located in states that adopted a generous Medicaid program. In the longer run the reimbursement of depreciation on capital expenditures as an allowable cost and other subsidies have permitted most hospitals to grow very rapidly with little control over the redundancy of specialized services in the community or the level of aggregate expenditure for hospital services. Similarly the transformation of indigent patients who were treated free or by ability to pay into citizens with vouchers who pay customary and usual fees led to a rapid escalation of physicians' incomes and ironically reduced consumer sovereignty and local needs as a constraint upon the individual practitioner's autonomy, ability to specialize, and define his or her role in the system.

The Evolution of the System, 1966-1976

In 1964 the Task Force on Health appointed by President Johnson pointed out that "in 1950 the average cost per day in a hospital was $15.92, by 1963, this had risen to $38.91, an increase of 149 percent while the consumer price index increased by 27 percent". By 1975 the expense per adjusted patient day in community hospitals was $128.26, an increase over 1963 of 329 percent.[4] In the same 12 years between 1963 and 1975 total health expenditures increased from little more than $30 billion to $118.5 billion. In fiscal year 1977 total expenditures for health care will be close to $150 billion, nearly 9 percent of GNP, or almost $700 for each resident of the United States. This enormous escalation in cost is the result of increased funds to pay for health care which have led to improved facilities, better trained health manpower in larger numbers, and greater utilization of medical services. The cost figures alone hardly begin to reflect the great changes that have been taking place in the last three decades, which were accelerated by the Great Society health programs and entitlements.

Just as virtually no home construction took place between

1930-1945, hospital assets decreased during the same period. Between 1947 and 1974 the Hill-Burton program allocated $14.5 billion for hospital construction and renovation of which $4.1 billion was Federal money and $10.4 billion came from state and local sources.[5] It is difficult to calculate total capital expenditures of hospitals for this period but since 1970 total construction costs for hospitals appear to have been in excess of $29 billion.[6] In addition, expenditures for medical equipment and supplies are currently $4.3 billion annually.[7] Although the total number of hospital beds has declined slightly in the last 10 years, the number of beds in community hospitals has increased from 721,000 in 1964 to 926,000 in 1974. The offsetting decline in other hospital beds during this decade was the result primarily of the development of outpatient treatment of psychiatric patients through drugs and community mental health centers, which led to a decline of 345,820 psychiatric beds, and successful treatment of tuberculosis with chemotherapy, leading to a decrease of 33,223 in TB beds.[8]

By 1976 all observers agree that virtually every community in the United States is adequately served with community hospital facilities. Rather than developing a method to subsidize expensive overhead facilities for use in emergencies, the problem has become one of rationing such facilities. It has become clear that permitting hospitals carte blanche in borrowing to do what they like and paying the loan back through Medicare, Medicaid, and private insurance reimbursement (the percent of hospital construction financed by debt increased from 32 to 58 percent between 1969 and 1974) can only lead to further loss of control. This proliferation of acute care facilities and resources has accelerated as private practitioners have begun to acquire brain scanners and other similar extremely expensive diagnostic and treatment equipment for use in their private offices. Indeed customary and usual reimbursement of fees combined with investment tax credits have made such equipment far more financially attractive to the individual practitioner or small groups of physicians than society could possibly desire.[9]

The increase in numbers and sophistication of medical professionals has paralleled the growing availability of health facilities and equipment. The financing of residencies through the GI bill after World War II was the mechanism by which most physicians began to receive specialist training. Through the fifties and into the early sixties there was very little increase, however, in the number of physicians being trained in American medical schools. In 1964 there were 269,552 active physicians in the United States. By 1974 this number has increased by 35 percent to 362,973 or 171 physicians per 100,000 population.[10] This increase was due in part to the increased enrollment in U.S. medical schools and in part to an influx of foreign medical graduates, 37,597 of whom were licensed during this period. Even if no more foreign medical graduates enter the United States, the increase in capacity of U.S. medical schools and the stock of physicians already in residencies will guarantee that by 1985 there will be more than 480,000 active physicians in the United States for a ratio of 207.2 physicians per 100,000.[11] This is a physician/population ratio which is only exceeded currently in California, Connecticut, Maryland, Massachusetts, and New York. And in each of these states far more physicians are engaged in research and training programs than will be likely in the nation at large.

This rapid increase in the number of well-trained physicians represents at once an opportunity and yet has the potential to reduce the effectiveness of the kind of medical system we are likely to have. As an opportunity, this increased number of physicians may diminish geographical disparities in physician distribution, rationalize the organization of medical practice, and lead to a reduction in physician compensation down toward the level earned by comparably trained professionals, while at the same time a proliferation of physicians may lead to an exacerbation of many of the most inappropriate developments in modern medicine.

The much-deplored lack of physicians in rural areas is a problem that is receiving increased attention, yet, even without the attention I believe that natural forces under way would alleviate it. The 10 states which had less than 100 physicians per 100,000 in 1965 (Alabama, Alaska, Arkansas, Idaho, Kentucky, Mississippi, North Dakota, South Carolina, South Dakota, and Wyoming) still are quite low with all but South Carolina and Kentucky below or very near the 100 per 100,000 ratio. These severe deficit states are generally the least populous; the combined population of all 10 is less than that of either New

York or California. Consequently 6,000 new physicians spread across these 10 states would lift the ratio in each state to 145 per 100,000. Six thousand physicians is comparable to one-tenth the number of physicians currently in residency training and is one-half the number in graduate training in New York. Given current budgetary stringency in many of the surplus states many of these physicians may emigrate to deficit states, some of which have recently experienced economic growth with the increase in prices of agricultural products, the growing demand for raw materials, and the movement of industry from the Northeast. Although there are also 145 counties out of 3,084 which did not have an active physician in patient care in 1973, they are sparsely populated and approximately 750 physicians would bring these counties up to an "acceptable" physician/population ratio of 140 physicians per 100,000 population.[1][2]

It is difficult to predict exactly how this increased number of physicians will affect the specialization and organization of medical practice. There are generally already far more specialists per capita in the United States than are found in other countries. The recent report of the main surgical organizations, *Surgery in the United States* states that 50-60,000 board-certified surgeons and 10-12,000 interns and residents could probably provide sufficient surgical care for the United States for the next 40 to 50 years. They estimate that an average of 1,600 to 1,650 new board-certified surgeons from 1972-1982 would maintain a stable surgeon to population ratio.[1][3] In fact the graduate training pipeline is currently producing surgeons at a rate far in excess of these stated needs. In September, 1973, there were 5,846 first year residents in surgical specialties. If one-third of the projected U.S. medical graduates and foreign medical graduate entries (5,000 entering graduate training per year after 1973) enter graduate training programs in surgery until 1980 and 95 percent eventually become board-certified, the annual 1973-1985 production rate of surgeons will be three times that necessary to stabilize the surgeon/population ratio. Looked at another way, by 1985 there would be approximately 46,000 more board-certified surgeons than necessary to stabilize the surgeon/population ratio. This would amount to an excess of board-certified surgeons roughly equal to the entire 1968 stock of surgeons.[1][4] Although it is true that there are approximately 30,000 non-board-certified surgeons, general practitioners, and osteopaths who currently practice surgery who could be replaced by these new specialists, there is no doubt that training programs could be sharply curtailed and the training of new surgeons reduced.

As physicians in general, and specialists in particular, become more available there may be attendant changes in the organization of the medical care system. If the training pipeline is shortened and many specialty training programs are eliminated, the rationale will no longer exist for many tertiary care facilities where most specialized components have been continued as much for training programs as for the care they actually provide. As a result specialized facilities and activities may be consolidated on a regional basis—leading hopefully to more intense specialty activity on the part of those specialists associated with the remaining tertiary hospitals and reducing or eliminating many procedures carried out by physicians less well trained.[15]

A second trend already under way is the increased number of multi-specialty groups of practitioners, *both* prepaid and fee for service. The more efficient utilization of specialists by prepaid groups than in the general community is well documented.[16] The number of physicians in multi-specialty groups increased from 24,349 to 39,311 between 1969 and 1975. This process may progressively lead to a reduction in business for unaffiliated specialists and may further reduce the demand for specialists.

As the training of specialists is reduced, training programs may shift from tertiary hospitals to the point where future family practitioners may serve apprenticeships in community physicians' offices. This would provide opportunities to learn more about public and social health problems, management of referrals, and serving as an ombudsman in organizing the use of several specialists for the individual patient and his family. Indeed, as citizens become more educated and demand a more active participation in their care, the physician's role may in many cases be principally that of an educator rather than either diagnostician or provider of therapy.

There are alternate scenarios to this one of natural adjustment to physician oversupply. Some believe that physicans have such an ability to generate new business for themselves that the larger number of physicians will lead to even more utilization of physicians' services. These analysts point to the fact that there are twice as many surgeons and twice as many operations in the United States as in England and Wales.[17] Or it is shown that

> The National Center for Health Statistics estimated that in 1973, 690,000 hysterectomies were performed in the United States. This represents a rate of 647.3 per 100,000 females—a higher rate than for any other major operation, one that, if continued in the future would result in the loss of uterus by more than half the female population by the age of 65 years.[18]

In addition to mobilizing additional technology to do excess procedures, it may be argued that additional physicians will undercut ongoing experiments with physician extenders, pediatric nurse practitioners, and other alternatives to the mainstream medical system.

The massive infusion of resources into the medical sector has, thus, changed the crisis in medical care from a crisis in supply and demand to a crisis of accountability. The resolution of this crisis will be determined in large part by the initiatives and decisions of the next few years at the national, state, and local level. With medical care costs escalating so rapidly, national health insurance, which many have characterized as a costly albatross, may have become a necessity in order to control costs and permit rational organization of the medical sector.

Putting the Individual and the Local Community Back Into Medical Care

Although it has had to be the Federal Government which guarantees, with its fiscal strength, the right to medical care, it is at the local level where the medical care is delivered that providers must be governed by citizen-consumers. As the entitlement to medical care is extended generally to all citizens and especially to those who currently least use it, the near poor or proud poor who do not receive Medicaid and the near old who are not old enough for Medicare,[19] local and individual choice must be built into the medical care system. This choice must be structured so that control may be exercised over both the quality and the comprehensiveness of health care available. In order to be effective there must be local initiative in regard to both facilities and the behavior of health professionals. These are objectives toward which new Federal programs such as the Professional Standards Review Organizations (PSROs) and Health Service Agencies (HSAs) are directed, but these programs lack the full participation of citizens and consumers which is necessary if they are to be successful. And these programs are somewhat isolated from the traditional public health concerns of health departments which ought to be included in any planning and regulation process.[20]

A. Developing Effective Health Planning

In order to mitigate somewhat the rapid escalation in cost of health care and the status competition between facilities which the new government resources for medical care made available, the Congress enacted Public Law 89-749, which established community health planning agencies (CHPs) at the local and state level. These agencies were designated broad health planning functions and in addition had some approval power over certain capital improvements in health facilities, if a facility did not obtain an approval it could be denied reimbursement for that capital expense in its Medicare and Medicaid rates. Although widespread consumer participation in the boards of Comprehensive Health Planning Agencies was mandated, most agencies have not been able to exercise more than limited veto power over the activities of the larger health care institutions. In some areas the agencies were captured by the larger hospitals, which were able to deny approvals to smaller potentially competitive institutions.

More importantly the CHPs served a passive function. They were charged with health planning, but they had neither resources nor operating authority to carry out such plans. Rather they had to wait to see what various institutions and professional groups in the community proposed and decide between them, or, as often happened, decide to approve all of them. The normal ambivalence of local government in a federal system—between efficient operation of local service delivery and acting as the agent of local agencies in mobilizing more resources from higher levels of government[21] —was exacerbated in the case of the CHPs. They were not rationing local funds; but rather they were deciding which institutions would have access to seemingly limitless Federal funds. The political pressures were virtually all in the direction of approval.

New Health Systems Agencies (HSAs) with broader powers

than the CHP agencies are in the process of being established. These agencies which were mandated under Public Law 93-641 are meant to provide local approvals for construction and programs which were formerly under both the CHPs and the Regional Medical Program. Further they have some approval authority over recipients of Federal grants from some of the programs administered by the Public Health Service. It was intended that these agencies be broadly representative of the communities in which they have authority, and that the state level HSA be made up of representatives of local HSAs. Since the HSA membership is appointed by a body designated by the Secretary of HEW and although in several states the real power is reserved to the state level, many have become concerned that the HSAs will be dominated by provider interests, that they will be resistant to evolving local concerns, and that they may have no more interest in economy and in rationing resources than the predecessor CHPs. A further item of concern is that while the HSA will have authority over hospitals and other institutions, private physicians' offices will go largely unregulated.

In regard to rationing capital there may exist a better approach still using the HSA. Since virtually every community has an adequate number of facilities and amenities available at present, perhaps all reimbursement of new construction through government programs, and through Blue Cross-Blue Shield which in essence is a quasi-governmental organization, should be halted. Similarly no reimbursement of procedures on new diagnostic equipment in hospitals or physicians' offices should be permitted. Instead, if a community wants additional facilities or expensive equipment, it should pass a local bond issue and pay for them in that manner. If certain regions or localities remain significantly deprived then special arrangements can be made. This would be far cheaper than current methods. It would provide a real political function to the HSAs to screen the projects to be included in the bond issue, and it would restrain the edifice complex of many by providing that concentrated discipline brought by paying for things out of one's own pocket.

Even this falls far short of governing the local health system. Regulating buildings and equipment alone without any control over the activities carried on is certainly partial control at best.[22] The Health Security Act proposed in several forms over the last decade would apportion a fixed amount of Federal money to local areas which would entitle all the citizens of each area to a specified package of services. How these services are made available and the facilities available would be largely a function of decisions of local government. The Health Security Act does not precisely stipulate how this local governance of the health system will take place.

B. Regulating the Provision of Services

It should be the function of government to enhance the ability of the consumer and the local community to monitor the care delivered and to organize alternatives to the professionalized mainstream system. In 1972 the Congress passed a number of amendments to the Social Security Act, including one which established Professional Service Review Organizations (PSRO) to monitor the adequacy and necessity of the care received by those covered by Medicare, Medicaid, and other Social Security Act medical programs. From the beginning the PSRO program has suffered from the fact that it is entirely comprised of physicians at the local level and that it does not apply to all patients receiving care. The malpractice crisis in fact may in part be the result of inadequate steps to reduce bad medical practice or to prevent physicians from practicing in areas in which they are not competent. Indeed with escalating malpractice premiums, many occasional and non-board-certified surgeons have found it economically rational to limit their practices.[23] One suspects that this limitation will improve the quality of care both by removing some marginal practitioners and by increasing the workload of those specialists who are left to a more appropriate level.

Approaches for monitoring the care that is provided have begun to emerge. Health authorities in several states are beginning to apply epidemiological techniques, through death records and other information to monitor the performance of individual medical care providers. Herbert Dennenberg, when he was the Pennsylvania Insurance Commissioner, published shoppers' guides to surgical and health insurance. Shoppers' guides to physicians in particular counties or regions are increasingly published. These guides generally publish information regarding a physician's specialty qualifications, hospital appointments, willingness to make house calls and other characteristics. Although there has been some initial resistance by physicians on "ethical" grounds, these guides have been increasingly well received by consumers. Yet another approach would be to provide information regarding performance. More than 100 years ago, Florence Nightingale proposed that hospitals should publish case specific mortality statistics. Even given all of the caveats which would be heard, this might be an excellent idea today when the mortality rate for a coronary bypass operation may vary from hospital to hospital between four and forty percent.[24]

Once the physician is chosen a useful technique would be for the patient to be routinely provided with copies of his or her medical records. Budd Shenkin and I proposed this three years ago.[25] We believed that this would lead to more patient satisfaction, improved continuity when the regular physician was not available, and decentralized peer review because no physician could be sure a patient would not take himself and his record to another physician for a second opinion. It was argued that this would lead to greater rewards from providing primary care for many physicians and would be functional in other ways as well. In the last several years the patient's legal right to the information on his record has become increasingly established.[26] Experiments in giving patients their records have been reported to be very successful.[27]

Armed with information concerning providers of care, the consumer and the community must decide what sort of care is appropriate. Advocates of a simplistic market approach have implicitly contended that universal insurance with the right coinsurance and deductables are virtually all that are required for appropriate patterns of utilization and provision to everyone. This approach disregards the degree to which providers of care are autonomous, and more important, the degree to which superior, often cheaper, alternatives exist to the approach which the professionalized system will deliver. In areas of great importance where patients or potential patients have the time to identify each other and combine resources, innovations like the LaMaze method, and hospices for the dying have been developed which deprofessionalize tremendously important life events and rehumanize that which has been over medicalized.

Other initiatives are needed to encourage and control innovations such as surgi centers, where minor elective surgery can be performed at a fraction of the normal cost, and home care for the elderly to prevent excessive institutionalization. It appears that significant cost savings would result from such programs, in part because as those patients who provide internal subsidies to the acutely ill are withdrawn from particular hospitals, the crisis in finance would force consolidation of acute care facilities and acute care activities. These programs which take place outside of institutions are particularly likely to proliferate and be not subject to easy monitoring. The participation of volunteers, community groups with an interest in the individual, and the profession of public health nursing will all perhaps have to be rediscovered and re-encouraged.[28] In the contemporary context these activities must be seen as acts of citizenship, not *lese majeste.*

The role of the national government in all this must be to provide broad entitlements to care, ensure that discrimination and special treatment are not taking place, encourage individual and community initiative, and gather information on system performance and health status of communities. At the state and community level, initiatives in the areas of environmental health, nutrition, housing, and education may have great impact on the health status of individuals. Such activities should not be slighted because the existing delivery system has been so effective at mobilizing resources. All of these warnings and admonitions are, it might be said, made necessary by the extra resources set free for medical care by the Kennedy and Johnson Administrations. The entitlements these programs established wiped out much misery and sorrow, and by affirming the basic right of all to inclusion in the medical care system, have left us who come later with problems of governance and choice, not problems of a permanent caste system. The part of the medical system for which we should feel shame has thus been largely removed. Now we must move to make these services more appropriate and responsive to individual and community needs.

References

[1] These statements regarding the objectives of the program and the campaign to enlist enrollees are a distillation of a number of memos internal to the White House which are available at the LBJ Presidential Library.

[2] Robert Stevens and Rosemary Stevens, *Welfare Medicine in America*, Free Press, 1974.

[3] Judith Feder, *The Character and Implication of SSA's Administration of Medicare*, Policy Center, Inc., Denver, Colorado, 1975, p. 15.

[4] Marjorie Smith Mueller and Robert Gibson, "National Health Expenditures, Fiscal Year 1975," *Social Security Bulletin*, vol. 39, no. 2, February, 1976, p. 4.

[5] Carol Cerf, *Trends Affecting the U.S. Health Care System*, Cambridge, Mass: Cambridge Research Institute, 1975, p. II-26.

[6] David Perry, "Medical Facilities Construction: How Much is Enough?", unpublished paper available from the author. His source is U.S. Department of Commerce, *Construction Review*, November, 1975, pp. 7-9.

[7] *Ibid.*, p. 9, citing U.S. Department of Commerce, *U.S. Industrial Outlook 1976*, Washington, D.C., 1976, p. 396.

[8] *Ibid.*, p. 2, citing American Hospital Association, *Hospital Statistics 1975*, Chicago, 1975, p. vii.

[9] See Stanley Shapiro and Stanley Wynn, "Cat Fever," *New England Journal of Medicine*, 294: 954-56, 1976 and letters to the editor, July 29, 1976, pp. 282-83 for a discussion of the proliferation of computer-aided tomography for private physicians' offices.

[10] American Medical Association, *Physician Distribution and Licensure in the United States*, 1964-74.

[11] Martha Katz, David Warner, and Dale Whittington, *The Supply of Physicians and Physicians Incomes: Alternative Projections of the Future*, Occasional Paper # 1, LBJ School of Public Affairs, 1976.

[12] *Ibid.*, p. 31.

[13] The American College of Surgeons and the American Surgical Association, *Surgery in the United States, A Summary Report of the Study on Surgical Services for the United States*, 1975.

[14] Katz, *et al., op. cit.*, pp. 17-18.

[15] *Ibid.*, p. 32.

[16] Hughes, E.F.X., Lewit, E.M., Watkins, R.N., Handschin, R., "Utilization of Surgical Manpower in a Prepaid Group Practice," *New England Journal of Medicine*, vol. 291, p. 759, 1974.

[17] John P. Bunker, "Surgical Manpower: A Comparison of Operations of Surgeons in the United States and in England and Wales," *New England Journal of Medicine*, vol. 282, pp. 135-144, 1970.

[18] John Bunker, Valentina Clark Donahue, Phillip Cole, and Malkah Nofman, "Elective Hysterectomy: Pro and Con," *New England Journal of Medicine*, vol. 295, pp. 268-269, July 29, 1976.

[19] Lu Ann Aday and Ronald Andersen, *Access to Medical Care*, Health Administration Press, Ann Arbor, 1975.

[20] C. Arden Miller, "Issues of Health Policy: Local Government and the Public's Health," *American Journal of Public Health*, December, 1975, vol. 65, no. 12, pp. 1330-1335.

[21] David Porter and David Warner, "How Effective are Grantor Controls," *Transfers in an Urban Economy*, Kenneth Boulding, Martin Pfaff, and Anita Pfaff, eds., Wadsworth Publishing, Belmont, California, 1973.

[22] Rosemary Stevens, "Regionalization of Health Manpower," Working Paper 6-44, Center for the Study of Health Services, Yale University, 1976.

[23] Sophie Carroll Weiss, "Medical Quality and Patient Outcomes: Malpractice in Perspective," Staff Report prepared for the Texas Medical Professional Liability Study Commission, April 15, 1976.

[24] George Crile, "The Surgeon's Dilemma," *Harpers*, May, 1975, pp. 30-39.

[25] Budd Shenkin and David Warner, "Giving the Patient His Medical Record: A Proposal to Improve the System," *New England Journal of Medicine*, September 27, 1973.

[26] Harold Hirsch, "Medical Records—Their Medico-Legal Significance," *The Journal of Family Practice*, vol. 2, no. 3, 1975, pp. 213-216.

[27] R. Bouchard, W. Eddy, H. Tufo, *et al.*, "The Patient and His Problem Oriented Record," in *Implementing the Problem Oriented System*, J. Hurst and H. Walker, eds., Medcom Press, 1973, and A. Golodetz, J. Rusk, and R. Milhous, "The Right to Know: Giving the Patient His Medical Record," *Archives of Physical Medicine*, March, 1976.

[28] Alvin J. Schorr, "Social Services After Eden, or, Who Promised Us a Rose Garden," Memorial Lecture for Richard M. Titmuss, Association of Directors of Social Services, Coventry, November 3, 1974.

SUMMARY William Levin

In reviewing the lengthy and complex history of the events that led up to the development of the legislation that has been implemented in the Medicare and Medicaid programs, Wilbur Cohen stated that it is much easier for legislation to be passed by Congress in an incomplete or imperfect form than in a form that includes all of the details of its implementation. This concept is exemplified in the actual experience with the implementation of the Medicare and Medicaid programs.

The intent of legislation that is passed, however, is commonly subverted by the guidelines and regulations that are developed to implement it.

It is clear from Cohen's comments that the efforts to pass the Medicare and Medicaid legislation spanned a period of at least three decades. He emphasized, as did Dr. Theodore Marmor, the bitterness which emerged during this period. Both attributed this bitterness to members of organized medicine; it is unfortunate that neither took cognizance in his discussion of the impressive contributions made by members of organized medicine since the implementation of this legislation.

Cohen emphasized, properly, the important role played by President Johnson in the final passage of the legislation and in the development of the program thereafter.

He attributed the desegregation of American society, in large part, to the implementation of Medicare and Medicaid legislation. Although he may have overemphasized this role of these programs, it is certainly true that segregation has been completely eradicated from hospital and clinic operations since Medicare and Medicaid have become a part of our society.

Finally, Cohen suggested that national health insurance should be extended in an orderly and graduated fashion and proposed that maternal and child health become the first programs for such extension.

Chairman Dr. David Hamburg quoted Mrs. Lyndon Baines Johnson, "Lyndon would have welcomed this. He never thought of the Great Society as laws cut in stone. Many of us look back on those years as a great laboratory in which many good minds were searching for new ways to correct old ills. Now, a decade later, whatever can be discovered about the successes or the failures that came out of the laboratory should, it seems to me, be a substantial contribution to the 1970s and beyond."

This statement of Mrs. Johnson's set the theme and emphasized the obvious conclusion that the development of such complex programs as provision of health and medical care for the American public must be a continuing and evolutionary process and should never be considered as having attained a state of absolute perfection. It is important that legislators, governmental administrators responsible for the implementation of legislation, the members of the medical and other health professions and the consumers thereof, agree to collaborate in the subsequent development of these monumental programs.

Subsequently, Professor Marmor expanded upon the historical events leading to Medicare and Medicaid legislation. He emphasized that the issue is guaranteeing *access* to medical and health care, although clearly, no legislature can alone guarantee accessibility to health and medical care. Education of the consumers—the public—must be undertaken to assure informed acceptance and implementation.

Dr. Karen Davis pointed out that "extension of an equal opportunity for a healthy life to all is not an easily obtainable goal, nor is it one that can realistically be expected to take place in a decade or perhaps even in a generation—as past neglect takes its toll for long periods ahead."

She also emphasized the difficulty in measuring the achievement of Federal health programs during the past 10 years because many extraneous influences, such as greater urbanization, increasing accidents, and rising death rates from cancer, have played important roles. On the other hand, she noted that many diseases have decreased both in incidence and in their impact upon the economy and upon society.

She concluded by emphasizing that national health security can and should be a reality. She pointed out that the funds for health resources development and effective controls for health care costs, developed in the first phase, should be carried over and expanded in the second phase to assure continued conversion to a more efficient and equitable system of health care delivery.

Dr. David Warner reviewed the impact of health care legislation on the delivery of medical and health care by private practitioners in a variety of settings—including rural areas. He summarized some of the effects that might be anticipated as a consequence of the creation of Health Systems Agencies.

He reminded us that the number of well-trained physicians has increased rapidly during the past 10 years and that present programs promise to accelerate this trend. He emphasized that it will be necessary to consider the problems of geographic and specialty maldistribution in terms of their influence upon the total problem of health and medical care delivery. He concluded with the statement, "The part of the medical care system for which we should feel a shame has been largely removed. Now we must move to make these services more appropriate and responsive to individual and community needs."

The panel discussion was initiated by Martha Griffiths, who reviewed recent legislation, and emphasized the power of certain individuals in Congress in guiding legislation through committees. She emphasized that the inclusion of Medicaid was accomplished with little discussion and with practically no opposition, despite the fact that Medicare had provided such a stormy focal point for congressional debate.

Adam Yarmolinsky commented that legislation introduced so far has not modified the structure of the health care delivery system in any fundamental way. As a consequence, he proposed that major changes are necessary in the organizational form of the system. He recommended the development of more health maintenance organizations as one of the more important methods to accomplish this end.

Dr. Ray Santos, a private practitioner, introduced a plea for more balanced consideration of the issues that are related to legislation on the delivery of health and medical care.

Dr. David Rogers cited certain statistics, such as a reduction in the death rates from coronary heart disease, as an indicator of the national achievements in the delivery of health care. He placed into perspective some of the problems that emerged at the outset of Medicare and Medicaid programs. Finally, he indicated his pleasure at what he perceives as a return to the optimistic conviction that "we can as a nation with pluralistic approaches really better the human condition."

Governor Patrick Lucey of Wisconsin expressed concern about the escalating costs associated with Medicaid and indicated that many of the states have gone as far as they can go or have actually overextended their capabilities in this area. He concluded with a plea for the development of cost controls before comprehensive national health insurance is completely phased in over the next two or three years.

Dr. James Haughton eloquently described the impact of OEO programs and concluded with the observation that consumers are now being heard by government and by other agencies in the development and in the implementation of major programs.

Dr. John Finklea, director of the National Institute for Occupational Safety and Health, presented the "unfinished agenda." He described the three goals of the program for which his Institute is responsible: (1) to make a work place a safer place, (2) to make it more healthy, and (3) to accomplish these ends without being excessively burdensome to the business community. He expressed the opinion that occupational health is one area in which struggle and contention are rising and that they are unlikely to subside.

Dr. Merlin DuVal expressed the judgment that the greatest single danger facing the United States at the end of its second century is traceable to the relatively rapid increase in a sense of alienation among Americans.

Dr. Kenneth Cooper emphasized the importance of prevention of disease rather than treatment and expressed deep concern over alcohol, smoking, overeating, heart disease, and so on. It was his contention that Americans should be taught maximum safeguards for the maintenance of health as individuals.

Bond L. Bible discussed rural health needs. He described certain models that have been developed in selected areas in the United States. It was his opinion that the interest in rural health represent an outgrowth of the health program of the 1960s and he considered that these developments speak well for the improvement of health services in rural areas in the future.

Alternative Health Plans

Several different proposals or approaches emerged in the discussion. Former Representative Griffiths spoke out for the immediate introduction of the Health Security Act, formerly the Kennedy-Griffiths bill, which would entitle all Americans to a package of benefits, distribute funds to regions and localities on a fixed annual basis, and require that a health budget for each locality be drawn up which would allocate funds for the year to come. This assertion crystalized the views of nearly all the participants and a number of alternatives to and difficulties with the Health Security plan were discussed.

Ted Marmor and Wilbur Cohen both felt that practitioners would not accept fixed salaries and that the administrative problems of immediately introducing Health Security would be overwhelming. They both proposed, in effect, introducing a kind of Health Security plan for children and mothers and then phasing in a national health insurance scheme.

Karen Davis also believed that the difficulties of introducing Health Security would be great and she advocated instead, as a first step, the total federalization of Medicaid and extending it to all of the indigent and the working poor. She stated that the Cohen-Marmor proposal would waste a lot of scarce resources and not solve the problem of cost control, the problem of access of low-income adults, or the problem of underserved areas. Governor Lucey made an earlier statement largely in agreement with her approach.

Dr. Haughton expressed concern that immediate entitlement of all to medical services, before the necessary resources are available to deliver the services, would primarly lead to inflation and additional frustration. In other words, he wanted to continue to encourage more appropriate geographical and specialty distribution of physicians before introducing universal entitlements.

Dr. Santos spoke of his belief that while the civil rights programs were necessary, he hoped that national health insurance would not interfere with traditional doctor-patient relationships and impose unnecessary bureaucratic impediments to free choice and prompt personalized care. Dr. Cooper, in response to a question, reiterated some of these points and called for increased attention to preventive behavior on the part of the individual. In particular he pointed to a life-insurance policy being considered by the Texas State Insurance Commission which would charge much lower insurance premiums to individuals who can meet certain criteria for healthiness.

David Warner pointed out that the Health Security Act does not stipulate adequately how the local health system will be governed and that there must be some way to work rationing and the entitlements out at the local level.

Adam Yarmolinsky said that he believed that not everyone could be included in national health insurance at once and that perhaps everyone over 60 and under 4 should be included at first. He also stated that he thought medical foundations are an interesting model that ought to be explored as well as health maintenance organizations (HMOs).

Dr. DuVal stated that the potential has already been created for a national health system. This potential exists in (1) the Health Planning, Resources, and Development Act (Public Law 93-641) to control facilities on a nationwide basis; (2) the Social Security Act Amendments of 1972 which created professional standards review organizations (PSROs) to monitor the cost and quality of professional care and authorized experiments by hospitals and other entities to control costs; and (3) the various health-manpower acts which Congress is now considering.

Dr. Rogers stated that the Robert Wood Johnson Foundation had supported model health practices in rural and urban areas, and new experiments with training health professionals, based on the prediction that in two or three years there would be some form of paying for care rendered outside the hospital. He strongly endorsed developing these new modes, but in tandem with developing a means for paying for these services. He said that he believes the current level of expenditure in the health system, around $700 per capita, was adequate for an effective, humane, dignified medical care system.

One of the important themes that recurred throughout the discussion was first enunciated by Secretary Cohen and deserves reemphasis. This has to do with the observation that policies are often easy to formulate and difficult to implement. The discussants reviewed the difficulties in the implementation of Medicare and Medicaid with the hope that by studying the mistakes that have been made, extensions of national health insurance can be implemented without committing again the errors that were made initially and are still being made in that program.

I would suggest that it is appropriate that we reappraise the attitudes of the emerging generation of physicians. It is my opinion that the physicians in the 1970s are quite different than those of the 1930s and 1940s. This younger generation of physicians *is* responding to the demands that society is making of them.

As an example, from my own institution—The University of Texas Medical Branch at Galveston—I can report that almost 60 percent of the graduating class of 1976 chose primary-care specialties for graduate training. This was done voluntarily, without any mandate provided by legislation. The same trend is occurring in medical schools throughout the country. I believe this is an excellent commentary on the social conscience of our younger health professionals.

I wish to reemphasize the plea that it is important for all who are involved in the design and implementation of health legislation to recognize that we are collaborators and not adversaries. The Federal establishment, the state governments, the medical schools, and the practicing physicians are of a common mind and have a common purpose. I believe that the majority of physicians and other health professionals will be important and effective contributors in the planning and implementation of national health legislation.

The panel touched upon some of the matters concerned with health manpower legislation. It was not a subject of lengthy discussion, but was repeatedly alluded to, especially in regard to rural health care. I would add that I perceive as an equally important (and perhaps quantitatively *more* important) consideration of planning the provision of health care for people in the inner cities. It is remarkable that even in cities with large medical schools and hospitals that make health care available at low cost or no cost, the neediest of patients often do not patronize them. The obvious conclusion is that it is going to be necessary to educate these members of our society as to the availability of health care and of the importance of taking advantage of it.

The question of fee-for-service or cost reimbursement or salary was one of the most sensitive areas touched upon. I am of the persuasion that fee-for-service is still the most effective way of maintaining a high level of motivation for physicians.

I would reemphasize the point made by Wilbur Cohen that whatever type of national health insurance legislation is written, it is essential that it be written in a way that will be accepted by the medical profession. If it is not accepted by the medical profession, it simply will not work.

Quality control of medical care delivery is essential. The PSROs, as they now exist, are by no means perfect, and in fact, are just getting tooled up. Hopefully, the PSROs are only a beginning.

Some of the criticisms which have been leveled at the implementation of national health insurance in the form of Medicare and Medicaid are possibly derived in large part from the imperfections of the legislation and from the sometimes chaotic state of the guidelines written by the Bureau of Health Insurance in the case of Medicare and by the various state agencies in the case of Medicaid.

In conclusion, I would stress the necessity for those in the government responsible for legislation and for administration of legislative enactments, to join together with physicians, with medical schools, with nursing schools, and other physician-extenders, so that they may mold, in a cooperative fashion, the best legislation possible and develop the best guidelines to implement the legislation. Let me reemphasize the plea for an abandonment of the adversary relationship which existed many years ago and which seemed to reemerge at times during the discussions. I really do not think it exists in the form in which it is perceived by some.

I would heartily endorse the recommendation for an orderly approach to planning of the various health systems, because without an orderly approach, chaos will result. The point to keep in mind is that we are concerned with caring for those who are sick and helping maintain the health of the largest possible number of the citizens of our country. These are our common goals and should serve as an ever-present continuing challenge.

PART

4

the right to a decent home in a decent community

Victor Bach

12

Visions Without Revisions: Urban Policy Orientations of the Kennedy-Johnson Years

Every period of policy innovation—whether for better or worse policy—is an organic consequence of events, forces, and changing conditions which give sudden currency to certain emerging ideas and concepts of public action. As such, the policy formulations of a period are as much the product of a field of forces grounded in hard-nosed, practical realities as they are the reflection of ethical or rational visions of societal action.

The forces that impelled the rapidly changing character of urban housing and development policy during the Kennedy-Johnson years, and the broadest policy realization of the national objective of "a decent home in a suitable living environment,"[1] were multiple in nature and intense. The increasingly successful struggle of the civil rights movement during the early 1960s had coalesced a major national constituency with a strong urban agenda. A network of committed professionals interested in redistributive change were succeeding in getting their ideas into currency—Michael Harrington's *The Other America*, the Cloward and Ohlin opportunity theory of juvenile delinquency, among other examples—and in gaining access to centers of Federal initiative. By mid-decade, the media had recognized the "urban crisis" and focused national public attention on the multifaceted nature of urban problems. A series of urban disorders, which took on major proportions in Watts in 1965, followed by conflagrations in Detroit, Newark, and other cities, were policy-shaping events which gave greater credence and priority to the articulated deprivations of urban ghetto communities.[2]

In 1968, an empathetic President, committed on the one hand to path-breaking strides in domestic policy and, on the other, to an abortive war in Southeast Asia, sought to maintain Democratic dominance with an increasingly disaffected urban constituency through the passage of major new programs during a turbulent election year. These concerns reverberated through Congress, as did those of the major interest groups. Among them, the housing industry looked toward declining housing starts and tight money;[3] it was prepared to place itself solidly behind new housing subsidy programs geared to volume production in the private sector. However diverse the forces were, they all seemed to be aligned in the same direction, toward broader Federal initiatives in urban housing and development policy. The national economic prosperity of the decade—"an economy of abundance"—made it possible to mount a sizeable and varied policy response to these forces.

By now, many of the more controversial policy innovations of the 1960s have become an accepted part of the public vocabulary, for example, the currency of rent subsidies and block grants. To recall their original impact against the limited Federal policy lexicon that preceded them is much like trying to remember how one learned to walk. One simply takes it for granted. Nevertheless, there are few areas of social policy in which turning back the clock over so short a time to the Kennedy-Johnson period involves such sharp ratchets of discontinuity as does housing and community development policy. One must move the time dial back past the New Federalist policies which have begun to make themselves felt since 1974; past the still-imposed, temporary moratorium on the housing subsidy programs which was first levied in early 1973; and past the turbulent experience of the Great Society housing and community development programs themselves which took place largely during the succeeding Nixon years.

This chapter is concerned with these policies at the point of formulation rather than in light of subsequent experience. What were the underlying policy orientations—the fundamental conceptions of ends and means—that were embodied in the evolving urban policy of the Kennedy-Johnson period? This examination of the "starting visions" upon which urban policy embarked during the 1960s is an attempt to bring some of those guiding conceptions into sharp focus in a way that permits them to be questioned and re-examined as policy values in terms of their relevance to present and future policy.

Shifts in Housing Policy

On the eve of the Kennedy inauguration, Federal housing policy had remained largely stable for a quarter-century, and it was a simple matter to assess past program experience. The mainstays were public housing and Federal Housing Administration (FHA) mortgage insurance, both legislated during the Great Depression of the 1930s as strategies of economic recovery through accelerated construction activity. A general consensus had been formed among the policy community about each of them. There were serious doubts about the viability of public housing as a major Federal strategy, even among the ardent housing reformers who had helped bring it into being. Catherine Bauer Wurster had already labeled it a "dreary deadlock,"[4] and Nathan Glazer subsequently called the massive, frequently problem-ridden public housing developments a "graveyard of good intentions."[5] Although there were, and still are, viable and cohesive public housing communities in a number of places, the negative imagery upon which such national assessments are made was well in place by 1960.

By contrast, the FHA mortgage insurance program was a generally acknowledged success. With its sibling Veteran's Administration (VA) program, it had been responsible for catalyzing the massive suburbanization and expansion of home ownership that occurred during the post-war period. Though the externalities that these movements imposed on the viability of center cities were partially understood, they were not yet a major source of policy concern. Against the scoffing of a few elite social critics at "suburban sprawl" and "mass consumerism,"[6] there were the large numbers of middle-income families who eagerly sought suburban, federally insured housing.[7] There was also the burgeoning FHA insurance fund—self-paying, actuarially sound—that had accrued a sufficient reserve to assure private industry there was a substantial profit to be made in insuring the mortgages of an emergent and stable middle class.

Although FHA and public housing were not conceived as paired strategies, by and large they represented the embodiment of Federal housing policy through 1959.[8] As such, they reflected a clear "dualism" in Federal policy, a sharp dichotomy of programs in terms of the benefits received and the constituencies served. While public housing served the urban housing poor— those defined as low-income who could ill afford standard housing in the private market—FHA served the mainstream middle class of American society. Public housing had been so designed.[9] In FHA's case, it was the result of actuarial caution and administrative discretion concerning the racial and income characteristics of home buyers. By 1968, the Douglas Commission on Urban Problems had the following to say of FHA:[10]

> The main weakness of FHA from a social point of view has not been in what it has done, but in what it has failed to do—in its relative neglect of the inner cities and the poor, and especially Negro poor. Believing firmly that the poor were bad credit risks and that the presence of Negroes tended to lower real estate values, FHA has generally regarded loans to such groups as "economically unsound." Until recently, therefore, FHA benefits have been confined almost exclusively to the middle class, and primarily only to the middle section of the middle class. The poor and those on the fringes of poverty have been almost completely excluded.

While this dual pattern seemed a reasonable allocation of Federal resources—higher public housing subsidies for the poor and lower insurance risk subsidies[11] for the middle class—it had other important distributive consequences. It relegated the urban housing poor to rental housing under public auspices at the initiative of local authorities, while it attracted an emergent middle class to home ownership and, thereby, extended its range of participation in the broader private housing market. It served to exacerbate long-standing patterns of urban residential segregation by income and by race. Increasingly FHA became a suburban phenomenon, while public housing located in the center city. As a consequence, the dualism of Federal housing policy served to constrain locational opportunities for the urban housing poor and intensify socioeconomic differences between center cities and their suburbs, particularly at a time of massive post-war inmigration to the cities from impoverished rural areas. As a whole, it sharpened the visible differences in housing consumption between the urban "haves" and "have-nots" in location, housing tenure, the other housing attributes.

The dominant theme of the evolving housing policies of the Kennedy-Johnson years is a gradual and increasingly massive erosion of this pre-existing dualism. Although the Section 221 rental program of 1961 excluded households eligible for public housing, it was the first to subsidize private rental housing for families, albeit moderate-income families. Early Federal fair housing initiatives barring discrimination in federally assisted and insured housing were undertaken during the Kennedy Administration. In 1965, after much Congressional debate in the face of strong administration support, the controversial rent supplement program was passed which was the first to subsidize newly produced, private rental units for occupancy by low-income families.[12] Amidst the stir created by rent supplements—whether the poor should live in "pueblos or palaces"—the Section 23 leased housing program slid quietly through the legislative process, a major innovation which allowed local housing authorities to lease rental units in the private market in order to relieve the burgeoning waiting lists for public housing. In the most radical departure from previously-held tenets of housing policy, the 1968 Housing Act embarked on a major strategy of subsidized home ownership for lower-income families with the section 235 program.[13] The Act as a whole was the capstone of the Great Society housing programs in the range of programs it offered, in its commitment to massive national housing goals over the coming decade, and in its incorporation of the private sector as the dominant means through which low-income housing needs would be met.

This catalog of new housing programs is far from exhaustive. The period from 1960 to 1968 is marked by a proliferation of Federal housing programs and an increasingly complex variegation in Federal housing activity, so much so that Congress subsequently made attempts to consolidate the programs legislatively. As a whole, the programs represented a breaking of the shibboleths of the earlier dualism in housing policy.

Shifts in Urban Development Policy

Prior to 1960, the cornerstone of Federal urban development policy was urban renewal,[14] and it retained its prominence through the decade within an augmented array of urban development strategies. By 1960, a relatively classic form of urban renewal had emerged in most cities. Constrained by the marketability of alternative land sites, influenced by powerful local development and commercial interests and by city officials interested in bolstering a declining tax base, guided by planners and architects with an urban-aesthetic orientation, local renewal authorities had nearly universally embarked on massive, long-range projects of downtown redevelopment and given lesser priority to the conservation or revitalization of older residential neighborhoods. Slums and lower-status neighborhoods located on prime land adjacent to the downtown centers were usually cleared and replaced by high-rise office buildings, luxury apartment towers, new retail commercial centers, and expanded public facilities.[15] By the early 1960s, it was recognized that those who bore the costs of urban renewal, with few compensating benefits, were the lower-income and minority families who had been forced to relocate, often within the context of an extremely tight housing market.[16] Although created in part as a residential program, renewal had succeeded in demolishing far more housing units than it had created.[17] The epithets of "the Federal bulldozer" and "urban renewal is Negro removal" were already at a stage of crystallization, and there was growing recognition of the values of residential rehabilitation, as well as some noteworthy attempts to move further renewal efforts in that direction.

During the Kennedy-Johnson years, the Federal repertoire of physical urban development programs expanded to include a wider range of actors, purposes, and neighborhood contexts. Federal matching funds were made available for the acquisition of open space by state and local public bodies, for parks, recreation, conservation, and scenic or historic purposes. Federal legislation gave teeth to local housing rehabilitation efforts by providing funds for housing code enforcement and for special rehabilitation loans and grants; such programs could be used in targeted, conservable residential neighborhoods outside of urban renewal areas. Categorical grants became available for specific purposes, including construction of multi-purpose neighborhood centers, historic preservation, urban beautification, and demolition of unsound structures. On the metropolitan level, there was funding support for regional or area-wide planning bodies, for construction of water and sewer facilities, and for financing to encourage the development of well-planned, new residential subdivisions. In short, the physical urban development policies of the 1960s significantly expanded the range of Federal concerns beyond urban renewal toward more fine-grained, multiple purposes at the level of the residential neighborhood and toward more macroscopic interventions at the larger metropolitan or area-wide level.

But the major shift in Federal policy away from its exclusive concern with physical development strategies occurred with the passage of the Model Cities program in 1966. Aimed at broad community development objectives—economic, social, as well as physical—Model Cities provided concentrated funding for "improving the quality of urban life" in targeted poverty neighborhoods of the nation's major cities. In a sense, Model Cities was the successor of a number of Federal community development programs begun earlier in the 1960s: the involvement under Kennedy of the President's Committee on Juvenile Delinquency with the Ford Foundation "gray areas" experiments, and the community action programs initiated under Johnson as part of the OEO poverty program.[18] In terms of Federal urban development policy, it was a major innovation. Its recognition of the complexity of urban change was apparent from its formulation, in the comprehensiveness of its functional concerns, in its encouragement of local flexibility and autonomy in program planning, and in its attempt to coordinate previously disparate Federal categorical programs, emanating from a number of independent agencies, in terms of their combined impact on the enrichment of the model neighborhoods. It had been conceived as a major experiment in coordinated Federal action to improve urban conditions.[19]

The Model Cities program was unique in concept and in some of its program mechanisms. It was an early realization of the block grant concept, an idea which steadily gained currency during the 1960s, in that it provided supplemental grants to local programs for the flexible funding of efforts which could not be supported within the existing Federal menu of categorical grant-in-aid programs. Although local Model Cities programs were to be administered through a city agency, the legislation called for "widespread citizen participation" and subsequent HUD guidelines sought to create a delicate balance in decision-making prerogatives between city hall and community participatory bodies composed of neighborhood residents. The embryonic HUD, created only a year earlier in 1965, was given the arduous, if not impossible task of serving as the coordinative Federal "hub" of the program, responsible for seeing that Federal action across a number of agencies was orchestrated in its impact on model neighborhoods. The creation of HUD itself had elevated urban affairs and concerns to cabinet-level status. Model Cities lent a new image to what had been considered a "bricks and mortar" agency, and registered a new Federal commitment toward a more comprehensive, broad-aimed, community-oriented urban development policy. By early 1969, when the Johnson Administration departed, 151 cities had been designated as Model Cities and those which had entered during the early stage of the program had only recently completed their first planning year and were beginning implementation.

Major Policy Orientations

Despite the proliferation and variegation of urban programs that occurred during the 1960s, it is possible to characterize the more basic, underlying policy orientations they shared within a few simple dimensions that illuminate the policy values that were put to the test during this period. Some of the more pervasive policy orientations were:

(1) *More direct redistribution of benefits to low-income groups.*

To the extent that the urban poor and near poor benefited from housing and urban development programs prior to 1960, they were largely indirect beneficiaries. It could be said that urban renewal resulted in a net increase in the local tax base which, in turn, increased local capacity to provide public services to the city's more marginal communities. Public housing had ceased to be considered a clear benefit by 1960, although it directly provided low-income families with adequate shelter at low rent. FHA and VA mortgage insurance programs served a suburbanizing middle-income constituency, which produced a filtering down of center-city housing opportunities for lower-income and minority households and contributed to substantial improvement in their housing.[20] But these were unintended consequences of Federal support for home construction and home ownership.

By contrast, the Great Society housing and development programs were strategies of "bottom-up" rather than "trickle-down" redistribution, growing out of a direct concern with the more immediate distributive effects on the poor and on minorities. The Model Cities program provided concentrated funds targeted directly at the more impoverished residential neighborhoods of the city. It was a clear example of the "worst first" priorities that were subsumed in the transition to community development. Moreover, the expanding array of small-scale physical development programs formulated during the 1960s, such as neighborhood facilities and housing rehabilitation activity, began to be qualified and targeted in terms of their location and access relative to lower-income subareas of the city.

In housing, the new series of subsidy programs were attempts to stimulate private market initiatives in the production and rehabilitation of housing units for direct occupancy by lower-income families. The 1965 controversy over rent supplements largely concerned its redistributive effects—whether new, privately-produced housing units should be federally subsidized for low-income occupancy in structures which, unlike public housing, might have sufficient amenities to attract unsubsidized middle-income occupants as well. The debate that occurred in the House is an astonishing indication of how far our policy conceptions have advanced since the early 1960s:

> . . . proponents reemphasized the great housing need in this country, citing the large number of substandard units and the misery of many families in our urban slums. The approach would fight urban slums. But backers frequently found themselves on the defensive . . . They also found the antagonists of the new approach to be vigorous and virulent in their amplification of earlier arguments. Phrases such as "across the board economic integration," "grabbing power," "aimed at changing social patterns," "an attempt to make the Federal Government the landlord of the entire American middleclass," "way of socialist state," "to force integration," "is the U.S. ready for collectivism?" clearly indicate the tone of much of the opposition. Proponents spent some time dealing with these emotional arguments, trying in effect to argue that it is not socialistic or collectivistic to involve private enterprise in housing families.

What was at stake was not merely the provision of "decent, safe, and sanitary" housing for the poor, the minimally adequate shelter standards public housing had provided, but a redistribution of residential opportunities. The Section 235 lower-income home ownership program legislated in 1968 promised even more

than a redistribution of residential opportunities; it sought to redistribute property ownership—its benefits and risks—and housing
statuses as they are normally reflected in urban society.

(2) The opportunity model of redistribution.

It needs to be understood that in attempting a more direct
redistribution of housing and urban services favoring the urban
disadvantaged, the Great Society urban programs followed an
opportunity model rather than a universal redistributive model.
Although opportunities expanded, not everyone stood to benefit.
To begin with, the programs provided selective opportunities
even among the urban poor. For every poverty neighborhood
designated for Model Cities enrichment, there were numerous
others—equally impoverished—that had no equity in the program.
The volume of low-income housing construction envisioned by
the 1968 Housing Act could satisfy, during its early stages, only a
small portion of the suppressed demand unleashed by the sudden
availability of subsidy funds. Although the idea of universal
housing allowances—income supplements to families for the
purpose of obtaining suitable housing—was growing in currency,
it had not attained any legislative momentum.[22]

Moreover, the emphasis on poverty which characterized the
Great Society programs as a whole was tied to a notion of
absolute deprivation rather than relative deprivation. There were
the poor or lower-income and, then, everyone else lumped into a
single category beyond Federal assistance. The working- or lower
middle-class neighbors of rent-supplemented families paid full
rents no matter how hard pressed they were. In its concentration
on hard-core poverty areas, Model Cities ignored numerous
working-class neighborhoods in marginal disrepair with scant
services, that had been long ignored by city governments tending
to make their capital investments in the newer, more profitable
growth areas.

Although the dynamics of the opportunity model of redistribution were not fully understood at the time the Great Society
urban policies were formulated, it is easy in retrospect to
understand some of its implications. The select character of the
programs and the "backlash" dynamics of redistribution made
the programs extremely vulnerable at the local political level. In a
number of cities, Section 23 leased housing was turned down by

city councils because of strong resistance from "ethnic" communities who stood to benefit little and feared intrusion from outside. The selectivity of Model Cities neighborhoods, representing a small, often powerless, local constituency, gave them little leverage with city halls and lent the program the character of "neighborhood turf" from the start. Within the context of a limited supply of subsidized housing units, the enormous demand—particularly for purchaseable units under the 235 program—gave builders and real estate brokers the upper hand in a potentially exploitive "caveat emptor" housing market. In short, the urban programs of the Great Society raised compelling questions concerning the dynamics of opportunity redistribution within the context of limited resources.

(3) Increased participation at the community level and at the consumer level.

Participation was seen as an essential correlate of more directly redistributive policies, both in the sense of community participation in developmental decision processes and in the context of consumer participation in the open housing market. Participation was the antidote for the alienation and disaffection of poverty neighborhoods and for the stigmatization of low-income housing opportunities that had occurred under earlier Federal housing policies.

Although Model Cities represented a backing-off from the early autonomy of local poverty agencies with respect to city hall and from the tenets of maximum feasible participation, it constituted the strongest crystallization of resident participation requirements that had yet occurred in Federal urban development programs. The legislative hearings on Model Cities in 1966 had established the administration's view that: "No precise formula for citizen involvement will be imposed . . . It will be up to the cities themselves to devise appropriate ways in which citizens will participate."[23] In contrast with the original Community Action Program, this was a clear deferral to the powers of city hall, if not a vote of confidence that local officials would conduct the program responsibly.

But early HUD guidelines made it clear that although the program was to be administered by a city agency established for the purpose, there was to be a formal participatory structure through which neighborhood residents would be represented in the Model Cities decision process from policy and program planning through program implementation and operation. The guidelines stipulated that "CP structures must have clear and direct access to the decision-making process of the CDA, so that neighborhood views can influence policy, planning, and program decisions."[24] The call for resident participation was extended in 1968 to local urban renewal efforts in a directive which required the establishment of resident Project Area Committees in each designated renewal area with "clear and direct access" to decision-making in all stages of the urban renewal process.[25]

The concept of maximum feasible participation incorporated in the poverty program had a clear function from the start in establishing the community legitimacy of an independently-based poverty agency blessed only by Federal designation. The function of resident participation in city-administered Federal programs is somewhat less certain. Intended to promote an effective grass-roots counterbalance to the formal statutory powers of city agencies and urban renewal authorities, leading to greater agency responsiveness to community priorities or at least to a meaningful dialogue, participation can also be thought as potential cooptation of community interests within a naive conception of consensual decision-making or simply as frustration and wasted effort. However, the underlying political calculus of participation is that access potentially leads to influence. It is this postulate which, despite the ideological ambivalences and operative dilemmas attached to formal participatory mechanisms, lies at the heart of the concept of participation and accounts for its durability through the Great Society programs.[26]

In urban housing policy, the erosion of the earlier dualism which had segregated federally-assisted housing from the private market has already been noted as a dominant theme of the 1960s. The new subsidy programs expanded the range of private market opportunities available to low-income consumers and the scope of their participation in both the rental and purchase markets. The values the Great Society attached to consumer participation in the open market, and its associated destigmatizing effects is nowhere more apparent than in the 1965 Section 23 leased housing legislation, which incorporated a "finders-keepers" provision allowing families applying for public housing to search out and select their own rental units in the existing market for leasing by the authority. Although the provision was rarely used by local housing authorities, it is significant as an approximation to the housing allowance concept.

But the potential risks and problems attached to large numbers of lower-income consumers negotiating the private housing marketplace were not at all addressed by the legislation. HUD equal opportunity efforts were established to help overcome discriminatory barriers faced by minority families in federally-assisted housing, but no other Federal resources were made available that would provide consumer-oriented resources to households attempting to optimize their choices within the newly-expanded range of opportunities. Although some housing submarkets were recognized to be potentially more exploitative than others—the speculator-dominated ghetto submarkets, for instance—the broader market participation legislation of the 1960s implicitly assumed that local housing authorities and FHA would serve as administrative watchdogs against abusive market practices.

(4) New opportunities through the old delivery systems.

The innovative and redistributive spirit of the urban programs of the 1960s obscures some of the more traditional tenets upon which the new policies were based. One of the less questioned and more pervasive givens was a reliance on in-kind delivery of urban and housing services rather than on income transfers with which lower-income families might effect their own priorities through their own expenditure decisions. Even the somewhat less radical notion of in-kind vouchers or allowances, which households could apply flexibly for the purchase of housing services, went largely unrecognized in the housing policies of the 1960s.

In housing, the conventional wisdom suggested that allowances flowing directly to consumers on a need-based sliding-scale would not in themselves promote a significant new supply response and would only serve to inflate rents in the existing supply without any associated improvement in new housing opportunities. The result was that the Great Society housing programs continued to rely on project subsidies, in which new units were selected for subsidy on the basis of builder initiatives and appropriate agency approvals, and subsequently rented or sold to lower-income families. The underlying rationale for project subsidies was that they could be geared to new construction and rehabilitation, so that subsidies augmented the available supply of low-cost housing and kept overall market price levels within reason. But as a consequence, private housing suppliers and bureaucratic intermediaries became the designated "gatekeepers" of the new subsidy programs:[27] their decisions determined the quality, location, and characteristics of housing to be subsidized and, often, the occupants to be selected. It was they who defined and bounded the broadened scope of market participation which subsidies permitted lower-income families, at times with disastrous results.[28] The project subsidy format also had a potentially regressive effect on the potential distribution of subsidies to eligible families. By tying subsidy amounts to the capital cost of construction, rather than directly to household income, eligible families at higher income levels could afford higher-priced housing and command higher subsidies.[29]

These counterproductive aspects of the housing subsidy programs are indicative of some of the establishmentarian, industry-oriented interests that lay beneath the merger of the private market and public subsidies, even within a significant attempt at housing redistribution. The deferral to established administrative interests is also apparent in the designation of FHA as the administering agency for the subsidy programs. By the middle 1960s FHA had become the target of continuing criticism because of its redlining of older neighborhoods and its cautious approach to minority purchasers.[30] During Senator Percy's low-income home ownership campaign of 1967, the Republicans had sought to create a National Home-ownership Foundation which had its own distinct identity, in functional as well as partisan terms, to administer the program. Even some prominent Democrats, Robert Kennedy among them, viewed FHA—despite its New Deal image—as inappropriate and ineffective in the low-income housing arena. In the Senate hearings, Senator Kennedy proposed the creation of a Low-Income Housing Administration within HUD, separate from FHA.[31]

The choice of FHA was, in part, a recognition of its considerable experience in mortgage credit approval and property appraisal and an attempt to lend the agency's blue-chip reputation to a controversial, new program. But in retrospect it is apparent that, despite its strong support from Congress and the housing industry, FHA was unsuited to the demands of a socially oriented program geared toward lower-income consumers. In their field operations, FHA insuring offices had related primarily to local builders and lenders, with whom they had developed stable, mutually productive, affiliations over the years. In its insurance function, FHA viewed itself as the protector of the lending institution; it seldom had any direct contact with the home buyer apart from the approval of credit applications submitted through the mortgate lender. Even its property appraisals were returned to the lender, rather than directly to the potential home purchaser. The successful operation of a new, lower-income home purchase program required that purchasers be carefully and sensitively screened and assisted, and that higher-risk properties be more carefully appraised and inspected than was FHA's custom in the middle-income submarkets. In short, it required a greater consumer orientation than FHA had ever exercised in the past.

In community development, there were parallel tendencies to rely on the established providers. To begin with, Model Cities objectives were inherently concerned with improved delivery of in-kind urban services to specified poverty neighborhoods, and most improvements were expected to occur through established local agencies normally providing those services. Whether the problems of poverty neighborhoods might to a considerable extent be ameliorated through income transfers to residents, rather than through improved service delivery, was imponderable if not entirely irrelevant to the fundamental concept of the program. So too was the question of whether increased income might have led many resident families to opt for alternative service configurations obtainable through a move and residence in other neighborhoods. The calculus of the Model Cities program hinged on an areal conception of urban functioning, and assumed a relatively stable resident population in the area that would stand to benefit from areally-concentrated service enrichment.

Moreover, the Model Cities program was to be administered by a specially created city agency directly responsible to the local chief executive. In recent years we have become too accustomed to notice anymore the particular irony of city administration of Federal programs of community enrichment and development targeted at the very areas cities have been prone to neglect in the absence of Federal aid. The Model Cities program was a step forward in the confidence it placed in city hall and in local political process; earlier Federal-urban programs had manifested a cynical distrust of city government, preferring to place program initiatives in the hands of paragovernmental authorities, such as renewal and housing authorities. New community participation requirements were a vestige of that earlier cynical mode, attempting to create a bicameral distribution of prerogatives under the program. Although Model Cities represented a step back from the early heydays of the Community Action Program and the autonomous poverty agency, it represented a step forward in the recognition of local government as a key functional and political nexus for community development.

These were some of the establishmentarian paradoxes that permeated the radically changing urban policy orientations of the 1960s. They are explicable in a number of ways: the Community Action program and the subsequent Green Amendment had taught the Federal Government a lesson about creating independent centers of local change without deferring to local powers. In housing, major interest groups had pressed for embedding new programs in the old and more familiar agencies. Or it simply seemed the best way of conducting the government's new social programs. The rapid pace of policy innovations during the Great Society was such that the poliferation of new benefits to be delivered discouraged major innovations in the delivery system. If one is shipping delicate merchandise, it seems wise to use established carriers. Given the strides which the new programs made in extending housing and community development opportunities beyond their narrow confines prior to 1960, it seems carping to suggest that they did not go far enough because they were bounded in these respects.

(5) Recognition of urban complexity and of the need for a more adaptive federalism.

The Model Cities approach to community development signaled a new Federal awareness of the complexity of urban change. Although the mandate for comprehensive planning and broadly-aimed intervention under Model Cities was excessively ambitious considering the short nine-month planning period prescribed and the limited funds available to each of the cities, it recognized the multiplicity of functional concerns that needed to be addressed in improving the condition of urban poverty areas: neighborhood physical improvements, housing, improved transportation access, education, manpower and economic development, recreational and cultural activities, crime reduction, health care, social services, and public assistance. Whether these issues could be addressed rapidly and effectively within the context of an uninitiated community participation effort remained an open question. The task of orchestrating disparate Federal agencies, in order to multiply their combined impact on the model neighborhoods, was left to HUD and to the persuasive powers of the President. This attempt reflected a telling assessment that the existing structure of Federal agencies was extraordinarily unsuited to the complexities of urban functioning and that a more coordinative and focused federalism was necessary to the urban task. Whether such coordination could be brought about among independent agencies reflecting diverse interests also remained an open question.[32] The program was valiant in terms of the urban-Federal questions it addressed and posed.

Most importantly, the Model Cities program moved toward a new form of federalism which recognized the limitations imposed on urban innovation by relatively rigid categorical programs, and the need for increased local autonomy and flexibility in determining priorities and appropriate program strategies. The supplemental grant provided under Model Cities constituted the first urban block grant for the funding of local programs which could not be supported within the available menu of categorical programs. The result gave Model Cities a hybrid character as a form of federalism, relying both on a battery of existing categorical programs and a block grant which could either fill the gaps and discrepancies between existing programs and local priorities or provide the "glue" that would bring the programs together as a more comprehensive whole. As a policy concept that attempted to wrestle with the issues of urban complexity, Model Cities represented a major innovation in Federal-urban relationships.

(6) Innovative on a massive scale.

The turbulent events and political forces of the 1960s called for rapid and responsive Federal action to the needs of the cities and their minority and lower-income populations. The policies of the period reflect an abundance of new and valuable ideas, and a political will to see that they were rapidly forged into legislation. In the rush of events and the need for action, it seemed wiser to act than to reflect cautiously on action. The result was that new ideas were cast into policy and implemented on a national scale before they could be experimented with and assessed on a smaller scale.

At the heart of the initial Model Cities concept, as formulated by the Wood urban task force, was an attempt to experiment with a new Federal approach to community development in a small number of cities. The suggested number ranged from two to five cities. To secure passage of the legislation, the number of first-round cities was increased to 75 and a similar number were to follow in the second round shortly afterward, all within the original funding level. Although the program called for radical changes in the usual behavior of Federal agencies and for significant shifts in local planning modes, the proliferation of Model Cities experiments—each of them with less resources to accomplish the original objectives—made the program extremely vulnerable from the start.

In housing policy the need for rapid action may have had even more telling consequences. The strongest example is undoubtedly the Section 235 program of lower-income home ownership. The program represented a new and significant opportunity for lower-income families, which had been tried on a demonstration basis by several non-profit sponsor groups who had conducted their programs on a custom-tailored basis. How families would fare in a widespread national program was still unpredictable.

In the absence of actuarial data on mortgage delinquencies among lower-income families, despite strong expectations that such homeowners would have periodic difficulty sustaining mortgage payments, Senator Percy had proposed a program of private mortgage relief insurance which would temporarily cover mortgage payments in the event of involuntary loss of employment, disability, or death on the part of a major wage-earner. The idea met with general agreement in Congress, but there was little time for studying the feasibility and costs of the insurance program. In the rush to legislate a major housing act in time for the 1968 elections, Section 235 was passed without the insurance component in place; the task of looking further into the insurance plan was left to the HUD Secretary.[34] Other innovations were necessary to make ownership subsidies rapidly deliverable. To encourage FHA to set aside their normal actuarial conservatism and move toward a high-risk program of low-income ownership, Congress created a special risk insurance fund which was not intended to be actuarially sound. During the legislative hearings, a mortgage failure rate as high as 25 percent was cited as within expectations for the program.[35] The House conference report explicitly mentioned this supplemental subsidy element of the program. Under the turbulent urban conditions of 1968, the program seemed worthwhile and necessary despite its acknowledgedly high risks. But to speed the passage of the legislation, the Congress had created a new form of subsidy which had not been fully accounted for in the authorization of funds for the program. In short, the 235 program went into implementation on a massive scale with a number of key questions still unresolved.

The Present Issues

The urban programs of the 1960s were visionary in the sense that they had their genesis in a strong redistributive agenda for urban America. As policy innovations, they were characterized by daring new conceptions of the Federal role in seeing to that agenda. But, no matter how well planned, innovations can be expected to carry a degree of uncertainty and risk. Moveover, the vulnerability of the innovative Great Society urban programs was further exacerbated by the tendency to forge them rapidly into legislation and to implement them subsequently on a national scale. Within the Federal context, the result is a near certain prescription for uneven program performance at best and a vulnerability to subsequent judgments of failure.

In an important sense, the art of program administration and implementation lies in its reckoning with the imperfections of yesterday's legislative visions and of today's program operations, and successfully resolving them through a series of compensating revisions. The widespread and rapid diffusion of policy innovations places a premium on administrative commitment to successful implementation, on the skilled planning of implementation, on careful monitoring of program progress, and on ingenuity in making the most appropriate and timely program revisions. Given their legislative imperfections and the subsequent complexities in their implementation, it is apparent that the urban programs of the 1960s needed alert and commited guidance mechanisms in their administration. Model Cities had been dependent from the start on bringing Presidential initiative to bear on Federal agencies. It was recognized that the housing subsidy programs would engender high but worthwhile risks calling for sensitive monitoring of program operations. But it was the fate of these programs to have been formulated late in the Johnson Administration and implemented largely under the succeeding administration. And it is mild to say that the succeeding administration was not fully committed to these programs—most certainly at the White House level—and that it was quicker to judge them failures than to correct and continue them. In that sense, the Great Society urban programs remain visions without revisions.

Nor do they seem to have been replaced by programs that have any clear vision of the present urban agenda. In the major cities, early trends in the Community Development Block Grant program indicate an emerging pattern of dispersed, small-scale public works and housing rehabilitation activity in the less seriously deteriorated neighborhoods of the city, and a reluctance to concentrate or invest community development funds in the most poverty-stricken neighborhoods where they are badly needed.[36] That this constituted a clear reversal of the priorities reflected in the Model Cities attempt is perhaps less important than that Federal funds are not being put to strategic use in dealing with the more fundamental issues of urban viability. With regard to low-income housing assistance, the new Section 8 program has accomplished little in its two years of existence—so far it has subsidized only about 35,000 units, a paltry record compared to the housing programs of the last decade.

But the present task of reassessing the urban policies of the 1960s goes well beyond the question of whether the old programs can be made to work and work well with a more effective and committed administration. Perhaps the most basic question is whether the present state of the national economy and a prevailing cynicism regarding the efficacy of Federal efforts will permit a renewed national commitment to the redistributive objectives reflected in the Great Society agenda. Given the recently accelerated economic decline of some of our major cities, there are also the hard questions concerning new priorities in light of the present urban condition. In an economy of scarcity, are policies aimed at distributive inequities likely to complement or conflict with emergent Federal priorities geared to urban survival? Even if there is a consensus on the importance of distributive objectives, the classical questions are still with us concerning the degree of reliance we ought to place on the in-kind delivery systems reflected in the programs of the 1960s as opposed to new income maintenance strategies as the appropriate means to improve living conditions among the urban poor.

Most importantly, the experience of the past decade is an awesome reflection of the complexities inherent in mobilizing Federal resources toward a coherent urban policy which is responsive to alternative local contexts and conditions. It raises the question of whether our present state of knowledge is sufficient to the formulation of a new generation of strategic Federal initiatives beyond block grants that can be implemented on a national scale. To the extent that the answers are presently hard to come by, what sort of urban experimentation and innovation are necessary before more effective Federal policies can be articulated, and where is the energy and initiative for such experimentation to come from? The experience of the formulation and passage of the Model Cities program is indicative of the political complexities inherent in attempting a more cautious, experimental federalism which comes to grips with basic aspects of the urban condition. Within the Federal context can we exercise the vision of Daedalus without risking the fate of Icarus?

References

[1] Title I, Housing Act of 1949.

[2] *Report of the National Advisory Commission on Urban Disorders* (Washington, D.C.: U.S. Government Printing Office), 1968, pp. 143-150.

[3] Chester Hartman, *Housing and Social Policy* (Englewood Cliffs, N.J.: Prentice-Hall, Inc.), 1975, pp. 137-138.

[4] Catherine Bauer Wurster, "The Dreary Deadlock of Public Housing," *Architectural Forum*, May, 1957, pp.

[5] Nathan Glazer, "Housing Problems and Housing Policies," *The Public Interest*, Spring, 1967, pp. 21-51.

[6] For a summary critique of then current anti-suburban thought, see: Bennett Berger, *Working Class Suburb: A Study of Auto Workers in Suburbia* (Berkeley: University of California Press), 1960, Chapter I, "The Myth of Suburbia," pp. 1-14.

[7] Herbert J. Gans, *The Levittowners* (New York: Random House), 1967.

[8] In 1959, Section 202 was legislated, subsidizing housing for the elderly.

[9] Laurence M. Freidman, *Government and Slum Housing* (Chicago: Rand McNally and Company), 1968, pp. 94-113; and Leonard Freedman, *Public Housing: The Politics of Poverty* (N.Y.: Holt, Reinhart and Winston, Inc.), 1969, Chapter 1.

[10] National Commission on Urban Problems, *Building the American City* (Washington, D.C.: U.S. Government Printing Office), 1968, p. 100.

[11] Henry J. Aaron, *Shelter and Subsidies* (Washington, D.C.: Brookings Institution), 1972, Chapter 5 supports the view that Federal underwriting of mortgage risk constitutes an indirect subsidy.

[12] Joe R. Feagin, Charles Tilly, and Constance W. Williams, *Subsidizing the Poor: A Boston Housing Experiment* (Lexington, Massachusetts: D.C. Health and Company), 1972, Chapter 3.

[13] .Christa Lew Carnegie, "Home Ownership for the Poor: Running the Washington Gauntlet," *Journal of the American Institute of Planners*, May, 1970, pp. 160-167.

[14] See collection of papers in: James Q. Wilson (Editor), *Urban Renewal: The Record and the Controversy* (Cambridge: The M.I.T. Press), 1966.

[15] Herbert J. Gans, "The Failure of Urban Renewal," *Commentary*, April, 1965, pp. 29-37.

[16] Chester Hartman, "The Housing of Relocated Families," *Journal of the American Institute of Planners*, November, 1964, pp. 266-286.

[17] National Commission on Urban Problems, *op.cit.*, p. 160, Table 2.

[18] Peter Marris and Martin Rein, *Dilemmas of Social Reform* (N.Y.: Atherton Press), 1969.

[19] Bernard J. Frieden and Marshall Kaplan, *The Politics of Neglect: Urban Aid from Model Cities to Revenue Sharing* (Combridge: The M.I.T. Press), 1975.

[20] Bernard J. Frieden, "Housing and National Urban Goals: Old Policies and New Realities," *The Metropolitan Enigma* (James Q. Wilson, Ed.) (Cambridge: Harvard University Press), 1968, pp. 170-225.

[21] Feagin, *et al.*, *op.cit.*, pp. 55-56.

[22] For a discussion of housing allowance, see President's Committee on Urban Housing, *A Decent Home* (Washington, D.C.: U.S. Government Printing Office), 1968, pp. 70-72; and Arthur P. Solomon and Chester P. Fenton, "The Nation's First Experiment in Housing Allowances: The Kansas City Demonstration," *Land Economics*, August, 1974, pp. 213-23.

[23] James L. Sundquist and David W. Davis, *Making Federalism Work* (Washington, D.C.: The Brookings Institution), 1969, p. 85.

[24] HUD, *CDA Letter No. 3*, "Policy Statement on Citizen Participation," October 30, 1967.

[25] HUD, *Local Public Agency Letter No. 458*, "Increased Citizen Participation in Urban Renewal Projects," June 24, 1968.

[26] Sherry R. Arnstein, "Eight Rungs on the Ladder of Citizen Participation," *Journal of the American Institute of Planners*, vol. XXXV, no. 4, July, 1969.

[27] For a discussion of the negative consequences of housing intermediaries, see: Bernard J. Frieden, "Improving Federal Housing Subsidies: Summary Report," *Papers Submitted to Subcommittee on Housing Panels*, U.S. House of Representatives, Committee on Banking and Currency, June, 1971, part 2, pp. 473-488.

[28] U.S. House of Representatives, *Investigation and Hearings of Abuses in Federal Low- and Moderate-Income Housing Programs, Staff Report and Recommendations*, Committee on Banking and Currency, December, 1970.

[29] Victor E. Bach, "Subsidizing Home Ownership Through the 235 Program: The Wrong Instrument for the Right Purpose," *Working Paper No. 2, Joint Center for Urban Studies of M.I.T. and Harvard University*, Cambridge, Massachusetts, January, 1971, pp. 6-9.

[30] National Commission on Urban Problems, *op.cit.*

[31] U.S. Senate, *Hearings, Senate Committee on Banking and Currency*, Subcommittee on Housing and Urban Affairs, July, 1967, part 1, p. 638.

[32] Frieden and Kaplan, *op.cit.*

[33] *Ibid.*

[34] Section, 109, Housing Act of 1968.

[35] The figure was quoted by Senator Clark: U.S. Senate, *op.cit.*, p. 83.

[36] Victor Bach, "The Community Development Block Grant Program: Local Experience in Six Major Center Cities," testimony presented to *U.S. Senate Oversight Hearings*, Committee on Banking, Housing and Urban Affairs, August 24, 1976.

Charles Haar

13

Housing Policy and Programs:
The Johnson Years

The periods marked by presidential terms can be useful milestones in evaluating the history, successes, failures, prospects, and aspirations of a social program, such as that of a national housing policy. In many ways, housing policy is a useful lens through which to view the Johnson Administration in toto. It sets forth, in microcosm, the broader hopes of that presidency, and reveals the underlying assumptions of much of that Administration. Its achievements, as well as its frustrations and mistakes, can be seen in the broader context as characteristic of the interplay of power, politics, and personalities that characterized the Johnson Administration.

Organization of a Department

What was immediately outstanding in the Johnson era was the setting up of housing as a major national priority. It was during the Johnson years that the long struggles, began spasmodically under Eisenhower, carried forward by John F. Kennedy but then defeated by a curious coalition in the Congress, finally came to rest with the creation of a national Department of Housing and Urban Development (HUD) in 1965. Thus, for the first time, cities and housing were given a voice in the Cabinet, presumably directly into the ear of the President; the Department would furnish a focus for the needs of the cities and those groups not being satisfied by the market enterprise system so far as shelter needs were concerned.

Unlike many reorganizations—which often take the place of policy when no other course occurs to the policy maker—the setting up of a cabinet department bore with it important substantive connotations. It called attention to housing as a claimant upon national resources and priorities. It meant new relations with the President, the Office of Management and Budget, and Congressional committees.

The Department exists today; but, many claim, with low morale and with uncertain mandate. Does this, to some extent, reflect a frailty in the design of the initial structure, or, on the other hand, is the uneasiness due to a lack of a sense of common purpose among the 15,000 people who work in the Department?

This question may be easily put aside as a subject for further examination, for which much can be said on either side, and for which evidence is hard to muster: who knows what would have been the result had other routes been followed? For instance, one of the major discussions we had on the Task Force that helped organize HUD concerned the Community Action Program. Should this mainspring of the War on Poverty be incorporated into the department? This merger might have cured what may be conceded to be a major functional difficulty of the Department—a concentration on physical planning and development. The Community Action Program undoubtedly would have put HUD much more into the forefront of human concerns, perhaps even to the point of economic development strategies in depressed urban areas. The Task Force did recommend this course to the President, with but one dissent. For whatever reasons, the President agreed with the dissent. In the case of both Presidents Andrew Jackson and Lyndon B. Johnson, a minority of one could readily emerge as a majority. A probable influence on the decision was that such a transfer would simply accentuate the position of HUD as a representative of minority groups and minority needs, rendering its relationships with the Congress and with the appropriation process even more difficult.

Organization of a housing department, especially one with the imperialist tag of urban development, is replete with puzzles, resplendent with paradox. One of the major programs that the Johnson Model Cities Task Force, chaired by Bob Wood, recommended for inclusion was that of the Bureau of Public Roads—a division was to be made between the intra-metropolitan and the inter-metropolitan portions of the highway trust fund program, with HUD to be in charge of construction within the metropolitan areas. We are all too familiar with the powerful impact of roads on the suburban-central city relationship, on the patronage, monies, and power that ride with construction. Had this program gone to HUD (as it might have, because at that time the Bureau of Public Roads itself was being transferred out of

Commerce) it might have given the department a different sheen.

And, while dealing with transportation's effect on housing and land use, another decision of the Johnson Administration must be taken into account—transferring urban mass transportation from HUD into the new Department of Transportation. In 1968, the DOT, as the newest Minerva of the Administration, had to receive special treatment. With this transfer in 1968 of a funded program out of HUD that could induce action on the local and metropolitan level for comprehensive planning, the erasure of "urban development" from the title of the Department was to all intents and purposes complete. Under the Romney secretariat, there was even less of an interest in transportation; it scrapped a complicated treaty that had been worked out in 1967 between HUD and DOT, which might have meant that the planning, especially on an area-wide basis, could have utilized the transportation fund for achieving comprehensive land-use goals. With this final clipping, HUD was to become predominately and overwhelmingly a housing department.

Yet it must be put down as a major Johnson achievement, one which only those who struggle to give housing a center for national concern and attention can fully appreciate. That setting up a cabinet department did not "solve" the urban crisis was foreseen. But, the potentiality of its being is a major promise.

Finance

The key to housing programs is the availability of capital and the price at which it is made available. This is a major strand in any housing program. It also relates to organization of a national department. For instance, if one were truly interested in establishing a powerful department—fashioned after the model of the McNamara Pentagon—control over the housing finance institutions would become crucial. Thus, the Home Loan Bank Board would be regarded as a crucial arm of the secretary in carrying out housing policy. Because of its dominance over savings and loan associations—the chief investors in residential real estate—it would help make available the flow of capital where required by national policy.

Without the secondary mortgage market the ability to move the production of housing is extremely limited. Under the

Johnson Administration, the Federal National Mortgage Association (FNMA) and Government National Mortgage Association (GNMA) were used widely at times of money shortage. There was a recognition by the director of the budget, if not by the President, that monetary policies often dealt unfairly with the housing and the municipal bond sectors. Under the guise of equality, which a general, impersonal setting of discount rates achieved by putting all would-be borrowers on the same footing, large corporations and consumer credit were inevitably favored by the banks. The sharp drought of money and the almost absurd roller-coaster effects on the construction industry (most recently seen in the housing drop from a 2.4 million starts per year to a rate of less than 900,000 per year in 1974) reflect a current willingness to make housing the weathervane of cyclical response. Under the Johnson Administration, while the Federal Reserve Board was dominant, and the Secretary of HUD had but a low-keyed voice in putting forth the claims of his constituents, nevertheless there was willingness to open up FNMA and GNMA to redress the balance. The invention of the Tandem Plan, the launching of the auction program, and the devising of the GNMA pass-through securities by the innovative Ray Lapin meant that FNMA was revitalized, and made into a strategic supporter of the housing programs. As part of the paradoxical way that accounting procedures rule us from the grave, and the strange way that the budget deals with capital items, FNMA was "privatized" in the Johnson years, leading to subsequent abuses which need not have taken place.

The power of financing leads to this interesting conclusion: all public policies on housing are not as effective in producing dwelling units (so long as we rely on the dynamism of the market mechanism) as a one percent decrease in interest rates decreed by the Federal Reserve Board. Hence, if any consistent approach to the housing industry is to be undertaken, a far closer relationship between HUD and the financial instrumentalities of government is crucial, whether this involves restoring the Home Loan Bank Board to HUD; or a new form of secondary market operation; or giving the Secretary some special role in the group upon whom the President relies for monetary, fiscal, and tax policy advice. This is one of the key questions that the Johnson Administration has left us.

A National Urban Policy

The organizational issue also raises an ideological one: the willingness to have a consistent and coherent national policy towards cities and the aggressiveness with which it is pursued. Many programs have come on the scene which might have been added to HUD to augment its ability to cope with the concentration of people and investments we call cities, which by their nature pose problems which are multi-faceted, multi-disciplinary, and range over the spectrum of human needs and desires.

For example, one lag—and this may be a surprising one to many observers of the Johnson scene—was the failure to put the Law Enforcement Assistance Administration (LEAA) into HUD. But for a peculiar quirk of history, this could have happened. When high-crime neighborhoods became an important issue in 1967, it became clear that the Democratic Party would have to develop its own approach and not leave this concern to the reactionary forces to take up as their issue. The Safe Streets Act was proposed and developed. At that time the Justice Department was reluctant to undertake its operation. Not used to dealing with congressional committees and lobbies, with trade-offs, with pressures, and content in its status as the conscience of the king, it did not wish to embark on a grants program.

Now think what might have happened had this been placed within HUD. Here is a program essential to cities—one that would go directly to mayors and strengthen the arm of city hall. Above all, it is a program popular with the middle class, extremely favored by the Congress, one which has money and one which would give the Department formidable staff and strength, and also an opportunity to carry out urban programs providing high-caliber municipal services where there was pressing need for safety, security, and domestic tranquility.

Programs such as economic development within the central dilapidated areas of cities or a variety of others could have changed the whole mien of the Department. In those circumstances the focus might not have been so much on producing housing—anywhere, anytime, with no consideration of where they are being located, how they are serving human needs, how they fit into the whole context of the environment, including access to jobs and transportation—as on how they help to preserve and enhance the potentialities of our cities.

Still another paradox emerges when housing is studied as a tool, and as a component part, of city building: the unintended consequence of high levels of housing production means housing that is located in suburban areas, attracting middle-income households out of central city neighborhoods, with consequent abandonment and concentration of poverty in older neighborhoods. To some degree, the Model Cities program was seen as a counter-strategy by the Johnson Administration, but, it must be conceded, the full interrelationship had not yet penetrated into the consciousness of policy makers at that time. How to expand the levels of production, thereby raising the housing choices open to all income groups, yet not adding to the financial woes of cities was a problem which was not resolved by the Johnson Administration.

Federalism

In many ways housing is the best test of how an administration really feels about the interlocking roles of the Federal Government, the states, and the cities. Unlike most other social welfare programs, housing presents an anomaly to the political theorist conceiving of municipal corporations as creatures of the state. For years, there had been a direct lifeline between the cities and Washington, bypassing the states. This was the essence of the public housing program and, later, of urban renewal.

So far as the Johnson Administration was concerned, Bishop Berkeley was wrong: not only is there an external world, but there is such a thing as a national housing need, and there is a definite role for Washington to discharge. There was, of course, recognition of the reality that regions and cities varied widely within this nation and that much depends upon local talents, local goals, and local desires. But by and large there was a sense of national purpose in Washington, a certain pride of authorship involving a belief that the Federal bureaucracy was learned, able, and hard-working. There was also a strong feeling that the President, elected by all the people, represented the different interests in society, often the poor and powerless, that were sometimes suppressed by city machines, and that he should be elected or defeated on the basis of what he did with regard to this constituency. Above all, there was a sense of a Congress and a working with the Congress. Under the Johnson Administration, it can be said that the Department was Congressional, with a Secretary accustomed to dealing with the legislature and highly adept at it, regarding his function as that of translating the President to the Congress and in turn bringing back its views and reactions. Hence there was a strong feeling of a national legislature's needs for satisfying its constituents, for cutting ribbons, for putting its programs through, and for its right to see what a program means and how it is carried out. This, of course, is in sharpest contrast with the subsequent Nixon Administration, which viewed Congress at best as an unruly partner. Moratoria occurred in 1973, impoundments throughout. What programs were to be carried out were to be developed at the state and local level away from Washington.

The past eight years have stressed the decentralization of HUD and its programs. But to what degree this cleavage represents contrasting philosophies of government is again unclear. In many ways, the difference in assigning responsibilities for housing to different levels of government may be said to represent clashing ways of sizing up things. It manifests different attitudes toward the very existence of a housing problem. So far as the Johnson Administration was concerned, the housing shortage was a problem to be met head-on and solved; the President's function, as laid out in his housing messages, was that of arousing the public recognition of what the less fortunate were suffering by way of deprivation in housing, as well as in opportunities for education, adequate health care, and employment. Men and women living at the margin of subsistence were a blight not befitting a Great Society. There was an eagerness to deal with the issue in Washington and a subordinate recognition was given to the role of the states and localities. By contrast, so far as the Nixon-Ford Administrations are concerned, the problem, while pressing, contained seeds of shame, something to be swept away, even at times to be denied, as in that famous pronouncement by President Nixon that the urban problem had folded its tent and gone away. That people were inadequately housed was due to their inadequacies, due to their failures to pick up the challenge of American society, to dig in heels, work hard, and prove themselves. Hence delegating it down (aside from federalist theory), meant that the problem was not there to be faced at the central office. Perhaps it would go away. Concededly, this "hot potato" version of block grants is an unfair characterization. But there is enough evidence in the speeches, in the stresses on balancing the budget, to support this perception.

With the Model Cities program, the forerunner of block grants, and the central program of its young years, HUD recognized the crucial role of locally developed, locally orchestrated, and locally implemented development plans into which housing should fit. But even here the type of close review that the Department insisted upon from Washington, indicated much more of a national view of the problem. This might have relaxed had the Johnson Administration continued. What one cannot escape from in dealing with the housing programs of the Johnson Administration is how unto Moses they are like: they came into sight of the promised land, the Douglas and Kerner Commissions having furnished the necessary momentum, and what the President was to call a "magna carta for housing" was enacted in the autumn of his Administration in the Housing and Urban Development Act of 1968. But it was never given to them to administer the programs they had advanced; they were not succeeded by Joshuas but by others who had a different program for carrying out the plans laid down most notably in the Model Cities Program and in their Sections 235 and 236 of the 1968 Act.

The balance between the cities, the states, and Washington, D.C. cannot be set for all times. There is much ingenuity in local government, as the recent uses of community development funds and housing rehabilitation programs attest. But the aggregation of local policies does not add up to a rational national housing or urban policy. The abdication of Federal responsibility, other than as a raiser of funds, entails a policy of neglect. The litany of ills encountered by our cities contains too many elements dependent on national intiatives, calls for massing of markets and of private enterprise, and demands skills and resources which no local governmental unit can muster. Federalism does not call for a withering away of national effort.

Housing and Coalition Politics

Much as the housing policy agenda of any administration must deal with central bank economics and fiscal policies necessitated by fears of depression or inflation, so it must cope with the pressing reality of coalition politics. This still is the key factor keeping the Federal Housing Administration within the Department, despite its heavy recent financial losses and despite the incursion of private mortgage insurance. FHA represents the middle-income and suburban parts of the coalition necessary to get housing legislation passed. Again and again in the omnibus housing legislation of the Johnson Administration, the sections on housing for the elderly, those for urban renewal areas, those for minority groups, would have been doomed without the presence of FHA.

For the political fact of life is that subsidized housing is a minority program. It cannot garner the votes necessary for appropriations, even with temporary triumphs in authorization, unless there is a perceived violent crisis, or unless there is powerful executive leadership combined with coalition tactics which can muster a majority of the Congress. Thus, the politics of interest groups and coalition is crucial if lower-income housing programs are to be viable.

This may change, indeed as it seems to be at present. For with housing costs continuously on the rise, and with no more than 20 percent of the population in many metropolitan areas able to purchase a home, housing inadequacy has become a middle-class issue. It is not only minority and lower-income families who are locked in, but young married and middle-class households who cannot afford homes in the current markets.

With this kind of coalition, a housing program capable of mustering broad support can be developed. But within the economic and political climate of the period, the Johnson Administration had to so limit, so shape, so combine, and so package its housing programs—often ingeniously, using the best resources of the public sector and the private sector to their mutual advantage—before the programs could be passed. This will constantly confront a housing program: how can it gain sufficient support to mount a national commitment to meeting the needs of an ill-housed minority of American families.

Housing and Civil Rights

Equal housing opportunity, the ability to live where one chooses to live, was emphasized very early in the Johnson Administration housing programs. The Model Cities program pivoted about this requirement. From its launching, there was an assistant secretary for equal opportunity in HUD, and the Fair Housing Act of 1968 was a major accomplishment of the Administration.

How far ahead of the public in this respect, as apparently in so many other aspects of housing production, was the Johnson Administration? Leadership should disdain the Gallup Poll approach, yet its findings were never too far from the President's arm; however, when convinced of their rightness, he was ready to venture his political capital for the programs that he deemed essential. In civil rights, the Administration's housing policy was closely related to the milieu of the Warren Supreme Court, with its stress on the dignity of the individual. The Johnson Administration, recognized the needs for equalization and eliminating all forms of discrimination and *Jones v. Mayer* was decided on about the same day as the Fair Housing Act was passed.

Naturally, this politically explosive approach was shunned by the Executive Branch under Nixon. But the courts continued to press the Johnson legislation to its logical end. And they wove together two separate areas which the Congress had seemingly absent-mindedly failed to interrelate.

The Shannon case is noteworthy for its beautifully elaborated opinion in which it pointed out something which people within HUD, as well as experts and decision makers outside the Department, tended at times to forget in the turmoil of dealing with burning issues of immediate consequence—housing policy is far more than the producing of shelter, it is also aimed at human dignity and private rights.

Carefully tracing the development and convergence of Federal housing and civil rights policy, the court concluded in *Shannon v. HUD* that "increase or maintenance of racial concentration is prima facie likely to lead to urban blight and is thus prima facie at variance with national housing policy." While HUD has broad discretion to choose between alternative types of housing,

> that discretion must be exercised within the framework of the national policy against discrimination in federally assisted housing. . . .Here the agency concentrated on land use factors and made no investigation or determination of the social factors involved in the choice of the type of housing which it approved.

In delineating a national housing policy, it is not enough to study Section Two of the Housing Act of 1947, with its statement of a decent home and a suitable living environment for every American family, nor the Housing Act of 1968, which quantified this need (26 million units of housing of which 2.6 million were to be for low-income and for sub-standard housing) so that there would be a deliberate target to aim at, by which to judge performance and evaluate dedication. As the Court pointed out, Congressional policy with respect to housing has to be found also in the various civil rights acts. So site selection, race relations, and opening up the suburbs have become the judicially decreed context within which housing policy is to operate.

This remains the ideal, and its legislative realization is a lasting achievement of the Johnson era. Its implementation is far more difficult, as the courts have found in the Gautreaux case. But slowly, piece by piece, public housing is going to be built that is nonsegregated and non-monolithic in nature. Slowly too, will the realization sink in of the metropolitan character of the housing market. The hope is that with new viewpoints, with the education which is part of leadership, with a strong role undertaken by a national department for citizens who elect and who pay taxes for it, there will be a deepening understanding of how housing in communities can be developed so that people can live in harmony not only with their inner selves but with their neighbors.

The Public/Private Melange

Under the Johnson Administration there was to be a creative mutual partnership with the private sector, with subsidy, support, and incentives being provided by the public sector. Even in the public housing programs, the invention and the later proliferation of the turnkey programs show the bent toward the private sector. The Douglas Commission pointed out that, in a way, these programs posed a last clear chance for private enterprise. Operating concurrently, the Kaiser Commission had pointed out reluctantly (in what turned out to be a wise admonition in view of the fiasco of Operation Breakthrough) that technology could not supply the whole answer. But by and large, government policy would stress housing production in the private sector.

Again, this is an uneasy balance in many sectors of the economy, but especially acute in housing. Housing for the lowest-income groups cannot be expected to be provided by the profit motive. Incentives and credit intermediaries have been shaped to stave off the spectre of government ownership, government building, government domination. But too often, for lack of institutional framework or of adequate supervision of the housing and appraisal industries, the results have been a perversion of public interest. For the groups (20 to 30 percent of the population) for whom the society as a whole is not working, a new system of providing shelter may be the next step in the reorientation of society's goals and priorities.

Your Money or Your House

Housing allowances, cash programs, and the like, have come to the political fore since 1968. This contrasts with the production side which received the Johnson Administration emphasis. Housing allowance experiments are presently being evaluated. At this point, it is not at all clear what they prove, as happens with many social science programs when they hit the reality of the fan. But when the moratoria on housing subsidies were declared by the Nixon Administration, and the stress in domestic programs went to income allowances for the poor rather than the typical housing production subsidies, this was regarded as a return to the "market". To many this seemed not a return, but a deliberate distortion of what the housing market is like. What the experiments seemed to demonstrate was the inability to appreciate the structural difficulties in the housing industry, the peculiar financial arrangements, the unique history, the conditions of no vacancy in many metropolitan areas which mean that increasing demand means inflation in prices rather than the production of new inventory.

One can hardly do better than to say that a blend (perhaps one *could* do better, by saying a wise blend) of both production and demand subsidies are necessary for effective housing programs, and that the proportion depends on individual local and metropolitan markets. But the proof of the value of the cash programs is still being awaited. More interesting—and this was a policy much debated within the Johnson Administration—is the broad question of whether a negative income tax, direct income maintenance, or some other conduit of turning money directly over to the poor might be a better way to satisfy the unmet needs of the housing market. In many ways, the turn of the Nixon-Ford Administration to the economists' stream of cash allowance rather than to a production approach can be seen as relief from coping with the intractability, intricacies, details, and hard-shell of the housing problem. While the Democrats may at times be said to throw money at the problem it may be better over the long-run for society than to cast dust upon the problem.

Presidential Leadership

Housing programs must share the fate of other domestic programs. Reform in the Great Society meant, in part, reasoning together. While housing to some degree was losing out on its internal metropolitan strategy, it ran into the unreason of war. For the major factor undermining housing strategy is that peculiar juxtaposition of domestic and foreign policy which has such great power over the fate of reform programs. Well aware of what war had done to Wilson's New Freedom and, still later, to FDR's New Deal, both of which had come to a halt in world wars, LBJ foresaw (with a prescient vision upon which he nevertheless proved unable to act) the effect of Vietnam on his Great Society. Housing could no more survive in the pressure cooker of the war than could other innovative domestic legislation. Reform, for many, requires a sense of guilt and shortcoming. To wage a war, however, other tones must be sounded: rectitude, belief in one's virtue and the nation's cause. Above all, the money was not there. Both tunes could not be played at once, which resulted in weakening the impetus for reform. Under the Nixon Administration, continuance of the Vietnam War drowned the nation's spirit even further, leaving little resolve to deal with the sorry condition of the cities.

Thus, in many ways, the Johnson housing programs represented a willingness to recognize a social problem, to deal with it, to marshall governmental resources, and hopefully, by action, to overcome. In many ways the administrations that followed the Johnson era paid lip service under the tenure of some secretaries, while others were dedicated to the production of housing as the records of 1970 and 1971 amply demonstrate. But there is a whole question of tone, of faith, and commitment—of the willingness or not—of a great nation to use its resources, to dedicate its ingenuity, to develop innovative institutions and arrangements, or to seek new combinations of public and private energies that can tap the best of each sector. The Johnson Administration was ready to lead. Indeed, it had a need to lead. Its willingness to try was in the main tradition of American political pragmatism and optimism, of belief in the responsiveness of institutions. That is the heritage it bequeathed to housing, a most difficult social problem which constantly changes its format and yields not to easy solution.

In learning from the past, we need to distinguish the transient and the tumultuous from the elements which are stable, more persistent, and more enduring, There are factors which have remained constant in the housing situation from the Johnson period to the current one: the existing stock of housing; the common elements of cities; the overwhelming force of the business cycle; the interests of Congressional committees; and migrations. So if man usually remains within the limits of possibility, as the great French historian Braudel reminds us, it is because his feet are stuck in the clay of those material conditions.

But then there are the more malleable features and the changes in those eight years: new migration patterns; changed attitudes on racial and economic integration; existence of state housing finance agencies; growth of private mortgage insurance companies; awareness of the plight of the older Northeastern and Midwestern sections of the country and of their dilapidated central cities.

So the interesting political puzzle of the 1970s will be to isolate those housing elements that are persistent and those where possibilities of action exist. The advances made in the Johnson era will form learning experiences and provide impetus for new action, but what is certain is that a return to these programs is no longer possible in the America of the 1970s, nor would that type of adherence to the old be understood by President Johnson. It is out of the new elements and out of a recognition of the new societal setting that a housing program for the 1970s will be forged. The return to liberal and rational politics will provide the thread of continuity.

A decent home is central to the American dream and to a stable family life. The goal of a decent home for every American is a worthy goal. These are the recurrent themes of the Johnson housing programs. With leadership, compassion, and efficiency, this goal can be attained.

Bernard Frieden
Marshall Kaplan

14

Community Development and the Model Cities Legacy

Federal aid for community development has raised troublesome issues from the New Deal to the New Federalism. Allocating money fairly to the cities, channeling it into projects that serve both national and local needs, giving Federal direction while allowing local flexibility, above all minimizing delay and red tape—these are chronic problems. Each generation of program designers and public officials deals with them in its own way.

The more basic issues of purpose—who is to be served, what types of programs shall be funded—are defined mainly by the priorities of each administration in Washington and by the political context of the cities. On these fundamental questions, we have come almost full cycle since the 1930s.

At that time, as the recent best-selling biography of Robert Moses reminds us, Federal community development aid meant municipal public works, with the benefits going mainly to well-off citizens and their neighborhoods. Even in Fiorello LaGuardia's "city of opportunity," a massive program of playground construction did little for the tenement and slum areas but concentrated on the more prosperous parts of New York. Lowest priority went to the three large areas where most of the city's black population lived. Of the 255 playgrounds Robert Moses built in New York during the 1930s, Harlem got one, Bedford-Stuyvesant got one, and South Jamaica got none at all. Harlem did get a new playhouse-comfort station in Riverside Park. Many of Robert Moses' buildings contained sculptural embellishments supposedly appropriate to their use or setting. The wrought-iron trellises in the Harlem playhouse were decorated with monkeys—an indication perhaps of Mr. Moses' biases and then prevalent social attitudes.[1]

From Public Works to Model Cities

The combination of Federal money and local public works construction did little to improve conditions in slum neighborhoods even after the invention of later Federal aid programs for urban renewal, highway construction, water and sewer facilities, and open space. Public officials and city residents both recognized that the great suburban boom of the 1950s left in its wake inner city neighborhoods suffering from poverty, physical deterioration, and civic neglect. When Lyndon Johnson's Great Society was ready for new Federal initiatives in the cities during the 1960s, this was the perception that gave rise to the Model Cities program.

Model Cities dealt head-on with the problem of how to move Federal dollars into the poorest urban neighborhoods, but by then the notion of what help was appropriate went far beyond the neighborhood parks and swimming pools of the 1930s. The nation had rediscovered poverty in the early 1960s and had found its causes to be varied and complex, calling for a wide variety of solutions. The spirit of the Great Society called for a more ambitious approach to community development, one that would go beyond the hardware of cities and give equal priority to raising the performance of school children, improving health conditions, training the unemployed for jobs, and bringing the poor fully into the political and economic life of the community. To this already formidable set of goals, the designers of the Model Cities program added another that was close to the hearts of both Federal and local officials alike: streamlining and reforming the Federal grant-in-aid system.

And Back to Public Works for the Well-Off

Before the Model Cities program could move very far, it met resistance from the Federal agencies whose cooperation was essential for its success, and then it came under attack from within the Nixon White House. Although the program continued to be funded at roughly the promised levels, repeated threats to close it down created a climate of great uncertainty which frustrated both Federal and local efforts to make it work. Eventually, the Housing and Community Development Act of 1974 replaced Model Cities with a different strategy of the 1970s: Community Development Revenue Sharing. The new approach, now being implemented, involved a consolidation of major Federal community development aids, including Model Cities. It provided a single grant allocated to localities on a formula basis. Washington imposed very few restrictions on how or where the money was to be spent, so long as expenditures were in accord with the broad purposes of the replaced programs and met several generalized objectives, one of which called for benefits to low- and moderate-income families.

Initiation of Community Development Revenue Sharing represents more than a managerial reform and a retreat from the unrealistically ambitious objectives of the Model Cities program. Early evidence suggests that local governments have used their freedom to shift funds quickly from poverty neighborhoods to other parts of the city, with at least tacit Federal approval. And despite the rhetoric of local control, national policy is once more encouraging the use of Federal money for public works projects and discouraging its use for public services.

From the point of view of poverty neighborhoods, the changes of program and strategy surely approach a no-win situation. During the 1930s, they were unable to get their share of public works funds for street improvements, playgrounds, and swimming pools, because they lacked political clout at the local level and because Federal programs did not give them special priority. During the 1960s, when Federal requirements worked in their favor and funds were available, hardware improvements were out of style. Instead, the money went for a diffuse range of public service activities that were more fashionable because they were seemingly innovative, experimental, and ambitious. But they were also high risk, and they left most poverty neighborhoods still impoverished in terms of community facilities. Now hardware expenditures are again fashionable; but in many areas the poor lack the political clout to secure facilities, and there are no Federal programs that send money directly into their neighborhoods. When will they ever get their parks, playgrounds, and swimming pools?

To give the urban poor a fair share of resources for community development and a chance to help decide what kinds of projects are appropriate, it is neither necessary not desirable to return to the Model Cities or categorical grant approach. Community Development Revenue Sharing, however, has rejected the valid purposes as well as the unworkable administrative features of the Model Cities program. In some areas of the country, it is becoming a wasteful public works program with no evident purpose of its own. In other cases, leakage of funds beyond the neighborhoods of the poor minimizes the rather fuzzy social priorities in the statute.

Early legislative attention is needed to redirect Community Development Revenue Sharing to its declared goal of helping low and moderate income people. The Model Cities program has generated ideas and experience that can be helpful in reshaping current community development activities, and in making overall Federal urban policy more consistent with key urban problems. We turn now to its history with this aim in mind.

MODEL CITIES AND ITS CONTEXT

If any one program represented or epitomized the Great Society (and its New Frontier inheritance), it was Model Cities. Here was an urban aid effort befitting, at least in concept, the emerging commitment of the Kennedy Administration to respond to urban poverty and the Johnson Administration's commitment to convert laudable objectives to action. Here was an urban effort that was directed, not at replacing, but at extending, and coordinating the numerous, hard won, categorical programs passed in the sixties. Finally, here was an urban aid effort, whose very genesis reflected the alliance between liberal academia and liberal politician, between the halls of Ivy and the White House.

Model Cities was partially the response of a rather open political system to outside events. Among them:

Civil Rights Movement/Rediscovery of Poverty

Martin Luther King's "I have a dream" speech in 1963 symbolized the spiritual content of the civil rights movement. Its political strength was reflected not only in the growing numbers of people taking to the streets, but in the emergence of a committed religious-liberal-labor coalition—a coalition ready to do battle for Federal intervention in a range of economic and welfare problem areas.

Because of the overlap between issues related to discrimination and problems related to poverty, the "movement" supported, indeed helped to generate, the rediscovery of the poor. Concern over racial and income issues, while not yet table-talk conversation, had apparently ɔecome an important White House agenda item at the time of President Kennedy's assassination.

Numerous cities in all parts of the country erupted in racial violence during the early and mid-sixties. While not as extensive and destructive as the riots which paralleled and came after the inception of Model Cities, racial troubles seemed all pervasive. Because there appeared to be a direct link between what key elements of the public considered to be the legitimate demands of civil rights activists and the response of state and local officials to these demands, racial violence, at least initially, prompted many people to favor a more active role for the Federal Government. Certainly, television exposure of Bull Connor's dogs attacking kids, and fire hoses turned on peaceful marchers, did much to create public support for civil rights laws.

Criticism of Categorical Programs

Stimulated by the liberal mood of the country after the assassination and pushed by the new President's activist predilections, Congress significantly increased the number and coverage of categorical aid programs between 1963-1966. Over 219 new grants-in-aid or assistance programs were established, more than doubling the total on the books prior to that time. By the mid-sixties, the aggregate volume of categorical monies was $12 billion.

No systematic overview guided program developers. To the contrary, most assumed that problems could best be attacked if they were defined discretely and handled with tailor-made strategies. This approach fit the pragmatism of the era and was politically acceptable. Also, it responded well to the many constituent groups yearning for Federal attention and Federal dollars. As important, it promised a reasonable local response to nationally determined needs. Would-be recipients were asked to meet legislative and administrative prescriptions concerning how, when, and on what to spend Federal funds.

Even before the ink had dried on the Presidential signatures below the new aid programs, many found fault with them. Some, according to their liberal detractors, were under-funded; too few, suggested others, were directed at changing local institutions or the way they treated the poor and minorities.

Resolution of complex problems was impeded, indicated

many, by the absence of a comprehensive, coordinated Federal urban aid effort. Cities could not easily make sense out of the confusing, fragmented Federal inventory. Always complicated, sometimes onerous Federal ground rules and program regulations were alleged to block locally innovative projects. The long delays caused by Federal reviews, the void between statutory objectives and administrative guidelines, and the weighty paper requirements associated with many programs, provided critics (both those in favor of Federal involvement and those opposed) with legitimate arguments in favor of reform.

Dissatisfaction with Urban Renewal

The then most visible Federal program for the cities, urban renewal, had few friends by the mid-sixties. Critics viewed it as exacerbating the difficulties of cities and of the poor by displacing taxable property and housing. On the right, those who disliked the program saw it as a threat to private ownership and labeled it "the federal bulldozer"; on the left, it was seen as a means to rid urban areas of the poor and minority groups.

Even for those who supported the program, its record was not a good one. From 1949 to 1963 almost 240,000 housing units were demolished in urban renewal areas and only about 70,000 were built or under construction in these same areas.[2] The poor and the minority family unquestionably received short shrift: · "At a cost of more than $3 billion the Urban Renewal Agency . . . has succeded in materially reducing the supply of low cost housing in American cities."[3]

In the process, Federal relocation regulations were not always met and very little attention was given to ameliorative social services.

Problems with the War on Poverty

Immediately after President Kennedy's death, the new Administration drew on work of the Council of Economic Advisors and the Bureau of the Budget to develop a bold new program for the nation's poor. The War on Poverty, administered by the Office of Economic Opportunity (OEO), was in part a response to the critique of earlier Federal programs. But it could not easily resolve its own inconsistent legislative mandates. Little wonder. The War's generals and troops were asked, on the one hand, to coordinate the operations of numerous Federal and local institutions and, on the other, to create parallel structures and encourage countervailing pressure groups. When faced with a choice, key OEO personnel generally made coordination a low priority item on their agenda.

Despite, or perhaps because of, OEO's visible success in creating thousands of Community Action Agencies around the country, the White House continued to feel the need for a new handle on urban policy. To the rising chorus of those who complained about the still unwieldy nature of urban aid programs, were now added the angry voices of many mayors demanding that Washington reduce the role of the poor in the War on Poverty.

Designing a New Program

President Johnson's massive electoral victory in 1964 gave him a mandate for strong leadership as well as a receptive Congress. His success in securing the establishment of the Department of Housing and Urban Development prompted renewed staff efforts to create new agendas for coping with the problems of cities. The Johnson White House typically looked for new ideas by bringing together advisors from outside the established Federal agencies. In Lyndon Johnson's view, the bureaucracy was "too preoccupied with day to day operations . . . too . . .dedicated to preserving the status quo . . . Moreover, the cumbersome organization of government is simply not equipped to solve complex problems that cut across departmental jurisdictions."[4]

In the fall of 1965, the President appointed a Task Force on Urban Problems, chaired by Robert Wood. It contained nine members, each with a well-known pedigree from academia, politics, labor, or the private sector. All were believers; that is, all shared a positive attitude about the ability of government to intervene successfully in the domestic sector. As important, most felt that the President and his White House staff could play a leading role in first defining and then carrying out urban policies and programs. applying presidential power to move recalcitrant agencies. None of the active members, however, had had much experience with Federal agencies. Unfortunately (in retrospect), no one was around to remind them of the obstacles most agencies would place in the way of reform and change—

especially when their turfs were invaded or their programs were tampered with.

After a few months of very private deliberations, the Task Force proposed a new "demonstration city program." It was premised on several guiding principles, all seemingly reasonable in light of the then current criticism of categorical aid efforts.

To resolve urban problems, the Demonstration Cities program (or Model Cities as it was soon called) would go further than the War on Poverty and require "the coordination of all available talent and aid . . . the mobilization of local leadership and initiative." To participate in the new program, cities would be asked to compete against each other. Competition would help limit program participants and permit the concentration of funds. Ostensibly it would permit the selection process to be based on visible commitments to the purposes of the program and local capacity to act effectively.

If initial local commitments to improve living conditions for low-income citizens passed Federal review and won approval, city hall would receive additional planning funds and ultimately a hefty allocation of discretionary "supplementary" funds as well as an assumed priority in tapping existing categorical monies. Hopefully, after a relatively short time (five years), the results would generate major and visible improvements in the quality of life in designated Model Neighborhood areas.

Despite the perceptions of some on the Task Force that city capacity was marginal and that Federal abilities to respond to city needs in a "coordinated" manner were untested (irrespective of Presidential commitment), the Task Force laid on both a heavy agenda. For example, cities, presumably led by aggressive elected officials, were to pick a neighborhood, engage in an extended, orderly, and comprehensive planning process, and implement a series of mutually supportive projects and activities. However, the proposed Federal prerequisites proved difficult to respond to, and politically out of sorts with local resources, conflicts, and needs.

For their part, the Federal Government, encouraged by an involved White House and orchestrated by the Department of Housing and Urban Development (HUD), was to:

• monitor and assure meaningful resident participation—a feat (irrespective of the statutory substitution of "widespread citizen participation" for OEO's "maximum feasible participation") not entirely without peril given the tensions in most poverty neighborhoods and wary attitudes of most local officials toward citizen groups;

- earmark existing grants-in-aid for participating cities—a task not calculated to please either non-involved cities or Federal program managers jealous of their prerogatives;

- provide technical assistance to hard-pressed city halls—a seemingly legitimate assignment without, however, clear definitions or available staff resources;

- develop performance criteria that would give cities maximum freedom in the use of Model Cities funds, but that would still guarantee their use for the benefit of the poor;

- evaluate overall program results—a doubly difficult assignment because of the broad range and number of program objectives, and because of the program's continuing dependence on the very agencies to be evaluated.

Surprisingly little was lost in the translation of the task force concept into legislation. While Congress quickly let it be known that political facts of life meant that more than a few demonstration cities would have to be involved, the task force itself had begun the dilution process when it recommended a total of 66 cities be included in the program.[5] Further, although Congress watered down Administration language requiring "measures to eliminate social and racial segregation," it left in language emphasizing the proposed program's concern of social priorities. Not too surprisingly, given limited funds, Congress joined with Administration spokesmen in obscuring the extent to which the new program could or would grant priority to participating cities for the use of the existing Federal inventory.

As finally enacted, the Model Cities program was a significant departure from previous Federal urban aid efforts. Taken as a whole, the legislation provided considerable latitude but not complete freedom for participating cities. For example, although the statute restricted the use of Model Cities funds to projects included in a city-prepared, HUD-approved plan, and projects in or related to a defined model neighborhood, it did not (unlike most existing categorical programs) require that funds be spent on any one problem area, or by any specific type of sponsor. While not the millennium, the new program came close to offering cities a flexible block grant for poverty neighborhoods.

City Response

Extensive evaluations are not needed to confirm the fact that the Model Cities program did not meet President Johnson's lofty expectations or even the more modest ones implicit in the statute. A casual tour of most model neighborhoods would show that unemployment remains a problem; that many families still live in substandard housing; that individual poverty is matched by the poverty of public services.

But a gross comparison between hopes and dreams, and actual results, is not enough to tell the Model Cities story. While the accomplishments fell far short of the promises, Model Cities did chalk up several noteworthy successes, especially in comparison with earlier Federal urban aid efforts. Among them:

Numerous job opportunities were opened to the poor and to minorities: Model Cities offered sustained employment opportunities to several thousand lower-income and minority individuals. Even during its early planning stages, close to 40 percent of all jobs were filled by model neighborhood residents. After the 1970 HUD guidelines firmed up resident employment requirements, close to 60 percent of all local agency positions were filled by model neighborhood residents, most of whom were poor. According to one analyst, city demonstration agencies on the average generated one job for every $10,000 in program funding.[6]

City involvement in the Model Cities effort opened up a broad range of city government positions to minorities. One recent California study has found that minority employment in city government increased faster in Model Cities communities than in other places; that many of the positions offered were at senior levels; and that minority employment in local government jobs continues to remain at higher levels in former Model Cities communities.[7]

Low-income and minority communities increased their political strength: Model Cities was in part a response to the problem many mayors and Congressmen had in confrontations with OEO-funded resident groups fighting the War on Poverty. More restrained Model City guidelines concerning resident involvement and a HUD staff that was less ideologically inclined on this subject than OEO's, led to different forms of citizen participation than occurred in the War on Poverty.

In some instances, such as Atlanta, city staff moved quickly and dominated the program, using residents to *legitimize* the results of their efforts. In other cases, as in Dayton, Ohio, residents pushed for and won the right to *control* the program's fate. Parity, or "double green light" situations, like those in Reading, Pennsylvania and Richmond, California, however, in which city hall and resident groups each had an informal veto over the other, seemed to produce the most promising plans for matching program resources to local needs.[8]

Life was not easy for most Model Cities participants. Hostility, anger, and frustration often pervaded discussions among residents and city officials. Federal deadlines and guidelines combined at times to block city efforts at defining feasible work programs, and in the process reduced mayoral involvement to ceremony and resident involvement to legitimizing local submissions.

No matter which system was used, the end result of most Model Cities efforts was an increased awareness on the part of residents of how to "play the game" and "get in the action." Political visibility and neighborhood organization resulting from Model Cities programs strengthened many resident groups to the point where they were able to win at least modest demands from city hall. Among the tangible outcomes were:

• Numerous residents were encouraged to run for political office (national, state, and local), and many won. The growing ranks of the elected black and Spanish-speaking officials throughout the nation contain many who entered politics through Model Cities positions and Model Cities training.

• While the data are not overwhelming, interviews with mayors of many Model Cities communities suggest that the program generated increased pressure to remedy disparities in public expenditures among city neighborhoods. As a result, many participating cities increased their budget allocations to model neighborhoods.

- Equally important, a number of mayors acknowledged the fact that without federally imposed performance criteria, they would not have been able to spend as much as they did in poverty neighborhoods and still survive politically. In effect, Model Cities ground rules provided a shelter, permitting them to share responsibility with HUD for monies spent in poverty areas.

- Although no startling breakthrough occurred to improve the quality of public services, most participating cities were led first to acknowledge (often publicly for the first time) and then to address service problems. Some ventured as far as challenging the monopoly of traditional (sometimes archaic) public institutions in delivering local services; some added programs and funds to the budgets of local institutions willing to experiment with new services.

- Reputable evaluations of local impact were never made. Unfortunately, we must rely on anecdotal evidence and local judgments. Perhaps, given the distance which must be travelled before public services meet even threshold criteria, and the relatively short life of Model Cities, the most telling comment is that Model Cities went further than other Federal aid programs in promoting self critique and new action. Indeed, resident insistence, combined with local perceptions of what HUD favored, resulted in a budgetary turnaround with respect to social services. Formerly, most cities relied on state and county agencies and outside non-local monies to provide social services, but in the Model Cities program, aggregate data indicates that more than 80 percent of local budgets went for social services.

Federal Management

Implementing the Model Cities program put the administrative capacity of the Federal Government to a severe test. The most impressive accomplishment, particularly in light of the subsequent debate over whether Federal strings should be attached to revenue sharing and community development funds, was HUD's success in limiting program reviews to broad performance criteria covering the most important Federal objectives. Only about two dozen out of the nearly 2,000 local projects submitted for HUD review were vetoed for lack of conformity to statutory guidelines. In effect, the review process, by substituting general objectives concerned with the purposes and beneficiaries of projects for administrative standards that prescribe the content of categorical programs, allowed cities considerable discretion, yet assured expenditure of limited Model Cities' funds for relevant purposes.

Most of the other lessons learned do not generate much confidence in the ability of either the Federal bureaucracy or the Congress to mount a coordinated attack on urban problems. Indeed, failure of the Model Cities program to live up to its promises must be attributed mainly to the various Federal participants. For example:

The program was overcommitted and underfunded: As indicated earlier, both the original Wood Task Force and Congress initially supported expansion of the program from a demonstration in a relatively few cities to an element of national policy in cities of all sizes and types around the country. While the ultimate extension of the program to 150 cities may have pleased those who wanted to spread the benefits of a new approach, it was not accompanied by any significant expansion of resources beyond the $2.3 billion proposed by the Task Force for only 66 cities. More important, there never was a legislative commitment to grant categorical program priority to participating cities. To the contrary, both the House and Senate committees involved in reviewing the initial legislation indicated clearly that Model Cities communities should not receive favored treatment with respect to existing aid programs. The House group was quite emphatic:

> Your committee . . . wishes to make very clear its intent that the demonstration cities program will not in any way change the flow of funds, as among cities, under existing grant-in-aid programs. The demonstration cities program does not provide any priority in the use of existing Federal grant-in-aid programs for cities which participate in the demonstration program.

Other departments did not support the program: Initially, hopes were high that the Model Cities effort would take up where the War on Poverty ostensibly failed. That is, HUD in administering the new program "in conjunction with" other agencies and under the direction of the President, was expected to develop a workable method of inter-agency coordination, particularly with respect to the use of other grants-in-aid.

Despite the intervention at times of both the Johnson and Nixon White House, statutory constraints combined with overwhelming departmental resistance produced little in the way of earmarked funds, flexible program guidelines, or technical assistance. Certainly, the Model Cities Program taught us something about the power of the Presidency. While the "Imperial Presidency" may be a phenomenon of foreign affairs, it has little bearing on domestic matters. The White House is not capable of providing *sustained* attention to a single urban program; it is not able to cut through bureaucratic rivalry, red tape, and statutory and administrative criteria. While most cabinet secretaries respond to White House pressure, most staff and programs are well insulated and they often outlive the tenure of the occupant of 1600 Pennsylvania Avenue.

Although precise figures are difficult to come by, it appears that HEW could scrape up only $65 million, the Department of Transportation $9 million, the Economic Development Administration $4 million, the Department of Labor $20 million, and HUD $400 million from their extensive inventories in any one year for use in the Model Cities program. Similarly, although most departments articulated a willing intent, most were not really able to overcome program manager, client group, and in some cases secretarial objections to simplifying Federal aid guidelines.

Federal technical assistance never became a fact of life, either. Most Federal personnel had problems understanding or dealing with varied city needs, priorities, and idiosyncracies; understaffed agencies found it difficult to put good people in the cities long enough for them to be helpful. A good deal of subversion went on under the guise of technical assistance; that is, many agencies used requests for technical assistance to strengthen the resolve of local groups they funded to avoid Model Cities coordination.

The program was shackled by unworkable planning guidelines: Many supporters of the Model Cities Program were convinced that without a federally prescribed planning process, participating cities would not or could not develop the capacity to spend funds wisely. Conversely, others who acknowledged the problems of federally imposed requirements in earlier aid efforts, and were more sanguine about the abilities of municipal government, were committed to minimal Federal involvement. Out of the continuous but rarely clear-cut debate between these two different factions emerged an overly rational, often academic, and almost always unworkable set of HUD Model Cities planning guidelines.

Federal requirements directed cities first to create a *new* planning mechanism responsible to their local chief executives. Subsequently, the new group was asked to prepare a comprehensive development plan incorporating a sequence of intensive problem analyses, a study of underlying causes, a comprehensive statement of goals, program approaches, projects and activities, and definitive budgets. Finally, to win HUD's approval, local plans had to incorporate citizen involvement, innovation, local coordination, and concentration of resources.

Political realities in the cities, combined with constraints of time, budget, and technique, led most participants to respond in form rather than substance to HUD's guidelines. Indeed, the process most cities used was closer to a system for "muddling through" than it was to HUD's concept of rational comprehensive planning. "Comprehensivity" diluted already limited expertise and made coordination and concentration difficult. Resident involvement, which generally translated into an understandable concern for basic services, often ran counter to Federal and staff concern for innovation. In this situation, much time and money were wasted and local priorities were often obscured.

The Bottom Line: What Was the Local Impact?

Even if Federal support had been more generous, less burdensome, and more predictable, could the local programs have delivered on their promise to improve living conditions and opportunities for poor people? Available evidence suggests that in many cases they could not. Although there are no systematic evaluations of the impact of local Model Cities Programs, we do have studies of similar projects undertaken as part of other Federal programs. Their findings are mostly negative.

The field of education offers the clearest example. More Model Cities funds were spent for local education projects than for any other purpose. We can make some judgment about their likely degree of success by looking at the far more ambitious Elementary and Secondary Education Act of 1965. Title I of this program provided more than a billion dollars a year to meet the special educational needs of disadvantaged children. Funding was both large and consistent. The program had widespread congressional support and by the mid-seventies was spending on the order of $1.5 billion per year. Yet every national evaluation that was made found the program had virtually no effect in improving the education of poor children.

In 1967, HEW commissioned a private consulting firm to evaluate the impact of Title I compensatory education. The results were disastrous. In the 11 school districts selected for study because of their reputed success, there was a very slight decline in average pupil achievement after a year of compensatory education. The only good news was that the lowest 10 percent of the pupils in school showed a slight improvement.

The 1967 findings were so threatening to Federal officials and school administrators that they blocked subsequent efforts to undertake similar evaluations. In 1968 HEW ran a survey which asked school districts participating in Title I to return questionnaire forms supplying achievement data. Out of 180,000 questionnaires mailed, fewer than 10,000 came back with usable data, and even these were too unrepresentative to permit any reasonable conclusions on achievement to be drawn. The following year, HEW's survey produced even poorer data.

Recognizing the political realities that prevented any systematic national evaluation, Federal staff instead used the bureaucratic technique known as "mining for nuggets." They searched carefully for successful local programs that could be described in case studies. The result was a description of "selected exemplary programs" and an "It Works" case study series. These nuggets, gathered in 1968, were used repeatedly to justify budget requests. However, follow-up studies found that even the nuggets tarnished quickly, since most of the carefully selected programs failed to show positive results beyond the first year.

How effective compensatory education was may also be gauged from the fact that state and local education agencies refused to supply even basic data on their operations. In 1972, 15 states sent in no reports at all, and Federal evaluation staff did not know the number of children participating in the Title I program. The commissioner of education, reporting to Congress in 1972 after six years and several billion dollars in Title I funding, had to search hard to find accomplishments worth mentioning. He claimed only that the data showed disadvantaged students progressing at a rate approaching the norm for other students, but he had to concede that even with a normal rate of progress, disadvantaged pupils would still remain behind others who had no learning deficits in the first place.[9]

Another favorite Model Cities strategy, the use of community development corporations to create jobs for the poor and to earn profits that could be used for neighborhood services, has also not fared well. Of 30 community development corporations funded by OEO, only a fifth were in the black at the end of 1972. Even so friendly a critic as Sar Levitan has concluded that community development corporations were "no more successful in establishing viable businesses in poverty areas than other establishment-run efforts."[10]

The failure of many Great Society programs to show demonstrable success in improving urban services or helping people learn new skills reflects a fundamental lack of knowledge of how to proceed. Model Cities, like other programs that emphasized innovation, uncovered problems faster than it could find solutions for them, even though it had some success in building new political awareness and creating jobs for the poor.

With hindsight, this experience suggests that Federal programs should not try to steer local efforts away from activities with a high probability of success into other fields with high probability of failure. Without Federal pressure to design comprehensive programs to get at the "root causes" of poverty and without similar Federal pressure on local communities to be highly innovative, most cities would probably have struck a different balance, giving greater weight to doing what they already knew how to do or what residents felt needed to be done.

COMMUNITY DEVELOPMENT AND THE NEW FEDERALISM

President Nixon's major initiative in community development grew directly out of his strategy for dismantling the Great

Society. In his 1971 State of the Union message he drew on the rhetoric of power-to-the-people in presenting revenue sharing as his program of Federal aid to the cities:

> The time has come now in America to reverse the flow of power and resources from the States and communities back to Washington, and start power and resources flowing back from Washington to the States and communities and, more important, to the people all across America . . . So let us put the money where the needs are. And let us put the power to spend it where the people are.[11]

The underpinning of President Nixon's new approach, General Revenue Sharing, became law in October, 1972. During its first five years it will provide $30 billion, allocated on a formula basis to all 38,000 units of state and local government in the country. These governments can spend the money in almost any way they see fit, subject to very few Federal restrictions.

Accompanying General Revenue Sharing as a part of the New Federalism were proposals to consolidate previous categorical aid programs into a series of new block grants that local governments would be able to use with great flexibility within general functional areas, such as manpower training, education, and law enforcement. One of these block grant programs, for community development, was included within the Housing and Community Development Act of 1974. It replaced the Model Cities program, urban renewal, water and sewer grants, grants for open space, urban beautification, historic preservation, and neighborhood facilities, and loans for public facilities and for housing rehabilitation—all of which were formerly administered as separate categorical programs. This special revenue sharing program is the New Federalism's major initiative in community development. It embodies the philosophy of the Nixon-Ford Administrations as surely as the Model Cities program represented the philosophy of President Johnson's Great Society.

Community Development Block Grants are too new to have produced much action in the field. Evaluation must be based on the plans that cities have rather than projects under way. Even from scattered and incomplete evidence, however, the way the program will work is already clear enough. The important news is: (1) there is less Federal red tape than in the older categorical programs; (2) hardware expenditures and public works are back in fashion; (3) poor people and minorities are no longer in fashion.

Cutting Red Tape

Community Development Revenue Sharing has unquestionably made it easier and simpler for cities to do business with the Federal Government. It consolidates seven different programs, each of which formerly had its own complicated application and review procedures. Now a single local application and HUD review are enough to start the Federal funds flowing for all the purposes of the seven predecessors. The new annual applications have been averaging about 50 pages per city, compared with an average of 1,400 pages per year under the earlier categorical programs.

HUD processing time has also been much quicker. Under Community Development Revenue Sharing, the total time from preparation of the local application to HUD approval and execution of a Federal contract has averaged only eight months. All the previous categorical programs for community development averaged more than a year for this process, and urban renewal averaged two-and-one-half years.[12]

If the purpose of cutting red tape is not only to reduce uncertainty and frustration among municipal officials, but also to speed the time it takes for Federal money to "hit the streets," then Community Development Block Grants must be rated as only a modest success so far. By the late spring of 1976, local governments had not yet spent the bulk of funds made available to them under the community development block grant program. Despite the financial squeeze in many communities and the repeated pleas for greater Federal aid, by mid-April 1976 the cities had been able to spend only a third of the $1.9 billion made available to them.[13] This record is comparable to the chronic underspending of funds under the Model Cities program, except that onerous Federal planning regulations were at least partly responsible for the Model Cities delay. Under the newer program, although some Federal regulations remain burdensome or confusing, red tape cutters should next look to city hall administrative and decision-making procedures.

A Return to Hardware

Model Cities, reflecting the spirit of its times, relied mainly on public services to achieve its community development objectives. Only a small amount of local expenditures under this program were for physical facilities, including housing and neighborhood equipment. The bulk of the money went for projects in education, health, manpower training, economic development, public safety, recreation, and miscellaneous social services.[14] This emphasis on software resulted from: Federal pressure to be comprehensive; innovative attempts to provide a wide balance of projects seemingly responsive to the interests of different resident groups; and widespread belief among urban technicians that previous programs had failed to help the poor partly because they were too concerned with physical rebuilding and not concerned enough for the social needs of residents.

As Community Development Revenue Sharing went into operation, it did not offer the cities a free hand in deciding on the mix of hardware and service activities. According to the law, public services may be funded only if they are related to physical development activity in the same area and only if the community has been unable to get support for them under other Federal programs. In addition, the joint House-Senate Conference Committee stated its understanding that no more than 20 percent of any community's funds were to be used for services in support of community development.

At the same time that social services require special justification, pressure from another source has been pushing cities to invest heavily in physical development once again. Almost 1,000 urban renewal projects and 400 related neighborhood development programs approved in the past have not yet been completed. Because HUD still has $4.7 billion in loan guarantees outstanding for urban renewal and neighborhood development projects, the agency has been urging local governments to use community development aid funds to complete these projects. Under the law, the Secretary of HUD has authority to deduct up to 20 percent of a community development grant to apply it toward the repayment of these temporary loans.

Not surprisingly, then, cities are choosing to concentrate 42 percent of their Community Development Block Grant funds in urban renewal and Neighborhood Development Program (NDP) areas in the first year. Similarly they report that 42 percent of their total funds are "clearance-related." Even outside urban renewal and other clearance areas, the great bulk of all the spending under Community Development Revenue Sharing is for hardware. According to approved first-year plans, only 4.3 percent of total funds will be for public services and another 7.7 percent for service-related facilities and equipment.[15] Significantly, former Model Cities communities account for 80 percent of the proposed public service expenditures.[16]

The new popularity of hardware expenditures goes beyond the completion of urban renewal projects. An analysis of community development plans in California cities shows that even those communities which never before received any categorical funding under HUD programs, are also concentrating their outlays on physical facilities and are investing virtually nothing in social service programs.[17] Hardware projects are attractive locally because they are one-shot investments followed only by maintenance costs, unlike service programs which may create clienteles that demand high budgets for years into the future. Further, hardware projects are tangible and visible and therefore traditionally good politics.

Beyond even these considerations, there has been a general disillusionment with human service programs, as their failure to deliver anticipated results has become increasingly well-known. The pendulum can swing too far, however, given the remaining need to find a way to improve basic community services. As important, in some cities poverty neighborhoods are reasonably well equipped with community facilities while important social services are unavailable or underfunded.

Who Benefits from Community Development?

The central question about Community Development Revenue Sharing (and also about the New Federalism at large) is whether it is bringing power to the people or power to the powerful. As a Federal aid reform it has succeeded in simplifying grant applications and in giving greater flexibility to local communities, but it has bought these merits at the expense of the poor.

First, the legislative history tells us something about the degree of commitment to the poor represented in this program. The original Nixon Administration proposal was concerned almost entirely with grant-in-aid reform and would have allowed local governments virtually complete freedom to decide on the use of Federal community development funds. As a result of objections from many members of Congress and urban interest groups, the law that finally emerged in 1974 moved further in the direction of establishing, as a national priority, aid to people of low and moderate income. This commitment is clearest in the provisions that Congress made for the allocation and distribution of funds. While keeping the total grant authorization at about the same level as categorical program outlays of the early 1970s, the law provided a new formula for distributing grant funds to eligible communities. The formula is based on the population of each city and on two other factors chosen to emphasize the social purposes of the program: the extent of poverty (given double weight) and the extent of housing overcrowding in each eligible community.

As far as the local uses of funds are concerned, the legislation does attach strings, but they are loose ones. The declarations of purpose have the ring of a bold commitment, such as "the expansion and improvement of the quantity and quality of community services, principally for persons of low and moderate income." But the application and review requirements are more equivocal. They call for each city to certify that its community development program "has been developed so as to give maximum feasible priority to activities which will benefit low or moderate income families, or aid in the prevention or elimination of slums or blight." But the law also authorizes the Secretary to approve applications for activities which the applicant certifies as meeting "other community development needs having a particular urgency." Similarly, the law requires each community to meet certain citizen participation requirements, but these have more to do with providing information and holding hearings than with assuring a significant role for citizens in policy making.

Since these requirements are vague and difficult to enforce, it is clear that local officials will make most decisions on the final use of funds subject to only a limited amount of Federal prodding. Why, then, should anyone expect local government to give higher priority to poor people in this program than it did with its own community development funds in the past?

Proponents of the New Federalism strategy made two major

arguments. One was that during the 1960s the poor and minority groups, because of Federal requirements, became better organized and more effective in local politics and that local government in turn became more responsive to them. This argument neglected the fact that Model Cities programs were limited to relatively few cities and that low- and moderate-income residents, without the certainty of Federal funds or Federal legitimacy, usually compete for resources in an unfriendly majority environment.

The second argument was that special revenue sharing funds would go directly to elected officials who in turn were directly accountable to voters and subject to political pressure from their constituents. Under the earlier categorical programs, in contrast, the bulk of Federal funds went to special purpose agencies such as local renewal authorities were not directly accountable to the voters and had their own special pipeline to Washington. The second argument neglected the importance of Federal prerequisites in beefing up the courage of many mayors. As one mayor indicated, "without being able to blame the Feds, I couldn't propose spending funds in the ghetto areas. . . The politics would kill me. . ."

The Allocation Formula

Despite Congressional intentions to distribute community development funds according to indicators of poverty, the legislative formula is actually shifting money away from cities with concentrations of poor people and into better-off communities. The full effects will not be felt until 1980, because cities where funding is being reduced will receive transitional grants during the first five years of the program. The new pattern, however, is already becoming clear. The Southern Regional Council's study of community development revenue sharing in the South[18] found that major new beneficiaries of the act include 75 urban counties consisting primarily of suburban communities with strong tax bases, low operating expenditures, and populations with incomes well above the low to moderate level. Most of these counties did not use the earlier categorical programs to undertake community development activities for the poor, and the Council reports growing concern over whether they will spend the $100 million they received in fiscal 1975 to meet the needs of low- and moderate-income people.

A more definitive study of California cities which looks ahead to 1980 formula entitlements demonstrates clearly that the allocation formula does a poor job of carrying out Congressional intentions for the targeting of funds. The authors, DeLeon and LeGates,[19] have identified 15 California "new money" cities that never received categorical urban development aid but will have community development funding; 41 additional "phase-in" cities that will get more aid than previously, and 23 "phase down" cities that will get less than previously.

The allocations formula shifts funds away from areas of black concentration. The new money cities are 0.6 percent black. Other phase-in cities are 3.7 percent black, while phase-down cities are 13 percent black. Cities that are older, and have more substandard and overcrowded housing, as well as a higher percentage of people below the poverty line, are hurt by the allocation formula. As an example, the percentage of population below the low-income level of 1970 was 5.4 percent for new money cities, 7.1 percent for other phase-in cities, and 9.3 percent for phase-down cities.

DeLeon and LeGates found that a city's allocation formula depends almost entirely on a single factor: total population. The formula gives about the same results as one that would distribute resources on a per capita basis. The reason is that the present formula fails to measure poor people as a proportion of the local population. City characteristics measured in total number rather than proportional share—such as number of poor people or number of overcrowded housing units—are highly correlated with total population size. Even the Congressional stipulation that the poverty measure be given double weight makes virtually no difference. In an alternate formula, DeLeon and LeGates gave the poverty component 20 times the weight of other factors and found only minor differences from the present distribution. Their simulation of other formulas shows that use of local proportion of population in poverty or inadequately housed will produce allocations that match resources to needs much more closely.

City Spending for the Poor

Once Federal money reaches a city, are poor people and minority groups now capable of competing against other interests to get a fair share of the money? Early experience with General Revenue Sharing is enlightening in testing the view that thanks to what they have learned under Great Society programs and to newly established Federal aid channels that operate through elected officials, the poor and the minorities can now look after their own interests locally. Under General Revenue Sharing no Federal agency attempts to steer local expenditures toward poor people or poverty neighborhoods. Although it is difficult to know who precisely benefits from most local expenditures under General Revenue Sharing, the Treasury Department's Office of Revenue Sharing reported that through June 30, 1973, the category of social services for the poor and the elderly received only 3 percent of total local spending.[20]

One of the very few strings that is attached to General Revenue Sharing requires nondiscrimination in programs paid for out of revenue sharing dollars. Many local groups have brought complaints of discrimination to the Office of Revenue Sharing (ORS). Where ORS records show the type of discrimination alleged, about half of these complaints concern disparities in local services, such as segregated location of park and health facilities, or unequal levels of service for street repair, sanitation, or water utilities in black and white neighborhoods. These complaints come from 17 states across the country, and ORS investigators have found substance to the complaints in at least half a dozen cases so far.[21]

Another insight into how well the poor are doing on their own comes from a California study in which the investigators interviewed public officials in 97 cities to ask them what percentage of their General Revenue Sharing expenditures they thought benefited the poor. Officials in two-thirds of the cities said they spent nothing at all on programs aimed specifically at benefiting the poor. In the other third, local officials claimed that some revenue sharing expenditures were intended to benefit low-income groups, but of these, three-quarters said that they spent 5 percent of less of their funds for this purpose.[22]

Under special revenue sharing for community development the poor are not left entirely on their own to fight for a share of the funds. Provisions of the law and of HUD's administrative processes directing local funds toward low- and moderate-income people are weak, but they are not totally useless.

For an overview of the results nationally, it is possible to locate locally planned expenditures in specific census tracts and then to characterize these tracts according to the median income of their residents. HUD's first annual report follows this procedure but uses a questionable yardstick. It classifies census tracts according to the relationship of their median income to the median income of the entire metropolitan area in which they are located. Census tracts with median incomes of 80 percent or less of the metropolitan area median are considered to be low and moderate income. According to this analysis, local communities plan to spend approximately two-thirds of the funds in low- and moderate-income neighborhoods.[23]

The problem with this measure is that in most large metropolitan areas the entire central city has a median income well below the metropolitan median. To determine whether a city is using its community development funds for low-income residents, a better yardstick would be the median income of the individual central city, rather than the metropolitan area including its suburbs. The National Association of Housing and Redevelopment Officials (NAHRO) surveyed first-year applications from 86 entitlement cities and found that only 12 percent of the community development funds were headed for low-income census tracts where median incomes were less than half of the city's own median earnings. According to the NAHRO study, another 39 percent of the funds are to be spent in moderate-income neighborhoods having between 51 and 80 percent of the city's median income.[24]

A closer look at the data in HUD's first year evaluation confirms that low-income neighborhoods are getting only a small share of the funds for new community development activities. Within the low- and moderate-income census tracts, as defined by HUD, nearly half the planned expenditures are for land clearance activities. The bulk of this money is undoubtedly going to complete existing urban renewal projects. Land clearance usually means the uprooting of low-income families and their relocation to other parts of the city. Demolition and relocation can hardly be considered benefits for poor people, especially at a time when the housing subsidy programs that might conceivably provide them with better places to live are either in suspension or not yet working. If we exclude money planned for clearance-related activites in low- and moderate-income areas—as defined generously by HUD—these neighborhoods will get only 34 percent of community development funds for the first year.[25]

Further, HUD's analysis of community development strategy in its 151 sample cities reveals a shifting of funds from the neighborhoods in worst condition to those that are somewhat better off. In comparison with recent expenditures under categorical programs, there is now:

> ... a greater emphasis on preventing and eliminating blight in the early stages of decay... Recipients are placing greater emphasis on activities in neighborhoods beginning to decline and those with decline clearly in progress. Those neighborhoods accelerating into major decline and nonviable, heavily abandoned neighborhoods receive less emphasis.[26]

Local Controversies

Several local controversies illustrate the difficulty low-income people are having in making the new community development system work to their advantage. For example, the Southern Regional Council reports that in Gulfport, Mississippi, local officials actively directed community development funds away from projects that would help the poor. In response to a city government questionnaire, residents listed the most important community development needs as housing rehabilitation, clearance of dilapidated buildings, storm drainage, street paving, street lights, and new sidewalks. Dissatisfied with these answers, local officials sent out more questionnaires. The new returns gave higher priority to building a central fire station, which then became the feature of Gulfport's first-year community development program.[27]

In Little Rock, Arkansas, a Southern Regional Council investigator asked the director of the Department of Human Resources how the city could justify spending $150,000 in community development funds to build a tennis complex in an affluent neighborhood. He claimed first that 99 percent of the money was going to low- and moderate-income areas, but then added: "you can't divorce politics from that much money. . .we must remember the needs of the people who vote. . .because they hold us accountable. . . Poor people don't vote."[28]

The Department of Housing and Urban Development, in a review of charges brought by the Southern Regional Council, explains that the central fire station in Gulfport, the tennis court in Little Rock, as well as a civic center and parking garage in Spartanburg, South Carolina, are all legally eligible activities. As for the contention that Gulfport failed to follow the results of its own citizen survey, the HUD review notes simply that "The statute makes very clear who makes the final decisions after it has followed the citizen participation process."[29]

In Alhambra, California, legal service attorneys representing three local citizens have gone to court to try to stop the city from spending $100,000—half of its total first-year community development grant—to enlarge a municipal golf course from 9 to 18 holes. The city put forward the golf course proposal under the statutory provision that allows HUD to approve activities for funding if the community certifies that they have "a particular urgency," even though they do not directly benefit low- or moderate-income families or help prevent blight. The city's own first-year application did not support this claim of special urgency and, in fact, ranked the goal of improving existing parks below seven other needs of higher priority. The statute gives the Secretary of HUD final authority to determine whether a local certification of particular urgency is justified, and the suit charges that HUD abused its discretion in this case.[30]

In Honolulu, a proposed Community Development Block Grant budget presented to the city council consisted mainly of public works and recreation projects having little discernible relationship to the needs of low- and moderate-income people. The proposal included a flood control project, several new bridges and road improvements, sanitary landfill operations, sewage facilities, and expenditures for the Honolulu zoo, several regional parks, and other recreation areas. During city council hearings in 1976, an attorney from the Hawaii Legal Aid Society argued that under the Federal statute, community development block grant funds are intended to benefit low- and moderate-income people and not to finance public works projects for the community at large. He threatened legal action if the council adopted the proposed program. The council then decided to revise Honolulu's plans.[31]

No matter how strong local resident groups are, the statutory definition of eligible activities allows them only limited and occasional leverage to influence the content of local programs. Further, current HUD requirements for citizen participation offer no more than a small opening into the local political system. Guidelines require each community to provide citizens with adequate *information* about the program, holding at least two public hearings to obtain their views, and provide citizens "an adequate opportunity to participate in the development of the application." But, the law is explicit in giving final authority for local decisions to elected officials.

One measure of resident involvement in decision making is the use of community development funds to pay for citizen participation activities. Although no national data are available, two surveys covering most California cities found that four-fifths of them spent no money at all for this purpose. Most outlays for citizen participation in California were a carry-over of former Model Cities activities.[32]

In short, cities can have about as much or as little citizen participation as they want and still receive their community development block grants.

Local experience has not yet been studied extensively and there are many variations from one community to another. Further, any judgments made in the first year of a new national program must be tentative. Still, the incomplete and early evidence at hand strongly backs these conclusions of the Southern Regional Council:

The 1974 Act, with the New Federalism approach it embraces, rests on the theory that local governments can be relied upon to carry out urgent national goals—in this case, the goal of improving the living conditions of urban persons of low and moderate income. But the fact is that local governments are not carrying out this goal with any consistency. Instead, they have been permitted to deviate at will from the national responsibilities that the 1974 Act supposedly places upon them.

. . . The very mixed achievements of Southern cities have shown that local diversions from the national purpose are not just occasional abuses, but rather form a pattern inherent in the implementation of the Act.

Clearly the most serious difficulty with the Act is that it fails to assure the channeling of funds to its low and moderate income target populations. . . The most important reason for this difficulty is the lack of political influence that low and moderate income groups exercise in the local community development decision-making process. Consequently, with an Act that relies so heavily on local political processes to carry out national objectives, legislative changes must be directed primarily toward strengthening the influence of low and moderate income persons in local community development decision-making.[33]

Comparing Community Development Strategies

Early returns show that Community Development Block Grants are operating very differently from the Model Cities program, but no more effectively in achieving national purposes. The purposes of the block grant program are in fact hard to identify. Our reading of the legislative background suggests that the following objectives are legitimate points of comparison for evaluating the two programs: keeping red tape to a minimum, giving local communities flexibility to select their own projects, delivering Federal resources to the low- and moderate-income groups for whom they were intended, and funding projects that are of benefit to their users.

The Model Cities program never succeeded in its attempts to simplify Federal aid management or to cut processing time for local applications. It gave the cities greater freedom to design their own projects than the categorical programs that preceded it, but Federal policy set the basic direction with an emphasis on social action and public service delivery. The program was a conspicuous success in channeling its resources into city neighborhoods where poor people and minority groups were concentrated. Local Model Cities projects were symbolically important at a time of great urban unrest, but our best judgment is that the services they offered were of little substantive value. They were more effective in helping the poor and minority groups to get public service jobs and to enter city politics.

Community Development Block Grants are a success in cutting Federal red tape, although the cities are still unable to spend Federal funds without long delays of their own. Under the new arrangements, cities are much freer than before to design their own programs. Washington continues to shape the character of local expenditures, however, this time favoring physical facilities and hardware investments. The block grant program is failing to target its funds into projects for low- and moderate-income neighborhoods: cities are taking advantage of the wide loophole the law provides to support activities that have nothing to do with families of below-average income, and HUD has readily given its approval to this diversion of funds.

Community Development Block Grants, as they are now operating, approximate a general revenue sharing program for public works. Cities are not funded on the basis of need, but according to a formula that amounts almost to per capita grants. Nor are the cities required to allocate their Federal funds to neighborhoods or projects on the basis of need: HUD relies heavily on their own good faith in complying with the statutory purpose of assisting people of low and moderate income.

If the overriding national purposes in urban development are to cut red tape and to encourage cities to spend more money on public works than they might otherwise choose to do, then this program may be a great success. What remains of a national commitment to improve living conditions in poor neighborhoods, however, is rapidly becoming a casualty of the legislative shuffle.

SALVAGING COMMUNITY DEVELOPMENT AND NATIONAL COMMITMENTS

Our assessment of both the Model Cities program and Community Development Revenue Sharing assumes that a continuing commitment to improve city slums and marginal neighborhoods is still the main reason for any Federal involvement in local community development projects. This assumption may be wrong. If it is wrong, community development block grants may already have served admirably to accomplish several political objectives. As a minimum, this program has given good cover to a retreat from the objectives of the Great Society, and has extricated Federal officials from troublesome local controversies across the country.

Yet, even from a political point of view, the Community Development Revenue Sharing program could easily turn into a major liability. It will soon be vulnerable to charge that it is little more than a $3 billion public works fund disguised by admirable statements of purpose while giving local governments free reign to spend Federal dollars however the most influential local citizens see fit.

Instincts for political preservation as well as residual social commitments—particularly among Congressional supporters of community development legislation—should both argue for early revision of the Community Development Block Grant program. We have some suggestions toward that end.

A guiding principle emerging clearly from Model Cities experience is that the American political system requires complementarity among programs for different interest groups. That is, programs for the poor are feasible politically only if there are, at the same time, similar but bigger programs for majority interests.

To this extent, a comparison of Model Cities with community development block grants is not entirely fair. Model Cities was only one of a handful of community development programs under the Great Society, and, of these, it was the only HUD program set aside explicitly for the poor. Community Development Block Grants, on the other hand, wrap together virtually all of HUD's Federal aid activities for urban development. Politically, it is close to impossible for HUD to turn its back on constituents who used most of its former categorical programs and to channel all-embracing community development funds primarily into slum neighborhoods. Even the lofty declarations of purpose in the legislation itself do not call on HUD to do this.

Still, as indicated earlier, Community Development Revenue Sharing is doing less than it could and much less than Model Cities did to give poor people a piece of the action. Between 1968 and 1972, the Model Cities program sent 18 percent of HUD's total community development aid budget into poverty neighborhoods.[34] According to the NAHRO study cited earlier, only 12 percent of current community development funds are going into comparably low-income census tracts, and much of this will be for clearance activities of questionable value to neighborhood residents.

Nor does our analysis of HUD data show that citizens of moderate income will be the prime beneficiaries of the new program. Excluding clearance activities, only a third of first-year community development funds are allocated to areas inhabited by moderate-income households. Most of the money will go for a combination of unfinished urban renewal projects, public works in the better neighborhoods, and facilities to serve an entire city, such as downtown parking garages. If the program continues on this course, the average citizen will benefit about as much as the average New Yorker did from 25 years of generously funded urban renewal projects in that city—which is to say that there will be some benefits, but they will not be very great.

Next Steps

We suggested in our book, *The Politics of Neglect*, that the basic components of the present Federal inventory—general revenue sharing, special revenue sharing, and the remaining categorical grants—meet the requirement for complementarity many times over and are capable of responding, in combination, to the political and administrative needs highlighted by the Model Cities experience. What is needed is a deliberate Federal strategy that recognizes the continuing, special claims of poverty populations to a fair share of national resources, and a willingness to deploy the three types of Federal aid (general revenue sharing, community development block grants, and categorical programs) according to this strategy.[35]

Among our specific recommendations:

Consolidate local planning: The Federal Government should use its leverage to have cities draw up spending plans for a broad combination of Federal aids as part of a single operation. Special purpose allocations to the poor and to families of average income are likely to be more defensible if they are seen as a small part of the total flow of Federal funds for a community, rather than if each individual Federal program is up for grabs before the city council. For this purpose, HUD and the Office of Revenue Sharing in the Treasury Department should consolidate the local reporting requirements for General Revenue Sharing and for Community Development Revenue Sharing. Further, their guidelines should encourage local communities to treat these as complementary programs, to plan their budgets for both on the same schedule, and to hold public hearings on the two programs together.

Permit categorical grants to be used as incentives: Categorical programs remain a primary source of Federal aid. They offer numerous opportunities to meet "complementarity" objectives. Some aids, continuing current practices, could be provided cities based on existing criteria. Others, however, restructured to provide for simpler administration and more strategic use, could play an important role in helping cities respond to commitments concerning reduction of poverty, elimination of discrimination, and improvements in local government management capacity. We would propose particularly that cities illustrating clear-cut efforts to attend to the problems of the poor and to their own administrative deficiencies receive priority in the allocation of categorical aids for social services.

Set specific income criteria and minimum budget allocations for community development grants: A most important step is to tighten the legislative requirements that community development block grants be spent primarily for activities that will demonstrably benefit low- and moderate-income families. The law should set realistic standards for measuring low and moderate income in relation to the median income for each community taking part in the program. Further, to provide mayors and councils with the political ability (shelter) to allocate funds to poverty areas, and low-income residents with a firm basis for claiming their rightful due, the law should establish a specific minimum percentage of funds to be used for low- and moderate-income families—on the order of the 80 percent requirement contained in the Senate version of the 1974 Act, which was deleted by the Conference Committee. Correspondingly, the law itself should set a low ceiling on the percentage of funds that can be used for local exceptions—that is, for other community needs unrelated to low- and moderate-income people.

Tighten standards for resident involvement in community development programs: To promote greater consistency between community development projects and the people for whom they are intended, we believe Congress should also tighten the requirements for citizen participation. The citizen role should, in our view, remain an advisory one, but present law does not provide even for a meaningful advisory role. The law should not prescribe specific procedures, but should state performance standards similar to those drawn up for the Model Cities program. They should, for example, require cities to offer residents of low- and moderate-income neighborhoods opportunities to comment on city proposals.

Let the cities decide on the mix of hardware and service projects: The extreme diversity of American cities argues against any attempts from Washington to prescribe the kinds of projects that will be most useful to local residents. Federal pressure in the Model Cities program led to an over-emphasis on human service activities; counter-pressure in Community Development Revenue Sharing is likely to lead to an over-emphasis on public works construction. Many of the older cities in the country are deficient in community facilities for their poverty neighborhoods; while many newer cities are reasonably equipped with hardware but have only marginal public services. City governments, with advice from their residents, are best equipped to decide what kinds of projects make sense to them and to be held accountable for the results. We believe the law should not continue to set more demanding requirements for service activities than for hardware.

Can these requirements for spending priorities and resident involvement be carried out without imposing the red tape burdens that made the Model Cities program so difficult to administer? We believe they can. In fact, the current application and review process is unnecessarily complicated and should be simplified. The law now requires each eligible community to submit an annual application containing a three-year plan, a comprehensive strategy, short- and long-term objectives, a one-year community development program, a program to prevent blight and provide improved community facilities, and a housing assistance plan, together with a program budget and several other local certifications.

If the statutory criteria determining who the beneficiaries are and establishing a resident role are stated clearly as performance standards, it should be feasible to do away with some of the current administrative requirements without sacrificing important national purposes. In place of the current community development plans, programs, and comprehensive strategies, each city should be required to submit only a brief statement of its objectives consistent with statutory criteria, and an annual statement of proposed projects. The Federal review should be based mainly on a post-audit after each year of operations, focusing on the consistency of actual expenditures with the community's annual statement and with the statute. If these requirements are to carry weight locally, the post-audit must be a serious one, carrying with it the threat of reduced subsequent grants if a city's expenditures violate statutory purposes.

Revise the basic community development allocations formula: In addition to these changes which would affect local uses of community development funds, the formula by which block grants are distributed among communities is badly in need of revision. The factors Congress included as indicators of local need actually have only a small effect on aid allocations under the existing formula. As part of an effort to redirect this program in line with its stated purposes, the formula should scale Federal aid for community development according to the proportion of poor people among a city's residents, and the degree of obsolescence of community facilities.

Although Community Development Revenue Sharing is off to a poor start in our view, if these recommendations are accepted it would provide a legitimate format for Federal aid to urban areas. Unlike Model Cities, it does not make unrealistic demands on a large number of Federal departments for support and coordination, nor does it call on local officials to supply a degree of coordination unavailable in Washington It is simple and straightforward to administer. Its aims are modest and realistic. Linked strategically, as we have suggested, to other complementary elements of the Federal inventory, the Community Development Program could yet offer cities increased opportunities to improve the quality of life for low- and moderate-income people.

References

[1] Robert Caro, *The Power Broker* (New York: Vintage Books, 1975), pp. 509-510 and p. 560.

[2] U.S. Advisory Commission on Intergovernmental Relations, *Relocation: Unequal Treatment of People and Businesses Displaced by Governments* (Washington, D.C., 1965), p. 24; William L. Slayton, Commissioner, Urban Renewal Administration, Statement in U.S. Congress, House Subcommittee on Housing, *Hearings: Urban Renewal*, 88th Cong., 1st Sess., 1963, pp. 421, 428.

[3] Scott Greer, *Urban Renewal and American Cities* (Indianapolis: Bobbs-Merrill, 1965), p. 3.

[4] .Lyndon B. Johnson, *The Vantage Point* (New York: Popular Library, 1971), pp. 326-327.

[5] Bernard J. Frieden and Marshall Kaplan, *The Politics of Neglect, Urban Aid from Model Cities to Revenue Sharing* (Cambridge: MIT Press, 1975), p. 49.

[6] Model Cities Services Center, *Model Cities: A Report on Progress* (Washington, D.C., June, 1971), p. 61.

[7] Rufus Browning and Dale Marshall, "Implementation of Model Cities and Revenue Sharing in Ten Bay Area Cities: Design and First Findings", paper delivered at American Political Science Association, September, 1974, Annual Meeting.

[8] Numerous studies of the model cities effort by the firm of Marshall Kaplan, Gans, and Kahn illustrate the effect of resident organization. See *The Model Cities Program: A Comparative Analysis of the Planning Process in Eleven Cities* (HUD, 1970), and *The Model Cities Program: A Comparative Analysis of the Planning Process in Twenty-One Cities* (HUD, 1972). See also Sar A. Levitan and Robert Taggart, *The Promise of Greatness* (Cambridge: Harvard University Press, 1976), pp. 169-187.

[9] Information on Title I evaluation from Milbrey W. McLaughlin, *Evaluation and Reform* (Cambridge: Ballinger Publishing Co., 1975), Chapters 3, 5, and 6.

[10] Sar A. Levitan and Robert Taggart, *The Promise of Greatness*, p. 266.

[11] President Richard M. Nixon, *The State of the Union Message*, January 22, 1971 (Washington: Office of the Federal Register), pp. 92-94.

[12] U.S. Department of Housing and Urban Development, *Community Development Block Grant Program: First Annual Report* (Washington: GPO, 1975), pp. 13-16.

[13] *Community Development Digest*, June 8, 1976, p. 4.

[14] The Urban Institute, "Survey Research Related to the Evaluation of the Model Cities Program: Second Quarterly Progress Report" (Washington, D.C., 1969), pp. 125-149; and Model Cities Service Center, *Model Cities: A Report on Progress* (Washington, 1971), pp. 41-76.

[15] Department of Housing and Urban Development, *Community Development Block Grant Program*, pp. 38-40.

[16] HUD, *Community Development Block Grant Program*, p. 31.

[17] Richard DeLeon and Richard LeGates, *Redistribution Effects of Special Revenue Sharing for Community Development*, Working Paper No. 17, Institute of Governmental Studies, University of California, Berkeley, 1976, p. 30.

[18] Raymond Brown, *et al.*, *A Time for Accounting: The Housing and Community Development Act in the South* (Atlanta: Southern Regional Council, 1976).

[19] DeLeon and LeGates, *Redistribution Effects* . . . ,p. 30.

[20] National Clearinghouse on Revenue Sharing, *Revenue Sharing Clearinghouse*, May-June, 1974, p. 2.

[21] Morton H. Sklar, William L. Taylor, *et al.*, "Civil Rights under General Revenue Sharing," *General Revenue Sharing Research Utilization Project*, vol. 2: *Summaries of Impact and Process Research* (Washington: National Science Foundation, 1975), p. 8; and Center for National Policy Review, *General Revenue Sharing: The Case for Reform* (Washington: Catholic University Law School, 1976), p. 8.

[22] John L. Korey and Catherine H. Lovell, "Implementation of Conflicting Goals: The Policy Impact of General Revenue Sharing in 97 Southern California Cities," paper prepared for 1976 annual meeting, Western Political Science Association, April 1-3, 1976.

[23] HUD, *Community Development Block Grant Program*, Table 4.1, p. 38.

[24] *Housing and Development Reporter*, vol. 3, April 19, 1976, pp. 119-120.

[25] Calculated from Table 4.1, HUD, *Community Development Block Grant Program*, p. 38.

[26] HUD, *Community Development Block Grant Program*, p. 30.

[27] Raymond Brown, *et al.*, *A Time for Accounting*, p. 51.

[28] Raymond Brown, *et al.*, *A Time for Accounting*, p. 53.

[29] Unpublished U.S. Department of Housing and Urban Development, "Review Comments: Southern Regional Council Report," 1976.

[30] *Garcia, et al. v. Hills*, U.S. District Court, Central District of California, CD No. 76-1014, dated March 29, 1976.

[31] Robert M. Harris, Legal Aid Society of Hawaii, "Testimony before the city council of the city and county of Honolulu regarding the annual budget bills and program of the city and county of the fiscal year, July 1, 1976 to June 30, 1977."

[32] DeLeon and LeGates, *Redistribution Effects . . .*, p. 30.

[33] Raymond Brown, *et al.*, *A Time for Accounting*, pp. 102-104.

[34] Calculated from HUD, *Community Development Block Grant Program*, Table E.5, p. 142; and Frieden and Kaplan, *The Politics of Neglect*, Appendix c, p. 271.

[35] See Frieden and Kaplan, *The Politics of Neglect*, pp. 234-257. This chapter describes the authors' proposals for amending Federal urban aid programs and their administration.

SUMMARY John Gallery

Since 1949 Federal urban policies can be divided into three general phases. Phase one consists of the era of urban renewal and categorical grant programs spanning from the Housing Act of 1949 up through the mid-sixties. Phase two consists of the Model Cities program initiated in 1968, and phase three, the Community Development Block Grant program established by the Housing Act of 1974. In many respects the Model Cities program is the key link between the programs of the past and those of the present. As Marshall Kaplan pointed out, the program arose out of the critique of urban renewal programs and the emergence of a consciousness of the poor that arose out of civil rights legislation. Thus it was an attempt to move from the fragmented system of categorical grants (210 separate urban programs had been created by the Federal Government between 1963-1965 alone) in the direction of consolidated grants as well as an attempt to refocus housing programs on the poor.

Considerable attention has been focused on the Model Cities program in recent years. Most of these evaluations have been directed toward the substantive results of activity in specific cities—that is the extent to which the program improved the delivery of services, created jobs, or improved the environment of the city. This emphasis tends to overlook the fact that one of the key differences between the urban programs of the Johnson Administration and those which followed was the attitude of the Administration. Mayor Richard Hatcher said, "During the New Frontier and the Great Society, there was present an element that, if it is present today, is there in a diminished form. That is, a feeling in the country and particularly in the cities, that someone really wanted to solve the problems that existed." This is particularly true of the problems of low-income and minority people in urban areas.

This attitude of wanting to solve the problems of the poor

resulted in definite shifts in emphasis from previous programs. While urban renewal programs had increasingly served middle-income families or central-city development interests, the Model Cities program was limited by its legislation to areas of the city where low-income and minority people were concentrated. In addition, the program required that the citizens directly affected should have a formal role in the process of planning and development. Because of this, said Gordon Cavanaugh, the programs need to be evaluated in terms of social accomplishments. "Mr. Johnson, and to some degree Mr. Kennedy, recognized that it was the process in the long run that could bring change for poor people." Cavanaugh noted that "the principal legacy [of the Model Cities program] is that the poor are a little stronger, considerably more self aware, somewhat more self-sufficient. Their vision of their own potential has been enlarged."

The failures of the Model Cities program, in other than these social accomplishments, help to expose the discrepancies between Federal rhetoric and action. Since 1949 Congressional housing legislation has stated its objective as providing a decent home and a decent environment for all Americans. As Cavanaugh said, "Historically what has occurred is that most of the resources of these programs have tended to serve not the poor who don't have decent homes, but to serve the broader community purposes and to benefit mainly middle- and upper-income citizens, institutions, or business concerns." In addition the resources provided have been woefully inadequate. As Floyd Hyde pointed out, "The Model Cities program, for example, was funded at a level of about $750 million a year, with which HUD was expected to improve the quality of life for citizens comprising three-fourths of the total population of the country." Kaplan has also pointed out the inability of Federal agencies to bring about the type of coordination between physical and social development implied by the Model Cities legislation.

In some respects the Housing Act of 1974 and the concept of block grants appear to be addressed to deficiencies of previous programs. For example, having recognized the inability of Federal agencies to bring about certain types of programmatic coordination, the block grant passes flexibility and jurisdiction to the cities, hoping that they will be better able to effect this coordination. According to Hyde, from a legislative point of view, "there isn't anything that could not be done in the CD block grants that was done in the Model Cities program." But in most administrative respects, as Bernard Frieden stated, the block grant program seems a retreat from commitments of the Model Cities legislation. Its most fundamental problems derive from the lack of commitment to urban problems by the Nixon and Ford Administrations. Kaplan stated that, as originally conceived, "The Community Development program was supposed to link community development and housing. Indeed cities have to submit a housing assistance plan prior to receipt of their annual CD contract. Unfortunately under the Nixon and Ford Administrations there has been a moratorium on housing programs. So cities submit a piece of paper that has no relevance to any other part of the Federal inventory, that lacks any sort of Federal commitment. The whole public sector housing policies have been set back several years because of this divergence between housing assistance and CD funding."

Some of HUD's policies in implementing the block grant program have further accentuated the funding problems. Hyde noted, "At the peak of the categorical grants that now compromise the CD block grant, HUD was serving approximately 1,100 cities in the country. Under the formula approach of the block grant somewhere between 1,400 and 1,500 cities should have received funds. However in the first year of the program HUD, with glowing accounts, pointed to its tremendous record of having funded some 3,500 communities with an additional 1,900 communities funded through county governments. HUD points to the objective of funding 4,800 communities this year with the same amount of funds and next year funding 7,500 communities."

Even the flexibility of the block grant approach, while it has given greater local control and reduced Federal red tape, has brought its own particular problems. Mayor Hatcher said, "Before the block grant approach became really entrenched, one of the protections that a mayor had was that he got most of the programs with very specific instructions as to how and where he could spend the money. With the block grants that is not there any more. As a consequence, mayors and councilmen are subject to a great deal of pressure from those who have the greatest amount of political influence." Flexibility at the local level does not insure that low-income people benefit from Federal programs. Indeed such an emphasis seems too politically difficult for mayors.

Cavanaugh said, "The programs that have succeeded most are those that have had the most Federal supervision and involvement. And when I say worked the best I mean those which have worked for the poorest people."

The political pressure away from low-income areas is compounded by a lack of citizen pariticpation in the block grant program. As Hyde said, "While cities can use block grant funds for technical assistance to citizen groups, they don't have to. And, as you might expect, about 90 percent of them or more have opted not to." Citizen participation, without some resources to get technical advice and to evaluate options presented by public policy makers, is forced to remain at a minimal level. No doubt, some of the resources of the cities are based on concern for the time involved in making certain types of decisions and in implementing programs. But, noted Cavanaugh, this limited point of view overlooks the fact that during the Model Cities era, "the broad participation of low-income people in our country was beginning to illuminate some very basic issues in our society." The elimination of formal citizen participation requirements and lack of funds for technical assistance has, perhaps, been more harmful to the development of meaningful housing and community development programs than any of the other things that have been mentioned.

General Deficiencies of Federal Policies

Some of the problems of Model Cities and CD block grants need to be viewed in a broader context of Federal policy. All too often Federal policies are developed on an individual basis, not part of a total system. This is perhaps dramatically clear in the case of civil rights legislation as it applies to housing. Cavanaugh said, "The Civil Rights Act of 1968 in HUD requirements makes it necessary to find housing sites for low-income people that are in better and more dispersed neighborhoods than in the congested areas of the inner core. That has been a constant battle with a whole series of losses. For as soon as you take a low-income housing project out of the deteriorated section of any community and try to bring it into a suitable environment, you meet vicious and usually successful opposition". The inability to implement such housing policies lies directly behind other urban issues such as school busing. "You cannot have an integrated school system in a segregated housing pattern," Reynell Parkins commented.

Federal policies have also been deficient in recognizing the complete housing problem in the country. According to Cavanaugh, "Two-thirds of the country's substandard housing does not exist in the urban metropolitan areas of the country but is in the rural sections of the U.S. . . . as in the South where half of the rural blacks are in substandard housing; Indian reservations where two-thirds of the people are in substandard housing; farm workers where 85 or 90 percent of the people are in substandard housing." For the most part these problems are only addressed by programs through the Department of Agriculture and while those are well run they hardly touch the problem.

One reason for the oversight in rural areas appears to stem from the lack of involvement of state government in housing programs. Outside of urban areas there are few governmental agencies capable of reaching dispersed rural populations. The states acting if necessary through county governments could provide some assistance in these housing issues. Even in urban areas, the potentially broader resources of state governments have only recently begun to be brought into the picture. Some part of this seems to stem from the direct relationships between the Federal Government and the cities; certain Federal programs might profitably be developed to provide incentives for state involvement in housing issues.

Lastly, all programs have suffered from inadequate Federal resources. Quite clearly, there are not enough public funds to solve all the urban problems in the U.S. or all the housing problems. "Even if we doubled or tripled the block grant appropriation it would be insignificant to do the task we are talking about," said Floyd Hyde. "Unless there is some fundemental institutional change such that local institutions that now spend something like $290 to $300 billion annually in local communities stop neglecting low-and moderate-income people, then $3 or $4 or $5 billion dollars of Federal assistance isn't going to make much difference." Often these financial institutions are highly insulated from citizen participation. Yet these decisions effect community development and the availability of housing as much as all the public programs. Both the Federal Government and state government through their regulating roles might give consideration to the way in which financial institutions make some decisions in these areas.

Some Ideas for the Future

Within the general discussions of the panel were a variety of ideas or suggestions about Federal policies for the future. Reference has already been made to the need for Federal incentives to the states and to financial institutions. The discussion on rural housing issues suggested the need for two housing departments or at least two types of programs: (1) an urban program that had a greater emphasis on community development and the provision of services than on housing stock *per se* and (2) a rural program that focused directly on the physical quality of housing.

The discussion of the Community Development Block Grant program included a wide range of recommendations. It seems clear that the grant funds should be focused more directly on low- and moderate-income people and their programs. This implied a return to a tighter set of Federal guidelines more in keeping with the focused provisions of the Model Cities program. Such a focusing of the block grant funds, however, might be politically acceptable only as part of a system of Federal programs. On the one hand, a refunding of some categorical programs, as Marshall Kaplan suggested, that provide some support to conservation of neighborhoods would be desirable. One might also look at a system of block grants that tried to cover the multiplicity of purposes originally assumed by the Model Cities program. This would recognize that the Community Development Block Grant is essentially a hardware program. A complimentary block grant system of social services seems essential, building off of the existing Title XX block grant for human services that is funded to the states and is not available to cities to develop their own corporation or programs.

Revisions in the legislation that would alter the allocation formula were also mentioned. These suggestions centered on changes that would give a real weight to low- and moderate-income persons and to age of housing. In all probability this would narrow the number of eligible communities and raise the allocations of older urban areas.

This complex system of Federal programs rather directly raised the issue of management. Frieden said, "If we agree that there is a need for a wide variety of programs. . .how can this be managed? Who can make decisions about how to combine different Federal programs? If we look at the recent record no institution looks too good. HUD was unable to manage even simpler things like 235 and 236 programs. If you look at the cities, they seem to be having trouble even spending their community development block grants. The states, by and large, have not been involved in urban problems." Though some remarks seem to suggest the need for Federal reorganization, there was also a concern for the feasibility of this. Putting all the parts of the Federal bureaucracy that affect urban America into one department does not measurably change anything. The often inconsistent policies of FHA vis a vis HUD bear this out.

Lastly there were suggestions made regarding the need of the cities for investment capital. Mayor Hatcher suggested that cities might try to find investors who would purchase existing public facilities and lease them back to the city. This would give the cities some immediate capital, the investment of which would cover the leasing arrangements. There was also mention of the use of value capture taxes on land values increased by public investment as well as the advance acquisition of land as ways of easing financial pressures on the cities.

The discussion was intended to focus on the Model Cities program and its successor programs. From my perspective, this tended to focus attention on the ways in which present programs could be restructured to return to a form of Model Cities program. In particular there was a strong emphasis on the ties between housing, community development, and social service, with little concern for the relationships between housing, community development, and economic development. Cavanaugh's statement was probably the only one addressed to this issue: "Programs that equip people for employment are shortarmed to the degree that the society has not expanded the structure for giving employment to the people who are trained. That situation has worsened in the intervening years and we still remain with very high unemployment rates particularly among minority people in this country. Unless we come to grips with that social programs will be playing catch-up first-aid kind of games."

This concern is further emphasized by the simple question of availability of money. We are in a period of declining funds. The major urban centers that need money are receiving less through block grants. There is not a national mood to substantially increase public spending. Even with a new administration in Washington it is unreasonable to anticipate dramatic increases in Federal urban expenditures.

These two things combined suggest that the future community development programs are ones that will link agencies such as HUD and the Economic Development Administration. Such programs will not only try to produce housing but also jobs—not in the sense of a public works bill, but as a sustained improvement in the economic climate of cities which recognize that, no matter how much public funds are available, the public sector alone cannot deal with these issues.

the right to equal educational opportunity

Douglass Cater

15

The Political Struggle for Equality of Educational Opportunity

In this video age, when memories are almost as fleeting as the images on the tube, events of only a decade ago appear as ancient history. My assignment is to describe the ideals and arguments which led to the programs for educational equality—and to examine the meaning of that experience. To achieve coherence, I must narrow my focus to the more formal education programs as viewed from the perspective of my former office in the White House. Essentially, this is a personal reminiscence based on nearly five years working for President Johnson with special attention to his education initiatives.

Perhaps the most encapsulating episode occurred before I went to work for the President. Having been deeply moved by Harry Caudill's *Night Comes to the Cumberlands* the eloquent description of economic and social erosion in Appalachia, I had determined to find out what the Federal Government meant to do about these disgraceful "pockets of poverty." Then suddenly during my journalistic investigations, I found myself in the midst of a vast governmental troop movement. The War on Poverty was being quietly mobilized in the upper ranks of the Federal bureaucracy.

I called on President Johnson two days after he sent his anti-poverty message to Congress, my first visit since he entered the White House. Having chosen as title for my article, "The Politics of Poverty," I queried him about his motivations for this major new endeavor. Wasn't it true that the poor didn't vote? How could he build a viable program against poverty in a capitol where constituency pressures count so heavily? Johnson heard me out, then leaned back and stretched himself. "I don't know whether I can get Congress to pass a single law or appropriate a single dollar, " he said with fierce intensity. "But I know one thing: before I'm through, no community in America will be able to ignore the poverty in its midst."

This, I believe, summed up his concept of the essence of the

President's role: to raise the consciousness of the nation. Despite later criticisms of "overblown rhetoric," Johnson believed that he could not set big goals with feeble phrases. He also knew what it took to pass laws and appropriate dollars. Not a single LBJ measure went to the Hill without the painstaking counting of heads to put together a decisive majority. Lofty ideals and hard political reality had a blending in his quest for educational equality as in the larger War on Poverty.

Antecedents to the War on Poverty

Consider the antecedents of that war. As the decade of the 1950s came to a close, the dominant image of America held by most Americans was of a quiet society afflicted with faint fears of becoming stagnant. Our chief concern was how to achieve a higher economic growth rate. J. K. Galbraith, often a pacesetter among idea men, had published his book, *The Affluent Society*, devoting only a limited amount of attention to the poverty in our midst and pretty much confining even this, as critics later pointed out, to "insular" rather than "endemic" poverty. John F. Kennedy based his 1960 campaign on the pledge to get America moving again; his rhetoric was mainly directed to stimulating a rising tide in the economy which would "float all the boats." On occasion, Kennedy voiced deep concern about conditions he encountered along the campaign trail—in the destitute hollows of West Virginia and elsewhere; but when he talked of millions of people going to bed hungry at night, even close supporters thought he was laying it on a bit thick.

The reality of that period, as we now recognize, was quite different. The American economy may have been stagnant but American society was in tremendous ferment. During the 1950s, there was a migration of more than eight million Americans into the metropolitan areas. Since World War II, nearly two-and-a-quarter million blacks had left the South and crowded into northern cities. Urban America was feeling an unbearable strain on its facilities—schools, welfare, hospitals, and clinics. Cities faced a rapidly growing crisis in their capacity to govern. Prosperous Americans were fleeing to the suburbs.

A few experts were seriously addressing these problems, but much of the scholarly literature was couched in a jargon that politicians could hardly comprehend, much less find compelling.

Translated, it revealed the distressing fact that at least 20 percent of our population lived in rather abject conditions. While this represented improvement over FDR's "one third of a nation," statisticians were estimating that those in the bottom fifth had been getting a stationary share of the nation's goods and services even as the gross national product had grown vastly. They were not simply confined to regional pockets such as Appalachia, but included millions living in city, town, and rural slum from coast to coast. They were caught in a rut of privation that seemed to deepen as the economy moved ahead.

Attempting to search out the poor and identify them, sociologists developed categories of families having "poverty-linked" characteristics: non-whites, families with no earners, families whose heads were females, males aged 14 to 25 or over 65, individuals with less than eight years of schooling, inhabitants of some farm areas, and families with more than six children under 18. These were the ones most apt to fall into the rut and, once in, have the most difficulty climbing out. In many cases, the condition was being passed on from generation to generation. A study made by one group reached the alarming conclusion that the poverty risks were on the increase: "Unless remedial steps are undertaken, there will be considerably more poor even with a more affluent America...Their poverty is the result of special circumstances, rather than of . . . the rate of economic activity. Their lot cannot be said to be the direct result of inadequate growth rate as they are not part of the economic structure . . . It will not do to argue—as most policy makers and economists do—that poverty will be done away with by policies aimed at bringing about full employment."

Caudill's book criticized national politics for ignoring the plight of his region even while dealing so generously with the nearby Tennessee Valley. Emergency Federal programs for Appalachia had mainly resulted in accustoming those dispirited people to life on the dole. Federal welfare, according to Caudill, had been dispensed in a way that reinforced the rule of the county courthouse satrapies, stubbornly resistent to progress.

Another eloquent book, Michael Harrington's *The Other America*, described regions less remote but just as isolated from the main stream in America. The poor, Harrington argued, had become invisible. Even those who huddled in the cities were not able to identify themselves or their problems so that others would pay attention. Harrington indicted a political system that could launch massive programs in agriculture, housing, and Social Security, while almost entirely neglecting the genuinely poor. Social Security did not cover them. Minimum wage laws specifically exempted them. Slum clearance, often labelled "Negro removal," only complicated their existence.

It was not an auspicious time for Johnson to launch the War on Poverty. Congress was bogged down on two related issues: civil rights and tax reduction. Kennedy programs directly aimed at poverty—the Area Redevelopment Administration and the Appalachian Project—were in serious difficulties, both having been rebuffed in funding efforts. As I wrote at the time: "The rise and decline of ARA suggests that the politicians lack the patience to allow time for a long range developmental program to prove itself . . . Poverty has so far lacked a power base in Washington capable of sustaining its claim."

Specific origins of an idea in the nation's capitol are always difficult to pinpoint, especially after a President sponsors the idea and thereby puts a premium on plagiarism. But this one seems to have had important beginnings in the Council of Economic Advisers (CEA), where it was stimulated not so much by a sudden feeling for the poor as by tough problems of fiscal policy. In early 1963, the CEA's Report had concentrated on the need for a tax cut, failing even to mention hard-core poverty. But as Chairman Walter Heller began to look beyond the tax cut, he foresaw an inevitable downturn in the government's rate of spending for defense, space, and related activities. On the evening before he left on his fateful trip that terminated in Dallas, Kennedy gave tentative assent to Heller's request to proceed with planning for a sizable anti-poverty program.

President Johnson's swift decision to move forward with this program was spurred by motives going deeper than economic pump priming. Growing up in the poverty-ridden Texas hill country, teaching disadvantaged Mexican-Americans, and serving as state director of the National Youth Administration had brought a passionate understanding of poverty's meaning. He was instinctively hostile to the dependency spawned by hand-out programs. As he declared in the Anti-Poverty Message to Congress, this was to be a struggle to knock down the barriers keeping one out of five Americans from sharing the fruits of America. "The great unfinished work of our society" would be to provide equality of opportunity so that the disadvantaged could lift themselves from poverty's rut.

Re-reading his message, one finds ample caution about both the dilemmas and the durability of poverty. The President stated flatly that it could not be accomplished by government alone. But neither did LBJ have doubts about using his "bully pulpit." As one scholar, Elinor Graham, has observed:

> The power of the Presidency to stimulate the news media into undertaking a massive effort to increase public awareness, if not to generate actual demands for government action, was dramatically demonstrated.

The Need for a Federal Role in Education

This serves as brief background against which to consider the birthing of programs for educational equality. The essential condition was to be equality of *opportunity*, not equality of *achievement*. But opportunity was to have a new definition for those who, because of disadvantage or handicap, were effectively barred from access to the good life.

Ignorance, as LBJ said repeatedly, was the most formidable barrier of all. This conviction, too, had been shaped by his beginnings when he nearly missed completing his own education. As a teacher he discovered what it meant to bring out the potential lurking in every child. He put education at the top of his priority list and maintained a simple faith in the value of schooling when many, even among the educators, were having doubts.

To establish a Federal role in education, however, held even greater political uncertainties than did the other areas of the anti-poverty program. Education is nowhere mentioned in the Constitution. Federal efforts to support it have succeeded at rare intervals: the Northwest Ordinance of 1787 reserving public lands for endowment of schools; the Morrill Act of 1862 assisting Land Grant colleges; the Smith-Hughes Act of 1917 providing funds for vocational education; the GI Bill of 1944 helping veterans go to college. But each of these landmark laws failed to bring wider breakthroughs. During the period following World War II, the effort to provide general school aid met repeated frustrations and defeats. Even the belated support of conservative Senator Robert Taft could not break the political stalemate.

Mounting needs brought special interventions. In 1950, the Federal Impacted Areas Act allocated funds to school districts containing large numbers of Federal employees—a formula, as four Presidents have futilely pointed out, bearing very little relationship to need. In 1958, shocked by the launching of Sputnik, Congress passed the National Defense Education Act (NDEA) to provide assistance for study of science, mathematics, and other courses deemed valuable in the competition with the Soviets. Even members of Congress who had once voiced fears of Federal encroachment went along with this measure setting firm priorities for school and college curricula.

In the early sixties, despite a mounting cry for general aid, there was continuing stalemate: the Elementary-Secondary Act was defeated by the segregation issue; church-state conflict blocked the Higher Education Act of 1962. Reporting on the last minute failure of this latter Act, I concluded glumly:

> Some skeptics on Capitol Hill dismiss federal aid to education as a program that doesn't really interest the public and therefore doesn't excite Congress . . . The trouble is not that there is too little pressure from the public, but that too much of it is conflicting pressure that seems to cancel itself out in the eyes of most Congressmen.

Representative Edith Green made the impassioned plea in the closing moments of the House debate:

> I say this—believe me with a heavy heart—if (representatives of the education profession) are successful in stirring up enough religious controversy on this, I do not think we will see an education bill in the Congress in the foreseeable future.

The underlying conditions of stalemate still prevailed when President Johnson took office. Two of his early achievements were to rescue the Vocational Education Act and the Higher Education Facilities Act from deadlocked conferences of the Congress.

It is beyond my present scope to trace the beginning of equal opportunity as a priority of Federal role in education. NDEA contained student loans based on need. The early anti-poverty programs had education components: Head Start for preschoolers, Job Corps training, and others. A number of Kennedy's proposals were incorporated in the Economic Opportunity Act of 1964: Adult Basic Education, College Work-Study, Neighborhood Youth Corps. But the most rousing commitment to those likely to be left behind in the quest for schooling came in LBJ's campaign speech at the Denver Colliseum on October 12, 1964. Bill Moyers, knowing of my keen interest, phoned me directly from the Colliseum so that I could hear the roar of the crowd greeting LBJ's declaration: "Every child has the right to as much education as he or she has the ability to take. I want this for our children's sake but I also want it for our nation's sake."

One significant development occurred in the report to the President shortly after the election by his Task Force on Education. Chaired by John Gardner, the task force described urgently the needs for broad school support, but concluded: "Of course, the political feasibility of general federal aid remains an open question. The church-state issue is unresolved . . . It is not part of our assignment to weigh questions of political feasibility. But we believe it is of crucial importance that other forms of aid—such as the major programs dealt with elsewhere in this report—not be held up while we go through one more agonizing tug-of-war over the church-state issue." Among these programs recommended by the Gardner task force, one entitled "Education of the Disadvantaged" led the list.

One other antecedent is worth noting. Senator Wayne Morse has been credited with the idea of including the unemployed among those to be counted in the Impacted Area legislation. Under Johnson's initiative, this idea was further extended. Why not consider the adverse impact on a school system of having to educate the economically disadvantaged? In retrospect, it appears a somewhat disingenuous linkage. Yet it provided the legislative technique for Title I of the Elementary-Secondary Education Act of 1965 which was tacked on to the Federal Impacted Area Act. Title I's first year authorization of $1 billion was larger than the funding proposed in any of the earlier unsuccessful attempts to provide general Federal aid.

No one can precisely measure the motivations of a political leader. I believe LBJ seized so enthusiastically on ESEA for two compelling reasons: to bypass the political stalemate of the past; and to deal with educational problems which concerned him most. Others may argue that Federal aid to education was an idea whose time had come, especially after the sweeping popular mandate of the 1964 elections. Those of us caught in the daily legislative strategies did not perceive it so clearly. I can recall at least a half dozen moments along the way when ESEA appeared in imminent danger of being blocked.

Political Accomodations

Three great political accommodations were involved. The first, in fact, was made the preceding year when, with Johnson's strong prodding, the Civil Rights Act of 1964 passed Congress. So far as the law was concerned, the issue of whether Federal funds could be expended for segregated purposes had been resolved.

The second accommodation—over church-state relations—complicated ESEA's path right up to the final passage. The U.S. Commissioner of Education, Francis Keppel, had conducted skillful negotiations with Catholic Church leaders, winning the concession that Federal assistance for the disadvantaged warranted approaches distinct from general aid. Funds were being directed to the child, not the school. The objective was to extend certain benefits whether the student was enrolled in a public or parochial institution. In specifics, this sharing would have to be worked out in the community and within the school system.

Justice Holmes once declared, "Some things must be stated obscurely before they can be stated clearly." This was the strategy of the church-state accommodation. Our predicament was how to maintain calculated ambiguity against efforts to force precise clarification. On one occasion, after Chairman Perkins of the House Education and Labor Committee had become too explicit about benefits the parochial students would share—alarming the public school lobby—we felt obliged to send a hastily written "further clarification" which restored an acceptable degree of obfuscation.

The third accommodation involved the formula for distributing funds. No legislative effort can survive Congress which does not show exquisite concern for which constituency gets how much. With ESEA, we were caught in a double bind: the Title I formula measuring "disadvantage" by the number of families below $2,000 annual income discriminated against the northern urban states where poverty can exist at higher incomes. On the other hand, the formula's provision to dispense aid on a ratio with each state's per pupil expenditure worked against southern states whose per pupil expenditures, in some cases despite substantial tax efforts, are considerably less than in the wealthier states. Negotiations to strike just the right balance were prolonged. We were able to show that the South, in aggregate, fared as well or better than under most other Federal formulas. As a last minute concession to northern cities, we agreed to count those families receiving aid to dependent children whose income rose above $2,000. One powerful and insistent claimant got slighted in the end: the growing suburban communities with large numbers of low-income workers.

But we had the votes and ESEA carried. Two members of Congress played a particularly noteworthy role. Representative Phil Landrum, the conservative Democrat from Georgia, took the lead in persuading his southern colleagues that it was time to get on with aid to education. Wayne Morse, Chairman of the Senate Subcommittee on Education, though already waging his strong protest against U.S. involvement in Vietnam, did not allow this to disrupt his daily cooperation with the White House on education matters. It was Morse, not the President, who conceived the Senate strategy of adopting the House version of ESEA without changing a comma. Morse had a standing feud with his fellow Oregonian, Representative Edith Green, who had fought unsuccessfully to amend the bill. He was determined not to give her a second opportunity which might have happened if the bill had gone to House-Senate conference.

I have dwelt on the politics of ESEA's passage because it represented a significant breakthrough. While the three accommodations have threatened repeatedly to come apart, they have prevailed with minor modifications and helped unleash the flood of education acts during the following three years. The political battle no longer raged over general aid. The Johnson education program was "categorical"; and equality of opportunity was a dominant theme running through most of the measures. This permitted the President to declare on the one-hundredth anniversary of the Office of Education on March 2, 1967:

> We are no longer satisfied simply with free public education. We have declared as our national goal that every child shall have the chance to get as much education as he or she can absorb—no matter how poor they are, no matter what color they are, no matter where they live.

Further Legislative Initiatives

With more than 60 education acts in all, merely to list some of the programs reveals the extent to which equal education had at last gained a secure foothold in Washington. It is even more revealing to describe some of the services for the disadvantaged which they supported:

Head Start to begin the attack on disadvantage at the pre-school stage;

Follow Through to build on gains made by pre-schoolers;

the scholarship-loan-work study package to provide means to continue education beyond high school;

— the Teacher Corps to attract the ablest teachers into the toughest teaching situations;

— community college supports to reach those unable to attend distant institutions;

— drop-out prevention;

— bilingual, Indian, and migratory worker education;

— community extension service to stimulate the universities to devote skilled resources to community needs, particularly in urban America;

— special support for the handicapped;

— aid for developing institutions serving large numbers of the disadvantaged.

Charges have been made that this was categorical aid gone wild. But it is well to keep in perspective the reality of those times: the educational reality that these categories of need were not being adequately addressed by the education system; the political reality that Congress was willing at last to pass categorical programs after two decades of failure to deal with unrestricted aid.

A candid assessment of the sixties must concede that Federal spending for these programs did not keep pace with promise, not even with the multi-year authorization levels contained in the legislation. War in Vietnam brought increasing pressures to restrain domestic programs. LBJ has been accused of contradiction because he continued to push for new legislaton even when failing to ask Congress for full funding of existing programs. But Johnson was convinced that once measures got on the statute books, they would survive no matter what the delay in implementing them. At the White House ceremony celebrating passage of the Elementary and Secondary Education Act, he paraphrased the old countryman when he first saw a train moving down the railroad tracks: "They'll never stop her." So he continued to drive the legislative locomotive right through his final months in office. The acts of 1968 reveal surprising gains for educational equality: the Indian Bill of Rights, School Breakfasts, Guaranteed Student Loans, Aid to Handicapped-Children, Vocational Education.

President Johnson cared deeply about getting start-up funding for these measures. In the fall of 1967, despite terrible budget stringencies, I watched him argue for more than an hour with Chairman George Mahon, of the House Appropriations Committee, to provide funding for the Teacher Corps and the International Education Act. Sitting in his small study just off the White House Oval Office, he pled with Mahon to cut twice that amount elsewhere in the budget if only he would allow start-ups for these two. The Chairman finally yielded on the Teacher Corps but the International Education Act never got its funding.

In the later budget battles during the Nixon Administration, Johnson's hope in putting statutes on the books was at least partly vindicated. Education programs faced especially severe tests because they represented "controllable" line items in the HEW budget, unlike such "uncontrollables" as Social Security and Medicare. But the political forces for education displayed amazing strength in boosting President Nixon's budget requests and several times overriding the Nixon veto. Charles Lee, former aide to Senator Morse who headed the Committee for Full

Funding of education programs, made the boast after one of these legislative victories: "For the past 50 years, Congress has been dominated by the politics of agriculture. Now more teachers vote than farmers. For the next 50 years, Congress will be dominated by the politics of education."

But Lee was over-optimistic and the victories have had limits. Head Start has been slashed. Other titles have been whittled. Sam Halperin, skillful HEW legislative strategist for education during the Johnson years, points out that title-by-title analysis reveals that funding for many of the programs has not kept pace with the inflation rate. Halperin divides Great Society education initiatives into three categories: equality of opportunity; educational innovation; and institutional support. Of these, he concludes, equality of opportunity has fared by far the best. The Nixon Administration picked up and, in places, developed the special commitment to the educationally disadvantaged.

In aggregate, Federal spending directly for education expanded nearly seven-fold during the sixties—Federal-state-local spending for education nearly tripled. Perhaps a better measure of the Great Society's impact: during 1960-1970, the percentage of the nation's GNP devoted to social welfare programs increased from 10.6 percent to 15.3 percent. Education's share increased from 5.1 percent to 7.5 percent. This meant a growth by almost 50 percent of national energies devoted to education.

The Impact of the Programs

Critics have raised serious questions about the efficacy of these energies. Before ESEA was in place, the voluminous findings of the Coleman Report on *Equality of Educational Opportunity* stimulated doubts whether Federal spending could close the gap separating the disadvantaged. According to the Report's interpreters, neither improving the school facilities nor reducing the pupil-teacher ratio could significantly affect student achievement. Other studies questioned how lasting were the effects of Head Start once the disadvantaged entered school. Discouragement took root among educational experts leading some, like Christopher Jencks, in his book *Inequality*, to conclude that education could not bear the heavy burden of overcoming disadvantage. Others, such as John and Ann Hughes in *Equal Education*, indicted the school system: "A painful first revelation was the discovery that the schools did not really know how to go about the business of educating the poor. A second revelation, following hard on the heels of the first, was the realization that the deficient child concept was no longer going to be swallowed by the constituency to whom it had been applied for so many years ... In turn, there was a third revelation: specifically, the schools had no real plan or general strategy for meeting the child needs that now were facing them."

There were ambiguities about these efforts to reach swift and definitive conclusions. As Ralph Tyler pointed out in *The Public Interest* in 1974, most of the statistical material on which Coleman and Jencks based their studies pre-dated ESEA "before schools became greatly concerned with the problems of learning encountered by disadvantaged children." Noting of their studies that "neither the test data nor the method of analysis ... could answer the question of what most children had learned in school," Tyler found that "most evidence" indicates:

There has been a steady increase in the number of Title I programs that are producing measurable improvements in the educational achievements of disadvantaged children, although there are still many programs that appear to be ineffective. These reports also show that improvements in learning can be maintained and increased when the program provides for a sequence of three to four years rather than one-shot efforts to help. But to bring the learning gains of disadvantaged children up to national average generally requires an expenditure per pupil that is 50 percent higher than the average.

Tyler concludes that "the right problems were selected for national attention. The country as a whole suffers from the failure of nearly one-fifth of our young people to learn what the schools are expected to teach them ... These problems were very serious and they were not likely to be solved by state and local efforts without Federal assistance. In most cases, they were not even recognized as problems on the local level until the Congressional debates and the availability of Federal funds brought them to local attention." But he also cautions that "fundamental changes in education would require the allocation, at least initially, of far more resources than were thought to be necessary when the programs were designed."

A somewhat separate criticism of the expanded Federal role in education has been that the Washington bureaucracy has usurped powers belonging to state and local authority. Though not always stated explicitly, the criticism arises in large part from a conflict of national and community purpose. Title VI of the Civil Rights Act forbids the use of Federal funds for segregated schooling, thereby involving the Federal Government in the community's most sensitive relationships. Title I of ESEA requires that funding reach the disadvantaged school child and not be blended into general school support—often frustrating to the financially hard-pressed educators. Undoubtedly, the effort to implement these measures has exposed bureaucratic ineptitude and arrogance. For higher education, the level of institutional support has not kept pace with Federal demands on the institution. The challenge is to develop better strategies for exerting Federal leverage. But the issue of whether a President and the Congress should assert educational goals to be pursued by Federal dollars will not be resolved by blaming the bureaucrats.

In *The Promise of Greatness*, Sar A. Levitan and Robert Taggart list their seven major conclusions growing out of the experience of the Great Society:

1. The goals of the Great Society were realistic, if steadily moving targets for the improvements of the nation.

2. The social welfare efforts initiated and accelerated in the 1960s moved the nation toward a more just and equitable society, mitigating the problems of the disadvantaged and disenfranchised.

3. The Great Society's social welfare programs were reasonably efficient, and though improvements need to be made, there is no proof that government endeavors are inherently wasteful or that there is any alternative to active intervention.

4. The negative spillovers of social welfare efforts were too frequently overstated and were usually the unavoidable concomitants of the desired changes.

5. The benefits of the Great Society programs are more than the sum of their parts, and more than the impact on immediate participants and beneficiaries.

6. The nation has continued moving toward a better society, despite efforts to check the growth of the welfare state.

7. By the mid-1970s, however, a plateau had been reached and new initiatives were required if the previous momentum were to be renewed.

To launch new initiatives will be a political task at least as challenging as those of the past decade. We recognize more clearly that equality of educational opportunity is a seamless web. It must involve the individual, prenatal to the grave, not merely in school but in the whole of his environment. I foresee real dilemmas in defining the Federal role. First, the courts are questioning the discrimination arising from educational resource allocation based on local property tax. Both Federal and state government will be obliged to assume larger shares of the total cost. Second, Federal aid to education could be stymied by new efforts at budgetary efficiency, such as zero-based budgeting, which bring added disadvantage to "controllable" items in competition with "uncontrollables." Third, there may be renewed dangers of polarizing the dispute between categorical aid versus revenue sharing. Finally, our relentless progress toward the "knowledge socicty" is steadily widening the gap between education's haves and have-nots.

President Johnson, when presented with such a laundry list of dilemmas, had the habit of leaning back and muttering, "Therefore?" To that query, I can only respond that the future will require a rekindled passion for educational equality, new definitions of what it means, and fresh energies to move toward its attainment.

Perhaps the best response was contained in the speech made by Lyndon B. Johnson four months before his death. Entitled "September Song" and addressed to the melancholia gripping the nation, the dying President declared:

Since the early presidency of Thomas Jefferson, this nation has been committed—as no other nation on earth—to education of all our children. We have valued the minds of our young as America's richest resource and we have honored that value by dedicating much of our wealth to development of those minds. Our purpose has been not to provide education for education's sake, but to equip our young people to be agents of change—questioning the past, challenging the status quo, changing the prospects of the human condition.

In our own very recent times, this long sustained national effort has come to fruition. Never before in any society have there been so many educated men and women—or so many young people enrolled in pursuit of education. Yet when we came face to face with young people who were questioning the past, who were challenging the status quo, who were working to change the prospects of the human condition—we have hestitated in doubt and sometimes in fear of the educated young.

Across the full breadth of our national efforts, I could repeat countless other parallels. Out of the very success of our system have come the qualms and doubts that contribute to the melancholy of this season.

Whatever may be your own perception of where we are and where we may be tending, let me say for myself that I see little today suggesting that our system is failing—but I see all too much which convincingly argues that by our doubts and hestitation we may be failing the promise and potential of our system.

Marian Wright Edelman

16

Title I of ESEA: Is It Helping Poor Children?

This chapter is an outside advocate's look at the effect of Great Society education programs, particularly Title I of the Elementary and Secondary Education Act (ESEA),[2] on poor children and on the institutional response of public schools to their needs.

ESEA was but one of more than three dozen Great Society programs designed to help poor children who traditionally have been neglected by America's social institutions and denied equal educational opportunity by school systems.[3] But it was perhaps the most significant in several regards: (1) its unprecedented provision of major Federal aid to local school systems; (2) its pinpointing of help for children with special educational needs— primarily poor children; (3) its establishment of Federal standards designed to push applicant school systems towards treating disadvantaged youngsters comparably to other youngsters; and (4) Title I's mandated evaluation requirements designed not only to demonstrate whether the money was reaching its intended beneficiaries but also whether the promise of substantial educational progress was being achieved.[4]

ESEA also gave teeth to the Civil Rights Act of 1964 which mandated nondiscrimination in federally assisted programs. By opening up new sources of information about local schools' performance to parents and the public, and by providing a role for parents in the Title I application process through the establishment of parent advisory committees, Title I catalyzed an outside constituency of parent and professional monitors which is developing into a new force in educational politics.[5]

Background

The Title I investment aimed at equalizing educational opportunity for poor children that began during the Johnson years more than doubled over the next decade.

TABLE 1 Title I estimated obligations[1] (1966-1977)

Fiscal Year	Title I Obligations (in millions)
1966	$ 747
1967	1,056
1968	1,049
1969	1,073
1970	1,140
1971	1,250
1972	1,570
1973	1,505
1974	1,461
1975	1,874
1976	1,900
1977	1,900
Total	$16,525

[1]Obligations are the amounts actually expended by a Federal program. They are approximately equal to appropriations for a program like Title I. Authorizations, on the other hand, have always exceeded the appropriation in Title I by vast amounts, and thus have borne no resemblance to the actual program expenditures.

Source: Prior to 1972, data from the *Digest of Educational Statistics, 1970,* Table 143, page 112. From 1972 through 1974, data are from the *Digest of Educational Statistics,* Table 147, page 159. Data for 1975 through 1977 are from the Supplemental Appendix to the *Budget of the U.S. Government, Fiscal Year 1977,* page 344. The figures for 1976 and 1977 are estimates, and do not appear in the main budget since President Ford has proposed to consolidate the Title I program into his Financial Assistance for Elementary and Secondary Education Act.

Not only did Federal expenditures increase overall, but a greater proportion of total educational expenses were paid for by Federal sources, including Title I:

TABLE 2 Federal, state and local shares of public elementary and secondary school budgets in the United States for fiscal years 1960, 1966, 1970, and 1975

	Percent of Total Expenditures for Public Elementary and Secondary Education					Total Expenditure for Public Education in Billions	
Fiscal Year	Federal Title I	Federal Other[1]	State	Local	Other[2]	Current Dollars	Constant Dollars[3]
1960	––	4.6%	35.4%	59.6%	0.4%	$15.9	$17.9
1966	2.8%	5.5	36.2	55.1	0.4	26.5	27.3
1970	2.8	6.0	39.5	51.5	0.2	40.8	35.1
1975	2.9	6.3	40.5	50.1	0.2	64.0	40.2

[1]The major programs other than Title I are (in various forms): aid to vocational education, aid to handicapped, bilingual, migrant, and American Indian children, Follow Through, Emergency School Assistance Act funds, and many supporting services to local and state educational authorities. All these increased faster than Title I.

[2]There is about $100 million per year derived from gifts, public school tuition payments from non-residents, endowments, philanthropic grants, and school fees charged to ordinary students throughout this period.

[3]Adjusted by the consumer price index to equal constant 1969 dollars. The increase in total education outlays on public elementary and secondary education from 1960 to 1975 represents an increase from 3.2 percent to 4.4 percent of the gross national product in both current and constant dollars.

Source: U.S. Bureau of the Census, *Statistical Abstract of the United States: 1975*, Table 178, p. 112 and Table 678, p. 414. Gross national product for 1975 is from the *Special Analysis of the Budget of the U.S. Government, Fiscal Year 1977*.

But a dozen years after ESEA's enactment, a flurry of questions remain as to whether Title I is really helping poor children. If so, in what ways? What have we learned from Title I about the impediments to delivering services to poor children? About the politics of educational reform? What does the Title I experience and current educational politics forbode for the future of categorical aid in education? Are there better ways of ensuring equal educational opportunity for poor children? In sum, what have been the consequences, intended and unintended, from this decade of experience, and from the expenditure of more than $16 billion from the Federal pocketbook?

Obviously, the answers to these questions will vary depending on who is being asked and what criteria they are applying. ESEA's birth was the labor of many midwives, each of whom had different reasons for and interests in aiding its passage.[6]

Civil rights groups and leaders like Adam Clayton Powell recognized the intrinsic importance of a Federal commitment to the needs of poor children, but also saw ESEA as a major vehicle for furthering the struggle against racial discrimination. And in fact, school desegregation progress over the last decade has been expedited significantly by adding the carrot of Title I of ESEA and the stick of Title VI of the Civil Rights Act. Between 1964 and 1973, the proportion of black school children in the South attending majority white schools rose from 1 to 46 percent. This was substantially aided by HEW compliance efforts backed by the threat to terminate Federal funds under Title VI.[7] Other groups, most notably the National Education Association, and some reformers in the executive branch of government, wanted to pierce the long-standing resistance to Federal aid to schools and get some needed financial help to local districts.[8] Still others, like the staff at the Bureau of the Budget, the Office of the Assistant Secretary for Planning and Evaluation, and some professional and academic educational reformers, viewed ESEA as a chance to catalyze reform of an antiquated educational bureaucracy, and hoped that it would improve the efficiency with which public funds are used.

Many of those who stood to benefit from ESEA had reservations about its provisions. The compromises made to win their support for the bill laid the groundwork for many of the problems of enforcement and implementation which have followed. Some state and local school authorities viewed ESEA as the best chance to get Federal relief, but they wanted to use it as general aid, and many of them resisted the Federal standards and compliance actions as meddling in local educational affairs. While they may have couched their complaints in the language of local educational autonomy, much of their desire has been to thwart effective Federal enforcement of civil rights. Similarly, while educational professionals welcomed the expanded job opportunities and status ESEA brought,[9] a number of them, particularly school administrators, resisted the reporting and other accountability requirements so crucial to Title I's success. A recent study of Title I evaluation efforts shows that educational officials' original resistance to participate willingly in evaluation efforts has not lessened with time.[10]

Assessments of the accomplishments of Title I have been frustrated by two key factors: (1) the illusive nature of measuring educational outcomes—"programs like Title I simply do not exist in the real world in concrete enough form to be evaluated;"[11] and (2) the failure of the Federal Government to enforce and monitor consistently the implementation of Title I. As one official of HEW's Division of Compensatory Education stated:

> Title I is a service-oriented program with predetermined amounts for the states. This sets the framework where the states are entitled to the money. Other than making sure that states got their money and making sure it was spent, there was no role for the Office of Education. I don't know anyone around here who wants to monitor. The Office of Education is not investigation-oriented, never has been, and never will be.[12]

In the first two years of program funding, 1966 and 1967, these barriers were beginning to be identified, and addressed. The first Federal regulations, issued late in 1968, clarified some of the basic premises of Title I, including who it was for and what it was meant to do. The early attempts at formal evaluation at least helped to identify the extent to which reliable local information was lacking regarding what public schools did with Title I money.

But the greatest frustration of the generous impulses behind Title I's passage—and other Great Society education programs as well—could not be regulated. It was the passage both of time and of the leaders who had wrung the promise of progress from the nation. By the beginning of 1969, the nation had elected a new President and had begun to slip back to its old habits. President Nixon immediately began to try to dismantle Lyndon Johnson's Great Society.

Current Politics of Title I

Title I in its present form is threatened by a convergence of different interests. Though President Nixon early in his Administration attacked compensatory education and threatened to cut Title I expenditures on the basis of evaluations showing it was not raising children's achievement levels, his attack became inconvenient when anti-busing politics rendered compensatory education a more politically palatable alternative.[13] President Ford sought to redirect ESEA's money into more discretionary local channels. At his request, a bill entitled "Financial Assistance for the Elementary and Secondary Education Act" was introduced in 1976. The proposed bill would have consolidated several Federal education programs, including Title I, into a new, single, educational grant for each state. This bill would have eliminated Federal restrictions which require states and localities to use ESEA funds for specific programs, and would permit states, subject only to broad limitations, to use Federal education dollars within their own discretion. The ESEA regulations enforcing program standards would be eliminated[14] as would the original mandated reporting requirements and parent participation in Title I's administration.

A number of state and local educational officials supported this bill. At hearings held by Representative Carl Perkins' Subcommittee on Elementary, Secondary, and Vocational Education, the National Association of Secondary School Principals, the National Conference of State Legislators, the Education Commission of the States, and chief state school officers from Florida and Pennsylvania all came out in support of the consolidation approach.

The move to redirect or drop support of Federal compensatory education efforts is bolstered by the voices of those in academia who question—after a decade of undeniably questionable achievement outcomes—whether any amount of money channeled through schools can make a difference in the achievement levels of poor children. Even poor parents, poor children, and some of their advocates, historically supportive of ESEA's promise and continuation, sometimes wonder whether ESEA's enforceability is so problematic that its resources might not be better spent entirely on jobs for needy families.[15]

Has Title I Helped Poor Children?

Given these variables, the question of whether Title I is helping poor children is bound to have a multifaceted answer.

Title I has not helped poor children as much as intended because it has been poorly enforced.

In 1969, the Washington Research Project and the NAACP Legal Defense and Educational Fund first scrutinized Title I and found:

1. The intended beneficiaries of Title I—poor children—are being denied the benefits of the Act because of improper and illegal use of Title I funds.
2. Many Title I programs are poorly planned and executed so that the needs of educationally deprived children are not met. In some instances there are no Title I programs to meet the needs of these children.
3. State departments of education, which have major responsibility for operating the program and approving Title I project applications, have not lived up to their legal responsibility to administer the program in conformity with the law and the intent of Congress.
4. The United States Office of Education, which has overall responsibility for administering the Act, is reluctant and timid in its administration of Title I and abdicates to the States its responsibility for enforcing the law.
5. Poor people and representatives of community organizations are excluded from the planning and design of Title I programs. In many poor communities, the parents of Title I-eligible children know nothing about Title I. In some communities, school officials refuse to provide information about the Title I program to local residents.[16]

Seven years later these problems persist. For example, in response to a law suit brought by low-income parents against the Pennsylvania Superintendent of Schools to enjoin Title I violations by the Philadelphia schools, a Federal district court found[17] Philadephia officials guilty of violating several of Title I's requirements or prohibitions. (1) Concentration[18]: Rather than concentrating its Title I funds on a limited number of educationally-deprived children, the school district of Philadelphia included 96 percent of the eligible children in its Title I program. (2) Supplanting[19]: Music and art instruction which was regularly provided to non-Title I children was paid for with Title I money when it was provided to children in Title I schools. (3) Comparability.[20] In 1970-1971, 102 schools representing 53 percent of the schools receiving Title I funds had comparability violations, and in 1971-1972, 138 schools were found in violation. In addition, the district court found that Title I's evaluation requirements were not met; that the state did not require the Philadelphia schools to institute Title I programs offering "a reasonable promise of substantial progress,"[21] that the program offered under Title I could not have helped low-income children to make educational progress, and that neither the city, state, nor Federal government did anything about it year after year. The evidence for this was uncontested by school officials.

Natonabah v. Gallup-McKinley[22] was a law suit which involved a challenge to racial discrimination against American Indian children by a county-wide school district in New Mexico. The proof not only showed inequitable capital expenditures and provision of services in general but also direct evidence that Title I equipment was located in ineligible, non-Indian schools; that regular educational services routinely purchased out of local and state unrestricted funds were, for Indian children, purchased with Title I monies and that parent advisory committee meetings held in Navaho communities where many parents spoke no English were nonetheless conducted in English.

On July 1, 1976, the Parent Advisory Council for the Centennial School District in San Luis, Colorado, filed a formal complaint with the Colorado Department of Education regarding the way the school district "consulted" with them over Title I projects. The parents said, in part:

> ... The Council was called together by the Superintendent and presented with a proposal. We were told that the plan was

to be sent to Denver the next day and therefore there was no time for changes. This is certainly not parent or PAC input in accordance and compliance with the Title I Act.

Further, it has come to our attention that the proposal which was presented to us that evening was completely changed and "reworked" by the Superintendent and Title I director of BOCS [a local Bureau of Cooperative Services] on June 8, 1976. We were never consulted on this new proposal.[2 3]

The Colorado State Department of Education Title I monitoring team reported on June 30, 1976, that the Centennial district had Title I aides performing playground and lunch duties for the whole school, and had replaced regular school teachers with Title I aides for many children, including most of those in the Title I programs. The district was paying for its whole guidance program from Title I, and calling the counselors "student advocates." Both Colorado state law and Title I forbid the replacement of certified teachers by aides or volunteers.

In a related area, HEW's Audit Agency reports on the Title I Migrant Program, more than a dozen of which were published between April, 1971, and September, 1975, have found almost endless violations of Federal regulations and state laws in the operation of these programs. The critical fact is that many of the abuses cited do not merely waste Federal money but, like the replacement of regular teachers by school aides in Centennial, Colorado, actually may work to lower the quality of education of poor children.[2 4]

These abuses are not atypical. Indeed, they are pervasive. They should serve to remind us of the underlying fact that necessitated Title I in the first place: The public schools have still not committed themselves to serving poor children well. While national programs like Title I can prod schools to provide better education for poor children, without strong Federal enforcement of specific regulations and local monitoring activity, merely increasing the resources of schools will not change the way schools act towards poor children.

But there is a positive side to the enforcement picture. HEW's audit agency now checks on Federal expenditures under ESEA, thus providing a new door for pointing up and challenging unsound educational practices. For example, *Title I: Is It Helping*

Poor Children? was based in substantial part on our review and analysis of HEW's own audit reports.

Title I applications also provide a new information source about local school practices. These applications and the Office for Civil Rights' Annual Civil Rights Survey are the two school documents available to the public containing substantial amounts of useful information about schools. The application is the only commonly prepared report that estimates the number of children who drop out of school each year. It is the only report that estimates the number of children in each school district who are institutionalized or who attend private school. The "targeting" pages of the Title I application contain the only estimates of the incidence of poverty for each school attendance zone within a school district. The Title I comparability report is the only widely prepared report that gives the per pupil instructional expenditures and the pupil-teacher ratios for individual schools.

Perhaps most striking, Title I evaluations are the only regularly conducted formal program evaluations in the vast majority of United States school districts. While the quality of the data is often very poor and almost never confirmed and compiled even on the state level (it is not even forwarded to Washington), the Title I application and its supporting documents remains the only nearly universal basis for an accountability review of public schools in the United States.

Some of the intended and realistic possibilities and effects of Title I have been misunderstood or overlooked.

President Johnson was a man of immense vision and immense practicality. I am sure he had few illusions about what ESEA alone could achieve, but he knew it was a beginning—a national commitment to the idea that poor children were entitled to the same education as middle-class children—just as the Civil Rights Act of 1964 ratified *Brown v. Board of Education's*[25] principle that black children were entitled to the same education as white children. These sound concepts were and are far away from 1965 and 1976 daily reality in schools throughout America.[26]

Title I was meant to help uncouple one link in the cycle of poverty: the link that permitted public schools to serve differentially or not serve at all the children of the poor. Too much of the debate on ESEA therefore has focused on the cognitive achievement of children, and too little on the equally crucial intended target of Title I: the institutional behavior of schools. Making schools accept poor children as rightful members of the educational process is no easy task and will take a long time, but the demand has been accelerated for them to perform better in this regard.

It is a basic fact of life that a school system that maintains a pattern of neglect and antipathy to poor youngsters, evidenced by unequal expenditures, racial discrimination, or disparate disciplinary and classification practices, is unlikely to raise achievement scores just by the injection of a few Federal dollars. We must be realistic in our expectations about change and resist the impatient cry of so many for instant results. You cannot pour new ideas into old vessels and expect these old vessels immediately to take a different or better shape. Like desegregation, the quest for equal treatment of all children regardless of income is going to be a long haul.

Title I alone was not meant and could not have been expected to do the desperately needed and hard job of changing schools' behavior or misbehavior towards poor children. The Great Society's panoply of programs recognized this. An array of educational programs combining incentives and enforcement powers was constructed. And we will never be able to separate out the contributions of the several different programs. Indeed, it may be exactly the breadth of the effort that played a critical role in what I do consider the shift of fate of poor children within the educational system in the last decade under the concerted impact of programs that ranged from Head Start through Upward Bound.

Title I alone, however, has made significant improvement in the schooling of poor children in some places. There have always been successful Title I programs; by anyone's criteria[27] —programs which have helped poor children learn school skills. But more importantly,

> Title I has worked to the benefit of a far larger segment of the student population than just the disadvantaged; it has benefitted education in general . . . In many school districts across the country Title I has been a catalyst for change . . . resulting in new approaches, better methodology, and geniune concern

about ensuring that each and every child learn basic skills and attitudes necessary to help him become a productive member of society.[28]

Great Society education programs and President Johnson's leadership created new levels of expectations and perception among poor and minority families and youth about the level of educational attainment that was possible.

Barriers to equality are subjective as well as objective. The symbolic impact of the hopes embodied in these programs cannot be ignored. The rate of college attendance of children from low-income families went up *immediately* after the introduction of the Great Society education programs. The explanation is not that these young people suddenly became smarter or more literate. The explanation is that poor children went to college at higher rates because (a) poor children *felt* that going to college was possible, and (b) college admissions officers *felt* that poor children were more acceptable as college students.

While data on education attendance rates by family income are rare, the Current Population Reports provides a series of college attendance rates measured by family income. Those college attendance rates are shown in Figure 1 for 1967—just after the start of the Great Society education programs; for 1969—before President Nixon's turnaround had any effect; and for 1973—after the Nixonian rollback was in full stride.

Nothing about this pattern could have been due to reading scores or particular changes of any kind in the characteristics of poor children—after all, the very first children to receive Title I programs in the lower grades in 1966-1967 have not *yet* graduated from high school! But we are looking at the response of a system to the changing social value of poor children. When the heat was up, the system began to retain and further the education of poor children. When Presidents Nixon and Ford turned and kept off the fire of social concern, school systems slumped back into somnolence.

When we make the same comparison for black children—rather than poor children—we find a strikingly different pattern. The proportion of black persons 18 to 24 years old attending college went from 10 percent in 1965 to 15 percent in 1970 and 16 percent in 1973.[29] White attendance at college in the same age range rose from 26 percent in 1965 to 27 percent in 1970 and then fell to 25 percent in 1973. President Nixon's onslaught slowed, but did not halt black educational progress.

I think the difference in the two showings stems from the fact that local constituencies for poor children wilted more under the Republican attack, while the civil rights movement held together around some key educational issues. That movement's fight resulted in Great Society gains which have continued right up to

FIGURE 1   Percent of primary families, by family income, with one or more dependent members (between 18 and 24 years old) enrolled in full-time college, as of October in 1967, 1969, and 1973

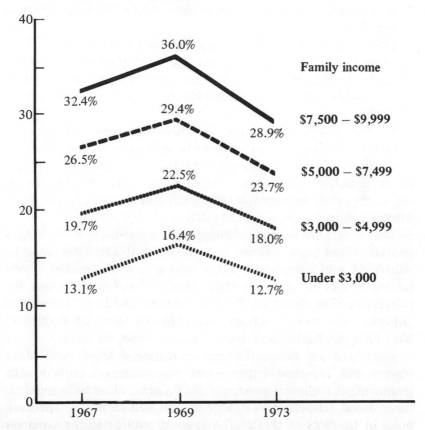

Percent enrolled in full-time college

the present. Black educational progress has been aided both by broad constitutional and other legal foundations, and by a greater willingness on the part of the public to perceive racial bigotry as unacceptable. Neither of these factors have played as significant a role with regard to guaranteeing equity for the poor.

During the last decade admissions officers and others have accepted the idea of affirmative recruitment of minority youngsters and geared their efforts in this direction. Equally substantial efforts have not been forthcoming for the children of the poor. This is not to say that black children have reached anything like *real* educational equality. Too many of them are enrolled in low-quality educational programs or programs with no substantial promise of adequate employment opportunities. But they are there, enrolled in educational programs, and accessible to further Federal initiatives in program support and legal enforcement. Now we must do the same for children, white, black, and brown, of the poor.

Title I and other Great Society education programs, by creating a set of expectations and the right of access to schools by poor parents and advocates, have given rise to an increasing tide of public demand for educational reform and accountability that will not go away.

Federal programs, merely by their statutory existence or monetary deluge, can do little to benefit groups that the other institutions of society have rejected. But those same statutes and rivers of dollars, when they are enforced and redirected by an organized and self-confident constituency, can bring about substantial progress towards equality.

The new and growing educational constituency of Title I parents, Head Start parents, and professional advocates must be cultivated and expanded. Their access to information about school decisions affecting their children and mechanisms for fostering enforcement of the law on their children's behalf can improve how public schools serve beneficiaries of legislation like Title I. Public and parent access must be enforced and strengthened in future Federal educational legislation. More formal and informal enforcement mechanisms, coupled with independent technical assistance for parents, must be mandated. Parents and schools must not be viewed and treated as opposing poles in the lives of children. And good public policy recognizes that institutions respond to those who make demands on them and not to those who don't. We must correct the imbalance of power in the educational process by giving parents a real voice in public schools.

We already see what parent involvement can do. By raising questions, by seeking information, and by challenging illegal school practices, parent groups are fulfilling the Congressional mandate and bringing about educational reform. This is called enforcement of the law and that makes sense if we are serious about getting the job done.

We must fight efforts to destroy or dilute parental involvement or to reinforce unequal power relationships in school systems, such as the proposed block grants. If poor children have had so much trouble getting the money that was expressly legislated for them, imagine how much harder it will be for them to get money under block grant or revenue sharing arrangements.[30] If school systems have been poor reporters under programs expressly requiring them to report, and setting standards against which to judge broadly their actions, imagine how much harder it will be to hold them accountable without any standards at all.

We cannot accept block grants. We must design better Federal, state, and local enforcement strageties that can use Federal money to accomplish the desirable national end of a literate and effective citizenry. Just what combination of incentive and paddle and the process by which it can be administered is the question we still have to resolve. Few, except the Republicans in their 1976 platform, anticipate that the Federal Government will get out of the business of providing financial help to elementary and secondary education.[31] But too many simply want the money without the strings that come with it. In my view, funds without goals and standards would be a great mistake, undercutting the movement towards educational equality that has begun in the last decade and leaving children of the poor with far less means to achieve the promise of opportunity intrinsic in this society.

The issue then is not whether Federal educational programs should be redirected away from categorical help for poor children. The issue is whether these programs will be enforced and strengthened to realize more rapidly the promise Lyndon Johnson saw. Schools do make a difference in the lives of children, and they should not be let off the hook of doing the job for poor children—all children—that they now too often only choose to do for some.

But schools alone are not enough. Title I alone is not enough. Uncoupling this one link in the cycle of poverty will not change the status of poor children in society. They will only be brought into the greater society by a decent job and income policy which will assure all American children families which can nurture, respect, and support them in every way.

Parents freed from survival needs will have more time to pay attention to what schools do with their children. And equally important, youngsters who can grow up in a society—go to schools, with the hopes that a job and dignity are at the end of the road—will feel better about themselves, will have hope in their futures. All of these strategies must be combined into a concerted and coordinated national effort. Lyndon Johnson started it. The final realization of his vision is up to the rest of us.

References

[1] In 1969, the Washington Research Project, the parent organization of the Children's Defense Fund, and the NAACP Legal Defense and Educational Fund issued a report entitled *Title I of ESEA: Is It Helping Poor Children?* (Washington, D.C., 1969).

[2] 20 U.S.C. 241 a-c. Title I is called "Assistance to Local Education Agencies for the Education of Children of Low-Income Families."

[3] Among the key Great Society programs which related to the educational needs of children were the Child Nutrition Act (1966); Civil Rights Act (1964); Economic Opportunity Act (1964); Education of the Handicapped Act (1968); Education Professions Development Act (1967); Elementary and Secondary Education Amendments (1966); Higher Education Act (1965); Higher Education Amendments (1968); International Education Act (1966); Model Secondary School for the Deaf (1966); National Defense Education Act Amendments (1964); National School Lunch Act Amendments (1962; 1968); National Vocational Student Loan Insurance Act (1965); Vocational Education Act (1963); and the Vocational Education Amendments (1968).

[4] See 20 U.S.C. 241 e(a)(1). For discussion of the impact of Title I's evaluation requirement, see Milbrey Wallin McLaughlin, *Evaluation and Reform: The Elementary and Secondary Education Act of 1965, Title I* (Cambridge, Mass.: Ballinger Publishing Company, 1975).

[5] Some of the groups which have monitored the implementation of Title I on behalf of poor children and their families are the American Friends Service Committee, the Lawyers' Committee for Civil Rights Under Law, the NAACP Legal Defense and Educational Fund, Inc., the National Coalition of Title I Parents, the Southern Regional Council, the National Advisory Council on the Education of Disadvantaged Children, and the Washington Research Project. See *Title I of ESEA: Is It Helping Poor Children?*, and Federal Education Project of the Lawyers' Committee for Civil Rights Under Law, *Newsletters* (January, 1976-July, 1976).

[6] For a good discussion of the historical setting and the politics of ESEA's passage, see Stephen K. Bailey and Edith K. Mosher, *ESEA: The Office of Education Administers Law* (Syracuse, N.Y.: Syracuse University Press, 1968), pp. 1-71; *Evaluation and Reform: The Elementary and Secondary Education Act of 1965, Title I*, pp. 1-32; and Jerome T. Murphy, "Title I of ESEA: The Politics of Implementing Federal Education Reform," *Harvard Educational Review*, vol. 41 (February, 1971), pp. 35-38.

[7] Marian Wright Edelman, "Winson and Dovie Hudson's Dream," *Harvard Educational Review*, vol. 45 (November, 1975), p. 420. For further discussion, see also Gary Orfield, *School Desegregation in Urban Society* (tentative title), forthcoming publication by Brookings Institution, June, 1977.

[8] Although the NEA had pressed "at least intermittently" since the end of World War I for Federal aid to education, following World War II its philosophy had been that such aid should be general, rather than categorical, and should not be given to parochial schools. "On these two positions, NEA found itself in general harmony with America's other educational groups." However, opposition to ESEA on these grounds was eventually overcome through a series of compromises. *ESEA: The Office of Education Administers a Law*, pp. 15-16; 44-45. See also, "Title I of ESEA: The Politics of Implementing Federal Education Reform," p. 38; and Douglass Cater, "'The Great Unfinished Work of Our Society': The Political Struggle for Equality of Educational Opportunity" (June 22, 1976), pp. 11-13.

[9] Average teachers' salaries rose at a rate of $240 a year between 1960 and 1965. After ESEA, teachers' salaries rose at a rate of $400 a year between 1965 and 1968. While this cannot be attributed just to Title I, it is probable that this new money into local education budgets facilitated increases. (Calculated from U.S. Bureau of the Census, *Statistical Abstract of the United States: 1975* (Washington, D.C.: U.S. Government Printing Office, 1975), table 214, p. 131.) Title I, by 1971, was paying the salaries of 116,000 teachers; 12,413 administrators and supervisors; 25,000 other professionals; and 123,000 aides and other non-professionals nationally. (Data from National Center for Education Statistics, *Consolidation Program Information Report (CPIR): National*

Estimates of Pupil Participation, Staff, and Expenditures 1972 (Washington, D.C.: U.S. Government Printing Office, 1975.) The 12,413 administrative and supervisory professionals paid for by Title I represents an unusual development of new upper level positions (Federal project directors, curriculum developers, program supervisors) that did not exist in public schools before ESEA. For example, in 1967-68 there were only 29,000 such supervisors in the nation. (Richard H. Barr and Geraldine J. Scott, National Center for Education Statistics, *Statistics of State School Systems 1967-68* (Washington, D.C.: U.S. Government Printing Office, 1970), Table 10, p. 27.)

[10] There have been three major evaluation efforts: The first outside analysis of Title I, done by General Electric's TEMPO Division, was commissioned by the U.S. Office of Education's Bureau of Research early in 1967. The TEMPO study picked exemplary school districts, and attempted to find out what gains Title I had made in those districts. The evaluators could not make firm conclusions, however, because local school officials had not kept enough specific data on which children received which benefits to permit a real analysis.

The next evaluation was a survey of over 400 school officials undertaken in 1968 by the Office of the Assistant Secretary for Planning and Evaluation (ASPE). But again, local school districts were unable to supply accurate data, and the OE evaluators estimated that at least 50 percent of the responding districts inaccurately reported the availability of achievement data. This pattern was repeated the following year with a third outside evaluation, Gene Glass's report, "Data Analysis of the 1968-1969 Survey of Compensatory Education (Title I)." In preparing the report (which was eventually suppressed by OE because its findings were so discouraging), Glass found local school officials even less cooperative in providing useful achievement data.

The only large evaluation of Title I done after Glass's 1968 survey was performed by the American Institute for Research (AIR). AIR easily found individual exemplary Title I programs. However, follow-up studies found that programs which were once effective often drifted back into general aid expenditures. See, *Evaluation and Reform: The Elementary and Secondary Education Act of 1965, Title I.*

[11] Peter Rossi, Book Review: "Evaluation and Reform: The Elementary and Secondary Education Act of 1965, Title I," *Harvard Educational Review*, vol. 46 (May, 1976), p. 264.

[12] "Title I of ESEA: The Politics of Implementing Federal Education Reform," p. 42.

[13] For a good discussion of Mr. Nixon's demand that compensatory education be shown as an effective alternative to busing, see *Evaluation and Reform: The Elementary and Secondary Education Act of 1965, Title I.*

[14] See Federal Education Project of the Lawyers' Committee for Civil Rights Under Law, *Newsletter* (April, 1967), pp. 7-8.

[15] Title I already provides jobs for the poor. About 176,000 of the 362,000 non-professionals (mostly teacher aides) employed were in Title I programs in 1972. (See CPIR, table C28, p. 93.) Many of the non-Title I aides now employed were hired on the basis of the popularity of the Title I aides. (See the National Advisory Council on the Education of Disadvantaged Children (NACEDC), *Annual Report to the President and the Congress* (Washington, D.C., 1976), p. 10.)

[16] *Title I of ESEA: Is It Helping Poor Children?*, pp. ii-iii.

[17] *Nicholson v. Pittenger*, 364 F.Supp. 669 (E.D.Pa., 1973).

[18] The Poorest attendance areas in a school district constitute the Title I "target area." "Eligible children" are all those residing in the target area. Title I money must be concentrated on the most educationally deprived of the eligible group. This is known as the "concentration" requirement, which is designed to prevent Title I services from being too thinly spread to have any substantial impact.

[19] Title I money is intended to provide *special* assistance to educationally deprived children. This means that Title I funds must supplement, not replace, state and local funds being expended in the target area. "Supplantation" occurs whenever school districts do not use Title I money in addition to state and local funds, but instead use Title I funds to purchase, for Title I eligible children, services that would or should be purchased for them anyway from state or local funds.

[20] Since 1971, the Title I regulations have required that per pupil instructional expenditures from state and local funds in schools in Title I target areas must be at least 95 percent of the comparable expenditures in non-target schools. This rule is known as the "comparability" requirement. Comparability is limited to specific types of expenditures and to dollar amount comparisons between target and non-target schools. The supplantation prohibition is broader than the comparability requirement in two ways: (1) it deals directly with the services offered to children, rather than just the cost of these services; and (2) it prohibits shortchanging Title I children in comparison to non-Title I children regardless of whether they are in the same or different schools.

[21] *Nicholson v. Pittenger, supra*, at 676.

[22] *Natonabah v. Board of Education of the Gallup-McKinley County School District*, 355 F.Supp. 716 (D. N.Mex., 1973).

[23] Letter to Victor Wall, Title I Director, Colorado State Department of Education, from the Parent Advisory Council for Centennial School District, San Luis, Colorado, July 1, 1976. This letter is only the latest in a series of complaints. Earlier letters resulted in an on-site monitoring report, Colorado Department of Education, Compensatory Education Services, June 30, 1976.

[24] For a summary of the Migrant program abuses, see Mark Masurofsky, "Title I Migrant Programs: Passivity Perpetuates a Non-Program for Migrant Children," *Inequality in Education*, no. 21 (June, 1976).

[25] 347 U.S. 483 (1954).

[26] While *all* children suffer from arbitrary and discriminatory public school policies and practices, the Children's Defense Fund has found that if a child is not white, or is white but not middle class, does not speak English, is poor, needs special help, is not smart enough or is too smart, school officials routinely decide that school is not the place for that child. We found nearly two million children out of school in this country and, for the most part, they are out not by choice but because they have been excluded. See our report, *Children Out of School in America* (Cambridge, Mass., 1974). For other examples of instances where school officials have decided that certain groups of children—generally non-white and poor—are beyond their responsibility and are expendable, see the following reports: Children's Defense Fund of the Washington Research Project, Inc., *School Suspensions: Are They Helping Children?* (Cambridge, Mass., 1975); Washington Research Project, Inc., *et al.*, *The Status of School Desegregation in the South, 1970* (Washington, D.C., 1970); American Friends Service Committee, *et al.*, *It's Not Over in the South* (Washington, D.C., 1972); Southern Regional Council and the Robert F. Kennedy Memorial, *The Student Pushout: Victim of Continued Resistance to Desegregation* (1973); and *Title I of ESEA: Is it Helping Poor Children?*.

[27] The early attempts to evaluate Title I by identifying achievement score gains among students in Title I programs were, as discussed above in Footnote 10, badly impaired by incomplete and inaccurate data from local schools. Other evaluations were subject to simple errors of statistical interpretation, overlooking the obvious fact that Title I programs were heterogeneous—working only in some schools, and working differently even where they worked at all. (For example, see Richard J. Light and Paul V. Smith, "Accumulating Evidence: Procedures for Resolving Contradictions Among Different Research Studies," *Harvard Educational Review*, vol. 41 (November, 1971), p. 441. The most recent "evaluation" of Title I—the Stanford Research Institute's compilation of data from state-mandated Title I program evaluations—actually showed an average gain of more than a month in grade-equivalent scores for every month of Title I programming for the children tested, and for a total sample size of over three million students. Finally, the National Advisory Council on the Education of Disadvantaged Children, in its Annual Reports to the President and Congress, identifies *1975, 1976 Annual Reports to the President and the Congress*.) Title I is neither an automatic success nor an automatic failure everywhere; rather, it is an opportunity that can be realized anywhere.

[28] NACEDC, *1976 Annual Report to the President and Congress*, p. 7.

[29] U.S. Bureau of the Census, Current Population Reports, Special Studies, series P-23, number 48, *The Social and Economic Status of the Black Population in the United States, 1973* (Washington, D.C.: U.S. Government Printing Office, 1974), table 49, p. 67.

[30] The effect of revenue sharing is no longer in doubt. It is now clear that local governments turn away from social needs and the needs of the poor when they escape Federal regulation and citizen participation. A study of revenue sharing in 14 cities and one state in the South found that:

With a few minor exceptions, revenue sharing funds were *not* used to meet social needs, were *not* used to replace Federal (categorical) funds which were withdrawn or cut off or threatened with cut off, and low-income and minority people were *not* involved in the decision-making process. On the contrary, revenue sharing funds tended to be spent in the existing pattern of local expenditures—roads, public safety, and the like—and to be used in ways which primarily benefited the white residents of the community.

In Mississippi, three-fourths of the revenue sharing allocation for colleges and universities went for football stadiums, field houses, and other athletic facilities. Ninety-two percent went to white institutions.

(American Friends Service Committee, Southeastern Public Education Program, *Revenue Sharing in the South: A New Tool of Discrimination* (Philadelphia: July, 1974), p. 1; p. 4.)

[31] See *The New York Times* (August 16, 1976), p. C-17.

SUMMARY Beryl Radin

Drawing from the experience of a range of programs developed during the Kennedy and Johnson Administrations, a panel of six experts seemed to agree that the goals of programs directed toward equal educational opportunity must be continued and reaffirmed. At the same time, however, the panelists suggested that some of the methods used to carry out those programs should be reexamined.

All of the issues discussed reflected a sensitivity to the marked difference in mood of the U.S. in the 1960s and today. Panel Chairman Harold Howe described the contrasting decades in his introduction to the session. He noted, "Today, we are talking in a very different time for education, in numbers of institutions, in numbers of students, in the interest of students in continuing on with education." Today is "a time of decline in enrollments in some segments of education, either declining now or projected to decline." In addition, today "students aren't quite so sure that education is the thing for them." Unlike the 1960s, education is not at the center of national concern. Howe continued:

In addition, the state of dreams about education has changed. In the 1960s, many of us—and I include myself—had dreams about the potentialities of education for bringing relatively quick solutions to major social problems. I, and others, have learned something about the reality of those dreams and have come to realize that the American belief that any problem can be solved and solved quickly is a belief more applicable to problems that are solved by technology than a belief that can be applied to problems of society.

While acknowledging that the political and social mood of the nation has changed during the past decade, most of the comments of the panel members did not suggest that they had wavered in their support of Federal programs and policies to meet the continued problems of unequal educational opportunity. Initially, most of the discussion was framed in two directions. First, the panelists seemed to respond to Teacher Corps Director William Smith's plea that, "We cannot be afraid to say, 'I am wrong.' " A belief that one can learn from negative experience supported discussion of such issues as the impact of too many programs; the failure to concentrate money or to adequately fund the programs; failure to concentrate on the achievement of children; failure to adequately understand the roles of the various groups within the educational system; failure to understand the political and administrative complexity of program implementation; and problems which revolved around evaluation techniques. The second direction of the discussion pointed to future programs. Panelists debated future directions for programs aimed at the achievement of equal educational opportunity by focusing on the form of the programs (consolidated programs, targeting, general aid or categorical programs); the level of public support for the programs; and the dimensions of a future Federal role.

A Compilation of Negative Findings

(1) Too many promises, too many programs.

Because of the unusual circumstances surrounding his Presidency, Lyndon Johnson was able to get an unusually large amount of major legislation through Congress. As a result, according to Samuel Halperin, former assistant commissioner of education and former deputy assistant secretary of Health, Education, and Welfare, "there was too much legislation for even the major programs like Title I to do anywhere near as much as they might have." Halperin noted that Johnson believed that there were "historic opportunities to pass major legislation" and that you'd better use those opportunities, force through your breakthrough, and then let another generation come around and tidy up the mess."

"By and large," commented Halperin, "the best energies of the Administration went into new creations, new promises, new ventures, rather than into the tidying up and the making work of these myriad programs." William Smith found that the new programs contained a great variety of objectives within them. He noted that program designers did not separate the objectives of one program from those of another.

(2) Failure to concentrate scarce resources.

Given the inadequate level of funding for the Federal education programs, the way in which those limited funds were spent determined whether the monies were able to make any change in the delivery of educational services. Albert Shanker, president of the American Federation of Teachers, noted that "the commitment in terms of funding has not been great enough in most cases to make a difference."

Shanker found that states and local communities have a "very great tendency to spread out whatever available funds there are." If funds had been concentrated, he noted, it might have made a difference. Shanker proposed that Federal programs be concentrated "very heavily on children of a certain age and on certain skills." He suggested that Federal policies requiring concentration of funds might allow local school officials to withstand the pressure "that you can't have one school that stands out with excellent services while the others seem to be starving."

(3) Failure to worry about student achievement.

Concern with the political and administrative problems involved in the implementation of the equal educational opportunity programs during the 1960s appeared to have overshadowed the question of student achievement resulting from those programs. Law professor Herbert Reid was concerned that "educational opportunity can become highly illusory" if we fail "to look at the educational system and make sure that it is producing." Reid noted that "this is a highly technological society and becoming more so daily." If, he commented, "the poor and disadvantaged do not get an opportunity, they are going to become castoffs in the society."

Albert Shanker shared Reid's appraisal. He argued that "the greatest shortcoming is that there has not been enough stress on the cognitive development." Stress on cognitive development, he noted, would go a long way in developing public support for education—particularly by parents. Shanker's position was supported by Marian Edelman who commented emphasis on basic skills is "what most parents want."

(4) Failure to understand the roles of various groups in the educational system.

A number of the problems which were identified by the panelists revolved around roles of teachers, parents, school boards, and others involved in educational decision-making. These role problems were identifiable in two ways: first, through an explication of the constraints and interests of the various groups involved; and second, by viewing the groups together as political actors within a total system.

Dr. Julian Nava, president of the Los Angeles City Board of Education, reminded the panel that a local school board is the group that has to "deal with stark reality, with vested interest groups." He noted that a school board has to make a school district function and has to deal with the demands created by Federal programs. Albert Shanker suggested that something must be done "to enable school boards to survive politically, to say that they have tried and failed." Unless we can do that, Shanker commented, "the public is not going to be willing to make investments."

Marian Edelman was concerned about the "insulation of parents in the community and the schools." One does not have to be talking about community control, she argued, to worry about community involvement. Rather, she said, "I am talking about giving to poor people the same kind of access and power relationships to schools that I, as a middle-class mother, have in the Newton schools." Albert Shanker and Marian Edelman agreed that alliances are necessary in the local community that serve both the interests of teachers and of parents. Edelman saw these alliances made up not only of poor parents but of parents of handicapped children, rich parents, middle-class parents, language minority parents, as well as black and white parents. Shanker, however, noted that community involvement has not been well defined. While agreeing that teachers, parents, community and political figures, and administrators all have to be involved, their roles have not been defined. "As long as that is the field of conflict," he commented, "we are not going to get very far."

The importance of the teacher in achieving educational change was also emphasized in the discussion. Harold Howe, looking at the Title I program in retrospect, noted that "not nearly enough Title I funds have ever gone into teacher opportunities and teacher retraining possibilities." Albert Shanker described the experience of many teachers—particularly young teachers—who walk into a classroom and "try everything that they learned in college in practice teaching and everything that they can remember that their teachers used." Yet, he noted, "when it's all over, they still don't seem to be reaching the students." This experience tends to push teachers to blame the children for not learning or to ascribe the problems in learning to the children's background.

"How do you change those attitudes?" Shanker asked. "The teacher in that room frequently feels very threatened in her or his whole professional life. The entire investment—not in money investment but in commitment to something—is shattered by that sort of experience."

While advocating an increased voice for parents in educational decision-making, Marian Edelman noted that "I don't see myself as anti-teacher. It's not going to serve my children to be out fighting teachers." Rather, she suggested, the issue is how to begin working with one another, "identifying common nexuses for entry points into the school system so that we can support each other."

William Smith cast the role question in a somewhat different framework. He characterized the relationship between groups with an interest in educational policy as a political process. "We should not, as educators," Smith argued, "be afraid to be involved in collaboration and recognize it as a political process." At the same time, however, he commented "that one of the things we must come to recognize is that we cannot solve political problems with education solutions to the problems that are political because we are very, very leery about admitting that they are political."

(5) Failure to understand the complexity of program implementation.

At least a part of the difficulty changing educational institutions with the programs of the 1960s were attributable to an inadequate understanding of program implementation. This problem had a number of components: failure to anticipate questions of administrative feasibility; failure to comprehend the complexity of institutional change; failure to anticipate the demands of new groups on the program resources; and failure to understand the level of change in intergovernmental relations created by the new programs.

Samuel Halperin found that "the Great Society gave very little attention to administrative feasibility, to the burdens that would be placed on administrative bureaucracies in the Office of Education, in the states, in the localities." According to Halperin, "the bureaucracy wasn't up to it; isn't up to it, and in my judgment, won't be up to it, as long as we try to do so very, very much with so very, very few people in the governments."

William Smith found that many of the programs were "characterized by noble intentions, but monumentally naive assumptions about the way complex educational institutions can be influenced to change."

Robert Bennett, former Commissioner of Indian Affairs, noted that the new programs of the 1960s included acknowledgement of the problems of the Indian people. The statement issued by President Johnson in March, 1968, he commented, "I believe was the first statement ever given by a President specifically on Indians to the Congress of the United States. Out of the 15 major goals in this statement, ten were education related." According to Bennett, those words sparked "an interest on the part of the tribes in the total spectrum of services offered by the Federal Government."

Julian Nava described a similar impact on the Mexican-American population. Johnson, Nava noted, "was the first American President, to say, in effect, 'I understand. I care and I will try to help you.'" The series of events that occurred during Johnson's Presidency "introduced another color into our spectrum: white, black, and now brown." "Without doubt," said Nava, "Johnson began an irreversible process, now underway among so called Mexican-Americans or Chicanos." The change in attitude by the Federal Government toward these groups—as well as others—created new demands on the already scarce resources available in states and localities.

The appropriate roles of Congress, other parts of the Federal Government, state government, and local government were also inadequately considered during the 1960s. Samuel Halperin suggested that there was very little attention to what is called "legislative oversight"—for Congress to ask "how things work, whether they might be better consolidated, or terminated or replaced by more effective delivery systems." He also noted that the flurry of activity in the 1960s left us with a "kind of a mess in which it's not clear who is really in charge." Although the Federal investment in education is about 8 percent of total expenditures, "there is widespread unclarity about who is accountable."

(6) Problems with evaluation techniques

The discussion about evaluation in the Federal education programs of the 1960s touched on several issues: the political difficulty of producing data indicating that a program failed; use of new criteria in the assessment of old programs; and the difficulty of separating the general trend of declining test scores from the target population.

Albert Shanker recalled that 13 out of 15 of the larger cities in the U.S. would not let Coleman in to test students and were thus excluded from the data that made up the Coleman Report. According to Shanker, these officials "didn't want the public to know how their students were doing compared to other students. And one can hardly blame those school boards and the mayors of those cities, given the political realities."

William Smith found "the difficulty of evaluation 10 years later is using new criteria that is based on what is appropriate now to assess old activities that were based primarily upon a different set of conditions." The legislation of the 1960s, noted Smith, "was not drafted by those cautious social scientists or by those business administrators who were concerned about the magic of the organizational bureaucracy but really by a bunch of passionate, true believers who then had the opportunity to have it watered down by a sympathetic and liberal Congress."

Herbert Reid noted that educational achievement, like so many social programs, is hard to measure. He described the recent press accounts of declining test scores and said "that the decline in educational standards cuts across class lines, race lines, sectional lines, any lines that you can think about."

Where Do We Go Next?

There was little disagreement on *whether* Federal programs aimed at the achievement of equal educational opportunity should be included in future policy agendas. As Julian Nava commented, "Only at the national level have you really had innovative, progressive efforts that approach equalizing opportunity." However, the members of the panel had varying views on the way that future funds should flow through the system as intergovernmental aid. Panel members also had different appraisals of the level of political and fiscal support that could be mobilized for future education programs.

Although he did not believe that Title I of ESEA should be changed, Samuel Halperin did argue for "some consolidation of many of these programs." But the movement toward block grants, according to Albert Shanker, "would widen the distribution and the choices beyond what they are now. And I think that they are too wide now." Rather, Shanker argued that in the past "the Federal Government did not tell the localities strongly and sharply enough where they had to go and what they had to do." Julian Nava characterized categorical aid "as something necessary, indeed, indispensable." While he hoped that targeted aid was transitional, it was now the only way that the disadvantaged would get assistance.

According to Halperin, the demand for general aid is coming "from most of the educational associations in Washington. They want general aid, if they can get it out of the existing Title I program, fine. If they can get it by dismantling other categorical programs, fine. Or if they can get new money, fine. But they are not interested in keeping the priorities on those who are most disadvantaged."

Albert Shanker, on the other hand, did not agree that education has lost its appeal, politically. He said, "the only monies that the American public votes through a referendum, year after year and continues taxing themselves more and more, is for education. I don't think you could pass a Federal budget or a state budget throughout this country by referendum and we keep passing school budgets." He argued that there is evidence that the public will continue this support.

Douglass Cater noted that "in the new competition of priorities in Washington or a renewed competition, education comes in at a disadvantage because it is a line item budget in a social budget [while] most of the other things have various kinds of devices for being uncontrollable."

Although the panel did not formally poll itself, there appeared to be a consensus among the members that a change in leadership in the White House, the creation of a Department of Education, and public recommitment to the goals of the programs of the New Frontier and the Great Society might give the goal of equal educational opportunity a renewed life.

PART
6

the right to equality under the law

Clifford Alexander

17

Equality Under the Law:
A Review of the Programs

At the heart of the Kennedy-Johnson Administrations was a commitment to providing equality under law for minority Americans. Surveying the programmatic attempts to achieve these goals stimulates two conflicting emotions: initially, an exhilaration created by statements of high purpose and energetic activity to reinforce this purpose with appropriate Congressional action; the other emotion is one of frustration when one sees how programs put into place by President Johnson have, particularly in the employment field, been emasculated and turned away from their original purpose.

While in the Eisenhower Administration only the judiciary was actively engaged in the fight to protect the rights of blacks and other minorities*, the increased protest in the South by young blacks and whites and increased public opinion in favor of civil rights met more sympathetic ears in the Kennedy and Johnson White Houses and in the Congress. President Johnson, in particular, captured President Kennedy's somewhat belated legislative initiative in 1963 and gave this legislation every emphasis and inpetus which a President has at his disposal. President Johnson's forceful sponsorship of civil rights legislation was much more a result of inner-felt purpose than it was the reflexive actions of a politician listening for the reactions of the voters.

Equal opportunity during the Kennedy-Johnson years should be viewed principally through three significant pieces of legislation—the Civil Rights Act of 1964, the Voting Rights Act of 1965, and the Civil Rights Act of 1968 (with particular emphasis on Title VIII relating to fair housing). But the 1960s contained much more. Court decisions and executive actions played an important and progressive role, particularly Executive Order

---

*A weak civil rights act was passed in 1957 which did establish the Civil Rights Commission; but little aid or comfort to minorities issued from the Eisenhower White House.

11246 regarding equal employment by Federal contractors, and the programs of the Justice Department and HEW to execute Title VI of the Civil Rights Act of 1964. Numerous Federal courts gave forceful support to the principles embodied in Title VII of the Civil Rights Act.

The achievements of the 1960s put programs in place to protect against discrimination in virtually every aspect of life— education, employment, housing, the administration of justice, access to places of public accommodation, and appropriate participation in the benefits of federally assisted programs. In the areas of voting and access to public accommodations, program enforcement followed legislative enactment. In other areas, and particularly in the area of equal employment opportunity, programs languished and enforcement ranged from uneven to nonexistent. Much of the burden fell back to the have-nots to secure their own rights and left aggrieved minorities pretty much to their own devices.

The Civil Rights Act of 1964

The Civil Rights Act of 1964 was a Congressional response to a broad range of events in the United States during the 1940s, 1950s, and early 1960s. The NAACP successfully initiated court actions to end racially restrictive covenants in housing, segregation in interstate transportation, and discrimination in publicly owned recreational facilities. These successes were capped in 1954 by *Brown v. Board of Education*—the triumphant climax to the NAACP's campaign against educational segregation in the public schools of the South. The NAACP and others had been successful as well in helping to register new voters throughout the South, and in the abolition of the "white" primary in 1944. In the 12 years following the outlawing of the "white" primary, black registration in southern states rose from a quarter of a million to nearly a million and a quarter.

The key dramatic point in the civil rights movement was in the area of public accommodations and access to public facilities with the direct action techniques of the Montgomery, Alabama bus boycott of 1955-56 led by Dr. Martin Luther King, Jr.

The South reacted forcefully to the Supreme Court's decisions and the successes of the NAACP and the Montgomery bus boycott. The reaction was the outlawing of the NAACP, intimidation against civil rights leaders, bringing on massive resistance to the Court's *Brown* decision, curtailing black voter registration, and the formation of White Citizens' Councils throughout the South.

The mounting violence brought on by the direct action of the blacks' protests, boycotts, sit-ins, and the like, was met by white resistance, and in some cases, outright murder. In 1963, police dogs, fire hoses, and cattle prods were used against marchers in Birmingham, Alabama. And on a quiet Sunday morning, a bomb exploded in a church in Birmingham, killing four young girls. In 1964, the violence escalated, with the murder of three civil rights workers in Philadelphia, Mississippi, and the murder by Ku Klux Klansmen of a black Army lieutenant driving through Georgia. Countless other blacks were intimidated and received not even token due process of law.

President Kennedy faced the mounting crisis forcefully in 1963, called it a "moral issue" on television before the nation, and introduced new civil rights legislation. The 1963 "March on Washington" further contributed to the broad national support for the bill. In 1964, President Johnson took command, and after a Senate filibuster, secured passage of the Civil Rights Act of 1964.

Although the Civil Rights Act of 1964 contains 10 titles we will concentrate here on Titles II and III regarding discrimination in places of public accommodation and in other public facilities, Title VI and its impact upon school desegregation and other federally funded activities, and Title VII and its mandate against discrimination in employment. The other titles are more or less supportive of these main initiatives and extended the Commission on Civil Rights and established the Community Relations Service.

Public Accommodations

One area in which the 1964 Civil Rights Act had a dramatic positive impact was in the field of public accommodations. As late as the early 1960s, segregation of restaurants, motels, hotels, and theaters was the rule throughout the South and in parts of the North. The freedom riders and the lunch counter sit-ins of the early 1960s were primarily responsible for enactment of the public accommodations sections.

With the passage of the 1964 Civil Rights Act, quick action was taken by the Justice Department to enforce the new public accommodations law. Within a few months after enactment, Justice brought several enforcement actions that tested the constitutionality of the public accommodations section. Actions were brought involving the Heart of Atlanta Motel in downtown Atlanta, and Ollie's Barbecue, a family-owned restaurant in Birmingham, Alabama. And in 1964, in two related decisions, the Supreme Court held the public accommodations sections constitutional. With passage and acceptance of Titles II and III, discrimination by hotels, motels, restaurants, and in public facilities virtually ended with clear public acceptance of the new law.

Desegregation of Schools and Other Federally Supported Institutions

The 1964 Civil Rights Act attacked the problem of discrimination and segregation in education in two ways. First, through litigation under Title IV of the Act, the Attorney General was authorized to bring lawsuits to eliminate unconstitutional discrimination by public schools and colleges. Second, through the leverage of Federal financial assistance under Title VI of the Civil Rights Act, schools and colleges had to end discriminatory practices as a condition to receiving such financial assistance.

Progress to desegregate public schools in the South has resulted directly from the enactment of civil rights laws. Ten years after *Brown v. Board of Education,* only three percent of the black school children in the South were attending public schools with white children. Five years after the passage of the Civil Rights Act of 1964, this percentage had increased significantly, with more than 20 percent of black children attending desegregated schools in the region. HEW's determination to enforce Title VI in conjunction with increases in federally funded education programs was the principal factor responsible for this significant acceleration.

Support for eradicating the dual school system in the South also came from assistance under Title IV of the 1964 Act, which helped to aid southern school districts in pupil desegregation. But, by 1966, funding for this valuable program was still at very limited levels, insufficient to induce voluntary compliance. For this and other reasons, attention turned to Title VI as a means of desegregating the dual school system in the South. Litigation could not be made to substitute for administrative proceedings prescribed by the Congress under Title VI. Revised Title VI guidelines were issued in 1966, but progress continued slowly. In the 12 years following the *Brown* decision, and two years after the passage of the 1964 Civil Rights Act, no more than 10 percent of all minority group children were attending integrated schools. Freedom of choice plans were still being accepted by HEW; however, many were seeking the elimination of such plans as an accepted, but ineffective method of compliance.

Title VI of the 1964 Act provides that no person in the United States shall, on the grounds of race, color, or national origin, be excluded from participation in, be denied the benefits of, or be subject to discrimination under, any program or activity receiving Federal financial assistance. Because of certain limitations in the statute, Title VI applies mainly to Federal loan and grant programs. A 1969 study showed that in 1968, Federal grant-in-aid payments under these programs amounted to more than $25 billion. Following Title VI's passage, a task force composed of representatives of the White House and other departments and agencies of the Federal Government went to work to develop regulations for enforcing Title VI. Progress continued to be slow, and as of May, 1970, several agencies had still not promulgated regulations implementing Title VI. The non-discrimination requirements of Title VI were applicable to public schools, hospitals and other health facilities; highway construction and public parks, covering in total more than 400 programs administered by 23 Federal departments and agencies. The programs covered by Title VI are those in which there is an intermediary between the Federal Government and the ultimate beneficiary of Federal assistance.

One area outside of education in which Title VI has had salutory results relates to practices in hospitals and health facilities. The Medicare program was enacted in 1965. In 1966, HEW conducted thousands of visits to hospitals to determine whether the requirements of Title VI were being met. Anxious to obtain Federal certification for Medicare, many hospitals quickly abolished discriminatory practices. By 1968, 97 percent of the nation's hospitals were committed to provide non-discriminatory services.

Title VI also came into play in the controversy surrounding the tax-exempt status accorded private segregated schools by the Internal Revenue Service (IRS). Many such schools were attended exclusively by white students and had been established in the

South as a means of avoiding public school desegregation. Many had received approval by the IRS as charitable institutions, thus exempting them from paying Federal income taxes. The question arose whether Title V of the Civil Rights Act authorized or required IRS to withhold tax benefits to racially segregated private schools.

The issue came to a head in 1967 when the IRS approved the application of 42 segregated private schools for tax benefits. The Supreme Court decided in *Coyt v. Green* that the Internal Revenue Code did not permit granting tax-exempt status to segregated private schools, or the deduction of charitable contributions. Although initially maintaining the *Green* decision was limited to private schools in Mississippi, the IRS reversed its policy in 1970, announcing that the tax-exempt status of private schools practicing racial discrimination would be revoked, although not basing its reversed policy specifically on Title VI.

Equal Employment Opportunity

Title VII of the Civil Rights Act of 1964 contained a clear, unequivocal statement of public purpose. Employment discrimination based on color, religion, national origin, sex, or race was prohibited and the Equal Employment Opportunity Commission (EEOC) was created. Of all the lofty civil rights pronouncements and goals, this was by far of greatest potential importance. Title VII has been the object of numerous Federal decisions, including significant action by the U.S. Supreme Court.

Unfortunately, few whites in power in the nation's private or public sectors shared Lyndon Baines Johnson's zeal for fairness in employment. When the proponents of a strong EEOC gave away its enforcement powers to the leaders of yesteryear in the Senate, it meant that the high purposes of the legislation would be deferred. Businesses and labor unions kept on discriminating, and knew that under the compromise legislation, there was little that the EEOC could do about it.

In the employment field, more than any other, the high purposes set out in Presidential rhetoric and legislative wording were to have little real meaning. From 1964 to the present, the black unemployment rate remains twice that of whites. Blacks earn $56 to every white $100, where in 1969, blacks earned $61 to every white $100.

The promise of legal protection against job discrimination, as it turned out, was an empty one; the basic flaw—the gutting from Title VII of the power to issue "cease and desist" orders against discriminators. Without this power, the Commission was forced to rely on persuasion, conciliation, and mediation. When a company or union did not want to conciliate after discrimination had been found, the *victim* had only one recourse—to bring suit in Federal court. Few, obviously, had the wherewithal to undertake this exhaustive and inappropriate step to enforce their claims.

President Nixon, with the help of Congress, did greater damage to the EEOC in 1972. Under the guise of giving the Commission more power, the Nixon Administration pushed legislation giving EEOC the right to sue in order to end discriminatory practices. The new "power" is and was a sham. While lawsuits lumber along, 150,000 complainants are waiting to have their charges investigated. More importantly, an administrative agency established principally to hear and act with speed on individual complaints of discrimination has turned into a frustrated marshmallow—powerless—inefficient—and most importantly, ineffective.

For the same reason that President Johnson saw terms and conditions of employment as a key to a more perfect union, others who were the traditional enemies of minority aspirations saw equal employment as the greatest threat to their order. Equal employment struggles lacked the drama of urban disturbances, peaceful demonstrators being manhandled, or ugly mobs overturning school buses. The drama is more low-key—more continuing—and more relevant than any of the other denials sought to be corrected in the sixties. A job is, after all, where adult America spends most of its waking hours. The fruits of labor are what give internal satisfaction to men and women. The source of frustration for minority America, first and foremost—now and then— was to be kept from earning or performing up to one's full potential.

The nation is far from catching up to Lyndon Baines Johnson's perceptiveness. He saw that if one could ease this frustration, not only would equity and fairness be served, but majority and minority Americans would be more prosperous. A greater contribution by minority Americans would lead to a wealthier nation, more at peace with itself. But sadly, the dream has not become a reality.

Executive Action to Foster Equal Employment

The most significant tool available to the government to promote equal employment opportunity is its capacity to terminate, suspend, or bar discriminating companies who do business with the Federal Government. The genesis of this concept is in executive orders issued during the 1940s, and in Executive Order 11141, issued by President Kennedy in 1961. Executive Order 11246 issued by President Johnson on September 24, 1965, was a firm step forward. It stated:

> The contractor will not discriminate against any employee or applicant for employment because of race, color, religion, or national origin. The contractor will take affirmative action to ensure that applicants are employed, and that employees are treated during employment, without regard to their race, color, religion, or national origin. Such action shall include, but not be limited to the following: employment, upgrading, demotion, or transfer; recruitment or recruitment advertising; layoff or termination; rates of pay or other forms of compensation; and selection for training, including apprenticeship. . . .

The executive orders took the appropriate legal position that it was within the power of the President to determine substantive standards for those who would do business with the Federal Government, thereby receiving Federal funds.

Under Executive Order 11246, President Johnson delegated his authority to suspend, debar, or terminate contracts of those who were judged to be discriminators to the Department of Labor. The Department of Labor established the Office of Federal Contract Compliance (OFCC). The potential power was immense. It was certain that the attention of a company would be obtained if millions of dollars worth of existing contracts were threatened, or if the company's future capacity to do business with the government was impaired. Far more than the complaint route formulated under the Equal Employment Opportunity Commission, the power under Executive Order 11246, later supplemented by Executive Order 11375, contained the leverage to effectuate rapid and substantive change in formerly discriminatory employment and promotional patterns.

Both Presidents Kennedy and Johnson were serious in their intent. But the seriousness of purpose was blurred as the responsibility was delegated. Despite all that was said, nothing was done. No government contractor lost a contract during the Kennedy-Johnson years. True, the executive orders led to certain significant substantive changes. The concept of an affirmative action plan was put into place, and many in the Johnson Administration worked toward its refinement in order that it would become an effective business tool to assure better utilization of minority and female talent. Government contractors receiving $50,000 or more in contracts were required to prepare affirmative action plans. The act of preparing the plans caused them to focus, as no other requirement had, on the deficiencies within their own organizations in the equal employment field. Certain companies took these deficiencies seriously and embarked on significant efforts to improve their utilization of women and minorities. Others, unfortunately, often, after complaining loudly about the burdens of dealing with the Federal Government, created inadequate plans which were a sure sign of their incapacity and/or unwillingness to utilize properly women and minority workers.

As the months and years went by after the issuance of Executive Order 11246, more and more companies realized that the government was less than serious in its purpose. Reorganization and delegation by the OFCC took place, and continues to take place up until this very day. As many as 17 agencies and departments who dealt directly with government contractors were given primary responsibility for assessing the adequacy of affirmative action plans and determining whether contractors should be debarred, suspended, or terminated. The few threats that were made of government action against discriminators, as time went by, were taken less and less seriously.

The one serious action that was taken came as a result of President Johnson's meeting with a group of black publishers, one of whom raised the discriminatory employment patterns of a company in his city. President Johnson authorized his White House staff to get the OFCC off the dime and eventually action was initiated just prior to President Johnson's leaving office.

Again, there was no doubt about his personal concern. The problems began to arise when those given the authority were asked to act. The action was not forthcoming.

President Johnson spoke to the issue of equal employment on occasions too numerous to list. He continually stressed the theme of unfinished business—providing full and fair opportunity to minority Americans. He tried to cajole the private sector and direct the Executive Branch to fulfill his wishes. In 1966, he held the only substantive and meaningful conference to address a wide panoply of issues affecting black and white in America—the White House Conference to Fulfill These Rights. He endorsed the Conference; he embraced its recommendations. He required reports of Cabinet members to carry out these recommendations. (And, in fact, some were carried out.) But in the employment field, the field of greatest importance to the President, and certainly to black Americans, substantive action did not follow with the same forcefulness as the pronouncements.

It might have been that had a President with commitment to these principles followed LBJ, we would have been further along today in our quest for equal employment opportunity. At least through LBJ's energy and strength, the enemies of equal employment had to hide under their rocks. But from 1969 on, the momentum was halted, and in many areas, reversed. Had there been some commitment at the top in the late 1960s and early 1970s, perhaps momentum would have caused a lessening of the economic gap between black and white. But we all know that the gap is widening again today. The remedy provided in Executive Order 11246 is still available to the government. Procedures, guidelines, and regulations assure that if any severe contractual action is undertaken, the affected company is significantly protected by due process. As part of the LBJ legacy, the procedures are in place now. It is for our nation to use them, firmly but fairly.

Equal Employment and the Federal Employee

The responsibility for providing equal employment opportunity in the Federal Government was placed in the Civil Service Commission by Executive Order 11246 in 1965. There the power resided until the 1972 amendments to Title VII of the Civil Rights Act of 1964. Then, statutorily, the Civil Service Commission was given a continuing role in allegedly securing equal employment rights for protected classes of Federal workers. The Civil Service Commission was directed to review and approve annually affirmative action plans and to evaluate the effectiveness of various agency equal employment opportunity programs. Further, the Civil Service Commission was to look at the merit system to see if it was flawed with bias. Federal employees were given the right, as were private sector employees, to institute litigation in Federal district courts on individual discrimination claims.[1]

In 1965, some of us questioned giving the Civil Service Commission the supervisory authority of providing equal employment opportunity in the Federal Government. The defenders of the Commission, however, ruled the day. Unfortunately, the programs under the aegis of the Civil Service Commission had done little to encourage affirmative action in the Federal Government, and less to insure a fair hearing to those who complained of discrimination based on race, sex, or national origin. The long-standing obstinacy and failure of the Civil Service Commission was obvious when one looked at the history of its activity—or more accurately, the lack of same—in equal employment opportunity. The activity of the Commission and, parenthetically, its own employment problems, provides a picture of exclusion of black people from positions of significance and authority within its own and the Federal employment structure.

The history of exclusion of minorities from Federal employment after the Civil War is a depressing one, and certainly not a precedent for progressive employment policies in the private sector. Some Presidents, and a continuous stream of bureaucrats, established and enforced a hiring mechanism that provided only a few of the lowest-paying jobs to minorities, and then when the quantity was increased, threw up roadblocks to the inclusion of minorities in the Federal employment structure in middle- and upper-eschelon jobs.

During the Administration of President William Howard Taft, racial segregation was set up in the Census Bureau. Subsequently, during President Woodrow Wilson's Administration, and consistent with his generally anti-black policy, the Department of the Treasury and the Postal Service were segregated. During World

War I, a new example of overt discrimination—tolerated in the military—was the requirement that black clerks who worked for the Navy be required to carry out their assignments behind screens.

Various forms of employment discrimination continued well into the Administration of Franklin D. Roosevelt. With the pressures of leaders such as A. Philip Randolph and the work shortages caused during the Second World War, opportunities were broadened, and in 1941, a Presidential committee on fair employment practices with the authority to investigate discrimination complaints was established. The Civil Service Commission was to conduct investigations of alleged discrimination. The Civil Service Commission, however, refused to examine those matters which it believed to be in the discretion of the discriminating agency, and saw no discrimination unless there had been a violation of the Commission's own Civil Service rules. No concept of affirmative action was even discussed until 1961, when President Kennedy established the President's Committee on Equal Employment Opportunity. The President's Committee had no statutory authority, and though it did initiate certain programs, its progress was uneven at best.

In 1964, the Civil Rights Act was passed, but Title VII, dealing with employment discrimination, did not cover discrimination by the Federal Government against its employees. There was, however, a basic statement of purpose which clearly indicated that it was against national policy to discriminate in employment based on race, color, sex, religion, or national origin. Despite this statement of national purpose, the Civil Service Commission, even into the 1970s, did not have a single black occupying a supergrade position throughout the entire agency. The Civil Service Commission gave lip service to its responsibilities under the Executive Order. But the rules and regulations it established served to blunt those who were brave enough to complain of discrimination. In 93 out of every 100 cases the Civil Service Commission sides with the agency and against the individual complaining of discrimination.

The Civil Service Commission treated with disdain the work of the Equal Employment Opportunity Commission, and the most basic statement of principle enunciated by the Supreme Court in *Griggs v. Duke Power* in 1971. While the Federal Government was rightfully attempting to correct tests and standards in the private sector that had a disparate effect on minority workers or potential minority workers, the Civil Service Commission was going in the opposite direction.

Both the Equal Employment Opportunity Commission and the Office of Federal Contract Compliance issued detailed guidelines on testing and employment criteria. The purpose of the guidelines was to establish for the private sector a relatively bias-free method of judging tests and promotional devices. The basic thrust of the guidelines was and is that tests and other employment devices, to be valid, must be job-related; that is, that there is a requirement that employers, if they are using examinations, tests, and other devices, show how the results of these tests relate to the job that is to be done by the prospective employee. If the tests do not have a job-relatedness and either maintain a system of past discrimination or are inherently discriminatory in and of themselves, they are to be discarded. This standard was wholly accepted by the Supreme Court in *Griggs v. Duke Power* in 1971 when it said that guidelines of administrative agencies must be afforded great weight and that any test or educational qualifications must be job-related. But in the period from 1965 through 1971, just as it had before, the Civil Service Commission continued utilizing an unvalidated test—namely, the Federal Service Entrance Examination.

The score on the Federal Service Entrance Examination was of overriding importance in the hiring of any employee who was required to take it. Yet, it had never been validated. This examination was utilized to screen applicants for 200 categories of Federal management, technical, and professional jobs in a great variety of Federal agencies. Additionally, in order to be construed as eligible for entry into many of these types of positions, a person was required to have a college degree or three years of work experience, this to be combined with a score of 70 or more in the Federal Service Entrance Examination. It is clear by any test of simple logic that no one examination can be substantially relevant to the requirements of over 200 jobs—unless we can make the uncalled-for presumption that people in those managerial, technical, and professional positions in various agencies really all do the same thing. Predictably, and probably to the liking of the Civil Service Commission, a disproportionately high number of minorities who took the examination failed to pass the FSEE.

When the 1972 amendments to the Civil Rights Act were passed, the Civil Service Commission's regulations still called for initial investigations by the agency being complained against for its own alleged discriminatory practices. Further, in the vast majority of cases, an agency finding was firmly upheld when reviewed by the Civil Service Commission Board. While the complainant could receive a hearing, the complainant's rights were severely limited because the finding of the Hearing Examiner was binding on the agency.

The final problem in the area of review was if the individual complainant were to file an action in Federal district court, it was likely at that point that only a review of the record would take place, as opposed to a trial *de novo*.[2]

Remedies that were consistently upheld in Federal courts against private sector employees were eroded through the practices of the Civil Service Commission. Once discrimination had been shown in the private sector and back pay deemed appropriate, the burden was upon the discriminating party to show that the individual was not entitled to this remedy. Under the Federal system, even after a showing of discrimination, the right to back pay is severely limited, and the charging party bears the burden of proof, even after a clear finding of discrimination. In many instances, again due to the Civil Service Commission's retrogressive policies, class allegations are separated from those of the individual, thus eroding a right that is commonplace under normal Title VII law. According to *The Federal Civil Rights Enforcement Effort - 1974*, prepared by the U.S. Civil Rights Commission in July, 1975, the Civil Service Commission issued examiners handbooks in April, 1973. The handbook gives instructions on preparing for and conducting a hearing. The handbook has no guidelines or any substantive information on what is Title VII law. The instructions in the handbook are contrary to the weight of authority under Title VII, and its description of discrimination speaks only in terms of disparate treatment. It says that the complainant has the initial burden to show disparate treatment. This is certainly contrary to Title VII law.

On page 79, the Civil Rights Commission goes on to say:

The findings and recommendations of the complaints examiner are not binding on the agency unless the examiner recommends a finding of discrimination and the agency has not issued a final decision within 180 days after the complaint is filed. If the agency rejects or modifies the decision recommended by the complaints examiner, or if the agency's decision is made when a hearing is not requested, it must set forth the specific reasons for its final action. During fiscal year 1974, 7% of final agency dispositions made a finding of discrimination.

The general anti-equal employment approach of the Civil Service Commission is continued as it carries out its responsibilities to review affirmative action plans. The Commission's affirmative action guidelines are a great deal weaker than those outlined in 41 CRF, part 60, which applies to private contractors with the Federal Government. The heart of the private contractor's responsibility is to develop a utilization analysis and work force analysis and establish goals and timetables where there is underutilization of minorities and women. The Commission does not require, however, that Federal agencies adequately determine where they have fallen down in utilizing minority and female workers. Most importantly, though everyone in the private sector is required to do it, the Commission does not require numerical goals and timetables of the Federal agencies whose affirmative action plans it has the responsibility to review. It is clear that this is a blatant and probably illegal refusal on the part of the Civil Service Commission to carry out its responsibilities as delegated through Executive Orders 11246, 11375, 11478, Title VII, and the 1972 amendments to the Civil Rights Act of 1964.

Not only in substance is the Civil Service Commission negligent. Its procedures call for an annual review of affirmative action plans; yet of the 47 national plans due May 1, 1974, just 13 were submitted at the appropriate time.

The Federal Government, as an employer, is a follower instead of a leader. Many private employers chuckle at the cynicism of their being required to adhere to rightfully stringent requirements of affirmative action plans, when the Civil Service Commission is playing footloose with the rights of those employees in protected classes who are in the Federal service.

The Voting Rights Act of 1965

The Voting Rights Act of 1965 has resulted in dramatic progress. As stated in *The Federal Civil Rights Enforcement Effort (1970),* published by the U.S. Civil Rights Commission,

> Before its passage registration of black citizens of voting age in the seven southern states affected by the law was less than 31%; by the spring of 1969 approximately 57% of eligible blacks in these states were registered. Black registration in these states increased by more than 740,000 persons since 1965; there are now more than 400 black elected officials as of 1970, compared with 70 in 1965.

However, passage of the Act has not resulted in full use of the franchise. For instance, the continuing economic dependence of rural blacks in the South constitutes a significant deterrent to their exercising their right to vote.

The Voting Rights Act of 1965 was developed because of the failure of earlier legislation to remedy discrimination in voting. The Civil Rights Acts of 1957, 1960, and 1964 focussed on streamlining traditional remedies available through the judicial process to enforce the Fifteenth Amendment. The 1965 Voting Rights Act, however, further strengthened judicial remedies, and provided additionally for direct Federal action for a variety of administrative remedies to overcome immediate or potential barriers to full and effective minority participation in the political process.

At the commencement of the Kennedy and Johnson years in 1961, the problem of denial of the right to vote appeared to occur in only eight southern states—Alabama, Florida, Georgia, Louisiana, Mississippi, North Carolina, South Carolina, and Tennessee. In these eight states, less than 40 percent of the total black population resided. Even in these eight states, however, with a total of 3.7 million non-whites of voting age, some 1 million non-whites registered to vote.

By 1965, the primary means used to keep blacks away from the polls were (1) literacy tests and other tests for voter registration, usually unfairly administered; (2) other obstructive tactics by voting registrars; and (3) the atmosphere of physical and economic intimidation that made blacks aware that politics was an activity for whites only. Not only were the illiterates disqualified by use of literacy tests, but the use of unfair tests, or unfair administration of fair tests, disenfranchised a large number of literate voters as well. The use of subjective understanding and interpretation tests, and even more extreme measures (such as Virginia's blank form, where applicants were required to supply the required information from memory without even a form to guide them) were a further bar to registration of blacks in any substantial numbers.

Mississippi and Alabama were the only two states to retain poll taxes during the 1960s. In 1954, of 500,000 voting age blacks in these states, only 22,000 (or 4.4 percent) were registered to vote. In Louisiana, a concerted campaign was conducted during the 1950s and early 1960s to minimize registration and voting by blacks. Agencies of the state's government including the legislature, cooperated with organizations such as the White Citizens' Councils to achieve this result. In addition to the wide latitude permitted registrars in administering voter qualification laws and establishing barriers to black registration on several occasions, black registrants were openly purged from the voter registration rolls.

The denial of the right to vote was not only a product of actions by registrars against individual blacks, but a concerted legislative effort on the part of various states to malapportion or gerrymander districts to deny blacks the right to vote or to weaken that voting strength. The courts were in the lead in finding that this gerrymandering procedure was a deprivation of rights under the Fifteenth Amendment. In Tuskegee, Alabama, in 1957, the Alabama legislature changed the boundaries of the city in such a way that all but 4 or 5 of about 400 blacks formerly voting in municipal elections were beyond the city limits. In *Gomellion v. Lightfoot,* the Supreme Court in 1960 ruled that when a legislature thus singles out a readily isolated segment of blacks for special discriminatory treatment, it violates the Fifteenth Amendment. The Section 5 provisions of the 1965 Voting Rights Act were clearly aimed at such actions by state legislatures.

Provisions of the Act

The Voting Rights Act of 1965 consisted of provisions, some of which are temporary, and others of which are permanent. The temporary provisions initially established in 1965 for five years were extended in 1970 for another five years. As a result of the Voting Rights Act Amendments of 1975, these provisions were extended for another seven years.

As for the general provisions, Section 2 of the Act sets out the prohibitions against imposition or application of any racially discriminatory voting qualification or prerequisite to voting.

Since enactment of the Voting Rights Act, more than 6,500 observers have been sent to cover elections in five southern states of which almost half were used in Mississippi. In 1974, 430 observers watched primary and general elections in Alabama, Georgia, Louisiana, and Mississippi.

In 1970, Congress found that in order to guarantee the purposes of the Act, an extension of the temporary provisions was required. With this five-year extension, Congress amended the formula contained in Section 4 to include jurisdictions that had in place a test or device as of November 1, 1968, and voter turnouts of less than 50 percent in the 1968 Presidential election. Also included was a five-year suspension nationwide of all literacy tests. The 1970 amendments also abolished durational residency requirements for Presidential elections and lowered the voting age to 18.

In August, 1975, Congress again prevented the Voting Rights Act from expiring. This time, the Act was extended for an additional seven years. It also added to the protections of the Act as follows. It prohibited for 10 years the use of English-only registration and election materials in any county in which five percent or more of the voting age population are members of a language minority group. Persons of Spanish heritage, Asian Americans, and Native Americans are considered language minorities. In addition, if the voting rate in the 1972 Presidential election was below 50 percent in such countries, the major provisions of the Act, including Section 5 preclearance, applied to the county and state for 10 years.

Impact of the Voting Rights Act. The March, 1965 march from Selma, Alabama, to Montgomery, consisting of 25,000 blacks and whites, focused attention on the need to guarantee the most basic of rights: the right to vote. It gave rise to a plea by President Johnson for the Congressional enactment of the Voting Rights Act of 1965. As a result of a court-ordered apportionment plan fashioned on the principles of the Act, in January, 1975, 15 blacks were elected and took their seats in that same state capital in Montgomery, as members of the Alabama legislature.

Between 1964 and 1972, the percentage of eligible blacks registered to vote in the 7 covered southern states increased from 29 percent to over 56 percent as a result of the registration of more than 1 million new black voters. There is no available estimate of the number of black elected officials in the South before passage of the 1965 Voting Rights Act, but it was certainly just a handful. By February, 1968, 156 blacks had been elected to various offices in the 7 states. This total included 14 state legislators, 81 county officials, and 61 municipal officials. By April, 1974, the total number of black elected officials in the 7 covered states had increased to 963; the total includes one member of the United States Congress (Andrew Young), 36 state legislators, 429 county officials, and 497 municipal officials.[3]

Section 3 describes judicial authority granted to apply the remedies established in deciding suits brought by the Attorney General under the special enforcement provisions of the Act. The Congressional finding that the poll tax is a violation of Fifteenth Amendment rights and is a basis for institution of suit by the Justice Department is set out in Section 10. Thereafter, with the Court's decision in *Harper v. Virginia State Board of Elections*, and the passage of the Twenty-Fourth Amendment, the payment of poll taxes as a requirement for voting was banned. A final permanent provision, Section 4e, defines Puerto Ricans educated in Spanish as literate if they have completed the sixth grade, regardless of their ability to read or write in English.

The heart of the 1965 Voting Rights Act was in the special provisions of Section 4 through 9.

Section 4 provides a nondiscretionary automatic formula or "trigger" by which states or their political subdivisions are covered or made subject to the Act's remedies. Section 4 prohibits the use of "tests or devices" as a prerequisite to registering or voting in any jurisdiction that maintained such tests or devices on November 1, 1964 *and* whose voter registration or turnout in the 1964 Presidential election was less than 50% of the voting age population. Section 5 freezes the electoral laws and procedures of such jurisdictions as of November 1, 1964 and prohibits enforcement of any changes of them until certification by the attorney general or the district court for the District of Columbia that the changes are not discriminatory in purpose or effect. U.S. Commission on Civil Rights, *The Voting Rights Act: Ten Years After (1975)*

This is what is referred to as the Section 5 preclearance procedure.

> Sections 6 through 9 provide for, but do not require, the assignment of federal examiners, to list eligible persons for registration by state officials in the covered states and counties; and observers to report on the conduct of elections in such jurisdictions designated by the attorney general. *The Voting Rights Act: Ten Years After (1975)*

The Act served the immediate goal of increasing registration by suspending literacy tests and other tests or devices in covered states and counties, and providing for Federal examiners to speed the registration process. It also looked prospectively by providing in Section 5 a mechanism for preventing jurisdictions from subverting the purposes of the Act by changing their electoral laws and procedures. During the consideration of the earlier civil rights act, establishment of a Federal examiners program was debated. By 1965, because of the failure of earlier legislation, it was acknowledged that some Federal presence was necessary. Examiners have been used sparingly and most served during the first few years after the Act went into effect. In fact only 60 counties and parishes have ever had examiners in the first 10 years of the Voting Rights Act's history (through 1975). Federal examiners have never been sent to North Carolina and Virginia.

The figures on increased voter registration obscure the disparities between white and black registration rates that actually exist within these states. In South Carolina, for example, the black registration rate approaches that of whites. This is so because the black rate is actually higher than the white rate in two urban counties and because the white rate has dropped substantially since 1964 in many black counties. Sheer numbers would suggest an overhwhelming success rate. In fact, however, offices held by most blacks are relatively minor and located in small communities with large black populations. One notable exception is the city of Atlanta. As of 1974, Mississippi, which is 37 percent black, had only one black legislator, who was elected in 1967. And as of November, 1974, there were 15 blacks in the Alabama legislature comprising 10.6 percent of the seats held; however, the black percentage of the state population was 26.2 percent. Nor are Mexican-Americans, Puerto Ricans, and Indians doing much better (where those jurisdictions are covered by the Voting Rights Act) than blacks in winning public office.

Section 5 preclearance procedures have become the focal point of the Voting Rights Act since its enactment in 1965. Section 5 and its history provide an index for the types of discriminatory practices that covered jurisdictions have attempted to put into effect. The language of the Act clearly showed that Congress intended a very broad range of subjects to be included under Section 5. The Supreme Court has interpreted the language broadly:

> The legislative history on the whole supports the view that Congress intended to reach any state enactment which altered the election law of the covered state in even a minor way. *Allen v. State Board of Elections,* 393 U.S. 544 (1969).

Seemingly minor changes in election law can produce a significant detrimental impact on minority participation or minimize the effects of their participation. Changes in polling places, registration times and places, qualification for office, schedules of elections, city boundaries, and redistricting are among the matters that must be submitted for preclearance under Section 5.

The structuring of properly apportioned legislative and Congressional districts and other reapportionment problems continue to threaten the adequacy of the right to vote by minorities. In 1973, a Mississippi legislative reapportionment plan was submitted that respected county lines, created multi-member districts and numbered post and residence requirements. The use of single-member districts through a subdivision of counties would have created a much larger number of majority black districts than did the legislators' plan which did not subdivide counties; single-member districts would also facilitate the creation of districts in which the black percentage is high enough to enable the electorate to have a chance to determine who is elected. In *Connor v. Waller,* the Supreme Court remanded the Mississippi reapportionment plan for Section 5 preclearance approval. But the Federal district court in Mississippi acted very slowly—so slowly, in fact, that the Supreme Court, in May, 1976, had to order the lower court to reapportion the legislature by June 17.

In Virginia, a redistricting plan provided for multi-member districts in the Virginia House for the cities of Hampton, Newport News, Norfolk, Portsmouth, and Richmond where black voters were significant. The attorney general's objections were withdrawn after a Supreme Court decision in *Whitcomb v. Chavez*, 403 U.S. 124, that removed the legal justification for its objections.

Another significant problem focusing on fair representation for blacks at the local level has resulted from annexation controversies. In Virginia, annexation in Richmond and Petersburg resulted in Section 5 objections and in litigation which reached the Supreme Court. In 1968, blacks elected three of the nine seats on Richmond's at-large elected council as a result of a slight black majority in population. Late in 1969, Richmond annexed approximately 23 square miles of adjacent Chesterfield County. The population of Richmond in 1970 after annexation was 58 percent white. The district court in 1974 found that the annexation discriminated against blacks both in purpose and in effect after the Supreme Court held in 1971 that annexations are covered by Section 5. Richmond submitted the annexation for Justice Department review. It was promptly objected to by the attorney general. The Supreme Court decided the case in *City of Richmond v. United States* in 1975, holding that an annexation reducing relative political strength of blacks does not violate automatically Section 5. The case was remanded to the lower court to determine if the city's annexation reasons were *bona fide* and not racially motivated (95 S. Ct. 2296).

The 1968 Civil Rights Act and Fair Housing

The 1968 Civil Rights Act, especially the Fair Housing Act of 1968, was a response to the conditions of segregated housing that existed throughout the nation. The Act includes 10 titles, although the most significant provision by far is Title VIII, the Fair Housing Act.

Title I of the Civil Rights Act of 1968 amends the Federal criminal code to prosecute those interfering with civil rights of others. It makes it a crime for any individual to interfere with federally protected activities by force or intimidation. These federally protected activities include voting, public accommodations, public education, public services and facilities, employment, housing, jury service, use of common carriers, and participation in federally assisted programs. The statute also protects officials or other persons, such as voting registrars, restaurant owners and employees, who have the duty to afford the protected rights involved under the Civil Rights Act of 1964 and the Voting Rights Act of 1965. These provisions making it a crime to interfere with federally protected rights were a response to the history of murder and racial violence of the civil rights period.

The same Title I also adds the Riot Act of 1968, which makes it a crime to travel in interstate commerce with the intent to aid or abet any person in inciting or participating in or carrying on a riot or committing any act of violence in furtherance of a riot. A companion provision—Title X—makes it a crime to teach or demonstrate the use, application or making of any firearm or explosive or incendiary technique that will be unlawfully employed in the use of furtherance of a civil disorder.

Titles II through VII have become known as the Indian Civil Rights Act. An organized Indian tribe recognized by the United States is prohibited in exercising powers of self-government to deprive residents on the reservation of a number of constitutional rights, including free speech, unreasonable search or seizure, double jeopardy, denial of property without just compensation, and habeas corpus. Also provided for is the development of a model criminal code governing the courts on Indian reservations, and other related judicial administration concerns. The consent of the United States is also provided states to give them jurisdiction over civil and criminal actions by or against Indians in the areas of Indian country situated within such states.

The key to the 1968 Civil Rights Act was Title VIII—the Fair Housing Act. But in the field of housing, legislation was only one weapon in the government's arsenal. The combination of Presidential Executive Orders, enforcement of Title VI of the Civil Rights Act of 1964, and the Federal Fair Housing Act of 1968, defined the response of the Kennedy and Johnson Administrations to the problem of equal housing opportunity. Other housing programs and legislation, such as the Model Cities bill, had the intention of fulfilling the pledges made in the 1949 Housing

Act—that every American is entitled to "decent, safe, sanitary housing. . . ."

The reason for the promulgation and enactment of equal housing opportunity orders and legislation during the Kennedy and Johnson years was evident from the denial of equal housing opportunity that existed throughout the history of this nation. One estimate states that from 1946 to 1959, less than 2 percent of the new homes provided through FHA mortgage insurance had been available to minorities. Early FHA handbooks were filled with biased references to blacks, their neighborhoods, and their alleged "shakiness" as credit risks. Even after the executive orders, a 1967 FHA survey of minority group occupancy found that less than 3.3 percent were reportedly sold to black families.

Residential racial segregation was perpetuated by large lot zoning limitations, minimum house size requirements, block-busting, etc. Redlining is a particular tool used by the home-finance industry to discriminate by its refusal to make housing loans within a certain area of a city.

The Federal Government which was heavily involved in housing, was a cause of this discrimination as well. Only in the 1960s did the government recognize the responsibility to insure equality of housing opportunity.

Significant Federal involvement in housing goes back to the 1934 National Housing Act, which created the FHA with its mortgage insurance programs. In 1937, the low-rent public housing program was enacted, and housing policy of the Federal Government took a different turn, aimed primarily at providing low-cost housing for low-income families. In public housing, the government adopted a policy of equitable participation which was not construed to preclude segregation. The majority of public housing projects produced during the first 25 years of the program's operation were all black or all white. Until 1962, this was a matter within the discretion of local public housing authorities.

The first step towards desegregation was President Kennedy's Executive Order on equal opportunity in housing issued in 1962. It was a limited order. Its command of nondiscrimination by no means affected all housing in which the Federal Government was involved. In the area of home financing, the order was limited to housing provided in whole or in part by loans insured, guaranteed or otherwise secured by Federal credit. Housing provided through mortgage insurance by the FHA and VA, representing 25 percent of the new housing market but less than 1 percent of the nation's entire housing inventory, were subject to nondiscrimination requirements. But conventionally insured mortgage lending was excluded from coverage. Moreover, the principal thrust of the order related almost entirely to housing provided through Federal aid agreements after the order's November, 1962, effective date.

Title VI of the Civil Rights Act of 1964 extended nondiscrimination requirements to many of the urban renewal and public housing units left uncovered by President Kennedy's Executive Order. Pursuant to regulations implementing Title VI, all urban renewal projects were subject to nondiscrimination requirements. In public housing, all low-rent housing projects still receiving Federal public assistance were also made subject to requirements, regardless of the date on which the contracts were executed. But even under Title VI, apartment houses built with the aid of pre-executive order FHA insurance agreements and housing conventionally financed by federally insured mortgages were still outside the scope of Federal nondiscriminaton requirements.

Thus, Congress acted in 1968 to pass fair housing legislation. Most of those who advised President Johnson on civil rights matters were opposed to any effort to obtain open housing legislation. Legislative strategists felt that there was no real chance of convincing a Congress to cover this important denial through any statutory action. Fortunately, as in many other cases, the President followed his instincts and, to a certain extent, his heart, and what became the Housing Act of 1968 was proposed. Legislative resistance was extraordinarily high. One week after the tragic shooting of Dr. Martin Luther King, Jr., in Memphis, the Congress, on April 11, 1968, passed the Fair Housing Act.

The Act provided for coverage extending to different types of housing in stages. By 1969, coverage was extended generally to private, non-federally assisted housing, except single-family housing and buildings containing no more than four housing units, one of which was owner-occupied. The final stage, effective on January 1, 1970, further broadened coverage by limiting the exception of single-family housing to such housing sold or rented without the use of a real estate broker. Since most single-family housing is sold or rented through a broker, this provision has the effect of bringing most single-family homes within the coverage of Title VIII.

Title VIII also expressly prohibits discrimination in financing of housing, the advertising of housing for sale, or rent, and the provision of brokerage services. Further, the practice of block-busting was prohibited. The Fair Housing Act, which prohibits discriminaton because of race, color, religion, or national origin was amended by the Housing and Community Development Act of 1974 to include a prohibition against sex discrimination as well. Unfortunately, Title VIII contained no enforcement provisions. The resolution of outstanding complaints was left to conciliation. The Executive Branch was given no authority to end a discriminatory housing practice. So, much as in the employment field, the statement of purpose was really all there was. The necessary enforcement machinery present in other substantive areas of law was missing.

The Executive Order and Title VI covered only a small fraction of the nation's housing inventory of some 70 million units. Under Title VIII, nearly 80 percent was subject to Federal nondiscrimination requirements as of 1970. However, under Title VIII, the enforcement burden falls largely upon the person discriminated against, except in cases of "pattern or practice" lawsuits, which come under the aegis of the Justice Department. The Department of Housing and Urban Development is charged with the principal responsibility for enforcement and administration of the fair housing law, but its enforcement capacity is actually non-existent. If under Title VIII, conference, conciliation, and persuasion fail, the Department of Housing and Urban Development can refer the matter to the Department of Justice. It has no authority to issue a cease and desist order, or to institute litigation on its own.

Two months after the Federal fair housing law had been enacted in 1968, the Supreme Court, in *Jones v. Mayer,* held that a provision of the 1866 Civil Rights Law barred all racial discrimination, private as well as public, in the sale or rental of property. The 1866 law, enacted under the authority of the Thirteenth Amendment, provides that all citizens of the United States should have the same rights in every state and territory as is enjoyed by white citizens thereof to inherit, purchase, lease, sell, hold, and convey real and personal property. The Court held this a valid exercise of Congress' power to enforce the Thirteenth Amendment and eradicate all badges of slavery, including racial discrimination in housing. The *Jones* decision rendered all housing, with no exception, open, without regard to race—at least as a matter of legal right.

In public housing, the pattern of all-white or all-black projects remained a rule even after the Kennedy and Johnson years. The Robert Taylor homes, a Chicago housing project, had 28,000 tenants in 1965. Three years after issuance of the Kennedy Executive Order, and a year-and-a-half after the enactment of the Civil Rights Act of 1964, all the units were occupied by blacks. Other Chicago projects were all white. In 1969, a Federal court in Chicago found that the tenant assignment and site selection policies of the Chicago public housing authority had a discriminatory effect, and enjoined the authority from continuing these practices in *Gautreaux v. Chicago Housing Authority*, 298 F. Supp. 907. This decision was affirmed by the Supreme Court in 1976.

Conclusion

The Kennedy-Johnson years, more than any others, focused on the denials of fundamental rights to black and other minority Americans. Minorities were represented in new and powerful places in the Federal structure. Legislation proposed and promised to protect minority rights in the field of employment, housing, access to public accommodations, the administration of justice, equal education, access to federally funded programs, and other fields.

A certain momentum was initiated. The momentum grew in intensity during the Johnson years. But the better part of the decade of the 1960s was not enough time to eradicate centuries of small-minded, bigoted customs, institutions, and laws.

The momentum continued somewhat after Lyndon Johnson left office, despite the immediate attempts of Richard Nixon and his minions to cut it back. But eventually, the adherents to "benign neglect" and the proponents of reversing the Kennedy-Johnson years ruled the day. Minority rights were treated as bothersome issues by many in authority. The media, with their short attention span, moved on to other vistas. And the country, in some ways changed in a lasting sense, settled back in other ways to the pernicious patterns of the past.

If there was one failing of great prominence in this field during the 1960s, it was that statements of high purpose were not followed by consistent, unrelenting enforcement. The appropriate mechanisms for protecting the early enumerated rights of minority individuals were often not there. Despite the unevenness of enforcement, positive residual effects of the legislative efforts, particularly of the Johnson years, remain with us. It will only be useful to review the high ideals of the Kennedy-Johnson years if the nation is now willing to continue the hard work that was started then.

References

[1] 42 U.S.C., Section 2000e-16(c).

[2] Fortunately, on June 1, 1976, the Supreme Court ruled that Federal employees charging discrimination are entitled to a trial *de novo. Chandler v. Roudebush,* 44 L.W. 4709.

[3] The covered southern states are: Georgia, Alabama, Mississippi, South Carolina, Louisiana, Virginia, and 40 counties in North Carolina.

Burke Marshall

18

Evaluating the Impact of the Civil Rights Legislation

The three acts dealing with race problems that became effective during the Johnson Administration—the Civil Rights Act of 1964, the Voting Rights Act of 1965, and Title VIII of the Civil Rights Act of 1968—comprise the most extraordinary effort at legislative control of racial discrimination in any society, at any time. The tides of public opinion have run so strongly in the few years since 1968 that this central fact has been swallowed up in impatience with other failures, and perceived failures, of the Federal Government. Yet even the the Reconstruction amendments and legislation were not treated until decades later by the other branches of the Federal establishment, except briefly by the executive in the period of military occupation, as a system of control of even government-sponsored, much less private, discrimination based on race. At the least, the laws passed in 1964, 1965, and 1968 put the nation on record for the first time as outlawing such discrimination.

To some degree this uplifting effort was bound to create expectations that exceeded its reach. In large part, this is because its visible beneficiaries were bound to be mainly people whose lives were individually and directly affected by racial discrimination, and those people were largely already middle class, or on the edge of it. The masses remained trapped by factors that could not be identified as directly caused by acts of racial discrimination, and were beyond the range of laws that dealt only with such acts. In addition, I believe that some failures were built into the goals and methods of particular parts of the legislation. This chapter is intended to identify as briefly as possible those elements of the statutes. Before doing so, however, it is necessary summarily to describe again the remarkable scope of the effort.

1964 Civil Rights Act

It is difficult even for those of us who had responsibility at the time for trying to eliminate racial discrimination to remember how totally pervasive it was, almost everywhere in the United States, when President Kennedy sent to Congress in June, 1963 the proposed law that became the Civil Rights Act of 1964. The public occasion for doing so was the widespread demonstrations, not riots, that had taken place in many cities following those led by Martin King in Birmingham in May of that year. The particular forms of discrimination being protested now seem so petty as to be ridiculous—for example, the refusal in Birmingham of the local outlets of national chains to serve blacks at sit-down lunch counters, or to hire even one black clerk as a sales person. But these forms symbolized a full-scale caste system, and they were protested by the civil rights movement, and protected by the white establishment, for that reason. Any responsive legislation accordingly had to be equally pervasive, and the bill proposed by President Kennedy was of that scope, at least in its effort.

Title I, dealing with voting rights, made the smallest advance in existing law even as proposed, and an even smaller one as enacted. Its effort was to simplify and speed up the program of county-by-county litigation that the Department of Justice was already engaged in, under the 1957 and 1960 Civil Rights Acts. The scope of the proposal was affected by the Department's experience in 1962, when it was unable to muster even a majority for cloture in the Senate in favor of an even more modest proposal. What effect Title I might have had eventually as the burden of litigation is not known, since the problem was dealt with on a wholesale basis less than a year later, by the passage of the Voting Rights Act of 1965.

Title II prohibited racial discrimination by hotels, restaurants, and other places of public accommodations. Politically this was the most controversial part of the 1964 statute when it was first proposed, in part because of ideological resistance to further Federal regulation of business for any purpose on the part of a number of Republican Senators whom simple arithmetic denoted as necessary for cloture, and final passage of the bill. An enormous debate developed briefly over the question of whether it was moral to ground such legislation for constitutional purposes on the commerce clause. The Administration favored this approach for legal reasons based on the scope of the Supreme Court decisions upholding the later New Deal legislation, rather than the Fourteenth Amendment, which most Republicans and some Democrats preferred because of distaste for those same Supreme Court decisions. The Administration wanted to avoid reliance on the Fourteenth Amendment because of the *Civil Rights Cases* of 1883, holding a Federal public accommodations law based on the Fourteenth Amendment to be unconstitutional. In the end Senator Dirksen, no doubt persuaded in part by the embracing of the proposed law by nationally based business, proclaimed that it was an idea whose time had come. Cloture was voted overwhelmingly, and voluntary implementation was immediate and massive.

Titles III and IV principally extended the authority of the attorney general to bring lawsuits for the enforcement of already declared constitutional rights to the fields of education and other public facilities, in the pattern of the 1957 and 1960 Acts in the field of voting. Title IV also provided for technical and financial assistance, through the Office of Education to school districts implementing desegregation plans. The political argument over these titles was in part a repeat of the one that took place over the proposed Title III in the 1960 Civil Rights Act, which would have empowered the Department of Justice to bring suit in Federal court to prevent the deprivation by state officials of any constitutionally guaranteed rights, including such rights as freedom of religion and speech, not just those involving racial discrimination. This was a liberal political issue, having no direct relevance to racial problems except insofar as it would have authorized government litigation to gain court orders permitting constitutionally protected demonstrations—a power that the attorney general did not want, and one that had to be opposed by the Administration in any event in order to cement the bipartisan agreement on the bill in the House of Representatives.

Title V extended the statutory life of the Civil Rights Commission, and also expanded its power to compel testimony in its investigations.

Title VI, like Title II, was an innovation in civil rights legislation, prohibiting discrimination as the ground of race, color, or national origin in any program receiving Federal financial assistance. This sweeping injunction against racial discrimination in all of the activities supported by billions of dollars in federal grants to state and local agencies, and private institutions, was necessary to meet a political problem, even though it was not at all clear that it was necessary to give the President the power to instruct the federal granting agencies to insist on racial fairness in the conduct of the activities they funded. The problem was the injection of race as a political issue into all proposals for Federal assistance programs, typically in such areas as health, education, welfare, or nutrition, through what came to be known as the Powell Amendment in the House and the Javits Amendment in the Senate. These amendments would prohibit the extension of financial assistance to any state or local organization that practiced racial discrimination, making such assistance unavailable as a practical matter in those days everywhere in the Southern states, and thus forcing Southern and border state politicians who might otherwise favor the legislation on its merits, to vote against it. If they could get away with it without notice, Southern politicians who opposed the legislation on its merits would vote for the amendment on an anonymous tally, as the surest way of defeating the entire proposal. Title VI was designed to eliminate this as a problem for individual bills, by prohibiting racial discrimination in all future federally funded programs as well as for those in existence. Termed the "billion-dollar blackjack" in the anti-civil rights literature, it was rightly viewed as an enormously important non-judicial weapon in the Federal civil rights arsenal.

Title VII prohibited discrimination on grounds of race, color, religion, sex, or national origin by all employers, trade unions, and employment agencies of significant size, and set up the Equal Employment Opportunity Commission (EEOC) as an investigative and mediative agency to implement the statute. Enforcement was left to the courts in the bill as enacted, either through suit brought by individuals discriminated against, or (in a compromise reached between Senator Dirksen and his group and the Administration) by the Attorney General where a "pattern or practice of discrimination" was alleged. The criterion of sex was added by opponents of the entire bill on the theory that its addition would eliminate Title VII, a strategy that did not work and might have had the political effect in reverse of increasing interest in the bill on the part of women's groups. The basic concession remained in the enforcement machinery, which was admittedly too cumbersome to be effective in view of the number of employers, unions, and employees who would eventually be covered by the statute.

The Right to Vote

As noted, the type of direct racial discrimination least affected by the 1964 Civil Rights Act was discrimination in voter registration. Elimination of such discrimination was the top priority of the Department of Justice, which had authority under the 1957 and 1960 Acts to bring suit in federal court for that purpose. It seemed plain that while the vote would not automatically bring other rights and opportunities, the absence of an effective political voice in blacks left the entire state and local government machinery most immediately affecting the daily lives of the people, including the police and the schools, in the hands of white politicians dedicated to the preservation of white supremacy and the caste system. I had occasion in the preparation of lectures to be given in March and April, 1964, while the 1964 Act was still pending in the Senate, to review statistically the results of some 35 law suits brought, mostly since the start of the Kennedy Administration, to enforce the right to vote. I found the results enormously disheartening. Except in special circumstances, the increases in the number of blacks actually registered were insignificant. In only two counties had the percentage risen above 40 percent, and in one of those the deterrent to registration had not been in the state voting laws or the attitude of the local registrars, but in organized private intimidation and retaliation which had been enjoined in a consent settlement. In 28 counties, there was virtually no change. The results also showed that what improvement could be accomplished required constant judicial supervision of the registration process by a determined and effective federal judge, such as Judge Frank Johnson of the Middle District of Alabama. There were few such judges available in the states where the problem existed.

In the lectures I described the sequence in one court case as follows:

Whatever the court's attitude, the suit in Forrest County shows the amount of court time and lawyer effort that may be necessary for any results. It was filed on July 6, 1961, and based in part on investigation which showed that of about 7,500 Negroes of voting age only 14 were able to register between 1949 and the spring of 1961, and none registered after 1954. The District Court refused to rule on a government request for preliminary injunction. The Court of Appeals reversed, but also issued an injunction pending appeal in March, 1962. The registrar disobeyed the injunction. On May 1, 1962, he was cited for contempt. This action had to be tried before the three judges sitting on the Court of Appeals panel and could not be set until September, 1962. It was tried for a week, briefed and finally submitted to the Court of Appeals on January 25, 1963. On July 15, approximately two years after the complaint was filed, the Court of Appeals found the registrar in civil contempt and ordered him to register 43 Negro applicants immediately and to cease other practices making Negro registration virtually impossible. The criminal contempt proceedings were held in abeyance until the Supreme Court decided whether Governor Barnett of Mississippi, the defendant in another criminal contempt case, was entitled to a jury. The civil contempt order was stayed for two months while the defendant registrar applied for review with the Supreme Court. Following that, the civil contempt order became effective. Yet subsequent examination of the treatment of Negro applicants led the government to conclude that further proceedings were necessary.

In the meantime, there has not yet been any hearing in the case on the merits. The number of Negroes of voting age who are now registered has increased to 200, over 2 percent of those in the county.

President Kennedy proposed in his 1963 message a step towards resolving such an impasse by authorizing federal officials to begin immediately to apply state voting standards on a nondiscriminatory basis. It was this proposal, of all those made by the President, that proved unacceptable to the bipartisan leadership group in the House Judiciary Committee. The result of that legislative defeat was continuing frustration with the blockages to black registration in the South, and finally the confrontation at the Selma bridge, dramatized on national television, in March, 1965. This event gave President Johnson an occasion to ask Congress to act to eliminate racial discrimination in registration and voting at one stroke, not by the process of litigation, but by immediate and effective substitution of Federal standards and processes for those of the states, in the states that met the statistical tests put forth in the bill.

The Voting Rights Act of 1965 accomplished nothing less than a Federal seizure of state registration machinery, in a manner that had not been attempted since Reconstruction, and had to be effected then through military force. Its constitutional basis was the Fifteenth Amendment, narrowly confined in subject matter, but plenary in its grant of Congressional authority where it applied at all. It proved politically possible because of the drama of Selma, because it applied to very few states, and virtually only in the South, and because the techniques of discrimination it outlawed, so vividly illustrated by the case history of Dallas County, Alabama, in the testimony of Attorney General Katzenbach, were totally indefensible and had been proved as a factual matter again and again in the law suits presented by the Department of Justice.

Housing

In 1968, spurred in part by the murder of Martin King, Congress passed the last of the civil rights legislation of the Kennedy-Johnson years in Title VIII of the Civil Rights Act of 1968. The statute prohibited discrimination in sale and rental of approximately 80 percent of the nation's housing, thus reaching the final important area of direct racial discrimination affecting people's daily lives. Ironically, the Supreme Court ruled in the same year, in *Jones* v. *Alfred H. Mayer Co.,* 392 U.S. 409 (1968), that the Civil Rights Act of 1866 accomplished much the same purpose, permitting private suit to prevent individual acts of the discrimination in the sale or rental of housing. Like the EEOC under the 1964 Act, however, the implementing agency under the 1968 Act, which was the Department of Housing and Urban Development (HUD), was given the power to confer, conciliate, persuade, and mediate, but no power to compel compliance, so that responsibility for enforcement is not accompanied by parallel authority.

Assessing the Impact

It is not too early to make an assessment of the impact of this legislative legacy, and to try briefly and tentatively to identify, based on that experience, what problems are susceptible to total or partial solutions by civil rights legislation. In doing so, there is no need to repeat or even summarize the massive detailed study made in 1974 by the Civil Rights Commission of the federal civil rights enforcement effort. Broadly, we know by common experience what has succeeded and what has not, or at least not yet.

We know the Voting Rights Act of 1965 has had a massive, direct impact and has largely succeeded in eliminating open discrimination in registration and voting. In Selma itself, in Dallas County, Alabama, the 2.1 percent of the blacks eligible by age who were registered to vote in 1965 has increased to almost 70 percent, and five members of the city council are black. In Mississippi, the absolute number of blacks registered has moved from 28,000 to more than 250,000 in the same period. There were less than 100 elected black officials in 1965; there were 1,944 identified by the Voter Education Project as of May, 1976. Dramatic increases have occurred in the states where the problem was worst—Alabama, Arkansas, Georgia, Louisiana, Mississippi, and South Carolina.

We also know that Title II of the 1964 Civil Rights Act was complied with in a massive way, immediately after its effective date. While racial discrimination is no doubt still practiced in isolated instances, and particularly in small and rural communities in parts of the South, no serious enforcement problem has existed since the constitutionality of that part of the statute was upheld in *Heart of Atlanta Motel* v. *United States*, 379 U.S. 241 (1964), and *Katzenbach* v. *McClung*, 379 U.S. 294 (1964).

Finally, on the positive side, we know that the elimination of open violations of the Fourteenth Amendment, by the maintenance of dual school systems, segregated parks, or all-white jury systems, is proceeding under Titles III, IV, and VI of the 1964 Act, as well as by private suit, to the extent that litigation is over pace and methods, but not over the need for action. This is true despite the retreat in principle by the Federal Government on desegregation in education, because of the busing issue, and despite the confusion and vacillations in the guidelines and enforcement measures by the various departments under Title VI.

On the other hand, it is plain that while there has been great symbolic progress in employment since the refusal of the Birmingham department stores in 1964 to hire any black sales persons, the enforcement of both Title VII of the 1964 Act and Title VIII of the 1968 Act is stuck in machinery that is not designed for its work. The Civil Rights Commission reported a backlog of charges in the Equal Employment Opportunity Commission exceeding 100,000 by March, 1975 (1974 Report, vol. 5, p. 529). The HUD compliance program under Title VIII has not generated many citizen complaints, without which no action at all is taken, but nevertheless is also burdened with a significant backlog, and a slow processing of those complaints that are received (1974 Report, vol. 2, pp. 34-35).

There are some general comments that can be made about this history to date. One is that continuing effective enforcement is a necessity if the rights created by this type of legislation are not to atrophy.

In part, this is simply a matter of writing and passing legislation that creates machinery that is at least designed to work. This is a matter of political difficulty, but it does not require new knowledge. HUD, for example, simply has no enforcement methods at all, and therefore is without the credible back-up of compulsion that is necessary to make conciliation machinery useful in persuading economic interests that have no other incentive to cooperate with it. This is a defect that can be corrected by Congress if the will to do so exists, and is one of the matters to which a new administration should turn its attention.

Enforcement Problems

In part, however, anti-discrimination legislation on a national scale appears to carry with it difficulties of administration and law enforcement that were unanticipated and are not susceptible to mechanical solution. This is certainly true of the enforcement of Title VII by the EEOC, and seems to be so of the implementation of Title VI by the many agencies involved in that business, although there the difficulties are at least compounded by the Presidential policies of the last eight years. There are several reasons for these difficulties.

First, the volume of complaints is magnified enormously by the fact that this federal agency has to deal with individual cases of alleged discrimination, as well as with the type of corporate-wide, or union-wide, and often industry-wide practices that federal regulatory agencies seem to be able to handle. This volume is swelled in turn by inclusion of sex as a prohibited reason for employment decisions of any kind.

Second, there has not yet emerged a fully accepted consensus as to what the EEOC is about—that is to say, whether the Commission's priority is to "a commitment to the merit principle," in Owen Fiss's phrase, or should be focused instead on current levels of employment of underrepresented groups throughout business and labor. The difference is significant, given the persistent imbalance of jobless blacks and other racial minorities, and other related barriers to job equality, especially in education and housing.

Third, the effects of this ambiguity are magnified by the constituency-oriented politics of the whole effort, starting with representational appointments to the Commission itself and permeating the staff, and ending with groups competing with each other.

Fourth, the rules of the game are still evolving through judicial and administrative decisions with respect to such matters as the proper use to be made of racial statistics and the fairest resolution of the problems of transitional inequity to white males who have been the random beneficiaries of past discrimination, through seniority systems and the like, or who are in competition with women and members of minority groups during a period of remedial action.

It is apparent that these problems cannot be solved by tinkering, even massive tinkering, with the enforcement machinery available to the EEOC. Many lawyers who have had intimate experience with the Commission's problem have argued that it could function much more effectively with the power to issue cease and desist orders, rather than depending on litigation in court. Any corrective legislation to this end should in my judgment concentrate as well on drastic simplification of process, with the elimination of the burdensome compulsory conciliation requirement and of the virtual necessity that all complaints of violations of the statute be taken to the Commission, even in the case of individual complaints against small enterprises. There is much to be said for individual enforcement through court without reference to an administrative process, particularly with the provision for the awarding of attorneys' fees. Yet the underlying factors I have just referred to would not vanish with these process corrections; they need attention as such at the highest level of government, as well as time for resolution.

In addition, the enforcement problem for the mass of the civil rights legislation is also partially one of effective management of the Federal Government as a whole. The 1964 and 1968 Civil Rights Act, particularly Title VI of the 1964 Act, created an enormously diffused responsibility throughout the Executive Branch for identifying and eliminating racial discrimination. The need for policy and administrative coordination in some central place was recognized, and after intensive study, President Johnson created the President's Committee on Equal Opportunity to fill this requirements, with Vice-President Humphrey as its chairman. The committee lasted from February, 1965, until late September of that year, when it was suddenly abolished, although its functions were to some extent taken over by the Department of Justice. It seems clear, however, that the civil rights legislation of the 1960s creates government-wide responsibilities and obligations, requiring government-wide attention, and that some Presidential management of the work to be done under the statutes is still necessary.

Limits of Legislation

Secondly, it is critical to realize that civil rights legislation can deal effectively only with direct racial discrimination itself, and not with its consequences or the legacy of its past. It became fashionable soon after the passage of Title II of the 1964 Act to deprecate its impact on the grounds that having the right to eat in restaurants was meaningless to the black masses who did not have the money to pay for a meal. This is of course true, but it has nothing to do with the purpose of Title II, which was intended only to prohibit refusals to serve prospective customers because of their race, and not as a kind of income-distribution measure. Similarly, it asks too much of an anti-discrimination law like the Voting Rights Act of 1965 to require it not only to eliminate all bars to blacks who want to register to vote, but also to do away with all factors, whatever they are, that results in blacks registering in fact in lower proportions to their population than whites.

Third, as a related matter, it is plain that it is much easier to achieve results through anti-discrimination measures when the economics of the situation favor elimination of racial barriers rather than their retention. Title II was immediately successful because the bulk of the businesses affected were losing revenue by practicing racial discrimination, and were on the whole anxious to abandon the practice so long as they did not have to do it on an individual basis, one-by-one. Title VII obviously is more effective in bringing minority group workers and women into jobs and promotions in a period of tight labor market and industry-wide efforts to recruit new workers. The legal difficulties, such as problems of unfairness to senior employees who are the random beneficiaries of past discrimination, and other difficulties in achieving transitional equity, as well as the greatest resistance to enforcement efforts, occur when unemployment is high and job opportunities are not abundant. Similarly no efforts at the enforcement of anti-discrimination laws in the field of housing have really been successful because of the perceived financial interest in segregated housing. It is plain that these involve difficult underlying problems of income distribution and wealth that must be addressed along with the prohibition against racial discrimination as such.

Administrative Control

Finally, it seems apparent that while there is no clear alternative to litigation to compel compliance with prohibitions, and especially constitutional prohibitions, against racial discrimination, litigation is nevertheless no substitute for placing control of the administration of whatever organization is involved in hands of people who do not want to discriminate. The beauty of the Voting Rights Act of 1965 was that it removed all discretion and all power to discriminate from the hands of the local officials until the process became self-correcting, and the political consequences of efforts to prevent blacks from voting became worse than having them vote. For a similar reason, as already noted, Title II of the 1964 Act presented no enforcement problems because those most directly affected by it, the businesses of public accommodations, needed an excuse to cease racial discrimination. Even the busing controversy has had no real effect in those school districts where the local board has wanted to deal with the problem of discrimination, rather than inflame it for political reasons.

Anti-discrimination laws as a category are, in short, designed to deal only with symptoms that reflect motives of profit and politics than can in turn be affected directly if they are understood and taken into conscious account. A transitional judicial method of accomplishing this in difficult situations, for example, would be the use of masters or receivers to administer the institutions that need correction, rather than an attempt to achieve that end by detailed judicial control and review of the decisions made by the managers of those institutions.

Such measures would, of course, bring renewed focus to the question of the burden of the transitional costs that cannot be avoided in the implementation of anti-discrimination measures like those of the Kennedy and Johnson Administrations. It appears that the debate concerning them—whether in the form of preferential treatment in recruitment and hiring, or school assignments, or faculty appointments, or in the effect of seniority systems established during a period of all-white employment, or busing—will intensify in the short term, and that its outcome in legal doctrine is still uncertain. Clearly no one can say that a white male who can prove he would have been admitted to law school, or appointed to its faculty, or promoted to a supervisory position, or not laid off, but for his race or sex, has no individual equity on his side when his personal and private actions have done nothing to contribute to the conditions that are being changed by law. It is also clear, moreover, that the courts are incapable of devising ways of redressing such unfairness as may occur and that the Congress has not done so. The result is justified because it is, as I have said, an unavoidable cost of eliminating great injustice, and because it is borne by a person who is at least a member of a class that still has the most other choices open to them.

Need for Innovation

There will come a time, however, when racial and sexual preferences cannot be justified in the name of transition under anti-discrimination measures. No matter how plain it is as a matter of legislative history that the target populations of those measures are blacks, and other minorities, and women, their fundamental concept is color-blind, and sex-blind. It is predictable that courts will more and more begin, as they already have, to heed claims by white males that they are being discriminated against because of their race or sex. Further, it is in the nature of anti-discrimination legislation that all it does at its best is to start people off equally without regard to race or sex. It does not handicap according to educational or economic or motivational or other advantages or disadvantages even if they are associated in some general sense with underlying racism or sexism in the society. It does not do what Lyndon Johnson often called for—especially in the civil rights symposium sponsored by the Johnson Library and the School of Public Affairs in late 1972*—bringing about equality in fact in the opportunities for success, or even in the essentials of a decent life.

There has been no attention at all to such a goal for at least eight years, and there is no real agreement as to the means by which the enormously complex and diverse American state could move towards it. The essentials that President Johnson referred to required solutions to the great, shared problems of the society —equality of educational achievement, not just freedom from overt racial discrimination; decent housing in decent neighbor-hoods, instead of immense urban slums and extreme rural poverty; and abundant job opportunities and incentives that are in fact available to those caught in the welfare cycle as well as those who are now unemployed because of national economic priorities. These problems require more innovation in national economic management, including income and wealth distribu-tion, which is at least in part the business of tax reform, and in urban revival, which is at least in part the business of new institu-tions, both broadening the political structures responsible through regional compacts and annexation, and narrowing them through such devices as community development corporations and decentralized community power bases. They involve extra-ordinarily difficult political obstacles and will require therefore political leadership and creativity of an extraordinarily high order. But they should not be the concern solely, or even pri-marily, of racial minorities, and the benefits of their solution should spread through the society. They are the agenda now.

*See *Equal Opportunity in the United States,* (Austin: Lyndon B. Johnson School of Public Affairs), 1973.

SUMMARY Dagmar Hamilton

From their formative years Americans are taught that the United States is a country of laws, with equality under those laws for all. But, until the Kennedy-Johnson years, "these platitudes about law were contradicted by the facts." This reminder by Clifford Alexander opened the panel discussion on "The Right to Equality," and Alexander noted that until the Kennedy-Johnson era, Congress had resisted any significant legislation in the field of civil rights.

Although Kennedy was tentative in the early months, what Alexander felt to be a strong commitment to civil rights became more than apparent in the year before Kennedy's death. President Johnson accelerated the pace; the 1964 Civil Rights Act, the 1965 Voting Rights Act, and the 1968 Civil Rights Act were all products of Johnson's deep commitment towards realizing the right to equality under law. The key, as Alexander saw it, was the quality of the commitment; unlike President Nixon, who followed him, President Johnson believed not only in the legislation which he fought for, but also in the implementation of that legislation through the use of his presidential office as a fulcrum of power. President Johnson "cajoled, persuaded, pointed fingers, sometimes bullied business, labor, and other elements to follow his lead".

Alexander was also quick to credit the black leaders of the sixties who, lacking elective office, were nevertheless able to mobilize their organizations to provide support and pressure. In words which evoked memories of Selma, Alabama; Philadelphia, Mississippi; and countless buses, lunch-counters and courthouse squares all over the South, Alexander paid tribute to the many hundreds of nameless blacks and whites who daily put their lives on the line to bring a conscience to a government without one.

The presidential leadership, the statutes, and even the efforts of hundreds of advocates were not enough, however; The momentum of the civil rights movement, in Alexander's opinion, was stalled and sidetracked by the election of Richard Nixon in late 1968. The courts, less partisan than the executive or legislative branches, of course continued to uphold the new laws, as well as the older civil rights statutes and the equal protection clause of the Fourteenth Amendment. But those problems which had not been solved or had barely begun to be treated were neglected or abandoned during the Nixon years. Alexander said, "It was like treating the 24-hour flu for a couple of minutes." (An even more apt analogy might have been the patient who, given a prescription for antibiotics to be taken over a period of 10 days, discontinues the antibiotic when he begins to feel better after the third day, only to find afterwards that the illness has returned full force because the bacteria have not been effectively killed off.) But whatever the example, Alexander's point was clear: the next President of the United States must pick up where President Johnson left off and provide the sustained leadership and attention necessary to achieve real equality.

In Alexander's eyes equality under the law means not only the basic rights which the Johnson Administration largely succeeded in implementing: the equal right to vote, "the equal right to public accommodations, etc.", but, also what Alexander regards as a basic right to equal opportunity for employment. Citing examples of the disparity between black and white earnings, Alexander said that blacks in 1975 were earning less in comparison to whites than blacks were earning in either 1952 or during the Johnson years. He concluded with an urgent plea for constructive action designed to end that kind of economic disparity.

Burke Marshall was quick to point out that the civil rights legislation of the 1960s was not designed to bring about absolute equality in all sectors. That legislation was intended to end overt racial discrimination and practices, he said; it was not intended to deal with the more complex economic and societal factors which trap masses of people in poverty, black and white alike. The fact that more blacks than whites are trapped may be relevant; nevertheless, Marshall sees this result not as an effect of overt racial discrimination, but as something beyond the reach of the 1960s civil rights legislation.

Marshall then examined within the context of their more (specifically) limited objectives, the three major civil rights statutes of the Johnson Administration. Starting with the most successful, Marshall said that the Voting Rights Act of 1965 had largely succeeded in eliminating open discrimination in voting and registration. Both in absolute numbers and in percentages of blacks registered to vote, dramatic increases took place in those Southern states where black disenfranchisement had been most serious. The number of black elected officials also increased (although as Clifford Alexander points out, many of these officials were elected only to very minor offices).

Marshall called attention to the 1964 Civil Rights Act, Title II, which dealt with public accommodations and was eventually upheld by the United States Supreme Court in 1965. With the exception of a few small rural communities, Title II effectively accomplished its intended purpose: to end segregation in places of public accommodation, such as hotels, motels, restaurants, theaters, etc. Titles III, IV, V, and VI of the 1964 Act also made it easier for courts to end open violations of the Fourteenth Amendment in such areas as dual school systems, segregated parks, and all-white juries.

Marshall was openly critical of other parts of the 1960s legislation, however, he singled out both Title VII, (Equal Employment Opportunity) of the 1964 Civil Rights Act; and Title VIII (Fair Housing) of the 1968 Civil Rights Act. In each instance, he said, "enforcement. . . is stuck in machinery that is not designed for its work". EEOC, which must handle single cases of alleged discrimination in employment as well as cases involving an entire class of persons (industry-wide or union-wide discriminatory practices) is so slowed down by the single cases that its backlog was well over 100,000 in 1975. HUD was given power to mediate, but has no power to compel compliance in cases involving discrimination in housing. Possibly, new legislation could be written which would give HUD enforcement machinery and thus put teeth into Title VIII; similarly, EEOC jurisdiction could be more sharply limited in order to eliminate individual complaints. The time saved could then be used more effectively to handle complaints with group-wide ramifications.

But legislation alone is not enough, Marshall warned. The more serious aspects of Title VII (1964) and VIII (1968) are not susceptible to mechanical solution. EEOC's priorities, for example, are still unclear. There is confusion over whether EEOC should simply apply, principles of merit; or whether it should take action on the basis of current employment levels for groups which are under-represented in business and labor. The basic ambiguity between the two positions seems to be reflected in what Marshall called the constituency-oriented politics of the Commission; and compounded by other administrative and court decisions which have for the most part failed to face up to what Marshall sees as a basic dichotomy between equality of opportunity and equality of achievement. Marshall appeared sympathetic to the plight of the white male who can prove that but for his race he would have been admitted to law school, hired for a particular job, or kept on in an industry making selective lay-offs. Arguably, such practices are part of the unavoidable cost of remedying great past racial injustices, he said. And arguably, this cost is at least borne by people who as a class still have most other choices open to them. But the time is fast approaching when racial and sexual preferences will not be justifiable in the name of transition. Courts are already beginning to be skeptical: an observation which probably came as no surprise to those who were aware of the California Supreme Court's decision on quota systems in the University of California system, and who had heard the rumors that the United States Supreme Court may agree to decide a *de Funis* type case on its merits during its next term.

The fundamental premise of equal rights legislation, according to Marshall, is to be color blind. In the long run, the equality that Lyndon Johnson called for at the Civil Rights Symposium in 1972 cannot be achieved simply through 1960s' type civil rights legislation. Rather, true equality will come only through solution of the great shared problems of job opportunities, decent housing, and educational achievement: problems which cut across racial and sexual barriers. The solutions will be extremely difficult; the political obstacles are enormous. But only if the problems are approached on such a broad basis by extraordinarily talented and creative political leaders will there be any hope, Marshall concluded.

Panelist Roger Wilkins agreed that the events of the 1960s had made it possible for him to have equal public accommodations; and that at the top levels of achievement in our society there are now a good many more blacks. Wilkins maintained, however, that racism and discrimination on the part of white Americans still run deep; and that the very success of a relatively few outstanding blacks has made it even harder for the poorest and least effective Americans to achieve equality. Some people look at achievers like Wilkins or tennis-player Arthur Ashe and deceive themselves into thinking that bigotry has ended; according to this conveniently Calvanistic rationalization, if all blacks are not achievers that is because " 'they didn't work hard enough' ".

To combat what he described as "this nation's natural predisposition towards racism", Wilkins called for two things: first, immediate Federal legislation to stimulate the economy and to provide for public sector jobs; and second, some kind of affirmative action to be continued over a long period of time. Wilkins clearly felt strongly about the latter; he saw it as a matter of "doing right" and of correction of past wrongs.

Althea Simmons chose the 1964 Civil Rights Act and the 1965 Voting Rights Act as the most effective pieces of legislation to emerge from the Kennedy-Johnson years. She shared with the audience her vivid recollections of what it meant, in personal terms, for Southern blacks to be able to register to vote for the first time in their lives. And in simple, moving terms she drove home what it meant to black Americans after the passage of the public accommodations law to be able to stop to eat and sleep after a long hard day's journey on the road.

She criticized Title VI of the 1964 Act not on the grounds that it is undesirable, but on the grounds that it has not been enforced. Under Title VI, Federal funds may be withheld from persons or agencies who discriminate on racial (and other) grounds. Unless the chief executive puts the power of his office behind the withholding, however, Title VI becomes hollow in effect. Ms. Simmons concluded that until we have a president as committed as was President Johnson to putting teeth into Title VI that we will be fighting not only those who discriminate but also those who should be policing the discriminators.

Harry McPherson agreed with Ms. Simmons and the other speakers that much of the sixties' civil rights legislation had been beneficial. McPherson observed that the changes wrought by the civil rights legislation of the sixties had created a "different universe" for those who were too young to remember what life was like before the legislation was enacted. He also noted that the earlier 1957 Civil Rights Act pushed through by then-Senator Johnson had paved the way for the later legislation, although criticized as being too weak at the time. McPherson added that Johnson, a Southerner with a deep commitment to civil rights and a sense of human compassion, may also have paved the way for the nomination and election of Southerner Jimmy Carter; and expressed hope that Carter would give the country a similarly committed leadership in the field of civil rights.

But McPherson was pessimistic about changing what he called "the social condition in America". He, too, focused on the unemployment rate, saying that as long as it remained high he saw no hope of solving the country's racial problems.

In the meantime, McPherson expressed concern over the possible inequalities imposed on some in the process of the move to equality for others. He said:

> It's not easy, it's not easy at all for me to live with what Burke [Marshall] described as transitional social costs.

Although he described himself (a white, middle-class liberal with children in private school) as one of those people who has not had to pay transitional costs, he felt that transitional mechanisms such as minimum quotas might well exact an excruciating price from those who feel it unjust to have to pay them.

This theme, variously referred to by Marshall and McPherson as "transitional costs", and by Alexander as "the phoney issue of reverse discrimination", was the central issue of Sidney Hook's remarks. Hook, a philosopher and former professor at New York University took sharp issue with the position that some sort of minimum quotas for minorities are necessary to assure equality of access in our society. To Hook, "reverse discrimination" is an important issue going to the heart of the concept of equal justice. According to him, "some of the proposed remedies against discrimination. . .demonstrably violate the letter and spirit" of legislation purportedly designed for equality.

Hook argued that on the face of it, "if you are opposed to discrimination you cannot be in favor of discrimination"—a statement which drew applause from the audience. Hook said that to discriminate against qualified individuals in favor of less qualified individuals who are members of groups which have been unfairly treated in the past is a violation of equality of law. Furthermore, such practices actually victimize persons who are in no way responsible for past discrimination. Hook argued that those responsible for past inequities are now gone, and that a statute of limitations should be applied to prohibit passing on the responsibility for past discrimination to new generations which had nothing to do with the original discrimination.

Hook also claimed that at least in higher education it is easier for qualified blacks to get jobs than qualified whites. To Hook, any lack of blacks in higher education is simply a function of inadequate supply. To impose minimum quotas here, he predicted, would eventually lead to a polarized rather than a pluralistic society.

Judge A. Leon Higginbotham, Jr., disagreed with Professor Hook. Higginbotham reminded his audience of a speech President Johnson had given at Howard University, in which Johnson had remarked that " 'we aren't all starting out at the same starting line' ". To illustrate his point that the starting line must be equalized, Higginbotham later referred to the Texas voting rights case in which it was proven that the State of Texas had for many years spent three times as much money in the education of a white child as it had in the education of a black. He implied that where a state institution discriminates so blatantly in the early years of education, the starting line will remain for many years unequal. Equality of basic elementary and secondary education is such an obvious prerequisite for equality of opportunity to begin equally at the college level, enter professional schools, and break into the job market that the starting line concept must be extended to any place along the ladder where state-sponsored discrimination is a major cause of the inequality of access. As long as the starting line remains unequal, by definition entrance into these other fields will be unequal; and this is where compensatory mechanisms make sense. Otherwise, realistically speaking, the vicious circle of inequality will merely continue—as poorly trained blacks from inferior colleges go out to teach other blacks, as disadvantaged blacks do not make it into law school, as less educated blacks fall further and further behind in the job market.

Compensatory steps have been taken in some areas—for example in the education and training of women—and these steps have benefited society, Higginbotham noted. Women lawyers and women doctors are a good example of the results of applying quotas affirmatively, he said; and he called for the positive, confidence of a Lyndon Johnson to overcome the problems of moving to a higher level of equality for all.

Bernard R. Gifford picked up on the need for compensatory mechanisms. Gifford said that the notion of compensatory justice was one of the great legacies left behind by Lyndon Baines Johnson.

Gifford paid homage, as did the others, to the Civil Rights Acts of 1964 and 1965. He said that this legislation had made it easier to move from a "racist" to a "racialistic" society; the former supported by law and theology, the latter less so. But Gifford pointed out that as long as income distribution curves continue to be characterized in racial terms, and as long as college faculties can be characterized in racial or sexual terms, inequality continues to exist. He maintained that in order to achieve equality here, the burden of suggesting alternatives to compensatory mechanisms such as reverse discrimination must fall on critics like Hook.

Gifford gave one example of an alternative which had worked in the New York City educational system. When faced with the necessity of layoffs, the Board realized that it would either have to lay off all of the recently hired minority supervisors with least seniority, or lay off a group of whites who had legitimate expectations of job security based on their seniority. In this instance, the Board was able to convince the union involved that neither choice was acceptable, and to come up with an alternative plan which cut salary increases in order to keep everyone on the payroll; presumably a much fairer solution.

Alexander, who was anxious to rebut Hook's argument, spoke eloquently and with passion of the need for affirmative action. He maintained that there is no lack of qualified blacks, yet the University of Texas has only one full black professor and his own school, Harvard, has only one or two. He said that setting targets, goals, and quotas is the only way to achieve serious change, and he called on whites and blacks alike to be less defensive and instead to get angry about the issues involved.

Hook, in reply to Alexander, returned to his own basic point that it is the individual person, not the ethnic/racial/or national group, who is the carrier of human rights. He spoke of the practical problems of compensatory justice, saying that it would hurt unjustly some people who as individuals were in no way responsible nor collectively guilty for collective guilts. For example, Hook said, in earlier days a quota system against qualified Jews operated to keep them out of professional schools. To bar their grandchildren from professional schools on the grounds that blacks were more deserving is to blame the wrong people for the prior unjustice and thus to polarize Americans and perpetuate the inequity. In Hook's eyes, the better solution would be to solve employment problems first and to provide jobs for all who are "qualified".

Hook did not say, however, how this solution would benefit those who are not "qualified", due to lack of earlier education or acquisition of particular skills.

Wilkins, in response to Hook, made two points about the word "qualified". First, Wilkins challenged Hook's assumption that if qualified persons were available, elite institutions would make choices based on the merits. His own experience on the *Washington Post* and *New York Times* editorial boards led him to think otherwise, he noted wryly

Secondly, in order to have equally qualified persons, Wilkins thought that tools like "reverse discrimination" were necessary to get from Point "A" (where the 1960s legislation left off) to Point "B" (where true equality of access would exist for all). Wilkins admitted that the present tools were clumsy, but reflected what was probably the feeling of all the blacks on the panel when he said he was distressed by Hook's unwillingness to recognize the need for compensatory tools. Wilkins, too, challenged Hook to come up with alternatives, saying that the lack of alternative proposals had been accompanied by "intellectual bankruptcy", and that not once had Hook really addressed the problem of how to achieve equality of qualification for blacks and whites.

Hook's answer to the problem of alternatives (which was also posed as a question from the audience) was to return to his plea for full employment. He expanded that theme by citing the need for remedial education, adequate housing, and what he referred to as an entire program of social change, expressed as "Social Democrats, USA".

A questioner from the audience asked how to apply equality under the law when the criminal justice system in New York is so overloaded that poor minorities spend three or four years in jail simply waiting for their cases to be heard. Since the burden of an inequitable bail bond system falls most heavily on blacks and minorities, what other alternatives might there be?

Judge Higginbotham's response to this question was to call for a resetting of priorities, so that both prisons and the arrest/conviction system could be improved. To do this, he warned, will take money; and there will have to be a greater commitment to more funding in these areas before any noticeable improvement occurs.

Conclusion

It is regrettable that some of the healthy emotion and feeling of the symposium does not survive to the printed page.

There were three major areas which the panelists addressed. First there seemed to be general agreement that the civil rights legislation was one of the strongest and best legacies of the Johnson Presidency. The public accommodation provisions (Title II of the 1964 Act) and the Voting Rights Act (1965) were particularly successful, although Clifford Alexander's caveat that the number of blacks holding important elective office is still disproportionate to the total black population must be noted. Burke Marshall's criticism of the failure of enforcement machinery for the cut-off of Federal funds provisions (Title VI of the 1964 Act) and his criticism of the housing discrimination provisions (Title VIII of the 1968 Act) were also well-taken.

Second, several panelists made the point that the use of the presidency as a place to speak out cannot be overlooked. Use of the presidential office to further the goals which the civil rights legislation was designed to accomplish is crucial in making those goals meaningful. There is almost always a time lag between the passage of an act which makes provisions for new laws to be executed and administered, and the actual implementation of these provisions. Unfortunately, much of the civil rights legislation never had a chance fully to mature; instead of being administered under the direction of a president genuinely committed to it, as was Johnson, it passed for eight years into the hands of a chief executive far less dedicated to making it work. Had Johnson had four more years, he might have spotted the deficiencies, worked with the legislature to create new enforcement remedies, and appointed people devoted to implementing its ends.

Third, there was real disagreement on the panel over what were proper legislative goals, and what may be beyond the reach of legislation. Increasingly the so-called transitional rationale is not enough for the courts, and not enough for some people. Given different circumstances and different leadership, however, the issue of equal treatment need not become as divisive as it potentially is. More innovative solutions such as the compromise in New York City hirings and firings described by Mr. Gifford, should be sought.

Finally, we may be able to find solutions that are not either/or solutions if we had more imaginative leadership and people devoted again to working out the spirit as well as the letter of the civil rights legislation. In this sense, the consensus of the panel was that solutions, if any, must be broader than the goals of the earlier legislation, and must encompass more jobs, more housing, more provisions for basic human needs, in order to achieve a society where there is no discrimination at either end of the economic scale.

CONTRIBUTORS

Clifford Alexander is a member of the Washington law firm of Verner, Liipfert, Bernhard, McPherson, and Alexander. He is a graduate of Harvard and Yale Law School and has been Chairman of the Equal Employment Opportunities Commission (EEOC), Program Executive Director of Harlem Youth Opportunities Unlimited (HARYOU), and host and co-producer of his own television show. He serves on the boards of several universities, corporations, and the NAACP Legal Defense and Educational Fund and is Secretary of the National Urban Coalition.

David M. Austin is Professor in The University of Texas at Austin Graduate School of Social Work and administrator of its Center for Social Work Research. Prior to joining the Texas faculty in 1973, he had been engaged in projects on community representation in community action agencies, youth services planning, community development, housing assistance, and public welfare.

Victor Bach is an Assistant Professor of Public Affairs at the LBJ School of Public Affairs. He has studied at MIT, was a fellow at the Joint Center for Urban Studies, and directed research at the Organization for Social and Technical Innovation (OSTI). His primary interests are in urban housing and community development policy and in policy research methodology. In addition to serving currently as a field associate on the Brookings Institution study of the Community Development Block Grant Program, he has been directing a two-year comparative field study of the impact of special revenue sharing on local community development efforts in six of the nation's major center cities.

Douglass Cater is Director of the Aspen Program on Communications and Society and a visiting professor at Stanford University. He was educated at Harvard University and has taught at Wesleyan, Princeton, and the University of California—San Francisco. He is former National Affairs Editor of *Reporter* magazine. He was a special assistant to President Johnson from 1964-1968 and is the author of four books, including *The Fourth Branch of Government,* and many articles.

Kenneth Clark is the President of the firm Clark, Phipps, Clark, and Harris, Inc. He received his Ph.D. from Columbia University and is

Distinguished Professor ·Emeritus from City College and retired President of the Metropolitan .Applied Research Center, Inc. He is the author of several books, including *Dark Ghetto,* and is a past President of the American Psychological Association. He is a member of the New York State Board of Regents, the Board of Trustees of the University of Chicago, and the Board of Directors of the Lincoln Savings Bank, and Harper and Row.

Wilbur J. Cohen is Dean of the School of Education and is a Professor of Education and of Public Welfare Administration in the School of Social Work at the University of Michigan, Ann Arbor. He was Secretary of Health, Education, and Welfare in 1968 and was Assistant Secretary for Legislation of HEW from 1961 to 1965 and Under Secretary from 1965 to 1968. He is a graduate of the University of Wisconsin and is the author of several books and a number of articles in the areas of social welfare and education.

Karen Davis is a Senior Fellow of the Economics Studies Program at the Brookings Institution. She received a B.A. in mathematics and a Ph.D. in economics from Rice University and has been a visiting lecturer at Harvard. She is a member of the Institute of Medicine and of the Health Advisory Panel of the Office of Technology Assessment of the U.S. Congress. She is the author of several books and monographs, including *National Health Insurance—Benefits, Costs and Consequences,* and many articles.

Marian Wright Edelman is Director of the Children's Defense Fund of the Washington Research Project, Inc. She is a graduate of Spelman College and received her law degree from Yale University. She has been Director of the NAACP Legal Defense and Education Fund in Jackson, Mississippi, a partner in the Washington Research Project of the Southern Center for Public Policy, and Director of the Center for Law and Education at Harvard University. She serves on the Board of Trustees of the Martin Luther King Memorial Center, Spelman College, and the Council on Foundations. She is also a member of the Yale University Corporation and serves on a number of other Advisory Boards and Boards of Directors.

Bernard Frieden is a Professor of Urban Studies at MIT. He has a B.A. from Cornell, a M.A. from Penn State, and a M.C.P. and Ph.D. from M.I.T. He has been a member of task forces constituted by the White House, HEW, and the State of Massachusetts. He has been a consultant to a number of foundations, corporations, and government bodies. He has written several books, including *The Politics of Neglect* with Marshall Kaplan and *The Future of Old Neighborhoods,* and a large number of professional articles and monographs primarily in the areas of housing and urban development.

John Andrew Gallery is Associate Dean of Architecture and Director of the graduate program in community and regional planning at The

University of Texas at Austin. He has also taught architecture and city planning at the University of Pennsylvania. Mr. Gallery's involvement with housing problems and city planning include working as special consultant to the mayor of Philadelphia, and service on the Philadelphia City Planning Commission.

Charles Haar is the Louis D. Brandeis Professor of Law at Harvard University. He received a B.A. from New York University, a Masters from the University of Wisconsin, and a Law Degree from Harvard Law School. He was Assistant Secretary for Metropolitan Development in the Department of Housing and Urban Development from 1966 to 1969. He has served as a consultant to the U.S. Congress and to a wide number of agencies at the local, state, and Federal levels. He has been on numerous Presidential and governmental task forces. He has published a number of books, most recently *The End of Innocence* and *Between the Idea and the Reality* and many articles in a wide variety of professional journals.

Dagmar Strandberg Hamilton is an Assistant Professor in the LBJ School of Public Affairs, and served as counsel to the U.S. House of Representatives Judiciary Committee during the Impeachment Inquiry of Richard M. Nixon 1973-74. During 1965-66, she was a lawyer with the Civil Rights Division of the U.S. Department of Justice. She was an editing and research associate for Supreme Court Justice William O. Douglas, 1962-73 and 1975-76.

Vernon E. Jordan, Jr., is Executive Director of the National Urban League, which works to bring advances to the minority community. He formerly directed the United Negro College Fund and the Voter Education Project of the Southern Regional Council. An attorney who practiced law in Arkansas and Georgia, Jordan has held Federal appointments on the Presidential Clemency Board and the Advisory Council on Social Security.

Marshall Kaplan is a principal in the firm of Marshall Kaplan, Gans and Kahn. He has a B.A. and M.A. from Boston University and a M.C.P. from MIT. He has directed numerous national evaluations and assumed a wide range of advisory roles to the White House, Federal agencies, state and local governments, as well as private community developers, builders, and community groups. He has published several books, most recently *The Politics of Neglect: from Model Cities to Revenue Sharing* with Bernard Frieden, and a number of articles concerning community development and planning issues.

Robert Lampman is Professor of Economics at the University of Wisconsin at Madison. He received his B.A. and Ph.D. degree at the University of Wisconsin. He has done a wide variety of research on income, wealth, and poverty in the United States. His books include *Changes in the Share of Wealth Held by the Top Wealth Holders* and he has written extensively on the economics of poverty.

William C. Levin is President of The University of Texas Medical Branch at Galveston since 1974 and previously served as professor of internal medicine and Warmoth Professor of Hematology at UTMB. He is a member of the scientific advisory committee of the American Association of Blood Banks and has served as chairman of the Cancer Clinical Investigation Review Committee of the National Cancer Institute, National Institutes of Health.

Robert Levine is Deputy Director of the Congressional Budget Office. He received a B.A. and M.A. in Economics at Harvard University and a Ph.D. from Yale. He has worked at the RAND Corporation and was President of the New York City RAND Institute from 1973 to 1975. From 1966 to 1969 he was Assistant Director of Research, Plans, Programs, and Evaluation of the Federal Office of Economic Opportunity. He is the author of numerous articles and studies in the areas of poverty.

Theodore Marmor is an Associate Professor at the University of Chicago. He received his B.A. and Ph.D. from Harvard University. He has taught at the University of Minnesota and University of Wisconsin, Madison. He has served as a consultant to HEW, the Heineman Commission, and many other groups and agencies. He is the author of several books, including *The Politics of Medicare* and many articles in the areas of health policy, income maintenance, and social policy.

Burke Marshall is a Professor of Law at Yale University Law School. He was Assistant Attorney General of the United States in charge of the Civil Rights Division from 1961 to 1965 and was General Counsel and Senior Vice President of International Business Machines Corporation from 1965 to 1970. He also was Chairman of the National Advisory Commission on Selective Service, appointed by President Johnson in 1967 to review the Selective Service system.

Ray Marshall is Professor of Economics and Director of the Center for the Study of Human Resources at the University of Texas at Austin and President of the National Rural Center in Washington, D.C. He received a B.A. from Millsaps College, an M.A. from Louisiana State University, and a Ph.D. in Economics from the University of California at Berkeley. He has taught at the University of Mississippi, Louisiana State University, and the University of Kentucky as well as at the University of Texas. He has been on the editorial board of several journals, president of regional and national professional associations, is Chairman of the American Economic Association committee on political discrimination and labor market studies, the Federal Committee on Apprenticeship, and is the Director of the Southern Regional Council's Task Force on Southern Rural Development. He has published more than 20 books and monographs and a large number of articles in the areas of rural development, manpower and employment policy, labor economics, discrimination, and health policy.

Beryl Radin is Assistant Professor at the Lyndon B. Johnson School of Public Affairs, The University of Texas at Austin. She has been a consultant to various groups, including the National Urban Coalition, National Urban League, Ford Foundation and U.S. Department of Labor, and was an assistant information officer for the U.S. Commission on Civil Rights.

Arthur Schlesinger, Jr. is the Albert Schweitzer Professor of the Humanities at the City University of New York. He received a B.A. from Harvard. He has taught at Harvard, has been a special assistant to President Kennedy, and has received the Pulitzer Prize in history and biography. He is on the Board of Directors of the Harry S. Truman and John F. Kennedy Libraries and the Ralph Bunche Institute as well as the Board of Trustees of the Twentieth Century Fund, the Robert F. Kennedy Memorial, and the John F. Kennedy Center for the Performing Arts. He is the author of more than 20 books, including *The Age of Jackson, The Age of Roosevelt, A Thousand Days,* and *The Imperial Presidency*.

James Tobin is Sterling Professor and Chairman of the Department of Economics at Yale University. He received his B.A., M.A., and Ph.D. from Harvard and has taught at Yale since 1950. He has been President of the American Economic Association, is a member of the National Academy of Sciences, and was a member of the President's Council of Economic Advisors in 1961-62. He is the author of well over 100 professional articles and several books primarily in the areas of monetary theory, economic theory, and economic policy.

David Warner is an Associate Professor of Public Affairs at the LBJ School of Public Affairs. He received his B.A. from Princeton University and his M.P.A. and Ph.D. in economics from Syracuse University. He has taught at Wayne State and Yale Universities, and worked in New York City for the municipal hospital system. He has been a consultant to the Twentieth Century Fund, the Ford Foundation, several components of the U.S. Public Health Service, and the U.S. Agency for International Development. He has written several books and monographs and a number of articles on health and education.

PARTICIPANTS

A Decent Standard of Living

Chairman

William Cannon
Vice President for Business
  and Finance
University of Chicago

Panelists

Wendell Anderson
Governor of Minnesota

Tom Bradley
Mayor of Los Angeles

Lisle C. Carter, Jr.
Chancellor
Atlanta University Center

Maynard Jackson
Mayor of Atlanta

Earl Johnson, Jr.
Professor of Law
University of Southern California
  Law Center

Steven A. Minter
Program Officer
The Cleveland Foundation

Jack Otis
Dean, Graduate School of
  Social Work
The University of Texas at Austin

Frances Fox Piven
Professor
Department of Political Science
Boston University

Health and Medical Care

Chairman

David Hamburg, M.D.
President, Institute of Medicine
National Academy of Sciences

Panelists

Bond L. Bible
Director, Department of Rural
  and Community Health
American Medical Association

Kenneth H. Cooper, M.D.
The Cooper Clinic, Dallas, Texas
Author, *Aerobics*

Merline DuVal, M.D.
Vice President, Health Sciences
Arizona Medical Center
The University of Arizona

John F. Finklea
Director, National Institute for
  Occupational Safety and Health

Martha Griffiths
Former Congresswoman
Attorney
Farmington Hills, Michigan

James G. Haughton, M.D.
Health and Hospitals Governing
Commission of Cook County

Patrick J. Lucey
Governor of Wisconsin

David E. Rogers, M.D.
President, The Robert Wood
  Johnson Foundation

Ray E. Santos, M.D.
Orthopaedic Surgeon
Lubbock, Texas

A Decent Home in a Decent Community

Chairman

Robert C. Weaver
Former Secretary, Department of
  Housing and Urban Development
Distinguished Professor of Urban
  Affairs
Hunter College of the City
  University of New York

Panelists

Gordon Cavanaugh
Executive Director
Housing Assistance Council, Inc.
Washington, D.C.

Richard Hatcher
Mayor of Gary, Indiana

Floyd H. Hyde
Former Under Secretary
Department of Housing and
  Urban Development
Urban Consultant

Reynell M. Parkins
Director, Housing Research and
  Urban Development
The University of Tennessee

Equal Educational Opportunity

Chairman

Harold Howe II
Former Commissioner of Education
Department of Health, Education,
  and Welfare
Vice President, Ford Foundation

Panelists

Robert L. Bennett
Former Director of Special Projects
American Indian Law Center
The University of New Mexico

Joseph E. Duffey
General Secretary
American Association of
  University Professors

Samuel Halperin
Director, Institute for
  Educational Leadership

Julian Nava
Professor of History
California State University,
  Northridge
Member, Board of Education,
  Los Angeles

Herbert O. Reid
Charles Hamilton Houston
  Distinguished Professor of Law
Howard University Law School

Albert Shanker
President, American Federation
  of Teachers

William L. Smith
Director, Teacher Corps
U.S. Office of Education

Equality Under the Law

Chairman

Louis Martin
President, Sengstacke Newspapers

Panelists

Bernard R. Gifford
Deputy Chancellor, New York City
Board of Education

A. Leon Higginbotham, Jr.
Judge, U.S. District Court
Philadelphia, Pennsylvania

Sidney Hook
Senior Research Fellow
Hoover Institution,
  Stanford University
Emeritus Professor of Philosophy
  New York University

Harry McPherson
Former Special Counsel to
  President Lyndon B. Johnson
Attorney; Verner, Liipfert,
  Bernhard, McPherson and
  Alexander

Althea T. L. Simmons
Director of Education Programs
National Association for the
  Advancement of Colored People

Roger Wilkins
Editorial Board, *New York Times*

INDEX

Other publications available from the Lyndon B. Johnson School of Public Affairs following symposia and conferences sponsored by the Lyndon Baines Johnson Library and the Lyndon B. Johnson School of Public Affairs, The University of Texas at Austin:

The American City: Realities and Possibilities ($3.00)

Educating a Nation: A Symposium on Education ($3.00)

Equal Opportunity in the United States: A Symposium on Civil Rights ($3.00)

Beyond Today's Energy Crisis ($3.00)

The Presidency and the Press ($3.50)

Women in Public Life ($3.50)

The Arts: Years of Development, Time of Decision ($3.50)

To order these or to obtain a complete list of publications available write:

Lyndon B. Johnson School of Public Affairs
Office of Publications
Drawer Y, University Station
The University of Texas at Austin
Austin, Texas 78712 (512) 471-5713